WILMETTE PUBLIC LIBRARY
1242 WILMETTE AVENUE
WILMETTE, IL 60091
847-256-5025

THE GREAT WAR AND THE MIDDLE EAST

THE GREAT WAR & the MIDDLE EAST

A Strategic Study

ROB JOHNSON

WITHDRAWN
Wilmette Public Library

OXFORD
UNIVERSITY PRESS

WILMETTE PUBLIC LIBRARY

Great Clarendon Street, Oxford, OX2 6DP,
United Kingdom

Oxford University Press is a department of the University of Oxford. It furthers the University's objective of excellence in research, scholarship, and education by publishing worldwide. Oxford is a registered trade mark of Oxford University Press in the UK and in certain other countries

© Rob Johnson 2016

The moral rights of the author have been asserted

First Edition published in 2016

Impression: 1

All rights reserved. No part of this publication may be reproduced, stored in a retrieval system, or transmitted, in any form or by any means, without the prior permission in writing of Oxford University Press, or as expressly permitted by law, by licence or under terms agreed with the appropriate reprographics rights organization. Enquiries concerning reproduction outside the scope of the above should be sent to the Rights Department, Oxford University Press, at the address above

You must not circulate this work in any other form and you must impose this same condition on any acquirer

Published in the United States of America by Oxford University Press
198 Madison Avenue, New York, NY 10016, United States of America

British Library Cataloguing in Publication Data
Data available

Library of Congress Control Number: 2016934366

ISBN 978–0–19–968328–4

Printed in Great Britain by
Clays Ltd, St Ives plc

Links to third party websites are provided by Oxford in good faith and for information only. Oxford disclaims any responsibility for the materials contained in any third party website referenced in this work.

940.4
JO

To my father, Keith Johnson (1937–2016), who knew the Great War generation well.

Preface

In Jesus College, Oxford, there is a portrait of Thomas Edward Lawrence, dressed in his signature flowing robes and adorned with *ghoutra* and *iqal*. The painting by Augustus John produced in Cairo in 1919, on Lawrence's return from Damascus, shows a weary and haunted man. War has taken its toll. The legend of Lawrence remains undiminished, even among the long lists of Oxford's luminaries, and 2016 is the centenary of the Arab Revolt in which he participated. As a scholar of Oxford, long troubled by the rather critical way in which the First World War is portrayed, it seemed to me appropriate to record the context of his endeavours, and how his aspirations, flawed and contradictory though they were, were unfulfilled. In recent decades, insurrections and wars in the Middle East have become a frequent occurrence, and it is often assumed that the First World War produced the conflicts that have plagued the region ever since.

The assumption that Western powers carved up the Middle East for their own ends produces widespread condemnation and there are frequent accusations of betrayal, connivance, and opportunism in most texts about the conflict. The chief problem with this assessment is that the decision-makers of 1914–19 are assumed to have been working towards a predetermined strategy. They were not. Strategy is guided by enduring interests but it is an iterative process, adjusted to meet new exigencies and calibrated to align ends, ways, and means. It is subject to friction, chance, and error. To attribute a master plan to the decision-makers of the First World War that could shape events in the later twentieth and early twenty-first century is erroneous: they were trying to win a war and create some sense of the post-war settlement, but they could not have foreseen the rise of republics, revolutionary politics, and fractured international relations over the next hundred years.

The violent jihadist movement calling itself 'Islamic State' began demolishing border posts between Iraq and Syria in 2014, claiming to have finally overturned the Sykes–Picot Agreement of 1915, which, they argued, had deliberately divided Arabs to weaken them and subject the people to

Western and Christian domination. The Islamic State movement militants were wrong. The Sykes–Picot Agreement had offered vague ideas about spheres of influence if the Ottoman Empire broke up, but not firm borders. The chief concern at the time was that Germany or Russia might try to dominate a Middle East where the Ottoman Empire no longer existed. The original Sykes–Picot Agreement was superseded even before the war was over and it was never intended to be any more than a vague understanding of areas of territorial responsibility, at least in Britain. Moreover, the Allies were not carving up some homogenous Arab state, since the Arabs were already divided by their own rival factions. Attempts to unite them failed, not just in 1916–19, but also in the decades that followed. Even the champion of Arab nationalism, T. E. Lawrence, was disillusioned by the lack of any prospect of Arab unity.

This volume on the First World War in the Middle East, and its immediate aftermath, is a strategic study, which concentrates on the higher level of war rather than on tactics and operations. The central idea is to identify, assess, and explain the most significant themes of that theatre, not as a 'military history' of manoeuvres and experiences but as a 'study of war' which illustrates the interactions of decision-making with the prevailing concepts, context, and changing conditions. While arranged chronologically, and by region, the work coheres with common threads: the making of strategy and the interaction between the planning and operations, between external forces and local actors, between aspirations and reality, and between actions and consequences. The premise of the book is that, while considered a 'European' war, the agencies and actors of the Middle East embraced, resisted, succumbed to, disrupted, or overturned the plans of external forces for their own interests, producing a region not simply the victim of Western imperial ambition, but full of all the contradictions that continue to characterize the Middle East today. In other words, the formulation of policy and strategic decision-making were constantly deflected and diverted by the hard reality of conflict within the Middle East, by its geography, its politics, and by the agency of the actors therein. War is not merely 'an extension of politics': war is a dynamic interaction of its actors, and the product of the friction of violent events. Contemporaries struggled with those dynamics, and tried to adapt their responses accordingly.

Despite the vast literature on the First World War, comparatively few works have dealt with the Middle East as a whole during the conflict and fewer still with the most significant and immediate consequences. The focus of the more specialist military studies has been individual campaigns, such as Gallipoli, Mesopotamia, or Palestine, yet, even in these examples, the emphasis has invariably been on selected parts of the Western operations (such as the Gallipoli landings in 1915, the fall of Kut in 1916, or the Battle of Megiddo in 1918). The Arab Revolt is usually described through the initiatives of T. E. Lawrence, but similar effort to lead local forces, by a variety of other officers, are less well known. British and Ottoman operations in 1918 in Kurdistan, Armenia, and Azerbaijan are also rarely analysed as frequently as the campaigns involving British and Indian forces on other fronts, despite the strategic consequences of the Ottoman defeat at Sarıkamış in the Caucasus or at the Second Battle of Kut in 1917. There are very few works, certainly in the Anglophone world, about operations on the eastern frontier, despite the enormous commitment of the Ottoman Army to that campaign, and the catastrophic losses they suffered there.

At the epicentre of the conflagration in the Middle East was the Ottoman regime. It was the revolt of the Young Turks and the accession of the revolutionary triumvirate, with its German partners, that marched the state into war: it was the stubborn defence of the old Ottoman Empire that determined the Middle Eastern campaign theatres of the First World War, and it was the defeat of the Ottoman Army that reordered the politics of the region. Moreover, it was the revival of Turkey that sparked conflicts in the Caucasus, in Anatolia against Greece, and a confrontation with the British in the Chanakkale. It was the emergence of Atatürk that inspired Middle Eastern leaders and intellectuals. Indeed, throughout the 1920s, from Egypt to Afghanistan, the Turks provided as great an inspiration an the Bolsheviks in the leadership of the region.

This book attempts to address the relative imbalance in the existing literature of the First World War, and, by drawing on selected archival collections, it tries to recover the strategic dimension of the Great War in the Middle East. As a study of war, the themes of the book reflect those connected both with the strategies of conflict and its immediate aftermath. They include the relative importance of diplomacy and the military calculations that led to certain decision-making, but also the elements that impacted upon the making of strategy, such as the forces, operational developments, revolts and insurrections, the growth of nationalist and transnational ideologies, and the internal security challenges both during and after the conflict of 1914–18. It also considers the strategic problems of peacemaking and post-war stabilization. To connect the analyses and provide the planning and decisions of contemporaries with context, there are descriptions and explanations of events at the operational level. There are references to individual thoughts and experiences to clarify the ideas of the period, but, at the same time, to show how aspirational or contingent decision-making was. Each chapter is arranged chronologically, and by region, showing the transforming effect of the war and the strategic developments that followed.

The inspiration for this book was not merely the centenary of the First World War but the ongoing conflicts in the greater Middle East and in particular the emergence of a violent and virulent manifestation of jihadism. The centenary occurred when Westerners were trying to come to terms with significant unrest in the region immediately adjacent to Europe, and its important historical antecedents. Above all, understanding the region and the decision-making of the past can have particular resonance in reaching a more informed judgement about the present and how to proceed.

It is too facile to attribute the recent conflicts of the Middle East entirely to a history of 'Western intervention', for, as this book indicates, there were significant internal convulsions that have played a part. The assumption that Westerners are the cause of the region's troubles is a refrain, frequently articulated, but rarely substantiated. This stems from the relative neglect of the First World War in the Middle East as a field of scholarship, or, perhaps worse, a reluctance to engage in understanding the origins of a problem that seems intractable. This unwillingness is curious given its significance. The European theatre has certainly overshadowed the study of the First World War. Had the operations of 1914–18 in the Dardanelles, Sinai, Palestine, the Caucasus, and Mesopotamia taken place *outside* of the context of the Great War, they would have been studied more determinedly, if for no other reason than their profound costs for the peoples who lived there. The First World War in the Middle East swept away 500 years of Ottoman domination, stirred nationalist sentiments, and created enduring international borders. The decisions taken in 1914–19 were important in the shaping of the modern Middle East, and while more modern political and ideological agendas are now used to judge them, there is merit in returning to the original decisions to examine what, in fact, lay behind them. The results are often surprising.

The 'Great War for Civilization', as it was styled by contemporaries, ushered in new ideologies and radicalized old ones—from revolutionary socialism to impassioned forms of atavistic Islamism; it created heroic icons, like the enigmatic Lawrence or the modernizing Atatürk, and destroyed others, like Enver Pasha, shot down by communists while leading Islamist revolt in Central Asia in the pursuit of a pan-Turkic imperial revival. The Great War was also a war for resources and national interests, where Britain looked to secure the oilfields of Persia, prevent the development of a continental railway from Berlin to Baghdad, and control strategic waterways in the Dardanelles and Suez. Germany and Russia too had interests to secure and they were prepared to go to extraordinary lengths to achieve them. For all sides internationally agreed standards about the conduct of war, so carefully demarcated before the conflict, were swept aside. It was a war fought for prestige in a region where the soldiers were acutely aware of the symbolism of Jerusalem, Baghdad, and Mecca.

Above all, the First World War was an imperial war. Many of the calculations of the decision-makers stemmed from concerns to secure their respective empires. Imperial prestige, thought vital to hold on to the allegiances of subject peoples, loomed large in the minds of politicians and military planners alike. Yet, it was a conflict where the very idea of empire was transformed and, in many cases, rejected. The Turkish redefined themselves more clearly once they had jettisoned their Ottoman territories. A stronger sense of Australian national identity was forged, especially at Gallipoli, at least for later generations. The war was the birthplace of Arab nationalism and insurgent resistance, although both ideal and method failed. For some, like the Armenians, Kurds, Druze, Azeris, and Georgians, there was a brief period of optimism, but their aspirations for independence were short-lived.

The British and French empires emerged even stronger from the conflict. The war was an opportunity for the British Empire to control regions that had posed significant security dilemmas in the past, and France fulfilled a long-cherished aspiration to acquire Syria. However, it was also the conflict that would impose burdens that Britain and France could not sustain, and within a few years there had to be significant readjustments in the relationship with Palestine, Egypt, and Iraq. The war established the new international institution of the League of Nations which, ideologically, represented a challenge to the *Realpolitik* of the European empires. The notion of 'self-determination' and the rights of small nations produced a direct contradiction of Britain's plans for federations across the Middle East.

This war provides a fascinating study of how decisions were reached on policy and strategy. It illustrates the importance of individuals and their assumptions, the prevailing values of the period, the agency of local actors, the friction of events, the dynamic of adaptation and escalation, and the effect of tactical and operational set-back or success on strategic plans.

Acknowledgements are due to a number of scholars who have assisted, challenged, and inspired me during the course of composing this book. Professor Sir Hew Strachan has been a great mentor and champion, but he has also worked to emphasize that the Great War was a truly global conflict, and, while the Western Front was undoubtedly prominent, this should not preclude the part played by other factors, including the Middle East, economic pressures, and the allegiances of the peoples involved. Hew Strachan has taught me the nuances and depth of strategic thinking, against which this work will fail to measure up, but it might, I hope, gain his approval at least in spirit. Three other colleagues at Oxford have been of particular assistance and it has been a great pleasure to listen to their thoughts as my own ideas emerged. Dr Adrian Gregory has frequently reminded me of the importance of culture and religion in this theatre of war, while Professor Edmund Herzig drew my attention to the value of Persian studies. Professor Eugene Rogan opened new perspectives on the regime in Istanbul through his excellent work on the 'Fall of the Ottomans'. Dr Metin Gurcan was a serving officer in the Turkish Army when we first met, but his energy, enthusiasm, and overwhelming hospitality were matched only by his objective and intellectual endeavour, and it is thanks to him that I gained access to obscure Turkish and Osmanli sources. Together we edited a book on the Turkish perspective on Gallipoli which led in turn to a firm relationship between the Changing Character of War Programme and the Turkish Staff College. While listing all the stimulating contacts in Turkey would soon exhaust this preface, it would be wrong not to cite Dr Haldun Yachinaya of Tobb University and Dr Alev Karaduman of Hacettepe University who have been so kind and helpful. I only hope they will forgive me for not including more from their respective disciplines of international relations and cultural studies in this book. For the Ottoman Army, I have relied on the work of two more colleagues, Erik-Jan Zuercher and Mesut Uyar, and I am grateful for their support. I have also drawn on the excellent work produced by Mustapha Aksakal and Bülent Özdemir, and I very much appreciated the support and advice that was given by Edward Erickson at the USMC University. For work on the British and Indian Armies, I owe much to my good colleagues Gordon Corrigan, Dr Kristian Coates Ulrichsen, Dr Ashok Nath, Professor David Omissi, Dr Kaushik Roy, and

Dr Andrew Syk. I am also indebted to Dr James Kitchen whose Oxford doctoral dissertation was of immense value and who co-hosted a conference on the subject of this book in April 2016. Armies have their own dynamics and agendas, and I was guided by the work of Professor John Gooch, the inspirational Professor Tarak Barkawi, the eloquent Professor Ashley Jackson, and the oracle of all French colonial matters, Professor Doug Porch. There are specialists on Germany who have been invaluable in developing my understanding of the role of the German Army in the region in the Great War, and who have guided me in one way or another. I should like to thank Professor Volker Berghahn, Professor Stig Foerster, Professor Juergen Foerster, Professor Anders Palmgren, and Professor Andreas Herberg-Rothe, the latter for assisting me to understand the finer points of Clausewitz. I have derived my thinking on strategy from Hew Strachan, but also Professor Eliot Cohen, who has always patiently fielded my insistent and erroneous thinking with grace and kindness. There are also iconoclasts who help in one's intellectual development in considering strategy: Professor Jeremy Black, Professor Patrick Porter, and Professor Tony King have taught me more than they will realize. In an entirely different way, I have had the pleasure of listening to Sir Lawrence Freedman, Professor Theo Farrell, and Professor David French at King's College London, and they have clarified that crucial link between strategy and policy. I have also found inspiration from other colleagues at Oxford, Professor Robert Service for his work on Bolshevik Russia, Professor Margaret MacMillan on the peacemakers, and Professor Theo van Lint on the Armenian question. On the value of diplomacy, I have been much assisted by my close friend Oliver Lewis, Sir Ivor Roberts, and the late Sir Jeremy Cresswell. I was also fortunate enough to make the acquaintance of several serving or recently serving military officers, including those who had been in position of great responsibility in past conflicts. Their insights, not least from the practical point of view, have acted as the antidote to the worst excesses of self-important theoreticians. General Sir John Kiszely was working on his own book on the making of strategy and I thoroughly enjoyed sharing insights with him. Major General Christopher Elliott also composed his own book while I was engaged in research for this one, and his thoughts on Iraq and Afghanistan as decision-making issues were very instructive. That both men of such seniority were so engaging and willing to entertain me made the process a true pleasure. There are many others who have had contributions to make, but I should like to reserve a special thanks for my former student, Elliott Bannan, not least for the references from the Australian War Memorial archives, and my Yale scholars, Allison Kolberg, Myron Zhang, Jiayi Shen, and Shimeng Xu for their archival support in 2015. I am immensely grateful to the team at Oxford University Press, especially Matthew Cotton, for their excellent advice and support. Finally, I need to thank my family and apologize for all the lost days and weeks when I was deep in this war. I know you think it's all over, but, to quote the CIGS, Sir William Robertson, 'I've 'eard different!'

Rob Johnson
2016

Contents

Note on Transliteration

There are significant problems in the transliteration of languages, and while Russian has a well-established system, there are more significant challenges with Arabic and Osmanli, not least because of the absence of vowels in the former and the different way in which the sounds of characters and words are pronounced in different regions. To add further complexity, language and proper names evolve, and place names change over time. The city of Karbala (كربلاء) is relatively straightforward, but Kut al Amara (العمارة والكوت), the site of the siege of 1915–16, is today simply Kut, while Amara, a city to the south in Maysan province, has grown significantly compared to the settlement of 1915. To impose some discipline on the problem, historic place names are used with references to modern names in parentheses where appropriate. English is used throughout, but certain key terms are not anglicized where this would mislead: so, the Ottoman forces are not referred to as Turkish, as was the case in 1914–18, except where ethnicity or a self-consciously Turkish national identity is established. The army formation known as 'Lightning' is retained as *Yıldırım* since to anglicize the term would risk misunderstanding.

List of Illustrations

List of Maps

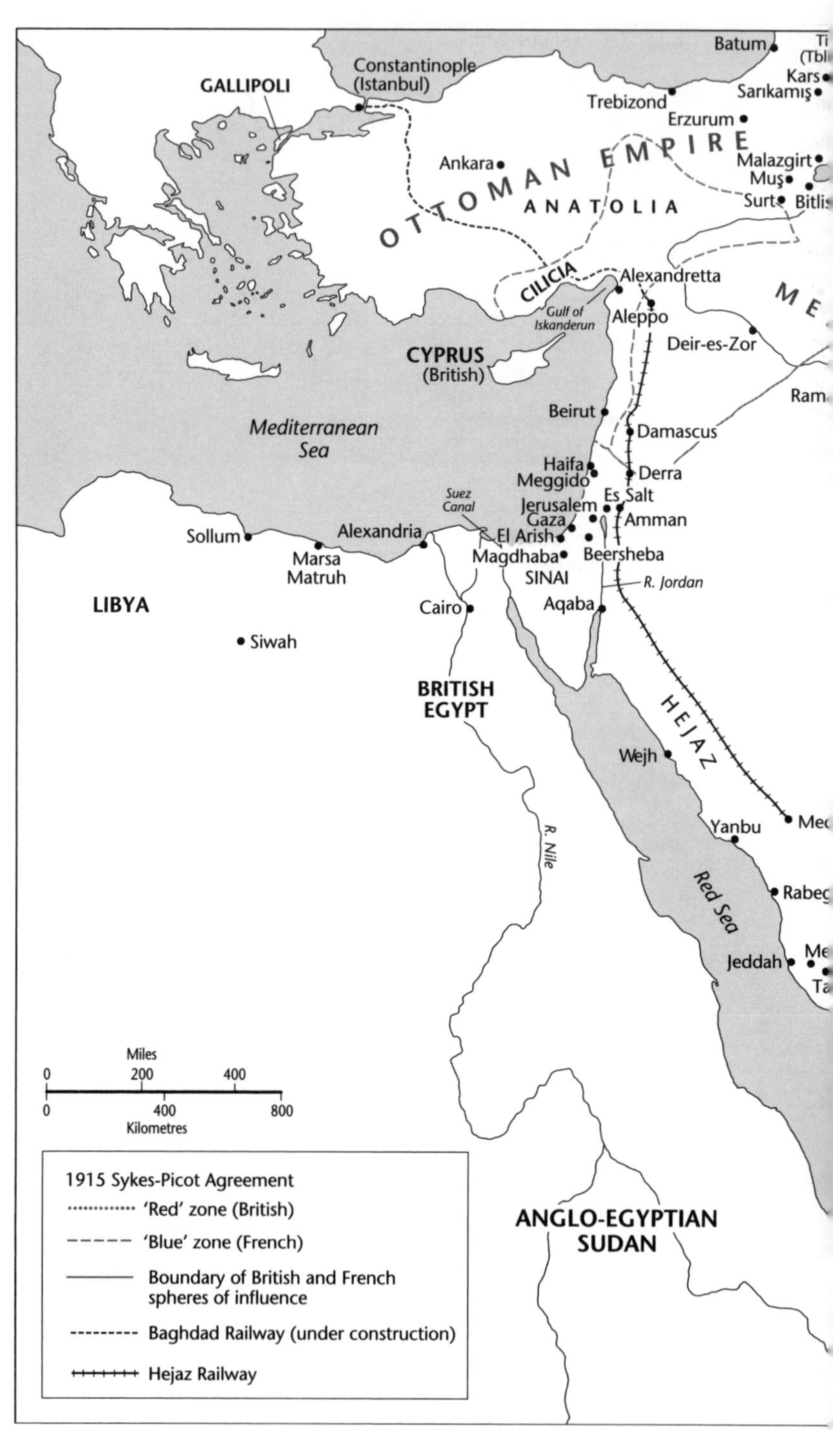

Map 1 The Middle East

AZERBAIJAN
Baku
Krasnovodsk
Caspian Sea
AFGHANISTAN
Tabriz
Enzeli
Tehran
Kirkuk
Hamadan
Qom
Kermanshah
Shargat
PERSIA
Baghdad
Kut
Hillah
Qurna
Mohammerah
Basra
Kirman
Shiraz
Fao
Bushire
Kuwait
INDIA
Persian Gulf
RABIA
Arabian Sea
ADEN
(British)
Gulf of Aden

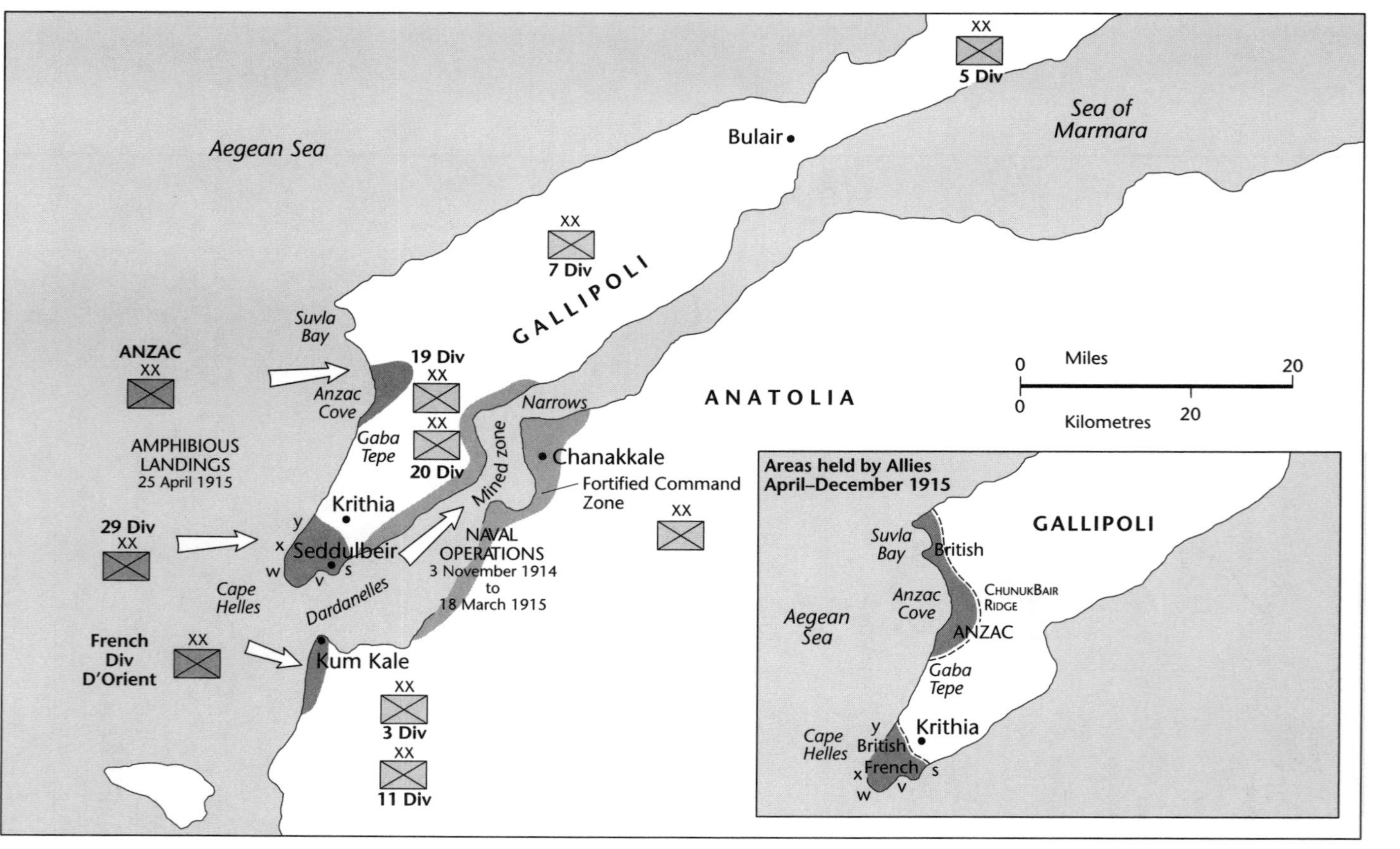

Map 2 Gallipoli, 1915–16

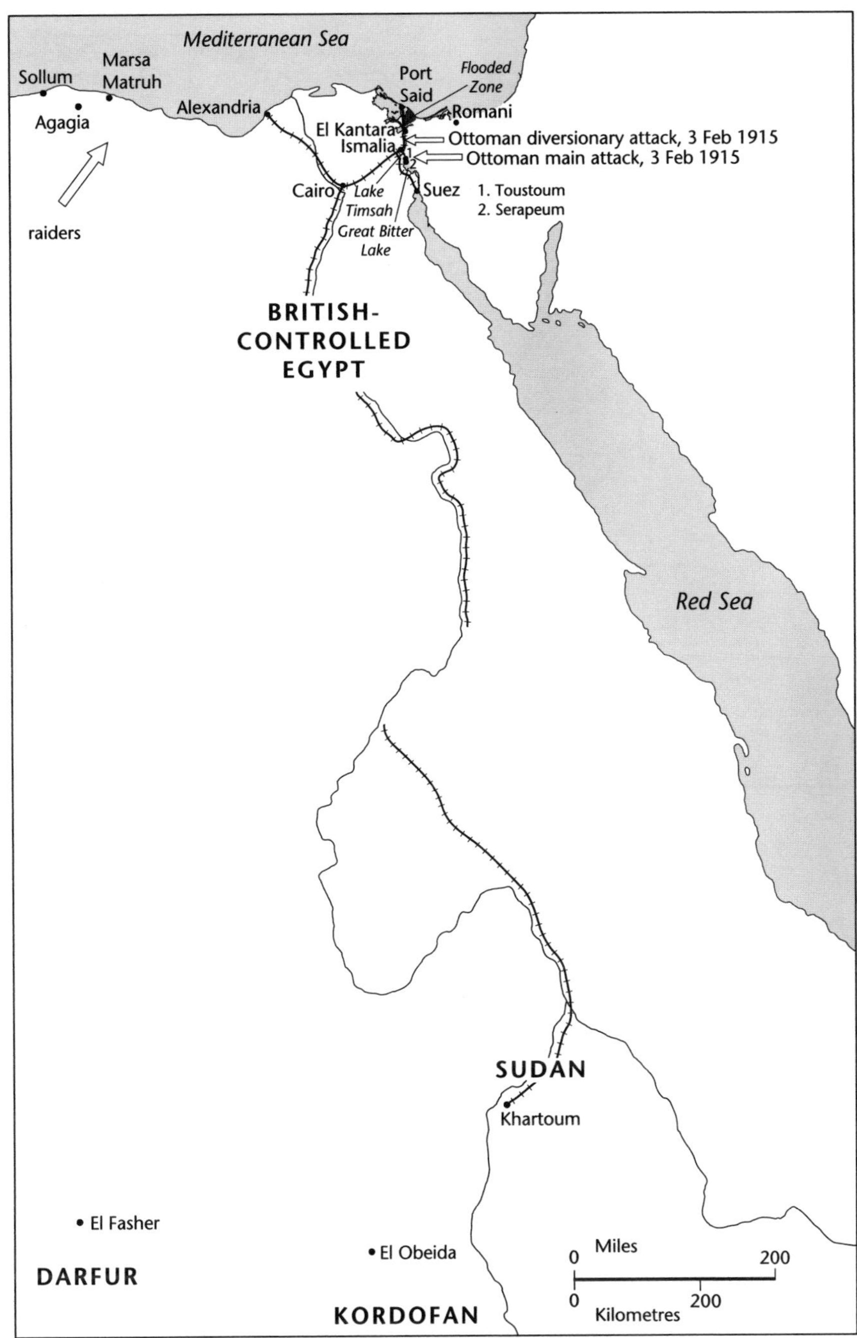

Map 3 Egypt and Sudan, 1914–15

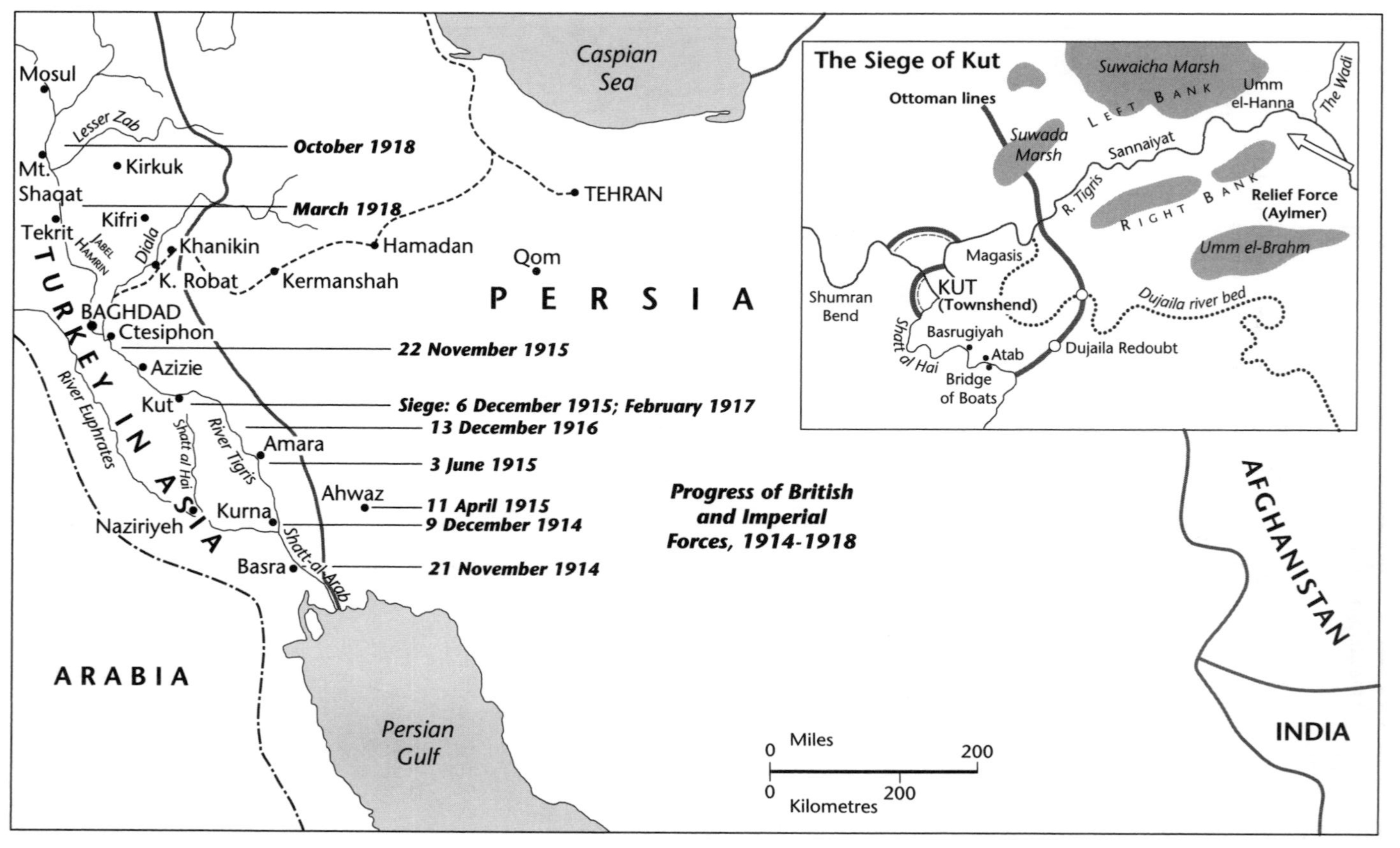

Map 4 Mesopotamia Campaign, 1914–18

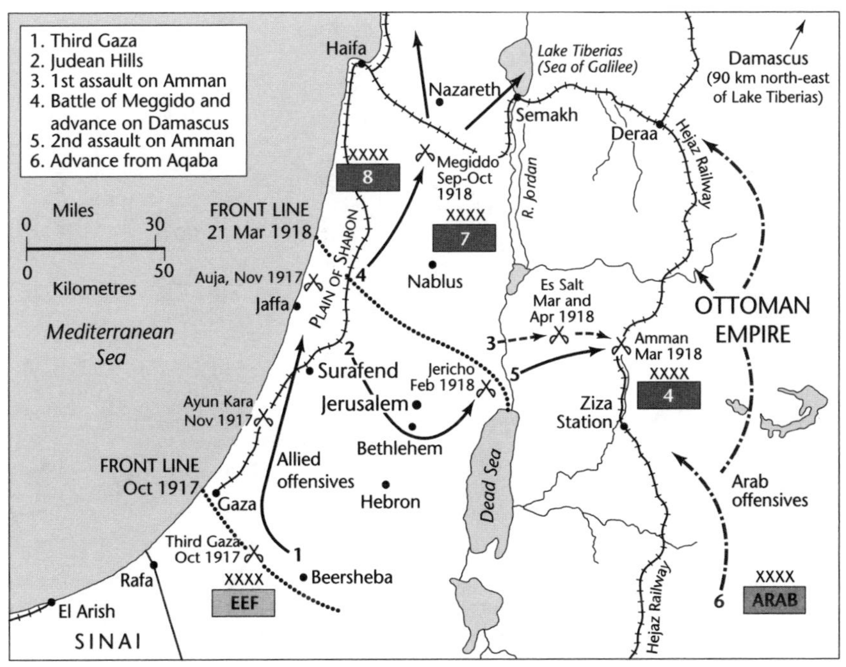

Map 5 Egypt, Sinai, and Palestine, 1916–18

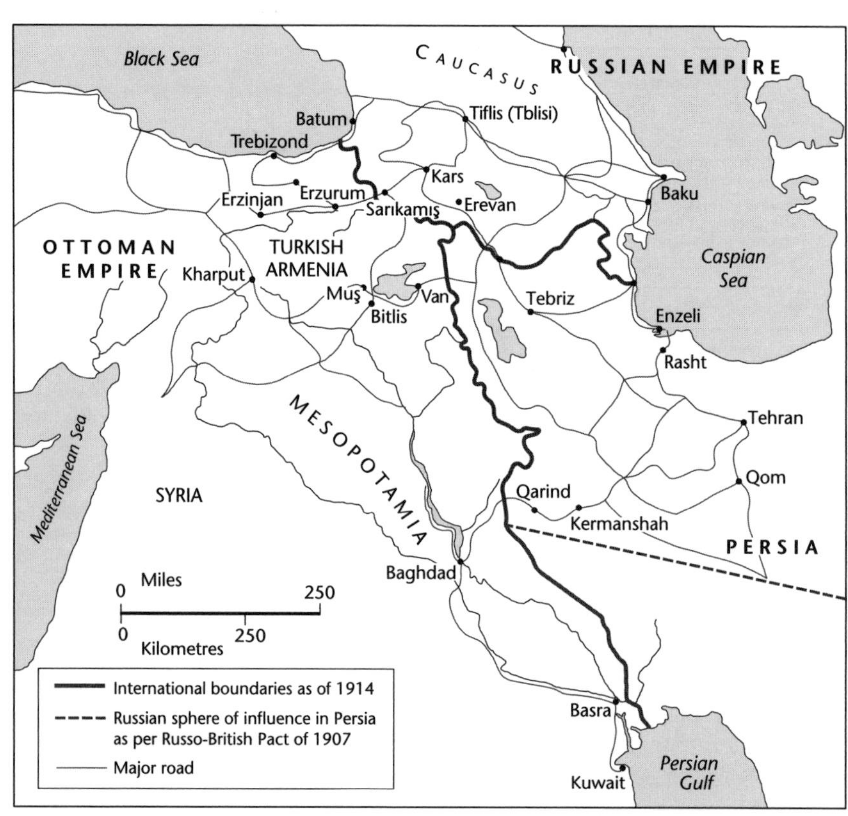

Map 6 Caucasus Campaign, 1914–18

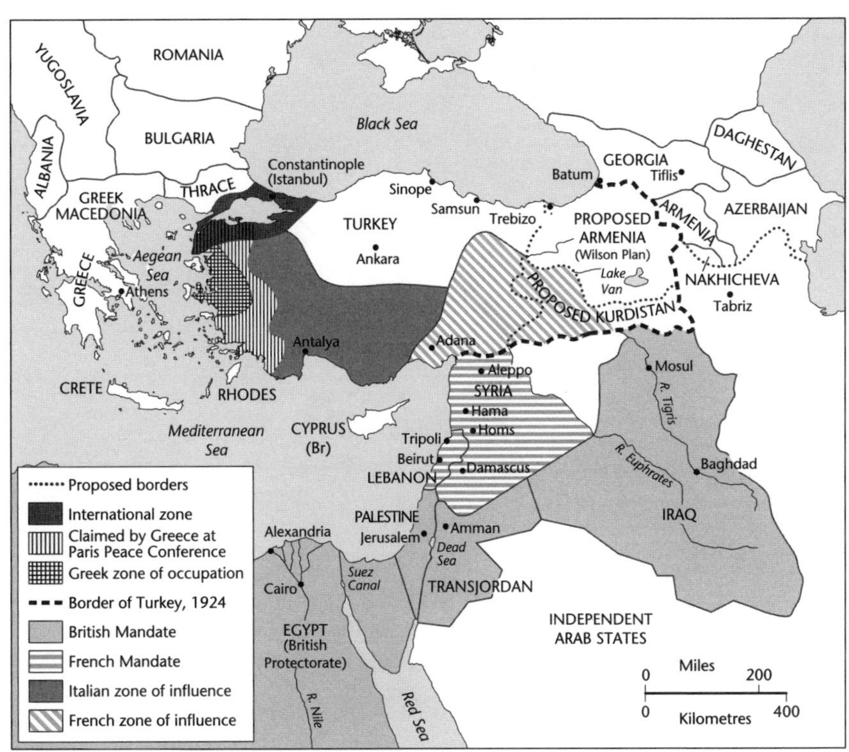

Map 7 The Peace Settlements, 1919–20

I

Ends and Ways

The Making of Imperial Strategy, 1907–14

The British Empire owes a great deal to 'side-shows'. During the Seven Years' War, which was also a great European War—for practically all the nations now engaged...were then interlocked in a great struggle—the events which are best remembered by every Englishman are not the great battles on the Continent of Europe, but Plassey and the Heights of Abraham; and I have no doubt that, when the history of 1917 comes to be written, and comes to be read ages hence, these events in Mesopotamia and Palestine will hold a much more conspicuous place in the minds and memories of the people than many an event which looms much larger for the moment in our sight.[1]

David Lloyd George, Prime Minister

It would be easy to regard [failed operations] as a chronic error, a delusion born of the spirit of the times; but there would be more sense in attributing them to a host of major causes, which we may possibly assimilate intellectually, but whose dynamic we will never comprehend as clearly as the men who were actually obliged to contend with them.[2]

Carl von Clausewitz, Prussian staff officer

In 1900, the British Empire was confronted with a geostrategic environment that was shifting profoundly, and with potentially far-reaching consequences. In Europe, a vigorous Germany was outstripping British manufacturing, commerce, and military capability. France, an old adversary, had just been faced down over disputed territory in the Sudan, but had concluded an alliance with Britain's other rival, the Russian Empire. The coming together of two powerful adversaries, combined with news of military set-backs in a colonial war in South Africa, was the cause of anxiety about the future security of the empire. There was also growing concern about Britain's naval supremacy, so long unrivalled around the globe. The 'two-power standard' whereby the Royal Navy possessed twice the number of vessels of any two other navies combined, was already in jeopardy and was soon to be neutralized by new naval technologies.

In the Middle East, the integrity of the Ottoman Empire, which had been Britain's bulwark against Russian expansionism in South-west Asia, was under threat. In the last decades of the nineteenth century, the Balkan provinces had broken away and established their independence. Russia had seized three provinces in the Caucasus. In North Africa, France annexed the Ottoman's old Mediterranean province in Tunisia. Cyprus and Egypt were already occupied by the British, but in 1908 Austria-Hungary annexed Bosnia-Herzegovina, and Libya was contested by Italy in 1911. The Foreign Office in London had to decide whether to shore up the Ottoman Empire, the so-called 'sick man of Europe', or to plan for its final demise.

Travelling further to the east, the relative decline of the Persian Safavid Empire, the eclipse of independent Central Asian khanates by the armies of the tsar, and the recalcitrance of decrepit dynasties such as Afghanistan and China, presented British strategists with another dilemma: how to protect Britain's largest and most valuable possession, India, against landward threats when its primary arm for defence was the Royal Navy. It was relatively easy to secure maritime trade at sea and to deter attacks on its smaller colonies with a large fleet, but it was more difficult to deter the European Great Powers from applying pressure on the British Empire in Asia, because there was always the risk that Britain could be drawn into costly occupations or unnecessary local conflicts, or forced to fight in the interior of the continent where its naval power could not be brought to bear.

Britain's preference was to project influence by other means—through diplomacy, consulates, financial services, infrastructural communications (such as the construction of railways, roads, and telegraph) and commercial concessions. However, specific crises sometimes forced Britain to demonstrate its power to the Ottomans, Persians, and the Arab fiefdoms, and to rival Great Powers like France, Russia, and Germany. In the Gulf, the Viceroy of India made a show of force in 1903, when he toured the area aboard a Royal Navy warship, and there were renewed attempts to maintain an influential presence in Tehran. The conclusion of a treaty with the emir of Kuwait, theoretically a domain of the Ottoman Empire, marked a change in Britain's strategic relationship with the region.

In essence, the methods of maintaining British strategic interests were furthered by four aspects of policy. First was diplomacy, using a system of

Residencies and Consulates with allies amongst the local elites, supported by an intelligence network that kept the British authorities abreast of local conflicts, shifting allegiances, and potential intrigues by other powers. This was augmented by agreements or the settlement of differences with other European empires, and, in the case of Persia, with a specific Anglo-Russian Convention in 1907. Secondly, there were spheres of influence through established relationships with local elites, or through loans, banking, building infrastructure, and military training teams. This contest for local support and the intrigue of the chief rival, Russia, was referred to in 1900 as 'The Great Game' although the title masked its serious nature.[3] Thirdly, buffer states were required. Persia, the Gulf States, and Afghanistan became the outworks in the landward defences of India while the hinterland of Egypt provided protection for the Suez Canal. Local rulers, including the shah of Persia, the sultan of Egypt, and the amir of Afghanistan, were granted direct financial reward or military aid. Fourthly, periodic military and naval interventions were used to reassert British dominance, such as the operations against Aden, Egypt, and Persia in the nineteenth century.

All these approaches were cemented by the notion of prestige, which was important in diplomacy but also acted as a means of deterrence. It was an idea that had to be reinforced constantly: Britain had to assert its power and demonstrate that it was both capable and willing to exercise force. In the second half of the nineteenth century, British policy towards Egypt, Persia, and the Ottoman Empire had sometimes lacked consistency as strategic considerations in Europe and India always came first. However, despite growing pressure from Russian intrigue and commercial rivalry from other powers, by the beginning of the twentieth century Britain appeared to have reasserted its exclusive control of the Gulf, ringed the region with compliant or allied states, and rationalized its relationship with its client regime in Egypt.

Before the outbreak of the Great War, British, Russian, and German intrigues and diplomatic negotiations designed to secure influence over the Middle East were therefore well-established, but there were new developments after 1905 which transformed the geostrategic landscape. The defeat of the tsar's forces in the Russo-Japanese War of 1904–5 and the aggressive commercial and political penetration of the region by German agents seemed to herald a more challenging period of rivalry for British planners.

A new climate of aggressive diplomacy had developed in Germany from the 1890s, but it entered a more strident phase in the early twentieth century. To some extent, it reflected the ambitions and anxieties of the kaiser,

Wilhelm II. Von Bülow, the State Secretary of the Foreign Ministry, echoed the kaiser's sentiments when in 1899 he announced that the new century would bring about a 'redistribution of empires and power'—and Germany would have to choose whether it was going to be the 'hammer or the anvil of world politics'.[4] Clustered around the imperial court were a number of extreme right-wing pressure groups variously demanding developments in the German armed forces, protection of the landed elites, and more assertive colonialism. One of these groups, the Naval League, predicted that unless Germany was able to expand it would either be 'choked in her [present] narrow territory or she will be squashed by the major world powers to which she will moreover have to send millions and millions of emigrants'.[5] Admiral Mueller asked von Tirpitz, the grand designer of the German High Seas Fleet, what should be done if the expansion of the German navy provoked a war with Britain, but he provided his own reply: 'Our answer must be... a *world war* which will lead our armies into India and Egypt.'[6] Max von Oppenheim, the former attaché of the German consulate in Cairo, and an advocate of closer relations with the Muslim world, persuaded the kaiser that the Middle East offered considerable potential for Germany. Believing that the Ottoman Empire would eventually be eclipsed, Oppenheim envisaged a *Drang nach Osten* (drive to the East) with colonial *Lebensraum* ('living space') stretching from the Bosporus to British India. The concept of a German empire across the ancient civilizations of the Middle East appealed to Wilhelm's vanity, and seemed to offer an outlet for the right wing's expansionist energies. Vehemently Anglophobic, Oppenheim would later author *Denkschrift betreffend die Revolutionierung der islamischen Gebiete unserer Feinde* (*Memorandum on Revolutionizing the Islamic Territories of Our Enemies*) on the outbreak of war in 1914 and he led the anti-British propaganda section of the Bureau of the East in Berlin.[7]

Courting Sultan Abdülhamid II in 1896, in spite of widespread European condemnation of Ottoman massacres of Armenians, which had just taken place, the German emperor was invited on a state visit to Jerusalem and Constantinople. It was an ostentatious state visit as the kaiser sought to present himself as the most prestigious monarch of Europe. Many in the British administration ridiculed Wilhelm's histrionics, but there was some unease at his attempts to win over Muslims given that such a large number of them lived under British rule. This unease was reinforced by the kaiser's support for the Afrikaners who fought the British in South Africa, the Germans' seizure of Tsingtao in China, and a rapid naval building programme—all of which seemed blatantly designed to threaten the British Empire. Few considered that it might be Britain's insistence on naval 'supremacy', despite claiming to uphold the free navigation of the seas, that was the cause of German antagonism.[8]

The result of the German posturing was that Britain looked to end long-standing rivalries elsewhere. In a House of Lords speech in the summer of 1903, Lord Lansdowne, the British Foreign Secretary, had warned Russia, and therefore put other Europeans on notice, that any attempt to establish naval bases in the Gulf would be 'resisted with all means at [Britain's] disposal'.[9] A decade later, Britain would issue a similar strongly worded statement against any German plans to establish a naval base in Morocco. Nevertheless, the government in London was reluctant to make dramatic interventions or put any further pressure on the Ottoman Empire or Persia lest it further destabilize the region. The British government of India tended to see changes taking place in the Middle East in a more pessimistic light. India's administration regarded Afghanistan, Persia, and the Gulf as strategically vital territories, which, if they fell into the hands of hostile powers, would make the defence of India prohibitively expensive and perhaps even untenable.

In 1900, the government of India was sufficiently concerned that it sent Major Percy Cox, an Indian Army officer in the Political Service and former Resident of Muscat, to southern Persia to monitor German intrigue and to befriend the local Persian elites by extending the informal networks that already existed. It was to prove a prescient decision, as Cox, schooled in the art of the Great Game, would go on to thwart German espionage during the First World War in the Gulf and, later, he would assist in the establishment of a pro-British state of Iraq.

The diplomatic breakthrough in Britain's new policy of concluding old enmities came soon after. In 1904, London and Paris celebrated an Entente Cordiale to settle rivalries in Africa, especially the Sudan, ending Britain's long-standing anxiety about French control of the headwaters of the Nile. Just three years later, St Petersburg and London concluded a 'settlement of differences' in the Anglo-Russian Convention of 31 August 1907. This demarcated spheres of influence in Persia and recognized the suzerainty of Russia over the Caucasus and Central Asia, and Britain over India, Afghanistan, and the Gulf. Following the protocols of the nineteenth century, the two spheres of influence that were defined in Persia—the north to Russia and the south to Britain, with a neutral strip between—were designed without consulting the governments in Tehran, Kabul, or Peking. None of the local authorities were given any opportunity to contribute to the definition of the territorial integrity of their own dominions.[10] Secretly, Russia also obtained Britain's approval for the eventual Russian occupation of the Bosporus, provided other powers agreed. While the strategic security of the empire and its buffer zones was the immediate driving force behind the agreement with Russia, the logic of Britain's Entente Cordiale with France in 1904 was also a significant factor.

There were other strategic problems to resolve, including Britain's ability to exercise naval command of the world's oceans. With new classes of surface ships and more-effective sea mines, submarines, and torpedoes changing the character of naval warfare, the joint statement of the Military and Naval Intelligence Divisions had been that the Russian Navy could only be tackled 'across the ruins of the French fleet', and that the Eastern Mediterranean, vital for seaborne commerce to the east, could no longer be considered a 'British lake'.[11] However, there can be little doubt that it was the new aggression of Germany that finally persuaded the British government of the need to bring to an end disputes with Russia and France it could not resolve by other means. In the face of the other nations' growing naval power, it had concluded the Anglo-Japanese Alliance in 1902 to augment its strength in the Pacific. In the law of unintended consequences, the alliance did much to encourage Japan to take on Russia in the Far East. The combined external defeat of Russian land and naval forces in 1905, accompanied by widespread internal unrest, demonstrated the tsarist empire's strategic weaknesses, and therefore offered an opportunity for Britain to conclude old enmities.

The sincerity of the Anglo-Russian Convention of 1907 may not have been questioned in London, but in India old suspicions remained. Intrigues in Persia did not abate and the Russians seemed just as active in trying to extend their influence throughout the country.[12] Yet, it was the arrival of German consuls in the region and their blatant attempts to win over the Muslim world to further their own commercial, political, and possibly territorial ambitions that tended to draw the Russians and the British, even those in India, into some semblance of cooperation.

What alarmed the British most was Germany's rapid naval building programme. The years before the First World War were characterized by widespread anxiety in Britain about the growth of the German maritime threat. It was ironic that the revolutionary new British design of the Dreadnought class of battleship, launched in 1906, gave the Germans the opportunity to expand their own fleet with a similar design at the same rate as the British. The kaiser and his naval chief, Admiral von Tirpitz, felt that, if it came to war, a decisive battle in the North Sea would force the British to be more compliant and accede to German demands for more colonies. Across Britain and the empire there was a growing concern that the Germans intended to usurp the power of the Royal Navy. This would appear irrational and meaningless in light of Germany's ultimate defeat in 1918, but to a nation that had grown used to the idea that its commerce, its worldwide empire, and its wealth were based on maritime supremacy, there was a genuine fear for the future. This made the far-fetched speculations about secret German invasion plans, or the fear that Britain was overrun with Teutonic spies already, all the more believable.[13]

Security of sea lines of communication depended on the Royal Navy but also on the stability of the region's states. Yet, in 1908, the Ottoman Empire, which lay alongside a significant part of the route to India, seemed on the brink of collapse. The sultan had spent twenty years trying to crack down on subversive elements in his domains but the discovery of a cell of the Committee of Union and Progress, colloquially known as the Young Turks, within the ranks of the Ottoman Third Army created a fear of a great purge, which in turn provoked a mutiny by some of its troops and their civilian accomplices.[14] Unexpectedly, their actions proved popular and soon other elements of the army had joined the disturbances. As in so many revolutions, the loyalties of the armed forces determined the course of events. Unable to rely on the allegiance of his soldiers, the sultan capitulated.

Within weeks, the revolution began to consume its opponents, and then its own supporters. Initially, the old regime's former gendarmes, spies, and thugs were treated to some rough justice. Then, when prices rose dramatically, protesting workers, who had initially supported the revolution, were attacked. New laws were passed curtailing strike action and banning criticism of the government. Opposition against the Committee of Union and Progress increased. Resistance began to crystallize around the unifying cause of Islam. The Young Turks were secularists, and the *ulema* were afraid that sweeping reforms would reduce their power in the Ottoman state. There were also divisions in the army: older officers were loyal to the sultan, while the junior officer corps tended to favour the reformist Young Turks. On 12 April, elements of the I Army Corps joined with the *ulema* of the madrasahs in Istanbul and marched on the parliament, demanding a new government and the reintroduction of Islamic law. The sultan seized the opportunity to overturn the secularists' power and Istanbul fell into the hands of the counter-revolution.[15]

The Third Army, which had spearheaded the coup the year before, now mobilized in defence of the revolution. From its base in Macedonia, it marched under the title of 'The Action Army' promising to restore the constitution once more. It reached Istanbul and suppressed all opposition, establishing martial law throughout the city. A new general National Assembly was convened and the sultan was deposed in favour of his younger brother, Mehmet V.[16] In the aftermath, enemies of the Committee of Union and Progress were targeted. So too were its fellow travellers—the Armenians of Adana, who had supported the revolution of 1908, were accused of being dangerous dissidents. In three days of massacres, 20,000 civilians were killed, their homes destroyed and their property looted. It was a vile and strange reaction, prompted by the atmosphere of fear and denunciation that prevailed in April 1909. It was also a dark harbinger of what was to come.

The weakened character of the Ottoman Empire prompted renewed ideas in Germany about the possibilities of carving out colonies in the east, on the ruins of the sultan's dominion. The much vaunted idea of a railway from Berlin to Baghdad raised the possibility that commerce would be drawn away from the coasts, on which Britain depended, to the interior, where the Continental powers like Germany and Russia would be favoured. Such a railway might also provide a strategic route for the deployment of German troops deep within the Middle East, or even the establishment of a Gulf port. Germany's ambitions were not limited just to the sultan's territories as they had Persia in their sights too. German agents were sent on 'archaeological expeditions' to gather intelligence, making their way into the Persian oilfields, and a number of German banks and businesses appeared offering low rates of interest to undercut the British-owned Imperial Bank of Persia. Wilhelm Wassmuss, a German consul, who was busily engaged in fraternizing with the Tangistani tribesmen in southern Persia along the Gulf coast, seemed to exemplify this form of meddling and intrigue.

Between 1911 and 1913, the Ottoman Empire was driven further into crisis, and looked towards Germany for support. On 29 September 1911, the Italians invaded Libya and overwhelmed the Ottoman garrison there. The Grand Vizier, Kamil Pasha, and his associates knew they were unable to defeat the Italians, especially when Britain and France announced their neutrality. But the Committee of Union and Progress, inspired by Major

Enver, an officer of the Third Army who had been prominent in the 1908 revolution, agreed to send volunteers to wage a guerrilla war.[17] Using the nomenclature *fedai* (those willing to sacrifice), the handful of Turkish officers made every effort to recruit local tribes. The most prominent group that emerged was drawn from the Sufi Senussi clans, and Enver played on their Islamic sentiments to mobilize and unite them against the Italians. Those of the original military garrison who had evaded capture were also brought into the guerrilla bands, and a specific intelligence unit, the *Teşkilât-i Mahusa*, was established, staffed with Libyan and Turkish personnel. The insurgent resistance followed its strategic logic: inflicting a steady stream of casualties and increasing the financial cost of the occupation.

The Italians responded in similarly logical terms. They secured the coastal towns and cities, where the majority of the population lived, and attempted to drive a wedge between the guerrillas and the people. They also escalated the conflict, bombarding Beirut on the Levantine coast in March 1912 and occupying the Ottoman islands of the Dodecanese. In May, they sent gunboats into the Dardanelles. A few months later, in October, they persuaded the Montenegrins to attack the Ottoman garrisons in the Balkans.[18] The Serbians, Greeks, and Bulgarians also mobilized against the Ottomans, thereby outnumbering the sultan's forces by two to one. The Greeks used naval power to wrest Crete and islands in the Aegean from the control of Istanbul, before advancing on Salonika and southern Albania. The Serbs and Montenegrins overran northern Albania, while the Bulgarians routed the Ottoman troops and marched to within 40 miles of the Ottoman capital. Besieged on all fronts, the sultan's government sued for peace.[19]

Divisions in the Ottoman ruling elite surfaced under the pressure of the Balkan defeat. The unionists called for the war to be continued, while the liberals believed victory was impossible. Enver, returning from Libya, seized the initiative and immediately launched a *coup d'état*: he and a handful of gunmen shot down the vizier's guards, killed the Minister of War, and took the Cabinet hostage.[20] The sultan, with little choice, approved the takeover and the policy of continuing the war.

On the front lines, however, the situation had rapidly deteriorated. Garrisons were mopped up piecemeal, and Edirne was starved into submission by the Bulgarians. The government in Istanbul again sued for peace and a treaty was concluded in May 1913 in London, which stripped the Ottomans of all of their European provinces. This sudden loss threw the Ottoman economy into crisis, while thousands of Muslim refugees poured into camps

Figure 1.1 Ismail Enver Pasha, War Minister and Deputy Commander-in-Chief with ambitious plans for Ottoman imperial regeneration

Figure 1.2 Mehmed Talaat Pasha, Grand Vizier and Minister of the Interior who was shot down by an avenging Armenian in 1921

in Anatolia. There was a sense of profound shock at the scale and rapidity of the defeat. As a result, the political turmoil continued. The new vizier was shot dead by a gunman, and the unionists, fearing a purge, decided to act first and with the utmost ruthlessness. Major Ahmet Djemal of the Railways Inspectorate, and a leading member of the Committee of Union and Progress, ordered the arrest and exile of all prominent critics. The sultan, clearly compromised and fearful that order was disintegrating, looked to the strongest faction to secure the state. He invited the unionists to form the government, and within weeks, Djemal, Enver, and Mehmet Talaat, a unionist leader and former postal official, established a revolutionary triumvirate with authoritarian powers.

In the Balkans, rivalries between the victorious states over the proposed borders sparked a Second Balkan War.[21] The Bulgarians found themselves fighting their former partners, and Enver seized the opportunity to lead a military column into Edirne. That summer, eastern Thrace was also recovered and Bulgaria called for a cessation of hostilities. Enver was lauded as a hero, but military victory could not substitute for the grave economic and strategic position the Ottomans were now in. The solution was for the regime to impose its will more strongly, with rigorous taxation and less tolerance for internal enemies.

For a brief period, the economy revived. Demobilization enabled agriculture and industry to resume and commercial activity returned. France made a loan of millions. Designed to encourage the Ottomans into further industrial and commercial development, it enabled investment in public works. Yet the unionists did not regard economic reform as their priority. They hoped to recover lost territory and to unite the empire through a successful, if limited, war. The first objective was to take back the Aegean Islands from the Greeks and thus remove the direct naval threat to the Dardanelles and the capital. In April 1914, notices of mobilization were distributed throughout the empire and there were preparatory calls for a holy war against Greece.[22] Russia, with the most to lose in terms of revenue through a closure of the Straits, urged restraint on both sides, but its inability to control these waters, so vital to its economy, gave rise to new strategic considerations of its own.

According to General Aleksei Nikolayevich Kuropatkin, one of the Russian Empire's most senior officers, the tsar wanted 'to seize not only the Bosporus but the Dardanelles as well'.[23] The security of the economy was only part of the equation, for imperial prestige, at a low ebb after the humiliating defeat at the hands of the Japanese in 1905 and a major internal revolt that year, required some dramatic compensation. The tsar therefore had other 'grandiose plans in his head: to take Manchuria for Russia, [and] to move toward the annexation of Korea to Russia. He dreams of taking under his orb Tibet too [and] he wants to take Persia.'[24] At a Council of Ministers on 13 January 1914, the tsar concluded that there should be plans in place to seize the Straits, especially in the event of a European war.[25] Anticipating a major conflict, the plans were finalized just three months later. Already in November 1912, Russia had tested its mobilization schemes for operations in the Balkans, a situation that almost led to a war with Austria-Hungary.[26] Indeed, while dominating the Straits and the Balkans were the strategic ends of Russian policy, the ways to achieve them in effect demanded the defeat of Austria-Hungary. In the subsequent crisis of July 1914, the Russian government initially considered a limited war, containing any conflict by mobilizing only on the borders of Hungary, but the logic of the Austro-Hungarian alliance with Germany necessitated their involvement, and thus, a war across the whole of Eastern Europe.[27]

The Ottoman Empire was constrained in its ability to fulfil its own ends of recovering lost territory, and stabilizing its revenues, by an absence of allies and the weakened state of its armed forces. To confront the Greeks, the Ottoman Navy needed more powerful ships. As a result, orders for two new Dreadnought-class battleships were placed with British shipyards, with a public subscription campaign to engage the passion of the people for the project. The army needed modernization and reorganization, and for that it needed military advisors. Here it turned to Germany. Ambassador Wangenheim described the Ottoman invitation as a unique opportunity to 'imbue the Turkish people with the German spirit' and the kaiser despatched General Otto Liman von Sanders in order to effect the 'Germanization of the Turkish Army' and make Germany dominant in Ottoman foreign policy.[28]

In late 1913 the appointment of Liman von Sanders to lead, rather than advise, the reorganization of the Ottoman Army provoked an international crisis. When St Petersburg objected in the strongest possible terms, he was assigned to command only the Ottoman I Corps, but this formation was at that time based in Istanbul with responsibility for the Straits. To the Russians, the Germans had effectively taken control of the Dardanelles by intrigue, and they announced their intention to seize Erzurum in eastern Anatolia as retaliation. The Ottomans took the view that Russia was now a direct existential threat to their territorial integrity and they looked to the Germans for diplomatic backing. Britain and France were concerned that Russia might attempt a *coup de main* and precipitate the final collapse of the Ottoman Empire, and the British Foreign Office suggested that Liman von Sanders might, instead, be invited to command II Corps, away from the Straits. The kaiser objected, and demanded that Liman von Sanders be promoted to field marshal, which gave him a supervisory role over the entire Ottoman Army, but he allowed a Turkish officer to take command of I Corps.[29]

The 'climb down' was unpopular in Germany giving rise to a sense of desperation amongst government officials in Berlin. Referring to the analogy of the demise of Napoleon, the kaiser remarked: 'Either the German flag will fly over the fortifications of the Bosporus or I shall suffer the same sad fate as the great exile on the island of St Helena.'[30] The bizarre idea of creating colonies in the Middle East by superimposing German rule over the Ottoman Empire was typical of Wilhelm's fantasy. The reality was that Germany was simply unable to create the exclusive economic bloc she had envisaged, and the Berlin–Baghdad railway, the artery of the proposed eastern empire, terminated in the mountains of Anatolia. The Baghdad section of the line was also embryonic. Most significant of all was the continued mistaken belief that the Germans could create a united pan-Islamic caliphate under the kaiser's benign leadership. It was a dangerous delusion in keeping with the notion that Wilhelm II was a beloved *Volkskaiser* (people's emperor) presiding over a nation that must either expand territorially or perish.

In strategic terms, what the British resented was all this disturbance to the established equilibrium between the major European nations, the so-called 'balance of power'. British foreign secretaries believed in using diplomacy to avert conflict and kept alive the old notion of a 'concert of Europe'. Britain was therefore trying to preserve the status quo in the Middle East, while Germany represented change and challenge. For the British, in terms of policy options beyond diplomacy, it was prestige and informal controls or influences that could reduce the need for physical and costly occupations, although that approach now seemed to be attended by greater risks.

British policy was essentially pragmatic. Given the impossibility of controlling every littoral along the maritime routes serving the British Empire, or extending security zones for its possessions deep into the interior of Africa, the Middle East, and Asia, the more subtle cultivation of local elites through bilateral agreements was the pragmatic and cost-effective solution. British interests in the Middle East and Mediterranean region were essentially the promotion and protection of trade, the security of India, the defence of the Suez Canal, and the exclusion of rivals from Egypt, Persia, Afghanistan, and the Gulf. Britain had the advantage of local agents; the personnel of the British and Indian Armies; other colonial auxiliaries in Egypt, the Sudan, and East Africa (who provided all the local security for Britain's residencies, consulates, and commerce); and the Royal Navy. Britain also had the strategic advantage that its enemies still had no comparable fleet in terms of power or reach.

However, there were a number of challenges. There were asymmetrical problems which were difficult to resolve, particularly intrigue by Germany, unstable buffer states, and unreliable allies. There were also broader strategic weaknesses to confront. The British government had to take a global view, and regarded the Middle East as relatively unimportant compared with the Mediterranean, Suez, or the Channel; but the British Indian government saw things differently and regarded southern Arabia, Persia, the Gulf, and Afghanistan as important elements in the security of the subcontinent, and the conflict of interest meant that policies with regard to the region appeared to be inconsistent. The fact was that the British Empire was not strong in land forces and simply could not afford to control the Dardanelles or occupy Persia or the Arab littoral sheikhdoms. The consistent aspect of British policy was that it needed the Ottoman Empire, Persia, and Afghanistan as bulwarks for its security, but the challenge was that they were weak and Britain found itself trying to shore up failing states. Diplomacy as a lever of strategy had its limits, and this fundamental dilemma was never quite resolved.

Making Strategy

For the Classical Mediterranean civilizations, strategy was the art of command and decision-making, but, by the late nineteenth century, war was transformed by the scale and range of new technologies and the 'mass' of industrial armies and navies. It was no longer possible to command, in person, formations of many tens of thousands along firing lines that extended laterally upwards of 30 miles and in great depth. Strategy was redefined as a plan of campaign, combining a clear objective with the 'how' it should be achieved. In the early nineteenth century, the influential Baron Antoine de Jomini had identified certain principles or guiding concepts that could increase the chances of success in campaigning, although his contemporary, Carl von Clausewitz, offered a more nuanced and comprehensive understanding of the nature of war and its dynamic effects.[31] Clausewitz realized that war was a total phenomenon, not just a series of military manoeuvres. He was particularly eager to understand enduring aspects of war which, if grasped, might ensure greater success. For this, he conceived of war as made up of a 'remarkable trinity' of passion, reason, and chance.[32] He argued that the essence of war is the passion of violence, with no 'natural limits', but identified a contrasting intellectual, rational search for objectives and techniques; and yet he cautioned that all war is subjected to friction, since wars are the realm of chance.[33]

In terms of solutions to this trinitarian nature of war, Clausewitz advocated rapid military adaptation to the new situation each war produced.[34] He noted that wars are not single decisive actions, but interactions, and the intensity of the struggle requires 'will' in the belligerent to endure its demands. Success also required the alignment of one's strategic 'ends, ways, and means', which he called the 'rational calculus' of war. To ensure the right objectives were sought he posited, famously, that war should be a continuation of a political policy, pursued by a variety of other means. He tended to advocate the full deployment and concentration of all available effort, and the exercise of strong will, which led him to believe that remaining permanently on the defensive could not produce the desired results in policy.[35] Thus, he argued that wars must be won by being on the offensive. He wrote that the focus of military effort should be concentrated at the enemy 'centre of gravity' (*Schwerpunkt*), in order to defeat them or coerce them to comply with one's own will.

Clausewitz had a realistic grasp of war, but he was still a man of his time and his work was criticized as impenetrable, impractical, or irrelevant. British critics pointed out that Clausewitz failed to offer a naval or economic dimension to the nature of war, even though these, with the exception of a brief expedition to Egypt, had been crucial in containing Napoleon and his land armies to Europe. Clausewitz also came in for criticism for failing to address aspects of technological development, and for his focus on state war-making at the expense of a study of guerrilla warfare. In his defence, Clausewitz knew all too well the embittered nature of a people's war, and his approach to strategy was formulated in part to avoid such protracted and problematic campaigns. There was more support for Clausewitz in his emphasis on the importance of willpower, arguing the purpose of war was to 'break the enemy will by destroying his means to resist'. Clausewitz also recognized the importance of thinking carefully about the formulation of strategy: while advocating a military education that would foster the *coup d'oeil* (instinctive insight) required by commanders in the heat of war, he noted the importance of well-trained officers in staff work that would overcome the complexity of getting an army mobilized, deployed to the right place at the right time, and therefore achieve the concentration of force at the decisive point.

The making of strategy is in part dependent on its geographical and temporal context, and variables such as time, economics, political culture, and what might be termed an orthodoxy in discourse all shaped the prevailing ideas of strategy and how they were constructed, accepted, and transformed. The location of resources, the continental or island status of the state in question, and the existence of choke points or avenues of commerce could all influence the making of strategy and create a number of assumptions and priorities.

In geographical terms, the Middle East was a cradle of civilization which, in antiquity, had depended on a 'fertile crescent' of cultivation in a region of deserts and mountain ranges, extending from the Jordan Valley in an arc south of the Caucasus and down the Tigris and Euphrates. The other great rivers, the Nile, the Amu-Daria (Oxus), the Indus, Diyala, Zab, Halys, and others formed the ribbons of settled land for adjacent civilizations and cultures, while coastal regions of the Black Sea, the Mediterranean, the Arabian Sea, and the Gulf produced their own seafaring cultures. Mountain ranges and arid regions, which channelled avenues of commerce and mobility, were the refuge of more impoverished and often warlike clans who preyed on caravans and more-settled populations.

This concentration of ancient civilizations made the Middle East the centre of three enduring world religions and a plethora of sects and factions, and their territorial claims were often based on their origin myths. This caused acute contestation of limited territorial space in cities such as Jerusalem and Constantinople (Istanbul). Moreover, it increased pressure to control vital resources, such as water in semi-arid regions, cultivable land areas, manpower, and even the possession of sites which formed the basis of belief systems. Historical influences also mattered a great deal: cultural behaviours were conditioned by actual and perceived experiences, be that past persecution, regeneration, or religious exceptionalism (such as the claim to be especially favoured by God). Religious arguments often prevented compromise and shaped very distinct identities and interests.

Overlaying these traditions is the history of a succession of empires and the conflicts that accompanied them. In the seventh and eighth centuries AD (first and second centuries in the Islamic calendar), the expansion of the Arab empire led to the establishment of a caliphate under the Umayyad dynasty. This collapsed through internal divisions and was overthrown by the Abbasids in 750 with a new empire centred on Baghdad. In the ninth century Shi'a Islam emerged through schism and there was further fragmentation of Arab and Islamic groups. North Africa turned to the Fatimid dynasty, while the Abbassids were defeated by the Seljuks of central Asia, part of a succession of waves of Steppe peoples from which the Turks derive their ancestry. In south Asia, more independent sultanates emerged, some lasting no more than the lifetime of one ruler, while others endured as hereditary systems. The fragmentation of the Islamic empire led to the various phases of the Crusades, and the territorial occupation of the coasts of the Near East, which, in time, became assimilated into the region's human fabric, although much older ethnic and faith-based societies such as the Jews, Maronites, Assyrians, Nestorian Christians, Kurds, Armenians, and Druze inhabited parts of the region. The Ottoman dynasty came to prominence between the 1400s and 1500s (800s and 900s in the Islamic calendar) in Anatolia, and, in the same period, so did the Safavids in Persia and the Mughals in South Asia.

In the eighteenth and nineteenth centuries, the rise of European empires posed a serious challenge to the Muslim states, and the economic take-off of the industrializing West created relative poverty in the Middle East. The flourishing of technology, science, mathematics, and learning, which had characterized the region in the medieval era, atrophied under the Ottoman dominion.[36] Some of the peripheries of the old Muslim world—including Aden, Egypt, the North African states, India, and Central Asia—were occupied by European powers.[37] In the Balkans, the indigenous Christian population, who had endured Muslim occupation from the sixteenth century, ejected the Ottomans with European backing, starting with the Greeks in the 1820s.

The geostrategic landscape in 1914 was therefore in a state of flux. The Ottoman Empire was economically weak, and had suffered multiple defeats over many decades. Some of the European powers, especially Russia, Austria-Hungary, and France were poised to dismember the sultan's remaining possessions, while Britain, as a maritime power eager to protect its sea lanes, saw strategic advantage in its preservation of the Ottoman regime against potential rivals.

Strategy is not only situated by geography and history, it is also an assessment of relative strength, of constraints, opportunities, and threats. It is a search for the exploitation of advantage, some 'edge' over an adversary, which may be time-specific. These aspects were strongly represented in Germany's calculations between 1912 and 1914. The sense of time running out, of gathering threats, or encirclement, and perhaps destruction, pervades the more alarmist German political and diplomatic literature of the period. The influence of military officers within the decision-making apparatus also created preferences for decisive solutions. In 1911, von Bülow, the chancellor, had argued that his policy of challenging the Entente powers aggressively was 'to confront France with the possibility of war, cause Delcassé [the French Naval Minister] to fall, break the continuity of aggressive French policy, knock the continental dagger out of the hands of Edward VII and the war group in England, and simultaneously ensure peace, preserve German honour and improve German prestige'. In the Ottoman Empire too, there was a deepening sense of crisis and anxiety, where military solutions seemed to offer a decisive escape.

Strategy is also the product of certain economic and technological developments. The relative power of European armies and navies in the late nineteenth century had enabled them to defeat almost every Asian and African state that they had encountered. By contrast, the Ottomans were struggling to keep up with the surge in technological changes taking place in Europe, although they possessed sufficient wealth and military power to suppress internal unrest and check some of the foreign encroachments. Britain was a leading economic power producing new technology, not least in warship design. Nevertheless, its economic base was dependent on relatively old systems and small units of production and it believed its leading commercial position in the globe was under threat. The United States and Germany were outstripping British manufacturing and heavy industry by 1914. The situation in Russia was far worse. While there were developed centres of industrial activity in pockets of the tsarist empire, the vast scale of the country worked against efficiency. In the first decade of the twentieth century, it was struggling to match the levels of production achieved by Germany. It was inefficient and badly structured to compete in the future. As a result, Russia too was looking for a decisive solution to avert a long-term decline.

These calculations remind us that strategy is made subject to domestic political considerations. The form of government and the direction of its policy, the resilience of the population, its prevailing ideology, and its 'will' to make sacrifices in the pursuit of policy all play a role in framing strategy. In 1914, the outbreak of war produced strong movements of popular support for their governments, even in colonies and otherwise peripheral territories. When war came, governments also exhibited firm resolution about the conflict, believing they were upholding important principles and ideas.

The purpose of strategy is to fulfil national interests, uphold values, and to put into practice the preservation of security, wealth, status, stability, influence, and political culture which is determined as 'policy'. Strategy is, in theory, subordinate to policy, and must be consistent with the prevailing strategic environment. Strategy is proactive, seeking to project forward a particular line of policy. Although strategy is about the use of force, and is therefore associated with war or confrontation, it demands a holistic perspective, incorporating a range of influences and drivers. In its ideal form, it would reflect the distilled wisdom of both one's own situation, one's allies, partners, and the adversary, but such comprehensive knowledge is obviously unobtainable and so strategy is often made in circumstances of doubt, anxiety, and pressure. Strategy is responsive to change and chance events (Clausewitz's 'friction'), and, once a strategy has been designed, it often challenges the status quo. Strategic decision-making is thus dynamic, setting out what must be accomplished and why, but decision-makers are constantly aware of the constraints and opportunities that can develop. That said, strategy is not as reactive or rapid as 'operational art' (the direction of military formations close to the front line or actually engaged in combat), and suggests a more enduring analysis which concentrates on drivers, motives, causes, and longer-term effects.[38]

In the making of strategy, certain perennial concepts often reappear, although not always with the same emphasis or relevance. Theorists of strategy concur that clarity of purpose, a definite aim, is vital. There is also some agreement on the value of adaptability, which is an essential requisite for survival. Various interpretations are placed on the value of coalitions and partners to create added strength, either moral or physical. In the theory, there are frequent references to 'weight', where the balance of an adversary can be tilted, undermined, or unsettled for some other exploitation. Opening up new fronts in the enemy's rear, for example, would compel an adversary to re-balance their forces, lose momentum, or even end an offensive.

Some enduring themes of strategy are much debated. There are invariably decisions to be made about the relative importance of mobility, the decision to go on the offensive, or remain on the more certain defensive, and the comparative value of concentration, dispersal, economy of effort, or full commitment. The varying importance of deception, surprise, and the possession of knowledge, or the use of information are also frequent areas of discussion amongst strategists.

There is agreement however on the dynamic interactive nature of conflict, which requires strategy to be a process of thinking through a set of problems, and the careful definition of an objective by study and calculation. Strategists have to acknowledge that war is inherently escalatory, and that the collision of conflict can have the effect of neutralizing advantages that, initially, seemed essential to achieving one's ends. In the First World War, the parity of the major powers created stalemates on all fronts for extended periods. To overcome the stasis, various strategies were conceived, some technological in character, others more concerned with restoring mobility, creating new threats to draw in and exhaust enemy resources, or generating widespread domestic subversion amongst the enemy's subject peoples. The dilemma was whether to try to bring about a decisive battle or whether to concentrate on exerting pressure on the enemy's government, economic capacity, and will of the people.[39]

War is, as Clausewitz repeatedly pointed out, the realm of chance. An effective strategy had to be able to manage unexpected outcomes, to consider the contingent, and to forecast the consequences of a planning process. For Clausewitz, unpredictability was not confined to events and unforeseen accidents, but to the passions of men. The sudden loss of will, the giddiness of victory that leads to overconfidence, or the overcautious commander could all make a difference to an otherwise robust strategy. Clausewitz was eager to cultivate a class of staff officer and leader who could compensate for these irrational tendencies. Preparation for leadership in war was to be cultivated where there was no innate 'genius'. Will and determination in leadership Clausewitz applauded strongly, regarding them as essential aspects of the trinity—that dynamic relationship between the government, the armed forces, and popular support—ensuring endurance, resilience in the face of hardship and loss, and an ability to calculate relative costs and losses, despite all the distractions of war. It was the basis of sound judgement.

Strategy is also dependent on the will of the population and their sense that the cause, for which the state fights, is just. The decay of that popular support might manifest itself first as dissent, but might develop into internal unrest, leading to revolt and even a full-scale popular revolution. Russia, Germany, and the Ottoman Empire experienced this collapse of public backing to varying degrees in 1917–18. Portions of the French and British imperial forces also rejected the war effort for brief periods. Lloyd George confessed that he was fearful that the Allied armies might panic and break when under immense pressure in 1918, but he discovered there was still a strong desire to resist, and, at home, he found a 'grim resolve imprinted on the faces of the people'.[40] Given the intensity of the Great War, what is surely remarkable is that the people, civilian and military, endured it for so long.

Contemporaries' Understanding of Strategy in 1914

The primary arm of defence for Great Britain and its empire was the Royal Navy. Lord Salisbury, the British Prime Minister and Foreign Secretary, to underscore the importance of maritime power to the United Kingdom and its empire, in 1887 concluded: 'we are fish'.[41] Britain's Royal Navy was twice as large as the next two largest powers combined. It possessed naval bases across the world. It could despatch expeditionary forces to reinforce any threatened point and in the nineteenth century it had mounted sustained operations to the Crimea, Persia, Abyssinia, China, and to Western and Southern Africa. Britain could not field armies of a great size, despite its colonial contingents, and there was some sense that the British 'way of war' was to operate on the peripheries of continents, making the decisive final contribution to the war efforts of others.[42] The exception was Britain's desire to maintain the integrity of certain small nations, including Belgium on the seaboard of the Continent, close to the shores of the British Isles.

New technologies and rival navies that had emerged by 1900 were not the most important challenge to Britain's hegemony. Rather, it was the political combinations against an isolated United Kingdom that mattered most. The Naval Intelligence Division concluded that control of the sea lanes in the Eastern Mediterranean, on which its East Asian commerce depended, could only be secured 'across the ruins of the French fleet', and, by extension, the fleets of France's Russian allies.[43] In the 1870s, cheap naval gunboats, a large naval 'estimate' (budget) and the neutralization of French power by Germany meant that Britain had been able to patrol its imperial seaways with relative impunity. Isolation had not been a significant political drawback and actually enabled it to avoid Continental commitments to conduct operations on grounds of its own choosing. By 1900, the strategic situation was radically different.

The British government therefore considered four 'grand strategic' options.[44] One was to continue to use diplomacy to negotiate on any dispute with its antagonists and avoid war. The second was to seek new alliance partnerships to share defence burdens. Thirdly, they could increase defence spending and emphasize the power of the Royal Navy as a form of conventional 'deterrence'. Fourthly, they could reconfigure their defence policy to meet future challenges, including the creation of a large conscript army trained for imperial garrison duty and Continental warfare.

The first option, diplomacy, was successful to a point. The problem was that the willingness of the Great Powers to work in a 'concert', as they had in the early nineteenth century, had started to unravel. Although there were conferences that settled international disputes, such as the crises of 1906 and 1912 over the future of Morocco, there was increased tension and distrust, not confidence and reassurance. International institutions can only function if there is sufficient will by the leading powers to compromise on their immediate national interests, and it is precisely at times of crisis that these powers will assert their own priorities. Britain's solution was to continue to work on pragmatic, bilateral agreements and focus only on areas of common concern, such as peace in the Balkans. In 1902, Britain established an alliance with Japan to shoulder some of its maritime security burden there, the second option, but it did not join either of the European alliance blocs, so this approach was limited.

Increased spending, the third option, was not a long-term solution. Britain's share of global manufacturing and commerce had fallen to 15 per cent of the word's output by 1913, and it had been overtaken by the United States and Germany. While its net income generation had increased (£6.2 billion in 1865 to £18 billion in 1900), there was an unwillingness to increase defence spending or alter the methods by which public finance could be extracted.[45] Worse still, the domestic debates of the late nineteenth century had been dominated by disagreements between the 'Blue Water' navalists and the British Army about spending priorities, precisely at a time when a comprehensive and unified scheme for imperial defence was required. There was no staff cooperation, both services developed their own intelligence branches, and there were advocates of each service prepared to fight it out in the press and in popular literature. In 1889, the Royal Navy won the debate on the grounds of providing the most reasoned defence of the United Kingdom and was awarded the Naval Defence Act with a budget of £21 million over five years. Nevertheless, relations with the army remained embittered when it came to Treasury awards, and Lord Randolph Churchill's idea of a united Ministry of Defence was drowned out by acrimonious discord.

The Royal Navy won the argument until the South African War (1899–1902), when naval supremacy failed to make any significant difference to the costs and difficulties of the conflict. What had begun as a short, colonial campaign to protect the British Empire against a small, aggressive rival, namely the Transvaal, became a protracted, often humiliating struggle costing £194 million.[46] It was a war that had briefly aligned Britain's rivals and critics, exposing the vulnerabilities of its isolation. At the same time, a revolution in military affairs was underway, particularly in naval technologies. Rival powers, possessed of the latest 'Dreadnought' warships by 1914, had rendered the 'mass' of Britain's fleets of gunboats obsolete.

The opportunity to enhance naval power through new technology appealed particularly to Imperial Germany, which placed enormous emphasis on the construction of capital ships. It was competition generated by these warship programmes and jealousy of naval power that led to a European land and naval arms race before the First World War, which, in turn, reduced the willingness of governments to trust their nearest rivals, and, perhaps, contributed to the outbreak of that war in 1914.[47]

Julian Corbett, who in 1900 was a naval historian and contemporary defence analyst, asserted that new technologies were no guarantee of success, arguing that strategy was far more important.[48] He had begun lecturing at the newly established British Naval War College, but he was critical of the intellectual poverty and 'amateurishness' of the Admiralty's strategic thinking, and was called in to assist in the reform of the navy's approach by Admiral Sir John 'Jacky' Fisher and the Director of Naval Intelligence. Thanks to his influence there was a new emphasis on strategic thinking, often through case studies, and on the planning process known as the 'war game'.

Corbett emphasized that naval strategy was not a separate branch of knowledge; it was intrinsically connected to the general principles of war. That said, he also pointed out that the maritime environment possessed unique characteristics when it came to warfare, and, naturally, navalists used this observation to argue for continued 'separation' and distinctiveness in resourcing and direction. He wrote: 'What is usually called Naval Strategy or Fleet Strategy is only a sub-division of a division of strategy, and... therefore, strategy cannot be studied from the point of view of naval operations only.'[49] His solution was to place greater emphasis on combined land–sea operations.

Corbett's famous contribution to thinking about naval strategy was to identify the importance of 'passage and communications', and that securing control of the sea was dependent on these factors. Yet what always mattered most was the *political* context. The purpose of blockades and amphibious operations, for example, was to change the political situation on land. The classic sea battle, regarded as the epitome of naval excellence in 1900, was for Corbett only relevant if it produced a clear political outcome. If not, it was merely an audacious risk and overemphasized the offensive over a far more certain strategic defence. Corbett's views were not always well-received. Naval historian Eric Grove has noted that 'experienced naval officers resented being told about their business by a dilettante man of letters . . . the fact that their lecturer was not a seaman clearly rankled, and his doctrinal views could thus be dismissed as not being based on mystical "sea sense"'.[50]

Corbett understood that what he was analysing was maritime and not purely naval strategy. He paid close attention to the developments of his age. By 1914 improved continental infrastructure, such as the extensive development of railways, threatened the unique importance of maritime power. His contemporary, Halford Mackinder, who was pioneering work on geopolitics, challenged the traditional faith in superior navies as the key to political hegemony.[51] However, Corbett used studies of historical conflicts to show the value of limited war, and how political objectives could be realized through a combined use of the levers of national power, including the nation's wealth and its commerce. For island nations, like Great Britain, limited war was an option that was effectively denied to Continental powers, for the vulnerability of their interests, lying adjacent to neighbouring states, would lead to the need to escalate war and mobilize their entire national resources. Yet, there was a paradox. At sea, rather than being limited to confined areas of operations, as the land environment was, maritime warfare was always potentially global.

Contemporary political advocates of a strike-force navy were eager to condemn Corbett's 'confusing treatise'.[52] But his understanding of policy and strategy was sophisticated: he realized that, in certain situations, maritime and naval forces might be less important than land-based ones. Above all, in the making of strategy, he understood the maritime environment was inseparable from the land, and subject always to political context. He concluded: 'The practical purpose [of teaching naval history] was to show how in the past the Admiralty never had a clean slate upon which to work out their plan of campaign. They were always hedged in by political and diplomatic considerations, which prevented them from following purely strategical lines.'[53] That observation was played out in the Great War in the Middle East in a very direct way.

There were, of course, equivalent ideas about land-based strategies in Britain. During the First World War, the *Daily Mail* journalist H. W. Wilson and a team of authors produced periodicals as an illustrated history of the Great War that eventually ran to thirteen volumes, and in one edition in 1916 Major G. W. Redway gave an explanation of Britain's strategy to the public.[54] He criticized the Clausewitzian fallacy of a quick victory which Germany had apparently gambled upon:

> In forming his plans [a commander will] first consider geographical conditions and seek inspiration from history (the art of war). He will thus learn that an immediate success may be gained by seeking out the main army and bringing it to battle in Napoleonic fashion, but, as an alternate course, he may refer to what Wellington called 'the sure game' and leave to climate, season, natural obstacles and spectral want the disintegration of the enemy forces.[55]

Contrasting the brute force of the German approach, Redway suggested that 'fighting takes place only as a means of overcoming opposition to the commander's designs'. The suspicion that Redway was seeking to explain the absence of any significant victory in 1916, and his advocacy of a long-term approach is further reinforced by his assessment of the initial successes achieved in Mesopotamia. Amid the praise for General Barrett, who commanded there, he wrote: 'While a crowning victory and the complete destruction of the enemy's fighting power are the ideals to strive for, experience shows that the generals usually have to be content with a half measure of success.'[56]

The assessment of strategy in the First World War revealed just how far tactical issues had thwarted traditional offensive strategic options. Redway admitted:

> Infantry in defence have a comparatively easy task, for, ensconced behind parapets of earth affording loopholes for rifles, they shoot from a rest at ranges already marked at a target of running men. Abundance of ammunition is handy. When a man falls his place is taken by a fresh man from the support, and the shooting is kept up even though the enemy is swarming over the trenches, for certain formed bodies called local reserves have been waiting for the opportunity for what the French call the 'offensive-return'.[57]

The ability of artillery to neutralize defences could also be countered by defensive artillery fire, and, reflecting on the conflicts of the preceding fifty years, which indicated the power of shellfire and protective earthworks, it seemed the Europeans had been 'slow to learn'. While gunners initially had placed a premium on locating and hitting a target precisely, so the *tir de barrage*, a curtain of fire through which assaulting infantry or enemy batteries had to pass, gained currency in 1915–16. This came with a concomitant rise in the expenditure of ammunition, which in turn created a strategic pressure on the munitions industries at home. In 1914, it was assumed guns would require up to 500 shells a day, yet in 1915 a single battery fired 3,100 shells in forty-five minutes. After expending 30,000 shells, the gun barrels were worn out. Light railway support to ferry ammunition, repair units, armourers, and workshops and to replace guns therefore became an essential requirement in sustaining modern operations.

The protracted character of trench warfare also drew comment regarding its effect on strategy: 'The salient feature of these long-drawn-out battles is the utilisation of strategic reserves—that is, forces that were in training or concentration when the battle began.'[58] The ability to transport forces to threatened zones, and to 'close down secondary theatres' meant that victories by attacking forces on one day could be prevented by timely reinforcements bolstering the defences on another, and the requirement to move forces in offence or defence placed far greater emphasis on the work of the staffs. In this context, a defensive strategy was valued for its ability to gain time, to conserve strength, to garner the support of neutrals, to rouse popularity at home, lengthen enemy supply routes, and compel an adversary to reveal their intentions and capability. It was this which appealed to the British as a description of their own approach at the strategic level, even when they used offensives at what we now call the operational level. Offensive strategy was seen as having value in bringing about the occupation of enemy territory which could, in turn, be used to supply one's army, but this aggressive exploitation was associated with Germany and the other Central Powers. However, in the Middle East, what may have begun as a counter-offensive in 1915 had developed into something more far-reaching by 1918.

British 'ends' in the Middle East in 1914 were to preserve the Ottoman Empire while attempting to dissuade the sultan and his governments from supporting German designs and intrigues. There was also a long-standing desire to see reforms implemented that would modernize the financial, economic, and political system and therefore make the Ottoman Empire more resilient. Throughout the nineteenth century, British statesmen had condemned episodes of brutal repression within the Ottoman domains, which only served to justify foreign intervention, particularly by Russia. Britain's regional ends were also closely connected to the policy of imperial defence. It was therefore ironic, as historian David Fieldhouse points out, that Great Britain, the country that was to lead the dismemberment and destruction of the Ottoman Empire, was the one country that had previously sought to preserve it.[59] The only area of defined British national interest when the war began was the outlet of Persian oil at Abadan on the Shatt al-Arab, close to the Ottoman city of Basra.

It was not until March 1915 that Britain articulated a set of wartime strategic 'ends' for the Ottoman Empire, several months after hostilities had broken out. The De Bunsen Committee, established by Herbert Asquith, the Prime Minister, was charged with formulating Britain's policy towards the Middle East and the post-war settlement.[60] The committee considered four options. The first was to partition the Ottoman Empire and reduce it to the rump of Turkish Anatolia. The second was to preserve the empire but, like Persia, demarcate zones of control and spheres of influence by other powers. The third option was to preserve or restore the Ottoman Empire as a purely Asian dominion, effectively reinforcing the outcome of the First Balkan War. The final option, which was the committee's recommendation, was to turn the Ottoman Empire into a federated state, with autonomous provinces.

The demand for a definition of British regional war aims had been prompted by the French, who had more interest in the future of the Ottoman territories. These had been expressed more than sixty years before, as a supervisory guardianship of the Christian holy places of the Near East, and a cultural link to Beirut, Aleppo, and Syria through the influence of Catholic missionaries and Christian populations, especially the Maronites. In material terms, France had invested in parts of the Ottoman economy, including the Near Eastern rail lines and its silk industry. Among the colonialist advocates of a stronger French influence in the Levant was François Georges Picot, a member of the lobby group, the Comité de l'Asie Française, but he had a number of allies within the French government. Picot, who had been a consular official in Beirut, was relieved of his duties just after the war broke out, which prevented him from carrying out a planned Maronite insurrection against the Ottoman authorities.[61] The British de Bunsen recommendation, to reduce the Ottoman Empire to autonomous provinces, did not meet the approval of Picot or the French Foreign Minister, Théophile Delcassé, who preferred the idea of spheres of influence. Nevertheless, the British suggested that, should there be a British operation against the Dardanelles or Alexandretta (today's Iskenderun on Turkey's Mediterranean coast), the

French would be able to contribute detachments in order to represent their interests in a later partition. This proposal was accepted by the French Minister of War, Alexandre Millerand.

The difficulty was that Russian war aims against the Ottoman Empire were far more extensive than those outlined by either Britain or France. The tsar wanted complete control of Istanbul and the Straits. Delcassé was again not in agreement, even though Sir Edward Grey, Britain's Foreign Secretary, was prepared to swallow the Russian demand. The result was that Picot and his colleagues in Comité de l'Asie Française began to lobby for a Greater Syria under French control, the borders of which would extend to Mosul in the east and Jerusalem, or even Egypt, in the south.[62]

In late November 1915, Sir Mark Sykes and Picot led the British and French delegations to decide on the future of the Ottoman Empire. Various schemes were discussed: the British looked to have a buffer zone for Egypt, the Gulf, and southern Arabia, and some supervisory role over Anatolia through the sultan of Egypt and the sharif of Mecca. The French argued they must have a Greater Syria. In the second round of talks, territorial allocations were debated, and there was inclusion of Greek and Italian interests. The approximate divisions were agreed, and then approved by Russia, in May 1916, although the Russian government gave secret assurances to France that it would argue in favour of France having Palestine, which the British had insisted be excluded from a Greater Syria.

The Ottoman war aims were even more complex and contested. The priority after the Second Balkan War had been urgent modernization, without which it would not be possible to fulfil their irredentist aims of recovery of the islands of the Aegean or territory in the Balkans. Suppression of all internal dissent was also thought essential to bring to an end the political turmoil of the years after 1908. Reflecting these priorities, Djemal was made Minister of Works and Enver became Minister of War, while Talaat was appointed Minister of the Interior. Beneath this agenda was the ideology of Turkish nationalism espoused by Ziya Golkap, who argued for a stronger state through a 'Turkish policy' in language, education, and political life.[63] It was a movement that on the one hand wanted to emulate European modernization, yet rejected foreign control of the economy. Moreover, while the loss of the Balkans seemed to herald the opportunity to make the empire a more self-consciously Islamic state, the growth of a secular Turkish nationalism was a reaction to this development and to the potentially stronger position of Arabs in the imperial apparatus.[64]

In essence, France and Russia were clear about their aspirations to dismember the Ottoman Empire, but, on the eve of war, Britain's policy was less well-defined. At the outbreak, London had to clarify what it wished to achieve—its 'ends'—and these were, in essence, defensive. For Britain, imperial security was the priority. The Ottoman Empire had an even more ambiguous agenda in August 1914. It did not join the European war immediately through unpreparedness. When each of the empires had decided on the ends of the war, they next had to consider how, and with what, these objectives were to be fulfilled.

2

Ways and Means

Armed Forces and Decision-Making, 1914

The Great War was an imperial war.[1] Not only were a share of the resources for waging the conflict drawn from outside of Europe, making the various global sea lanes and continental lines of communication strategically important, but the authority and prestige of political control exercised by Britain, France, Germany, and the Ottoman Empire depended on their military or naval capabilities, and their monopoly of force. The points of strategic vulnerability for the British Empire were twofold: one, its religious composition and the capacity for Islam to be used to mobilize resistance to the Christian or secular authorities; and two, the overwhelmingly non-European ethnic composition of the empire with a corresponding dependence on indigenous sub-imperialists to maintain order, provide labour, and maintain the flow of trade. The British were dependent on a degree of consent to their imperial authority, which could be jeopardized by subversion or defeat.

A declaration of war by the Ottoman Empire would make it easier for the British to justify war in order to persuade their Muslim subjects to participate. Nevertheless, there were some misgivings about asking Muslim troops to fight their co-religionists in Ottoman territories.[2] The sultan's declaration of Islamic holy war on 14 November 1914 was thus convenient in making this a defensive war for the British Empire, but it did not entirely extinguish its concerns. During the conflict, only a small proportion of Muslim soldiers deserted or resisted their imperial masters, largely because of national, ethnic, and linguistic differences, and, amongst the troops of the Indian Army, there was a stronger corporate loyalty to the British than to the caliph.[3] Even so, the allegiances of Muslim soldiers were an unknown quantity for the strategic planners of 1914.

If the British and French empires were vulnerable, the Ottoman Empire was regarded as so weak and dependent that it might fail altogether if pressed hard. In the nineteenth century, Britain's policy had been to offer qualified support to the Ottoman Empire, largely as a bulwark against Russia. Propping up the Ottomans had required pressure for financial and governance reform and few believed the regime of the Sublime Porte would ever manage any substantial reorganization. Indeed, the prevailing assessment was that the 'Sick Man of Europe' was in terminal decline. Not that this was welcome to the British either. If the Ottoman Empire broke up, it would have strategic implications. Provinces that lay close to the sea route to India in the Eastern Mediterranean and the Arabian Peninsula might create vulnerabilities for Russia or Germany to exploit.

British assessments of weakening Ottoman military capabilities were not unreasonable, and based on recent observations of the Balkan Wars. After a series of set-backs between 1912 and 1913, the Ottoman Army was still considered unready for significant operations during a period of much needed reform. Germany's assessments were similar. The kaiser's decision to despatch General Liman von Sanders as senior advisor, and his instruction to 'Germanize' the Ottoman forces, was as much a recognition of the empire's

Figure 2.1 Otto Liman von Sanders, who organized the Ottoman Fifth Army on Gallipoli in 1915 and the last-ditch Ottoman defence of Palestine and Syria in 1918

incapacity as it was a vague attempt to spread German influence in the region. Historian Hew Strachan notes that Ambassador Wangenheim in Constantinople (Istanbul) thought Russia would make a far better partner for German aspirations in the Middle East and that Turkey was too 'dependent'.[4] While the Ottoman Army made rapid progress in its transformation, it was still untried and unready in 1914: the war came too early even for the Turkish reformers to be confident about its performance. The army was crippled by shortages in almost every sphere, including artillery, rifles, horses, and transport, and Enver believed it would take at least five years to rectify the most acute problems.[5] Consequently, the Ottoman strategic objective in 1913 was to find partners to recover its position in the Balkans, and it had considered France, Russia, and Britain. Germany was the last of the Great Powers to be approached, and an alliance was concluded at a comparatively late stage, on 22 July 1914.[6]

The British were far more concerned with the growing German threat to the Middle East, and believed, at the outbreak of war, that the kaiser's ambitions could be checked by an operation against the Ottoman Empire. Once again, there was a strategic threat that Britain could not ignore. Germany owned the Anatolian Railway Company and its much-vaunted purpose was to construct a railway from Berlin to Baghdad. The railway would link central Europe's economies with the resources of the East, circumventing the maritime strength of Britain, France, and the United States.[7] Moreover, the kaiser's self-promotion as friend of the Muslims, with rumours of his secret conversion to Islam, while regarded as histrionics, could not be ignored entirely. Indeed, German designs to raise a holy war against British and French control in Muslim lands were not a *canard*.[8] Once the war had broken out, Turkish and German missions of subversion were despatched to Egypt, Persia, the Gulf, and Afghanistan.[9]

From the British perspective, Constantinople was never sincere about its initial 'neutrality' in the war. On 29 July, London impounded two Ottoman Dreadnought battleships (the *Sultan Osman* and the *Reshadieh*) which were under construction in Britain, a not unreasonable decision in light of German and Ottoman hostility. The seizure of the vessels was legal under British contractual law, but the popular reaction in Constantinople was angry condemnation. Then, on 2 August, just after the outbreak of war in Europe the Ottomans signed a secret treaty with Germany, followed by a similar agreement with Austria-Hungary on 5 August. Here was the smoking gun: these moves effectively ended the Ottoman Empire's neutrality.

In the second week of August, two German cruisers, the *Goeben* and the *Breslau*, escaped the Royal Navy in the Mediterranean by passing through the Dardanelles. They reached Istanbul, where they were transferred into the Ottoman Navy.[10] On 15 August, the façade finally dropped when the Ottoman Navy was, as far as the British believed, transferred to German control. The British thence regarded the Ottoman Empire as a *de facto* belligerent, readying an expeditionary force of the Indian Army to secure the oil in southern Persia with a landing near Basra, diplomatic overtures to Greece, and a naval blockade. As First Lord of the Admiralty, Churchill was a particularly strong advocate of a closer alignment with Greece, Romania, and Bulgaria against the Ottomans.[11] As operations unfolded in Europe, on 1 October the Ottomans closed the Dardanelles Straits to all Entente shipping. In an instant, Russia's export trade, dependent on the waterway, was thrown into crisis.

Strategically, the British had lost the Ottoman Empire to the Central Powers, but the leaders in Berlin and Vienna had been unable to affect the decision-making process in Istanbul, where operations against the Greeks and Serbians were the strategic priority, an objective that would have brought the Ottomans into collision with Russia and the Entente in due course. As it was, the Ottoman government engineered its entry into the war by pre-emptive naval strikes against Russian Black Sea ports on 29 October 1914.

The Ottoman Empire's strategic decision-making was dependent on the triumvirate of Enver, Djemal, and Talaat.[12] These men, the Turkish dictators of the ruling Committee of Union and Progress, were considered 'power hungry and beset by petty jealousies, which compromised their ability to work effectively together'.[13] Despite later claims that Germany had engineered the Ottomans into the war, it was the ambitions and militaristic outlook of this triumvirate which not only prompted Ottoman action but also their grandiose strategic schemes.[14] The German ambassador, Hans von Wangenheim, encouraged the Young Turks, but the German Army actually took a different line. Liman von Sanders and the German military mission did not think that the Ottoman Empire was fit to take an offensive role and their concern was that its armed forces should limit themselves to a defensive strategy that focused on denying the Dardanelles to the Entente powers. Nevertheless, in Berlin, there was strong support for the strategy of revolution against Britain's colonies around the world, by appealing to both nationalistic and pan-Islamic ideology amongst the peoples of Africa and

Asia.[15] The vehicle for this policy of revolutionary war was the call to arms to all Muslims.[16]

When the Ottoman triumvirate announced it would launch two offensives in 1914, one into the Russian Caucasus, and the other into Egypt, there was some dismay in German military circles. Resourcing two major offensives simultaneously, particularly after a prolonged mobilization, caused some officers to doubt the competence of the Ottomans. There had also been months of procrastination: the Ottomans had resisted joining the war in August and had refused to cooperate in joint action with Austria-Hungary. Relations had been so strained that the German military mission to the Ottoman Empire was almost withdrawn. Nevertheless, the prospect of an Ottoman campaign into Egypt to seize the Suez Canal would cause serious strategic and reputational damage to the British. At the very least it would compel London to divert troops from the Western Front. That said, Germany and the Ottoman Empire saw the attack on Egypt differently. For Berlin it was 'a means to an end', but for Djemal 'it was an end in itself'.[17] Djemal expected that an Ottoman offensive across the Suez Canal would ignite an Islamic revolt against the British.[18]

Enver, in contrast to Djemal, believed the strategic objectives of the empire were the recovery of the lost Balkan territories and the annexation of the Russian Caucasus, northern Persia, and the 'recovery' of Turkestan and northern Afghanistan. This 'pan-Turanianism' appealed to the idea that all Turkic peoples were linked by heritage and language.[19] It was a manifestation of Turkish nationalism within the Ottoman Empire but its ideas were not popular, even within the Ottoman Army. Enver therefore ensured that members of the Committee of Union and Progress were given senior command appointments to see through the invasion of the Caucasus.

There seems to have been little consideration of the consequences of a set-back to either of the schemes.[20] Yet, it was the failure of both offensives that drew the Entente into counter-attacks and placed the Ottoman Empire on a defensive footing on every front.[21] Indeed, it meant that the empire was soon engaged in serious fighting not on two fronts, but five. Worse still, it soured relations between the Ottoman leaders Enver and Djemal on one side, and the Germans on the other.[22] Cooperation continued, but there were conflicts of interests and contested priorities throughout the war. Moreover, interpretations differed. The German conception of any revolt in Egypt, for example, was that it would be nationalist in character, a view that was distinctly at odds with Djemal's idea of a unifying, pan-Islamic cause.[23]

Yet neither had bargained on Britain's ability to maintain the support of the Egyptians through the indigenous elites, particularly their assurances about 'self-government' after the war.[24] At the same time, the nationalists were divided and disorganized, just as they were inside Ottoman Syria and amongst Arab factions. The leadership of the Egyptian nationalist party, the *Wafd*, did eventually manage to mobilize popular protests in 1919, but this only proved possible because of the hardships imposed by the conditions experienced during the war. As was to occur elsewhere in this theatre, revolutionary motives and capacity were completely exaggerated by each of the major powers.

Means: The Ottoman Armed Forces in 1914–18

Reform of the Ottoman Army was literally the first priority of the Committee of Union and Progress after the defeats of the Balkan Wars.[25] Before the war, on 3 January 1914, Enver took personal control of the reorganization, establishing agreements with Britain, France, and Germany to send, respectively, naval, gendarmerie, and military advisors. The German mission recommended changes to the Ottoman system of conscription and therefore the methods of mobilization. The objective, for both Germany and the Ottoman Empire, was to raise a larger army more rapidly: it was envisaged that the Ottoman Army would eventually number 500,000 men. By 2 August 1914, when the secret treaty with Germany was concluded, some 12,469 officers and 477, 868 men had been enlisted.[26] The rapid recovery from the casualties and discharges of the Balkan Wars, and from the loss of the conscripts that would have been available from the Balkan territories, was made possible by clamping down on the widespread practice of exemptions (which excluded over half of the annual eligible numbers) and limitations on taking personnel from certain communities.

The response to the outbreak of war was mixed. While units in western Anatolia reached their full strength quickly, the proportion of men coming forward in eastern Anatolia, Mesopotamia, and other Arab territories was much lower. The XII (Mosul) and XIII (Baghdad) Corps, for example, never reached full strength because of evasion and desertion. Formations in Yemen and Hejaz were not mobilized at all. The manpower shortages that plagued the Ottoman Army therefore started in 1914, and became progressively more acute. While the original age of conscription was 20–45 years

Figure 2.2 The Dardanelles: the view from the stern of HMS *Agamemnon*, the vessel that took part in the ill-fated naval attack of March 1915, and appeared off Istanbul in 1918 to accept the Ottoman surrender

at the outbreak of war, it was extended to 18-year-olds in April 1915 when the Allies landed at Gallipoli, and was further extended to men up to 50 the following spring.[27] The empire was supposed to be able to produce 2 million servicemen, but it took a full year of war before these numbers were actually in service. In 1916, the army numbered about 2.5 million, and, by 1917, despite significant losses, there were 2.8 million under arms.[28]

The men allocated to the infantry were initially expected to serve for two years in the regulars, the *Nizam*, and then spend twenty-three years in the reserve (first line *Ikhtiat*; second line *Redif*, and then a militia, the *Mustahfiz*), although in the other arms it was three years of service and just seventeen in the reserves. The reserves had a standing cadre to manage mobilization, but the training of reserves was practically non-existent. Students and other socially elite groups were granted shorter terms or exemptions, and the physically unfit were expected to pay a tax for their exclusion. Jews and Christians were not permitted to join the fighting forces but could be allocated to labour battalions. Manpower and equipment shortages were problematic. The administration and logistics of the army was its weakest point, despite German efforts to improve matters. Uniforms and basic equipment were usually in short supply. By the midpoint of the conflict, strict orders had to be issued to prevent issued sandbags being cut up and used as clothing.

At the outbreak of war, there were four armies, but during the war this was increased to nine. Nevertheless, the increase in scale was illusory. In peacetime, a *Nizam* division was made up of thirteen infantry battalions, a squadron of cavalry, and twenty-four field guns: a total strength of 15,000, which could be brought up to a war establishment of 19,000. In reality, divisions were barely half that size. Yet there are also accounts that show desperate measures were imposed to overcome the haemorrhaging of casualties, sickness, and desertion, including the impressment of teenagers and old men. By the end of the war, despite these exigencies, Ottoman armies were no larger than divisions. In an extreme example, the Ottoman First Army declined from 200,000 men in 1914 to 3,000 men in 1917.

The army was organized into divisions, each of three regiments which themselves consisted of three battalions. An infantry battalion could field twenty-four officers and 700 men, at least in theory. Alongside the battalions, the army possessed sixty-four separate machine-gun companies, and the relative density of machine-gun units across the army, compared with the British Army and the imperial forces, was a particular strength. Cavalry regiments were made up of five 100-man squadrons, and these were augmented by Kurdish and Arab irregular horsemen, who, while titled 'volunteers', were often not. Neither regular nor irregular cavalry was well-mounted, and horse management was poor. More enthusiasm could be found amongst voluntary irregular units, or from Muslim *muhacirs* ('refugees') who had been displaced by the Balkan Wars or from the Caucasus. Men released from prisons and placed into irregular bands for war service were also eager to fight, particularly if there was some chance of material gain. Yet, irregular units were notoriously unreliable. The 20,000 Kurdish cavalrymen in the Caucasus at the outbreak of war had dwindled through desertion to just 3,000 by November 1914.[29] Large numbers of deserters became brigands in Anatolia and the Caucasus, joining the insurgent bands that plagued isolated logistics units in Mesopotamia or stragglers in the long retreats.[30]

There has been some debate in recent years about the numbers of Arabs serving in Ottoman units. It was long argued that the defence of the Gallipoli peninsula was conducted by units that were overwhelmingly Anatolian 'Turkish' in ethnicity.[31] Critics noted that two of the regiments at Gallipoli were from Aleppo, and only one, the 77th, was under the command of

Colonel Mustapha Kemal. This, it was thought, demonstrated that Arab soldiers, rather than Turks, had played a key role in checking the initial British and imperial landings. The difficulty with this thesis is that the troops that had been stationed at Aleppo before the war were not all locally recruited. Enlistment data did not record the ethnicity of the recruits, but there appears to be some evidence to show that the Aleppo regiments consisted of a mix of groups, including Turks, Nusayris, and Turcomans. In other words, the ranks were filled with men that would best fit the description of Ottoman, rather than Arab or Turkish. The issue of ethnicity affects assessments of the number of Arabs in the army as a whole. There are various estimates, and the figure of 300,000 is sometimes used, which would represent some 20 to 25 per cent of the fighting strength of the army in 1915. If correct, this would make a striking contrast with the much-vaunted claims of those that focus on the success of the 'Arab revolt': its Hashemite leaders mustered some 6,000 volunteer fighters, but this is dwarfed by the number who remained loyal to the Ottoman regime. One final qualification is needed, however. Of those in Ottoman service, the number of genuine volunteers was small. Captured Allied soldiers recalled seeing men from Mosul brought in under duress, 'roped together by the shoulders and further secured in pairs with wooden handcuffs [and] strings of footsore Arabs arrived to be trained'.[32]

By contrast, the *topkhana* (artillery) was the *corps d'élite* of the Ottoman Army. Many batteries were armed with the latest German 75 mm Krupp field guns although there were older varieties, especially in heavy artillery. German influences in the structure of the Ottoman Army were mirrored in equipment: the infantry carried Mauser rifles, operated German signals equipment, and were supported by German aircraft. Moreover, German officers served on the staff of all headquarters. Indeed, of the seventy-three staff officers in Palestine and Mesopotamia in 1917, all but nine were German.

The Ottoman Navy was another weak point of the empire. Apart from two German vessels, the rest of the fleet was small in scale and aged. The capital ship *Messudieh* was sunk by a British submarine in the Straits, leaving four battleships, two cruisers and thirty other vessels but the Ottomans were dependent on German U-boats for any 'strike' capability.

Means: The British Imperial Forces

The Royal Navy possessed the world's most powerful fleet, and, on the eve of war even Germany, its most committed rival, could only muster half the number of Britain's battleships and armoured cruisers. While the main focus in 1914 was to ready the Grand Fleet of the North Sea to contain and defeat the German Kriegsmarine, squadrons were based around the world, including the Mediterranean.[33] Assisting the surface ships in long-range reconnaissance were aircraft of the Royal Naval Air Service (RNAS), which, during the war, improvised in bombing and ground attack.[34] By 1917, despite some losses, the Royal Navy was perhaps even more formidable. It could deploy sixty-one battleships, twelve battlecruisers, and twenty-four 'heavy' cruisers (each with a displacement of over 9,000 tons); eleven cruiser squadrons (one in the Mediterranean); sixteen flotillas (each up to twenty vessels) of destroyers; as well as submarines, monitors (semi-submersibles), seaplane carriers, merchant cruisers, and Q-ships (merchant vessels converted into submarine killers). It was the vast armada of the Royal Navy that could transport land forces to any coast in the world, and protect sea communications on which vital supply lines depended. As a marine capability, it could land two brigades of the Royal Naval Division and could place aloft twenty-seven squadrons of the RNAS, each with between eighteen and twenty-four aircraft. Moreover, the firepower of naval gunnery was significant. In the early weeks of the war, the Royal Navy were able to bombard Aqaba (on the Red Sea coast on what is now Jordan), the forts at the limits of the Dardanelles, and threaten Alexandretta. Indeed, there was great consternation in the Ottoman government that the British could land troops on practically any coast of their territory, and, if the Dardanelles were breached, then Istanbul would be entirely at the mercy of British guns.

The Royal Flying Corps, which was a branch of the army until the creation of the Royal Air Force in May 1918, experienced rapid growth during the war reaching 179 squadrons on the Western Front and in Italy by 1917. Nevertheless only small contingents could be spared for service in the Egyptian Expeditionary Force, in Mesopotamia, or in support of the Arab revolt, although the few machines that were used made a significant difference to reconnaissance, the direction of artillery, and ground-attack operations.

The British Army was a small, volunteer force in 1914, and while perhaps perfectly suited to expeditionary warfare against small states, was inadequate for fighting the scale of a Continental adversary such as Germany. The British Expeditionary Force (BEF) that deployed to France at the beginning of the war was not designed for a European war. Richard Haldane, the Secretary of State for War (1905–12), had predicted in 1906 that 'our wars... require an Army wholly different from that of any other nation [whose] possible work may vary between the defence of India,... to some small war in a Crown Colony'.[35] The Committee of Imperial Defence, established in 1902, was, as its name suggests, focused on the British Empire's security, although the Army Council (1904) and the General Staff (1905) looked at closer cooperation with France. The coordinator was, in theory, the Chief of the Imperial General Staff (CIGS), but in 1914, the ailing General Sir Charles Douglas was unable to take a lead and he died two months after the outbreak of war. The Director of Military Operations was Major General Charles Edward Callwell, a colonial soldier, but when Kitchener was appointed as Secretary of State for War, he did not even consult him. In contrast to the First Lord of the Admiralty, Winston Churchill, who held regular meetings with the First Sea Lord and his staff, Kitchener was 'a one man show'.[36]

The BEF was much lauded for its sacrifice in 1914, not least because it retained its cohesion despite catastrophic losses, but it was not sufficient. Moreover, the Territorial Force, which had emerged from the 1908 reform of the Yeomanry, Militia, and Volunteers, was also far too small for the tasks with which it was presented. In 1914, the Territorials were dispatched hastily to several colonial stations in order to release regulars needed in Europe. The regular reserves, divided into four categories of readiness or service conditions, filled the gaps. Conscious of the urgent need for manpower to augment this small army, Kitchener famously called for more volunteers in order to create 'New Armies'. The response was overwhelming, with 33,000 a day coming forward in September 1914. In July 1915, the initial flood had slowed and a National Registration Act, and the Derby Scheme of October that year, allowed for a further reserve or manpower to be created. Still the demands increased, and in January and July 1916 conscription was introduced for unmarried and then married men between 18 and 41 years of age. Such was the severity of the crisis in 1918 that the age of service was extended to 51, although the system was brought under civilian control as the Ministry of National Service in November 1917. In total, some 2.6 million volunteered and 2.3 million were conscripted.

In 1917, the British Army had five armies in Europe, with the First Army under Sir Henry Horne (I, XI, XIII, Canadian, and Portuguese Corps); the Second Army under Sir Herbert Plumer (IX, X, I and II ANZAC); the Third Army under Sir Julian Byng (III, IV, VI, VII, XVII Corps, 4th Cav Div); the Fourth Army under Sir Henry Rawlinson (XV Corps and 1st Div), and the Fifth Army under Sir Hubert Gough (II, V, VIII, XIV, XVIII, XIX Corps), while the Cavalry Corps was led by Sir Charles Kavanagh, and possessed four divisions. Forces were also required in the colonies to maintain the imperial garrisons, not least in the protection of the Suez Canal. In the Middle East, the two principal armies were the Egyptian Expeditionary Force (initially under Sir Archibald Murray, then Sir Edmund Allenby) and the Tigris Corps (led by Sir Stanley Maude until his death that year when he was replaced by Sir William Marshall). The composition of these forces varied, with an increasingly large component being made up of Indian Army personnel.

The standard organization of the British Army was the Division, with Corps and Army groups regarded as a special wartime requirement. Each Division consisted of four brigades although in 1918, manpower shortages had reduced this to three with a corresponding increase in the number of machine-gun companies. Each brigade was made up of four battalions supported with twenty-four machine guns. In 1915, the number of heavy Vickers machine guns per brigade was doubled, and in 1916, a brigade would possess forty-eight Lewis light machine guns and sixteen Vickers. The infantrymen would also be backed by trench mortars that could hurl projectiles on a high trajectory into enemy fortifications. Divisions had their own artillery support, which also increased steadily from the 1914 establishment of fifty-four field guns and one heavy battery of four 60-pdrs.

The expansion of the British Army during the war, and the creation of New Army divisions, had threatened the cohesion of the regular forces' regimental system, which was thought to be crucial to its success. To maintain *esprit de corps* and a sense of identity amongst the New Army formations, they were given regimental affiliations and numbered accordingly. No new regiments were created, with the exception of the Heavy Machine Gun Corps and machine-gun units, so battalions were given the 'parent' regimental number. When a Territorial battalion was deployed, it was replaced with a Territorial reserve battalion with a fractional number (such as 1/4th Battalion), and when that was replaced in turn by another new battalion, it would adopt another fraction (2/4th). In 1915, the third reserve battalions were being formed as 3/4th. The effect was to inculcate in every soldier a belief that he was part of a longer regimental heritage which had a reputation to preserve and enhance. Brigadier S. W. Hare, in encouraging his new Fusiliers prior to the landings at Gallipoli, invoked the regimental victories of Albuhera (1811), Minden (1759), Delhi (1857), and Lucknow (1857), which, apparently, had a tremendous effect on the soldiers' sense of purpose.[37]

The outbreak of war was greeted with tremendous enthusiasm in Australia and the government of Andrew Fisher offered firm support to Britain.

The troops that came to form the ANZACs, a derivative of the title Australian and New Zealand Army Corps, earned a reputation for courage, rugged endurance, and strong cohesion or 'mateship', but they were also criticized by British senior officers for a lack of discipline, indifference to authorities they disapproved of, and rowdy behaviour. Australian soldiers insisted on addressing officers by their first names, which infuriated the class-conscious British officer corps, but the Australian defiance was in itself a reaction to the often patronizing manner in which senior commanders spoke of the 'colonials'. Anecdotes are legion. In one incident, perhaps apocryphal, during delicate negotiations between Ottoman and British officers over a temporary truce on Gallipoli, an ANZAC soldier simply wandered in and demanded to know which of the bastards present had seen his kettle. This wonderfully irreverent behaviour caused great amusement, and admiration, amongst British troops. Yet it was their fighting prowess and recklessness that earned the highest plaudits. Unsurprisingly, Australians have ever since been held in the highest regard, and the greatest affection, by their British military counterparts.

The Australians refused to countenance conscription and the 332,000 men who served overseas were all volunteers, formed into five divisions. Of particular note was the Desert Mounted Corps, which conducted operations in Palestine. It was a force dominated by personnel from Australia and New Zealand, supported by the British Yeomanry Mounted Division and a multinational Imperial Camel Corps. The commander of the force, 'Light Horse Harry' Chauvel, remains a national icon in Australia, and the achievements of the various Light Horse regiments are celebrated on ANZAC day, the date of the landings at Gallipoli.[38]

The New Zealanders managed to field a force in the Great War that, proportionally, represented fully one half of the eligible male population. There was equal enthusiasm for the war in New Zealand as there had been in Australia and Britain, and the National Government, formed in 1915, remained resolute in its support of the war effort. In 1916, like Britain, the government introduced conscription. The forces sent overseas consisted of mounted infantry, with an almost universal experience of horsemanship, and Territorial regiments that retained a provincial title for identity and cohesion. Their contingents distinguished themselves on all fronts of the war, but their achievements in courageous mounted attacks in Palestine and their doggedness at Gallipoli, particularly in August 1915, drew particular admiration.[39]

The Indian Army had begun its existence as the auxiliary 'Native' contingents of the contracted army of the Honourable East India Company in the 1740s, and in the nineteenth century there had been three separate, geographically based 'Presidency Armies', with the troublesome North West Frontier region under the direct control of the governor general. After calls for amalgamation, there was a period of reform between 1895 and 1903, and a single Indian Army was created by Lord Kitchener, the then Commander-in-Chief of India. Old 'presidency' titles were, in theory, abolished, but various names and nicknames survived. Crucially, units retained traditions and customs to reinforce their identity and regimental *esprit de corps*, including a selective diet or eating rituals.

To 'stiffen' and supervise the Indian Army, and provide it with heavy and field artillery, British regiments were brigaded with two or more Indian ones. The arrangement was known by the name 'the Army in India'. The proportions of British and Indian troops and the long-standing article of faith that Indian troops should be equipped only with light mountain guns were legacies of the Indian Mutiny. It was considered to be a sensible precaution not to equip its servants too powerfully.

In 1908, to ease administration, the Indian Army was divided into a northern and southern army, but the strength of the force was in its ability to garrison every part of the subcontinent, despatch troops to pacify the frontiers, and, if necessary, deploy independent brigades overseas. Before the Great War, there were thirty-nine regiments of cavalry (not including contingents of bodyguards), ninety-five single-battalion regiments of infantry, twelve single-battalion pioneer regiments, and eleven double-battalion regiments (39th Garwhals and the ten Gurkha regiments).[40] There were three units of sappers and miners (for engineer operations), mountain artillery, ordnance units, logistics teams, medical units, and administrators. *In extremis*, especially on the frontier, there were Imperial Service Troops, local auxiliaries trained, for the most part, to a standard acceptable to the Indian Army. There were also militias, levies, and scouts, who provided some regional security, especially to British political officers and constabulary. There was a pool of European and Anglo-Indian volunteers who could be called on to protect installations such as the railways, and there were also sizeable private armies directed by the Princely States, such as the Hyderabad Contingents, the Central India Horse, and the local units of the other Princely States such as Malwa, Erinpura, and Deoli, where the quality varied between anachronistic retainers to more modernized troops.

The legacy of the nineteenth century was not limited to titles and organization, but also the source of manpower. The Mutiny of 1857 effectively ended recruitment from Bengal, where the revolt had begun, while, for reasons of prejudice, men from the rural south were not considered particularly energetic or 'martial'. By contrast, Bombay, Punjab, and the mountainous north seemed to produce especially warlike groups, and the Indian Army recruited from them extensively. Thus, for example, while there were just 5,588 Madrassis and 3,000 Tamils from the south in the army in 1904, there were 31,000 Sikhs, 32,000 Punjabis, 14,000 Gurkhas, and 11,000 Rajputs.[41]

The other peculiarity of the Indian Army was the organization of the officers. Each infantry battalion had twelve European officers, and subordinated to them, regardless of experience, were seventeen Indian officers carrying the viceroy's commission. Together they commanded 729 ranks and forty-two civilian 'commissariat' followers. In the cavalry, the proportions were the same. There were obvious cultural differences between British and Indian Army units, and they were also evident amongst the officer corps.[42] In the Indian cavalry, the legacy of being 'irregular' and under the personal command of pioneering individuals gave rise to an attitude that praised initiative, carried disdain for parade-ground precision (while exhibiting pride in the most splendid Indian uniforms), and cherished the horses and the Indian cavalry soldiers, the sowars, above all else. The fact that troopers owned their own mounts (the sillidar system) made the men particularly attentive to the endurance of their animals.

In the Indian infantry, Claude Auchinleck, who saw action in defence of the Suez Canal and in Mesopotamia during the war, described an atmosphere of respectful relations between officers and men. He wrote: 'there was no question of ordering them about—they were yeomen really and that made all the difference'.[43] The more senior and experienced Indian leaders known as viceroy's commissioned officers, despite their subordination, were the most respected of all, and guided young British subalterns in their role. They were referred to as 'God's Own Gentlemen'. In contrast to most European armies which expected their 'native' soldiers to learn the Europeans' language, in the Indian Army every officer had to learn to speak to his soldiers in their vernacular, not least because he was regarded as the neutral arbiter in any local disputes.[44] The emphasis on personal leadership led to a tendency to lead from the front in combat, but that had its own attractions for young British officers. The appeal of command in the Indian Army was so high that, in 1913, of the top twenty-five cadets at the

Royal Military Academy Sandhurst, twenty of them opted to join the Indian Army.[45]

In 1914, the motivation of the Indian Army was not in doubt. A hierarchy of prestige, based on 'fighting quality' and physique, ran through the different ethnic groups that constituted the army, and each was eager to assert its martial prowess.[46] This competitiveness existed between units recruited on the basis of territorial demarcation as much as on ethnicity, and it was common in 'mixed' units where companies were made up of a particular 'class'. The 6th Bengal Lancers, for example, consisted of one Muslim squadron, one Hindu, and one Sikh, with the headquarters squadron made up of troops from all three 'classes'.[47] Half of the regular army was drawn from the Punjab, and even regiments designated with particular regional titles might actually contain a cross-section of more competitive groups.[48] However, there was also a trait amongst some groups to enlist for the 'fight' rather than identity per se.

At the tactical level, certain experienced regiments of the Indian Army, such as the Frontier Force and the various battalions of the Gurkhas, were highly accomplished, able to use field craft and the skilled use of fire to defeat guerrilla fighters on the frontiers. However, units with little experience of mountain warfare were unsuited to the modern conditions of combat.

At the higher command level, a General Staff was created in 1903 to manage the complexities of training, military policy, operations, plans, intelligence, and deployments. However, while relieving the Commander-in-Chief India of many tasks, the General Headquarters had still to manage a high volume of minor administrative matters and there was no clear chain of command to the divisional level. Moreover, the Commander-in-Chief had to combine the duties of Military Member of the Viceroy's Council (1906) and responsibility for military supply (1909). Divisional commanders were burdened with administering not only their three infantry brigades, a cavalry regiment, their artillery, and their pioneers but also all the additional formations in their area of responsibility, including militias and volunteers, even though these would not be the units under their command in wartime. Indeed, when a divisional headquarters was deployed, these other militia and volunteer units were simply abandoned, with no plan for continuity in such an eventuality. Moreover, while there was a surplus of this additional manpower, there was a paucity of vital ancillary services, including medical and administrative staff.

Worst of all, there were far too few staff in each headquarters. In 1906, 'A' staff of the General Branch, directed by the Chief of Staff, were concerned with training, discipline, and personnel; while 'Q' staff were concerned with equipment and supply. The following year, a Staff College was established at Quetta, ending older systems of patronage or dependence on the British Staff College at Camberley. The only tragedy of this excellent reform was that it was too late to produce senior staff-trained officers before the outbreak of war in 1914.

The Indian Army of 1914 was a long-service professional force but one of its fundamental flaws was that it lacked sufficient trained reserves to be able to regenerate itself in the event of significant casualties. Frontier fighting had required well-trained units with the cohesion to withstand demoralizing insurgency, but casualties had, on the whole, been light.[49] The fighting had offered sufficient hazard to reinforce one's personal *izzat* (honour) or sense of fate, demonstrate attachment to one's officer and unit, and earn decorations and promotion without a high probability of death. The Afghan and Pashtun tribes' habit of murdering the wounded and mutilating the dead meant that heroic efforts were always made to recover casualties, which again reinforced cohesion. Service in Indian regiments tended to deter the rapid turnover of personnel and therefore it was hard to generate a large cadre of reservists. To qualify for a pension, soldiers had to serve twenty-five years. By contrast, three-year short-service men, who could take opportunities for periodic retraining, were few and far between and in any case insufficiently trained to be useful. Often, sickness and civilian employment rendered ex-soldiers unfit for further military service. The result was an army of some experience in mountain warfare, cohesive, with a strong sense of its exclusive identity, but without any notion of formation level operations or high-intensity European war, and unable to draw on a large pool of trained reservists.

In India, despite all the concerns about the loyalty of Indian subjects in the nineteenth century, there was particular enthusiasm for Britain's cause at the outbreak in 1914. When the viceroy declared war on India's behalf, unfashionable though it may seem today, there was a sincere response from many Indian leaders and organizations: the All India Muslim League, Punjab Provincial Congress, the Princely States, and many thousands of individuals expressed their loyalty to the British Empire. Gandhi, not yet well-known across the subcontinent, tendered a resolution to the Indian National Congress for unconditional service to the empire. Offers of money, horses, medics, hospital ships, and ambulances were made, and twenty-one of the twenty-seven princes' Imperial Service Troops contingents were mobilized.

The Nizam of Hyderabad committed his troops to the war effort and gave 60 lakhs of rupees (£400,000). The Maharajah of Mysore gave a further 50 lakhs (£333,000). Enthusiasm and cohesion were not in doubt: the Jodhpur Lancers, for example, were even commanded by their septuagenarian Regent-Maharajah, Major General Sir Pratab Singh.

Four expeditionary forces were mobilized, far more than had been planned for. It was to the credit of the pre-war planners that the Indian Army at least had a scheme for mobilization and deployment in place when the war broke out. India had two infantry divisions and one cavalry brigade available for immediate operations.[50] But the requirement to expand this deployment rapidly caused disruption and overwhelmed the depots. The Lahore and Meerut Divisions (Force A) were assembled and despatched urgently to France. Indian Expeditionary Forces B and C, barely at brigade strength, went to East Africa, ostensibly to secure the coast and neutralize the German naval threat to shipping in the Indian Ocean but also to protect the British railways into Kenya for whose defence there was insufficient manpower.

In October 1914 the government of India believed the invasion of what were, in terms of sovereignty, Ottoman domains at the head of the Gulf would be 'provocative' and might precipitate belligerence. However, urged on by the India Office in the British government, the 16th Infantry Brigade of the 6th (Quetta) Division was diverted from Force B bound for East Africa and renamed Force D.[51] Initially the objective for Force D was simply to assert a military presence at the Shatt al-Arab and it landed at Fao, on the Gulf coast (today in Iraq), on 6 November 1914.[52] But once war had been declared by the Ottoman Empire, following its aggression against Russia, Force D was ordered to advance northward toward the town of Basra, which it captured on 21 November. To cover its expanding area of control, the 16th Infantry Brigade was soon augmented by the arrival of the 18th Brigade, while a third brigade arrived in January 1915. In due course another infantry division would be deployed, as proposals were made for an advance up the River Tigris toward Baghdad, particularly when operations in the Dardanelles stalled in the summer of 1915.[53] These deployments went well beyond the pre-war planning assumptions.

The government of India had no mechanism for long-term force generation, and, as far as the campaign in southern Mesopotamia was concerned, the piecemeal approach to deciding on objectives meant improvisation for every phase of operations. There has been much criticism of this situation, since the 1917 publication of the Mesopotamia Commission onwards, but the context is crucial: both the British and Indian governments were struggling to manage their resources and make the transition to a war economy.[54] It had long been established that, in the event of crisis in the Middle East, British expeditionary forces would form the bulk of the military effort, not Indian. In other words, no one had foreseen that it would be the Indian Army that would form the bulk of the forces for the invasion of Mesopotamia and of Palestine, and thus, in effect, bear the brunt of the fighting against the Ottoman Empire.

Ways: British Decision-Making

The primary decision-making body at the strategic level in 1914 was the British Cabinet. The Prime Minister, Herbert H. Asquith, had been in office since 1908, following a Liberal landslide election victory in 1906, and he had endured a number of domestic political crises with some patient and careful negotiation. Industrial disputes, disloyalty of leading army officers over the future autonomy of Ireland, and women's suffrage had been dealt with by deferring decisions as often as making them, and Asquith had a reputation for a 'wait and see' approach. By contrast, two members of his Cabinet, David Lloyd George, as the Chancellor of the Exchequer, and Winston Churchill, the First Lord of the Admiralty, had reputations for dash and energy. Both were also outstanding orators in the House of Commons.

The Cabinet was soon overwhelmed by the business of war as well as the business of government. It was therefore decided, on 25 November 1914, to establish a War Council, made up of members of the pre-war Committee of Imperial Defence. Its role was to focus entirely on the strategy of the war, and the three most prominent members were Asquith, Churchill, and Lord Horatio Kitchener of Khartoum, the former viceroy of Egypt who was made Minister of War. Kitchener estimated that the war would last at least three years and therefore Britain had to work closely with the French until such time as new manpower could be mobilized from volunteers in Britain and across the British Empire. His perception that, in the west, Germany was too strong to be defeated, led him to advocate the alternative course of knocking its eastern partners out of the war. In this assessment he got the enthusiastic support of Churchill and Lloyd George. Kitchener was single-minded but was impatient with politicians, especially Asquith and his Liberal colleagues, who he felt were not energetic or ruthless enough to prosecute the war. As a result, Kitchener did not work closely with the Cabinet and insisted on his own line of action. This meant it was easier for his Cabinet colleagues to blame him if things went wrong, and he was later accused of not providing sufficient resources to support the operations in Gallipoli in 1915.

In essence, Kitchener insisted on military primacy in the making of Britain's strategy. His experience of unquestioned supreme command and independence in decision-making in his campaigns in the Sudan (1896–8) and South Africa (1900–2) gave rise to a certain aloofness. Yet, as a former Royal Engineer, Kitchener was thorough, and he was all too aware of the inadequacies and shortages in the early stages of Britain's war effort.[55] Even his most ardent critics admitted that it was Kitchener who was instrumental in making armies and organizing Britain's industry for a long war.

The set-backs to the Dardanelles campaign prompted the leader of the Conservatives, Andrew Bonar Law, to insist on a coalition government, which was formed in May 1915. The result was an enlargement of the country's decision-making body, with Asquith, Sir Edward Grey (Foreign Secretary), Kitchener (War), Bonar Law (Colonial Secretary), Arthur Balfour (First Lord of the Admiralty), and Arthur Henderson, the Labour leader (Education).

Figure 2.3 Field Marshal Sir William Robertson, Chief of the Imperial General Staff, who prioritized the Western Front over the Middle East

Churchill was made Chancellor of the Duchy of Lancaster, but, criticized for the Gallipoli operations, he resigned soon after. Lloyd George was given the appointment of Minister of Munitions to try and resolve the shortages in production and supply. Nevertheless, while Kitchener became less influential in the War Cabinet because of the lack of progress in the Dardanelles, Sir William Robertson, the CIGS, ensured that the army was the primary strategic decision-making body.

In November 1915, in another attempt to streamline decision-making, Asquith announced that a new War Committee would be formed consisting of just five men. He remained as Prime Minister, and he appointed Lloyd George, Bonar Law, Balfour, and Reginald McKenna (the Chancellor of the Exchequer) as his committee colleagues. While the munitions crisis eased as British industry geared up for war, there were still challenges and set-backs: conscription was introduced in January and July 1916, despite Liberal opposition; Irish republicans tried to seize control of Dublin, and were defeated; Anglo-French cooperation improved but the joint operation on the Somme in July did not produce the anticipated breakthrough on the Western Front. In June 1916, when Kitchener was lost at sea, to replace him Lloyd George was appointed Secretary of State for War. Yet, by the autumn of 1916, there were bitter disagreements about the conduct of the war, and, crucially, the higher direction of the war. Asquith appeared to be content to leave the key strategic decisions to Robertson (CIGS) and his commander on the Western Front, Sir Douglas Haig, but Lloyd George thought the 'westerner' strategy, which focused the war effort on France and Flanders, was not achieving results. Worse, the Dardanelles and the Mesopotamia commissions of enquiry were investigating what had gone wrong in these two campaigns, and consequently why the eastern strategy had failed.

Frustrated by the absence of 'push and go' in the apparatus of government, in contrast to his own direction of the Ministry of Munitions, Lloyd George insisted on 'a fight . . . to the finish – to a knock out'.[56] He demanded that Asquith cut the War Committee down to four members with absolute power, and, in the killer blow, he insisted that Asquith was to be excluded. Lloyd George was refused and he resigned, and Asquith, with his Cabinet split, also resigned, expecting his colleagues to support him. They didn't. Lloyd George had agreed in advance with Bonar Law and a handful of leading Conservatives that Asquith had to go. They agreed that Lloyd George was the man to head the new Cabinet, and, with Bonar Law's consent, Lloyd George became Prime Minister on 7 December 1916. Immediately, he summoned Arthur Henderson, Sir Alfred Milner, the former high commissioner of South Africa who had run the civilian administration during the war of 1899–1902, and Lord Curzon, the former viceroy of India who had considerable administrative experience. Bonar Law became the War Council's spokesman in the House of Commons and the five-man executive was supported by co-opted members of the Cabinet, including Churchill, recalled as Minister of Munitions, Balfour as Foreign Secretary (replacing Grey who had insisted on initiating peace talks with Germany), and the earl of Derby as Minister of War. The establishment of Lloyd George's War Council did two things: it centralized power and led to the more ruthless prosecution of the war. It also reasserted civilian primacy in the making of strategy for the first time since 1914.

There were other changes in the primary decision-making organization at the top of the government. The king was also emperor of India, although it was the Cabinet's Secretary of State for India who determined British policy for India. The actual administration of India was led by the governor general or viceroy, who served for five years. Charles, Baron Hardinge of Penshurst, held the appointment until 1916 when he was succeeded by Frederic, Baron Chelmsford. The viceroy executed his policies through a six-member council, and had a further sixty-one members for legislative functions. The provinces of British India were divided between governors, lieutenant governors, and chief commissioners but the entire administration was only 6,500 strong in 1914. The army in India was the largest standing military force in the British Empire, and, as such, the government of India had an influential role in the war effort. India was assigned responsibility for security and operations in the Far East, South East Asia, the Indian Ocean, East Africa, Persia, and Mesopotamia, and, later, for the provision of troops to Palestine, Syria, Egypt, Central Asia, and the Caucasus. Moreover, India was expected to find not only manpower, but supplies, foodstuffs, and equipment, from sandbags to steam locomotives. When this proved beyond the capacity and organization of the subcontinent, the government of India was given much less freedom of action in its decision-making. London imposed its will through the War Council and the War Office.

By contrast, the leaders of the dominions of Canada, Australia, New Zealand, South Africa, and Newfoundland were invited in March 1917 to the first Imperial Conference, along with the Secretary of State for India. The purpose was not just to coordinate the direction of the war across the globe, but to recognize the enhanced status of the dominions as partners, not subordinates. The success of the annual conferences resulted in the elevation of Jan Smuts, the former Afrikaner guerrilla and now loyalist, to the War Cabinet.

Lloyd George made a further, more significant change in November 1917, when he persuaded the French to accept the establishment of a Supreme War Council. Appointing his approved military representative, Sir Henry Wilson, the Prime Minister tried to relegate Robertson and Haig, and thus achieve full control of British strategy. His success was in despatching General Sir Edmund Allenby to capture Jerusalem, but the relative neglect of the Western Front meant the British Army was less well-prepared than it might have been to face the massive German spring offensive in 1918. Nevertheless, the structure of government remained unchanged throughout the remaining months of the war. Lloyd George was effectively a dictator in Britain, possessing considerable powers. His oratory added to his capacity to persuade others and get his way, but, in the end, it was this power that was be his undoing.

In his memoirs, Lloyd George reflected on the difficulties of civil–military relations in the making of Britain's wartime policy. He drew attention to the initial tendency of civilian leaders to allow the military and naval officers to design strategy, and the disputes that followed when he and other members of the War Cabinet tried to assert civilian primacy. With a combination of eloquence and frustration, he wrote: 'Every prolonged war has at one stage or another produced differences or disputes between the civilian government and the Generals in the field.' He continued that it was 'inevitable that there should be argument as to reinforcements and supplies between those who have to use them and those who have to furnish them'. But he warned: 'No country has unlimited resources at its command, and a wise government will mobilise its strength to its best advantage.'[57] He believed all generals in the war had underestimated the home front, 'and yet that is where the war was won and lost'.[58] With increasing ferocity, Lloyd George argued that the politicians had provided the manpower to the generals, but they had too often squandered those lives 'in the prosecution of doubtful plans and mishandled enterprises'.[59] He subsequently described with anguish operations he considered 'futile and ill-conceived', 'militarily foolish', or 'psychologically . . . insane'.[60]

He then asked the critical question: 'should we have interfered in the realm of strategy?' To this question he admitted: 'This is one of the most perplexing anxieties of the government of a nation at war.' The reason was simple: 'civilians have had no instruction in the principles of war, and to that extent are complete amateurs in the methods of waging war'. But then he added that 'strategy is not entirely a military problem', noting, in reference to the Suez Canal, 'the passing of the gates of India, the Far East and Australia is not by any means principally a military question for Great Britain'. He condemned the idea that strategy was just a case of 'victory-in-battle'.[61] Instead, domestic political, alliance, and imperial considerations were as important. His verdict was that 'the defeat of the Turko-German Army in Palestine was an Imperial necessity'. Lloyd George concurred with Sir Alfred Milner that one of the outcomes of the war was a more consolidated, closer British Empire able to assert itself in every region of the globe.[62] Jan Smuts encouraged Lloyd George to regard the Middle East as part of a future 'Southern British World'.[63] In the critical winter of 1917, the government had established first an Imperial Forum and then a succession of Imperial Cabinets. Although Lloyd George saw much of the conquered Middle East not as long-term colonies but bargaining counters for future negotiations, it was noted how his familiarity with the imperially minded War Cabinet led him to despise 'That mob [in the Commons], this rotten assembly at Westminster'.[64]

The one issue he felt the military would not permit interference with was the decision whether or not to conduct 'a great battle'. When these large engagements failed to achieve their initial objectives and became prolonged, again Lloyd George asked his readers to consider: 'Should governments intervene or leave the decision entirely to the soldiers?' The implication of his words was an emphatic 'no' to decisions made entirely by soldiers.

Lloyd George argued that had the Balkans theatre been pursued instead of the endless hammering at the Western Front, then the way would have been open to cut supply routes to the Ottomans and their defences in the Dardanelles. While admitting that cooperation with France took precedence, he tried to assert that failing to make the Balkans as a major theatre 'was one of the strategical blunders of the war'.[65] He admitted that his colleagues in government had permitted the fighting on the Western Front to continue as the primary scene of operations because conducting operations 'is mainly a decision for the generals', but he made no mention of his own endorsement for the Dardanelles and Gallipoli campaign without the resources it required.[66] As one historian put it, 'The army at the Dardanelles, never adequately supported, was in effect allowed to moulder until threatened with destruction from either the enemy or the elements.'[67]

Instead, Lloyd George focused on his decision to create a Supreme War Council as an antidote to generals with 'a ridiculous cavalry obsession', their 'inadequate brains', and their 'amateurism'. Without acknowledging the role that cavalry had played in 'his' victory in taking Jerusalem in 1917, Lloyd George posited that 'the Generals had to be helped out by the politicians' in the crucial questions of munitions, tanks, aircraft production, mortars, shipping, and hydrophones. He firmly believed that the British Army's insistence on obedience and seniority had confined their best talent to 'the slime' of the trenches and stifled intellect in the senior officers. His assessments became a popular explanation for the high casualties of the war and Britain's failures to achieve victory sooner, but Cabinet records and correspondence shows that the political leaders struggled to define their objectives, manage the dynamics of conflict, or align their ends, ways, and means any more successfully than the military men. Disputes between the military and civilian leaders jeopardized the conditions in which an effective and agreed strategy could be devised. British ministers could not agree and did not assert themselves over the direction of the Great War as a result.[68]

Strategy and decision-making is affected by group dynamics and it is subject to all the advantages and flaws of human interactions. The unchanging nature of war provides a degree of continuity for planners, and they can also be aided by certain enduring principles., These include simplicity, adaptability, a focus on timing or synchronization, the search for an 'edge' over the enemy, and the need to be comprehensive in nature. Sound strategy must also pass four tests: it must be politically acceptable, feasible, suitable to the context, and sustainable both in terms of national resources but also the will of the people.[69] In the examples of the Great War in the Middle East, the national strategies of the major powers, and the popular movements involved, did not pass the essential tests of strategy.

Ways: the Cairo Administration and the Arab Bureau

The British position in Egypt was peculiar: although, in theory, Britain maintained only a Consulate General in the country, along with the other Great Powers, the role of the British official was not merely diplomatic. The Consul General was the key decision-maker of the 'Protecting Power', and the 'ultimate authority in the country in all those matters which [Britain] chose for the moment to regard as calling for the exercise of its control'.[70] Despite sovereignty officially residing in Ottoman hands, Egypt was dependent on the financial and military management of European interests, and, following Britain's military occupation of 1882, Egypt was, in effect, directed by London. The occupation continued to ensure the control of the Suez Canal, the vital artery of British commerce which, in financial terms, was largely owned by the British government.[71] Retaining such a strategic point was regarded as crucial after 1885 when other European powers began to acquire colonial territories in Africa: if Britain withdrew, it seemed inevitable that another rival nation, such as France or Germany, would seek to take over the weak Egyptian state and thereby threaten to choke off the Suez route. British administrators, such as Lord Cromer, had therefore set out to consolidate control of Egypt with programmes of fiscal restructuring, public works, legal reforms, and improvements to agriculture and irrigation.

An Egyptian Army was also reconstituted, largely for border defence against incursions from the south and west, and to assist in the maintenance of order in the Sudan, Egypt's former colony. The jihadist movement of Mohammed Ahmed, 'the Mahdi', in the 1880s, and his successor, the Khalifa Abdullah el-Taaishi, had necessitated the raising of Sudanese troops and a joint Anglo-Egyptian expedition into the Sudan in 1896–8 under the command of Kitchener. The new British administration that was established in Sudan was unencumbered by the legacies of the Ottoman system and was not yet subject to the criticisms of nationalists in the way that the Consul General in Cairo was.

The security of Egypt was maintained by a relatively small force. Major General the Honourable Julian Byng commanded just 5,000 troops in Egypt and General Sir Reginald Wingate, the governor general of Sudan, had an even smaller contingent. When the war broke out, the immediate concern was the security of the Canal and railways, and the initial plan was for regular British troops in Egypt to be replaced by units of the Indian Army. Within days, the Indian troops were designated to go straight on to France while Territorials were sent out from Britain to provide the security for Egypt instead. Lieutenant General Sir John Maxwell, with long experience of service in Egypt, was appointed the commander of the new garrison which gradually increased over the next few months.

In the initial weeks of the war, the closure of cotton markets affected the Egyptian economy adversely. The fact that so many relied on the cash crop's success was a cause for concern for the British authorities, because serious internal unrest could overwhelm the local resources of the garrison, particularly if that disorder was combined with an offensive by the Ottomans. The concern with disorder was also perhaps an issue of institutional culture: uprisings were regarded by British officials as evidence of poor governance or management by local pro-consuls, although some have argued that there was a 'paranoia' resulting from the undemocratic and prejudiced nature of colonial authority.[72] The result was a strong focus on ethnographic or 'human intelligence' in order to intercept sedition and conspiracies. Markets, ports, and centres of potential resistance were kept under surveillance, and efforts were made by civil administrators and police forces to keep abreast of public opinion. There was concern to monitor any possible foreign political influences, reflecting a fear of the 'hidden hand' of rival powers. The antidote was to ensure that loyalist elements, drawn from the social elites of the Egyptian sultan, political leaders, landowners, and the religious scholars, the *ulema*, were kept close to the administration.[73] In peacetime this system ensured order, but in wartime, in Egypt, it took on strategic significance.

Gathering intelligence beyond the borders of Egypt and the Sudan was nevertheless embryonic in 1914. There was a significant reliance on 'open source' information, relayed by neutral consulates within the Ottoman Empire, and on prisoners of war. One of these, Lieutenant Muhammed Sharif al-Faruqi, an Arab officer from Mosul who deserted at Gallipoli, gave the impression that all Arabs, even those within the Ottoman ranks, were eager to rise up in support of the pro-British Sharif Hussein of Mecca against the government in Istanbul.[74] Transferred for interrogation to Cairo, Faruqi's testimony was influential in encouraging a pro-Arab policy in British strategy.

The Arab Bureau, established in January 1916, was designed to be a coordinating body for precisely this combination of political and military intelligence across the region. Consequently, it was as concerned with Arab opinion as it was with Ottoman military capabilities.[75] Officially, it reported to the high commissioner of Egypt and was, as such, one branch of the Sudan Intelligence Department. As a result, its product and its direction were, in theory, directed by the Foreign Office in London, but the nature of its contributors made it virtually an autonomous policy-making organization. Staffed with talented and ambitious individuals who shared an interest in directing the affairs of the entire region, it regarded itself as independent in all but name of both the government of Cairo and of London.

The driving force of its approach was therefore the consequence of the composition of its staff. Those who had come from military intelligence derived their experience from the operations of the Egyptian Expeditionary Force in 1914–15, while personnel from the Cairo Residency had a background focused on gathering and analysing local information. The third influence was the staff drawn from the Foreign Office Eastern Department, which gave the Arab Bureau a regional perspective. They were all 'Arabists', familiar with local languages and experienced in their understanding of British policy in Egypt, Sudan, and its neighbours. Consequently they found it difficult to separate the purely intelligence roles of collection, collation, and analysis from the business of giving advice and exercising influence. The small size of the bureau gave its members homogeneity in their opinions and a sense of unified purpose. The first bureau chief was Colonel Gilbert Clayton, former director of military intelligence in Egypt, and Clayton was on close terms with Sir F. Reginald Wingate, the governor general of the Sudan, and then his successor in 1917, Sir Lee Stack, who had been the director of intelligence in Cairo in the decade before the war.

The Arab Bureau was housed in the Savoy Hotel in Cairo, and consisted of between ten and twenty members, some of whom were career military and diplomatic staff, and others university-educated experts co-opted for their experience of working in the region alongside military intelligence. The deputy director, Captain Kinahan Cornwallis, was a former Sudan Political Service officer who had read Arabic at Oxford. Thomas Edward Lawrence, also an Oxford man, had travelled extensively in the Near East and, before the war, had worked on the British Museum's archaeological excavations at Carchemish in Syria and assisted Captain, later Colonel, Newcombe in a survey of the Sinai. It was Newcombe who designed the wartime sabotage offensive against Ottoman railways in the Hejaz, until his capture in 1917. David Hogarth, who took over from Clayton as bureau chief, had also attended Oxford and was curator of the Ashmolean Museum there, as well as being a leading archaeologist of Arabic antiquities. It was this collective interest in the Arab world that led the bureau to advocate the formation of an Arab state, going well beyond their original task of intelligence.

The influence of the Arab Bureau was not confined to Cairo. In Persia and then Baghdad, once it had been captured in March 1917, Sir Percy Cox, Sir Percy Sykes, and their associates shared a similar outlook. Cox was the consul at Muscat and British Resident at Bushire (a strategically important city on the Persian side of the Persian Gulf), where he had such a strong supervisory role that he was nicknamed 'King of the Persian Gulf'. Before the war, Sir Percy Sykes had been the British consul at Meshed in northern

Persia and Kashgar in western China, spreading British influence in order to prevent northern Iran or western China falling under Russian control, but in 1914 he was redirected to form a regiment of local auxiliaries entitled the South Persia Rifles.[76] He proved so successful in the task that he advocated southern Persia should be declared a protectorate of the Indian Empire, a move which was resolutely rejected by Lord Curzon in the War Cabinet. Nevertheless, an intense study of the anthropology and shifting alliances of the peoples and clans of the greater Middle East was a unifying characteristic of the *corps d'élite* of the Sudan Political Service, the Arab Bureau, and that other great institution of government and intelligence, the Indian Civil Service.

The basis of the work by these agencies was to gather information but, at the same time, seek to encourage the local elites to pursue a particular line of policy. There was considerable faith in the idea of indigenous hierarchies who could persuade populations to avoid confrontation with the British or elicit information about conspiracies which might disrupt British policy. Nationalist and militant groups within the British Empire could often be presented to local elites as trouble-makers who could cause those same local elites to lose their status or British privileges. Historian Chris Bayly described the process as constructing an 'empire of information' to control an 'empire of opinion'.[77] That at least was the aspiration. The British often struggled to keep abreast of local developments, and, as the war demonstrated, rarely controlled or influenced local actors beyond the frontiers of the British Empire in quite the way they had anticipated.

Intelligence assessments were influenced, and prejudiced, by the assumptions of the age. Taken from a British perspective, stereotypical behaviours were frequently elevated to a permanence and generalization that, today, analysts would collect under the heading 'culture'. For a security-conscious empire, cultures and behaviours that were a potential threat, or might be categorized as useful in a 'martial' sense, were given prominence. Yet, the focus was invariably on local elites and leadership. If a community, clan, or region was given to 'fanaticism', then it became all the more important to win over and co-opt the chieftains, elders, prominent religious figures, or sheikhs. There was a strong emphasis on British officials, agents, and governors learning the local vernacular languages in order to detect signs of unrest, treachery, or potential partnerships.[78]

The British Empire represented an opportunity for many local dignitaries who possessed authority or could convince the British they were worthwhile allies. Nevertheless, the threat of force was also a powerful incentive. The British often referred to the tendency of Asians and Africans to seize upon any weakening in the imperial apparatus for their own gain, producing a frequent call to avoid any military defeats. Imperial accounts also noted an alleged preference of Asians and Africans to be on the 'winning side'. This seemed to contrast with a British sense of themselves as a people who adhered to principles rather than passions, but, at the same time, it showed that, as long as the British maintained an appearance of strength, they would not be challenged. Part of the reason why these views were sustained was the importance of the armed forces in maintaining security in the peripheries, or beyond the frontiers, of colonial control: the interior of southern Arabia, Darfur, and the fringes of the Sudan, northern Somalia, and Afghanistan were dominated by military assessments.

In Egypt and the eastern Mediterranean, as we have seen, the priority for Britain was the defence of the Suez Canal. Given the priorities in Europe, only the minimum necessary garrison was to be retained, and Egypt was to be more of a staging-post and training base for British and dominion soldiers travelling to Europe. Sir William Robertson recognized the importance of the Suez Canal but felt the absolute priority, in men and material, was defeating the German Army on the Western Front.[79] General Sir Archibald Murray described the strategic requirement to furnish men to the European theatre as his 'bible of the war'. Defeat in France would mean that 'Palestine, Egypt, Tanganyika, West Africa, and Mesopotamia mattered not'.[80] As Hew Strachan put it, all 'efforts outside Europe in 1914 were designed to restrict the war, to eliminate Germany as a global force, to drive its cruisers from the seas, to close down its African and Pacific colonies'.[81] Nevertheless, the British Cabinet conceived of a plan that would, if successful, knock the Ottoman Empire right out of the war, set in motion the desire of the other Central Powers for peace, and force Germany to the negotiating table, or, if isolated at last, to certain defeat.[82] In 1915, the site of that masterstroke was to be the Dardanelles. But first, they would have to defend the most critical artery of the British Empire, the Suez Canal, against an unexpected attack.

3

The Strategic Defence of Suez and the Failure of Pan-Islamism, 1914–15

The Suez Canal was undoubtedly a strategic point, and, when the British government became the largest shareholder in 1875, it was described as the 'key to India', a location vital to the security of the British Empire.[1] Commercially, it had reduced the travel time from Britain to Australia to seventeen days, and the steady increase in volume of traffic made an important contribution to the wealth of British businesses. From a naval and military point of view, it was a vital passage for the movement of ships and manpower to any threatened point in the empire. Pre-war planners had assumed that protecting the canal that linked Alexandria, the port that served the route to the United Kingdom and the west, and Suez, the point of embarkation for India and the east, would depend on holding the territories to the east and west as well as the maintenance of naval supremacy in the Mediterranean and the Arabian Sea.

Before the war Egypt had a small British garrison of 5,000 men, but the primary defence of the Suez Canal and the Eastern Mediterranean was in the hands of the Royal Navy.[2] Nevertheless, after the outbreak of hostilities in 1914, the proximity of the domains of the Ottoman Empire, and the weakness of the sultan's fleet, made the security of the Suez Canal from any landward threat the priority. As a result, General John Maxwell, who commanded the garrison in Egypt, drew up a scheme of defence of the Canal Zone, making full use of the hastily assembled reinforcements—Territorials from Britain, the regulars of the East Lancashire Regiment, and the 10th and 11th Divisions from India. Geography was in Britain's favour: the Ottoman Army would have to traverse the arid tracts of the Sinai to reach the canal, while the British forces held a strong position. The sea approaches were secure with a flotilla of ships; the canal itself was a significant obstacle, and troops could be moved to any threatened point along its length by a railway and road. Out to the east, patrols provided early warning, while deep in reserve the remainder of the garrison could be held in concentration.

Maurice Hankey, the Secretary of the War Cabinet, noted that 'The Committee of Imperial Defence in 1909 had recommended that a serious invasion of Egypt could best be met by a landing at Haifa.'[3] Churchill had suggested that either an attack or a feint at Gallipoli would deter an Ottoman attack and 'give us control of the Dardanelles' where 'we could dictate terms at Constantinople'.[4] A successful naval raid under the direction of Sir Richard Pierse on the railway at Alexandretta, and the cooperation of the Ottoman governor who wished to avoid the bombardment of his port, 'helped to form the opinion in our mind as to the degree of resistance which might in all circumstances be expected from Turkey', wrote Churchill. He concluded that 'we were not dealing with a thoroughly efficient military power'.[5]

Imperial defence relied not only on the military dispositions along the Suez Canal, but on the ability to co-opt, coerce, or subdue internal opposition. There was great concern that Egyptians might not accept British control, particularly if they were compelled to fight the Ottoman Empire. There were memories of the Arabi Pasha nationalist revolt in 1881, led by the Egyptian army, which had rejected foreign domination and prompted British military intervention. There was also concern with periodic outbreaks of violent jihadism, typically described as a universal threat of 'fanaticism'.[6] To the south, in Sudan and Somalia, this threat was still live, and any additional unrest in Egypt would place the system of imperial defence under considerable strain. Moreover, the prospect of the caliph of the Ottoman Empire calling for a pan-Islamic resistance to the subjects of the British Empire was regarded as a serious threat.[7] The development of newspapers, the increased popularity and accessibility of making the Haj to Mecca, and the emergence of a pan-Islamic doctrine of resistance, exemplified by the late nineteenth century writings of Jamal-ud-din al-Afghani, had spread networks across the Muslim world. Worse still was German interest in subversion. Days after the outbreak of war, the German chancellor, Bethmann Hollweg, warned: 'One of our main tasks is to gradually wear England down through unrest in India and Egypt, which will only be possible from there.'[8]

Part of the British anxiety was its legitimacy in Egypt. Despite the presence of the British administration from 1882 onwards, Britain was officially

Figure 3.1 The Hertfordshire Yeomanry on the banks of Suez Canal during the Egyptian campaign

only in a supervisory position. In 1914, Sir Edward Grey, the Foreign Secretary, had advocated the annexation of Egypt in order to resolve the dilemma, but the Acting Consul General, Sir Milne Cheetham, was concerned that annexation would provoke the very resistance they sought to avoid. However, when war with the Ottoman Empire was imminent, the British Residency abolished the embryonic Egyptian Legislative Assembly, issued a proclamation to the effect that Britain now assumed full responsibility for the defence of Egypt without requiring Egyptian participation, and, a month later, declared Egypt a protectorate. Following a well-established imperial procedure, the local pro-Turkish Khedive was deposed and replaced with his pro-British nephew, Hussein, thus ensuring a local face to this foreign coup. On the departure of Lord Kitchener, the British Agent, who took up his position as Secretary of State for War, the first high commissioner, Sir Henry McMahon, was appointed. Nevertheless, it was the British and Indian Army that came to dominate the domestic affairs of Egypt, culminating in the establishment of martial law in 1916.[9] General Maxwell, who exercised command of the country in 1914–15, nevertheless managed to use his personal touch to make the transition to a wartime system as palatable as possible.

The declaration of war on the Ottoman Empire, on 5 November 1914, provoked the anticipated condemnation of Britain by the caliph. The British were prepared for the five fatwas that called on all Muslims to rise up against their British and French colonial masters. In the Balkan Wars of 1912–13, Turkish demands for support against the Christian Serbs and Greeks had given a strong indication of the likely trajectory of Ottoman propaganda. One of the chief targets the British had anticipated was the Indian Army, of which one-third were Muslim. However, with the banning of particular newspapers and a sense of vigilance, the threat soon abated. The British appealed to the class-conscious Muslim princes and aristocrats to show responsible leadership, and they were attuned to the desire of the Muslim middling classes for order and stability. A handful of young activists were identified in urban areas, but rural hinterlands were unmoved, where the routine of agrarian life was dominant. The Ottoman Army that later advanced across Sinai had in its baggage a great volume of pan-Islamic propaganda, and some of it was directed towards Indian troops, but there is no evidence of its effect or even of its distribution.[10] Ultimately, the credibility of the British Empire was to be determined by military achievements or set-backs rather than subversive literature.

Djemal Pasha, the former Minister of Marine and now commander of the Ottoman Fourth Army, had expected to overwhelm the small British garrison at Suez in order to ignite a general Egyptian uprising.[11] Despatching 25,000 men in two divisions (the 10th and 25th Infantry Divisions) and supported by artillery under the German advising officer, General Friedrich Kress von Kressenstein and the German Chief of Staff, Werner von Frankenberg, Djemal had expected that 'the Egyptian patriots, encouraged by the capture of Ismailia by the Turkish [*sic*] Army, would rise *en masse*, and Egypt would be freed in an unexpectedly short time by the employment of quite a small force and insignificant technical resources'.[12] This was to be a classic *coup de main*—a sudden march across Sinai and the seizure of the most significant strategic point of the British maritime empire, before the British had a chance to react.

The strategy actually owed more to German encouragement than Djemal had admitted. In September 1914, the German Chief of the General Staff, Helmuth von Moltke, had urged General Liman von Sanders to press the Ottomans to launch operations 'against Odessa . . . and Egypt [as they appear to be] the most promising', while the German ambassador in Istanbul,

Baron Hans von Wangenheim, believing an amphibious attack against Odessa to be too demanding for the Ottomans, suggested concentrating its forces against Egypt.[13] He argued that German financial support to the Ottomans would be dependent on making 'the push against Egypt', even though he admitted that the operation there held out no real advantage for the government in Istanbul. Indeed, there seemed to be little consideration given to the consequences of even a successful mission. The canal might be blocked, perhaps, but two divisions would be insufficient to hold the Canal Zone, not least because land lines of communications, across the Sinai, were precarious. As General Kress von Kressenstein later complained, he had insufficient camels to sustain his force.

It is likely that Wangenheim did not expect the Ottomans to succeed. His purpose seems to have been only to have tied British and Imperial troops to the defence of Egypt and thus prevent their arrival in Europe.[14] The Young Turks, by contrast, had their own agenda. They favoured the recovery of Egypt from the British and shared the idea of a general Muslim uprising against the Entente powers, prompted by a military victory. Enver Pasha had described the objective as a personal initiative, but one which would protect the Straits: 'I want to start an offensive against the Suez Canal to keep the English tied up in Egypt and thus not only compel them to leave there a large number of Indian divisions, which they are now sending to the Western Front, but to prevent them from landing a force at the Dardanelles.'[15]

Djemal had made no secret of his mission from the outset. Tasked to raise an army in Syria, he was hailed in Istanbul by crowds on 21 November as 'the saviour of Egypt'. As he set about assembling his army, the British were receiving reinforcements of their own at Suez. By that November, some 50,000 British and Empire troops had assembled, while a steady traffic of Territorials heading out to India and regulars returning, as well as the movement of mountains of stores, underscored the strategic importance of the Canal Zone. Djemal had raised a similar number of forces, but many of the irregular volunteers from across the Levant could not be supplied, while lines of communication required protection, rendering his strike force no more than the strength of a single corps augmented with untrained levies. Djemal later claimed that he 'staked everything upon surprising the English', but his precautions for operational security were non-existent.[16] Later he claimed he expected only to cross the canal and establish a defensive position, a combination of strategic offence and tactical defence, where he could defeat British counter-attacks.

Figure 3.2 Ahmed Djemal Pasha, Naval Minister and then governor of Syria who crushed Arab nationalists and yearned for a Pan-Islamic unity

Djemal also made appeals to local Arab leaders, in the hope he could create both momentum and the legitimacy of a multi-ethnic, Islamic, and thus truly Ottoman offensive. Wahib Pasha of the Hejaz brought up much of the Ottoman garrison from Mecca, but it was noticeable that neither Sharif Hussein, nor his son, Ali, made any move to support the campaign. Moreover, it was not until January 1915 that the force selected to attack the canal could be concentrated at Beersheeba, the last supply base in southern Palestine, or the supply depots built up, in 15-mile intervals, across the Sinai. Heavy rains had filled all the wells and created temporary lakes which relieved pressure on the crucial supply of water. Pontoon bridges, telegraphic equipment, and medical supplies were accumulated, but the project suffered from a lack of rail transport south of Syria. Gilbert Clayton, the head of military intelligence in Cairo, had nevertheless concluded that up to 100,000 Ottoman troops and volunteers could cross the Sinai in under two weeks, and Cairo had had two of its intelligence officers, Leonard Woolley and T. E. Lawrence, carry out reconnaissance work to confirm the calculations a year before the war broke out.[17]

For the British planners, the defence of Egypt was to be augmented by a thrust against the Ottomans in Syria. In 1907 and again in November 1914, the Committee of Imperial Defence had considered an amphibious operation in the Levant, with options for landings at Haifa or Alexandretta, where communications between Turkey and the Arab south could be severed. Sir Charles Callwell, the Director of Military Operations, and Lord Kitchener had both given serious thought to the plan, but the lack of available manpower meant it was shelved in January 1915.[18] Assumptions about imperial defence made in peacetime, when reserve divisions could be shuttled to objectives with impunity, were no longer viable.

The view expressed by General Maxwell was that the Sinai desert was 'a great ally' in that it presented a serious obstacle to the movement of any enemy force.[19] Nevertheless, he had ordered that defences be constructed in eastern Egypt from November 1914 onwards. As part of the preparations, gaps were cut in the Canal in order to flood certain sections of desert some 20 miles to the east, reducing the length of front to be held by the garrison to about 70 miles. Naval launches carried out patrols, while four British and two French ships added to the overall mobile fire support available. When intelligence reports confirmed that the Ottomans intended to cross the desert to the canal, there was some incredulity, for, throughout 1914, the War Office had assumed the main effort of the Ottomans would be the Caucasus. Yet the first Ottoman patrols skirmished with the Indian picquets (outpost lines) in late January, confirming the news of a Sinai offensive.[20] Air reconnaissance noted Ottoman troop concentrations, prompting final revisions of British defence plans.[21]

At the tactical level, it was difficult for the British to discern the main thrust of an attack, particularly as most movements were conducted at night and Ottoman probing attacks were designed to screen the main effort. A sandstorm on 1 February added to the difficulties in reconnaissance. Moreover, the decision to station the entire force on the western bank, creating a linear defence of the Canal, deprived the British depth in their ability to gather intelligence or to conduct disruptive operations of their own. Lord Kitchener later summed up the situation in his criticism: 'Are you defending the Canal, or is the Canal defending you?'[22] To some extent, there was a political motive at work: Britain was eager to demonstrate that it was not violating the rights of neutral powers to freely navigate the Canal, and it could show that the Ottomans were the aggressors, but, even so, the defensive mentality gave the initiative to the Ottoman Fourth Army.

Djemal's troops advanced to make their crossing of the Canal on the night of 2–3 February, initially at Ismailia, with subsequent attacks at Kantara (Qantara) and El Ferdan. Artillery was positioned so as to attempt to sink one or more of the ships on the Canal, in the hope of blocking it.[23]

The attempts to cross at night were discovered, and, at Toussoum, a Punjabi battalion under Colonel Geoghegan poured rifle and machine-gun fire into the metal boats and their Ottoman crews. The local detachment commanders, Major Skeen and Captain Morgan, not only neutralized the entire crossing, they also mopped up the forty or so men who actually got across the Canal. At Serapeum, another Ottoman attack was broken up and 300 were taken prisoner. At daybreak the remaining Ottoman detachments were cleared from the eastern bank and their pontoons were destroyed by gunboats. The Ottomans remained in depth, using artillery and occasionally making sorties to drop mines into the Canal at night. All bar one of these attempts failed, and the steamer *Teresias*, while damaged by a mine, was deliberately run aground to prevent the canal from being closed.[24] The bulk of the Ottoman force was nevertheless withdrawn, against General Kress von Kressenstein's advice, and it concentrated again at Beersheeba. For the loss of 200 killed, 381 wounded, and over 700 prisoners, the Ottoman offensive had failed. The British losses were 162 killed and 130 wounded.

The failure of the offensive against Suez was a significant set-back to the promise of a universal jihad. The sudden loss of momentum, not only in Suez, but at Sarıkamış in the Caucasus and in Mesopotamia, broke the mystique of a regional uprising under the banner of Islam. Ottoman ambitions had been unrealistic. Djemal had promised not to return until he had 'conquered Egypt' but now, much chastised, he and his Fourth Army were marching rearwards into Palestine. It had not been, as he later claimed, through a loss of surprise that he had failed, but a totally unrealistic strategic plan. Outnumbered, on extended lines of communication, lacking air support for reconnaissance, and operating against a prepared position, Djemal's chances of success were minimal.

Nevertheless, the ease with which the British had seen off the Ottoman offensive, and their successes on the lower Tigris in Mesopotamia, fulfilled an assumption, long held by British planners, that the Ottomans could be defeated relatively easily. Serious consideration was now given to mounting an offensive towards Baghdad, and naval operations were designed to force a passage through the Dardanelles. While there was some criticism later about Maxwell's decision not to pursue Djemal, and make this a three-pronged assault on the Ottomans, the British were not yet in a position to make an advance from Suez. The Ottomans lost some 7,000 camels in their retreat, and there is no reason to doubt that a similar fate would have befallen any hasty and ill-prepared counter-offensive. Moreover, Maxwell's priority was to maintain his strong position at Cairo, a central location from which he could radiate his defences not only eastwards but also west and south, to deter tribal risings.

The Ottoman strategy against Egypt was to launch offensives on multiple axes. So, while the Fourth Army advanced from the east, irregular forces from Libya and the Sudan, inspired by the cause of pan-Islamism, would attack from the west and from the south. The Senussi of Libya were to be supplied with arms by a neutral steamer and German submarines and then orchestrate an offensive.[25] This was not a guerrilla strategy like the one which had been used against the Italians in 1911–14, but a coordinated attack that would ignite a revolution within Egypt and overwhelm the British. In January 1915, Nuri Bey, Enver's half-brother, and Jafar al-Askari, an Ottoman staff officer from Mosul who had been trained in Berlin, left Istanbul to make contact with Sayyid Ahmad, the acknowledged leader of the Senussi order. The following month, they found Sayyid Ahmad in a strategic dilemma: while willing to assist the Ottoman cause, he was under pressure from the Italians, contained to the south by the French in Chad and dependent on supply lines from Egypt, where the British could, at any moment, cut him off. His priority was to continue his war against the Italians. He may also have had concerns that, even if he joined the jihadist cause, the Ottomans might try to assert themselves over his territories. The Istanbul government needed him for their own purposes, to add to the authority of their holy war, which was supported by the sultan, but not by the sharif of Mecca. Interestingly, Jafar al-Askari would most probably have shared the sharif's suspicions, for he was a member of the secret Arab faction al-Ahd which was pledged to defend the Ottoman Empire but also, at the same time, to resist Turkish nationalist domination.[26]

Jafar al-Askari used his twenty-strong training team to assist in turning the Senussi into a more effective force for 'conventional' operations. The core of the Senussi was the Muhafiziyya, a collection of 400 committed religious students, while the rest were made up of tribal irregulars. The Ottomans had brought in machine guns and mountain artillery to increase the firepower of the host, but in just a few months it was clear that the key tactical advantage of the Senussi was their mobility.

What they did not possess was the element of surprise. Sir John Maxwell had been kept informed of the arrival of the Ottoman training team, and the French had intercepted one Ottoman supply ship in June 1915, seizing its munitions and bales of inflammatory propaganda. What Maxwell lacked was the means to deter the threat.[27] He had already had to dispatch the 28th Indian Brigade under General Sir George Younghusband to Aden when the Ottomans approached the port, and the lion's share of reinforcements were needed for the operations underway at Gallipoli. Moreover, there was evident trouble brewing on the borders of the Sudan in Darfur. On the western border of Egypt, the actual line being indistinct, security was dependent on Egyptian guards, but the inhabitants were mainly Bedouin living in large oases. If these were induced to join the Senussi revolt, the border could not be held. At this point, a last ditch attempt was made to turn Sayyid Ahmad with an offer of a large subsidy, but, no doubt fearing that the Senussi leader would delay any assault on the British indefinitely, in November Nuri Bey and Jafar al-Askari provoked hostilities by making raids on the Egyptian border guards at Sollum.

The attack on Sollum, small in scale, was accompanied by concomitant civil unrest in Alexandria, suggesting that the Ottomans were broadly correct in their assessment of the revolutionary potential of their offensive. The fact that the isolated Egyptian border guards were withdrawn, in order to concentrate their forces 120 miles to the rear at Marsa Matruh, also seemed to indicate that further pressure now against the British—even a minor victory—might set in train the breakdown of order elsewhere. The Awlad Ali clans who lived astride the border joined the revolt soon after, and 134 Egyptian Coastguards also deserted to the Senussi cause. There was every indication that the offensive was now building momentum.

The British had gathered together a Western Frontier Force under General A. Wallace to check the Senussi advance and restore confidence at a time when fortunes on other fronts were at a low ebb. The troops were from a mixture of units, most of whom were the rear echelons of the formations in Gallipoli. The Yeomanry brigade provided a mobile arm, and the infantry brigade a ground-holding force, while a detachment of the Egyptian Public Works Department and logisticians made up the rest of Wallace's contingent. Two aircraft were also found, serviced, and deployed. As this indicates, it was not regarded as a front-line formation, as most of the personnel had not completed their basic training, and what they faced were some highly experienced and motivated guerrilla fighters and a select team of artillerymen and machine gunners. Worse still, the British troops had almost no experience of desert warfare and were outnumbered by over 1,000 men.[28]

Nevertheless, on 11 December 1915, in the traditions of colonial campaigning, the British went on the offensive, attacking the Senussi at Wadi

Senab in an action that lasted two days. A second thrust was made at the Senussi on 25 December at Wadi Majid, surprising their forces. Hemmed in on three sides, and shelled by warships off the coast, the Senussi could not hold their positions and were driven off into the desert. The British attack was so effective that the tribal forces were routed. In the finale of the campaign, the Battle of Agagia, which featured a reckless cavalry charge by British Yeomanry into Ottoman machine-gun fire, the Senussi were again thrown into headlong retreat. Jafar al-Askari was amongst those wounded and captured. The shock of the casualties and defeats had a deleterious effect on the morale of the Senussi. There was a steady flow of desertions, and, while they retained Sollum, protected and resupplied by German submarines, the offensive into Egypt was clearly over.[29] The effect in Egypt was immediate: pro-Senussi demonstrations soon petered out.[30] The British continued to drive the Senussi back, and fought further skirmishes before operations were concluded with the recapture of all Egyptian territory, including Sollum, in February 1916.

In the Sudan, rumours that the Ottomans had taken the Suez Canal and had invaded Egypt seemed to make little impression on the Darfuris or the peoples of the Khordofan.[31] However, intelligence that the Senussi and their Ottoman accomplices had made contact with Ali Dinar, the sultan of Darfur, prompted the British to reinforce their more isolated posts with camel-mounted troops and contingents of infantry. Ali Dinar had defected from the khalifa's revolt in 1898, when the British under Lord Kitchener had been poised to defeat the Sudanese at Omdurman, and the British had permitted him to retain an autonomous fiefdom based on the desert city of El Fasher (today called Al Fashir in Darfur Province). However, it was known that he was a jihadist with extreme views. In late 1915, Sir Reginald Wingate, the governor general of the Sudan, discovered that Ali Dinar had joined the Ottoman cause.

In the first few months of 1916, Wingate decided to reinforce the perimeter of Darfur, but any operation towards El Fasher and its hostile garrison of 5,000 men would necessitate crossing hundreds of miles of waterless terrain with a scratch force. As they approached El Fasher in a gruelling march, the Darfuris made a series of attacks. At the village of Beringia a determined assault necessitated the formation of a 'square' of soldiers, closely packed and facing in every direction, which was a tactical anachronism belonging to warfare in the previous century.[32] The Official History noted: 'the assault was delivered with that fanatical bravery in which few races can match the tribes of the Sudan, despite the fire of two mountain guns and four sections of Maxim machine guns manned by British detachments'.[33] Sticking to their ground, the British cut down the skirmishing Darfuris and then counter-attacked. Coupled with an air attack by Lieutenant J. C. Slessor, the British drove relentlessly on to Ali Dinar's capital and harried the tribesmen into the desert. His followers began to turn against him. Hungry and suffering from disease, many of his men surrendered, and the British continued to overrun his stocks of ammunition. When his family gave themselves up, it was clear the end was near. On 5 November, a British flying column intercepted his camp, and Ali Dinar was found dead—shot in the head—but whether by British fire or as the result of betrayal is not known.[34]

The Senussi revolt was finally extinguished when a force known as the Light Armoured Car Brigade advanced on the Senussi headquarters at Siwa. Although engaged with artillery, the motorized column defeated all resistance and Sayyid Ahmad concluded a peace with both Italy and Britain. Nuri Bey refused to capitulate and continued his resistance until November 1918, although Sayyid Ahmad was taken by German submarine into exile in Ottoman Turkey.

At the operational level, despite the tactical difficulties of using an inexperienced force to defeat a much larger, highly motivated formation, the Senussi were not strong enough to overwhelm the British forces in Egypt's Western Desert. The strategy could only succeed if there was coordination with the Ottoman Army and if the Egyptian people joined the jihadist cause. Consequently, while the Senussi revolt constituted perhaps the most 'successful of the Turco-German initiatives in revolutionary wars', that was hardly an accolade when all of the revolutionary initiatives launched by the Ottomans and the Germans failed.[35] It is interesting to note that Berlin believed that if the Sudanese and Senussi had succeeded, the Germans could have used the Arabian peninsula and the Sudan as the conduit through which supplies, munitions and men could contribute to the expansion of German conquests in *Mittelafrika*.[36] The value of the Senussi was in their guerrilla warfare prowess, using the desert hinterland to evade the British and therefore keeping the flame of resistance alive. They launched their last significant assault on the British as late as April 1917, but, in the end, the only strategic value of the Senussi revolt to the Ottomans and the Germans had been to tie up British forces.[37] That said, even second-echelon troops, albeit with some reinforcements in the shape of armoured cars and aircraft, had contained and then defeated the Senussi offensive. Sudan and Egypt remained firmly under British control, Sayyid Ahmad was forced to conclude his resistance to Italy, and Ottoman assumptions about pan-Islamism had proven to be illusions once more. At the strategic level, one is driven to the conclusion that this was an unmitigated Ottoman failure.

Germany had also failed to recognize the limits of its own ambitions. It had opened negotiations, through Ambassador Wangenheim, with the Egyptian Khedive, Abbas Hilmi, without Ottoman approval.[38] While the Germans hoped to foster Egyptian nationalism through him, the Ottomans were eager to reassert their anti-nationalist imperial control. The Egyptian nationalists were themselves divided: the Watan party claimed to be both patriots and pan-Islamists, but were really no more than a protest movement which had collapsed even before the war broke out. The Umma party was opposed to the Ottomans and had faith in progressive British socio-economic reforms as the route to eventual independence. The idea that the Egyptian Army might be subverted was also hopeless. Most of the regiments were stationed in the Sudan and were remote from political intrigue. Any thought that the Egyptians would rise up against the British once the Ottoman Army approached the Suez Canal was a fantasy without any evidence, but it had been the basis of the assumptions behind the planning.[39]

The Ottomans were faced with limits to their ambitions in southern Arabia where the authority of the Ottoman Empire was contested. The port of Aden presented a possible entry route for the British to the Hejaz, and, more importantly, the means to win over Arab leaders against the sultan. Aden had been acquired as a strategic coaling station on the route to India in 1839 when an agreement with the local ruler, the sultan of Lahej, broke down and Britain had occupied the port. By the terms of the subsequent agreement, the territories of the sultan of Lahej were rendered a British protectorate. Settlements were also made with nine other prominent clans adjacent to the port, and commerce began to flourish. The Ottomans disapproved of the British incursion and made their own attempts to reassert their sovereignty of the region. In 1849, they had garrisoned Tihama, and local disturbances led to calls by prominent imams within the Zayid clans for Ottoman assistance in restoring order. However, Ottoman forces were defeated in their efforts to take Sana and the highlands. It was not until 1873 that they successfully occupied the region, but despite trying to promote certain tribal leaders at the expense of others, the Ottomans experienced difficulty in exercising control over this periphery of the empire, and, in their efforts to introduce the modernizing 'Tanzimat' reforms from the late

1870s, they generated further resistance in the Yemen *vilayet* (province). The insurgency that developed there in the 1880s spread from the northern highlands after 1904 under the leadership of Imam Yahya Hamid ed-din al-Mutawakil. In 1911, exhausted by the costs of the counter-insurgency, the Ottomans concluded peace with Imam Yahya and gave his Zayidis full autonomy in the northern highlands. In return, they confined themselves to the south. The agreement proved strategically valuable, for the imam maintained his material support of the Ottoman forces in Yemen throughout the fighting. Nevertheless, the Ottomans were unable to quell another local rebellion by Idrissi, emir of Sabayyeh, on the Red Sea coast, and that continued right through to 1914.[40]

In April 1915, the British concluded a treaty with the Idrisids, offering autonomy and protection if they would take up arms against the Ottomans. The move had been prompted by the prospect of an Ottoman *coup de main* against the port of Aden, at the outbreak of the war, but it was the build-up of a British Indian garrison at Aden, and the driving of their forces across the Sheikh Sa'ad peninsula, that convinced the Ottomans that they needed to take further action. In June 1915, they advanced on the Sheikh Sa'ad peninsula, and tried, but failed, to land on Perim Island (also known as Mayyun) at the southern end of the Red Sea. Intelligence arrived in British hands indicating that an Ottoman division was en route via Lahej to seize the port. Major General D. L. B. Shaw decided to take the initiative and disrupt the Ottoman offensive, and, at the same time, demonstrate his willingness to protect the Idrisids and the local sheikhs as promised. With a squadron of Indian cavalry sent ahead to Lahej, a force of just 1,000 men set out to reach the town before the Ottomans could arrive in force. On 4 July, the advanced parties of both sides collided in what degenerated into a confused night fight in the town.[41] The Arab civilians who had been transporting the British baggage fled at the first encounter and Shaw was compelled to withdraw to reorganize. The Ottomans pursued slowly but by late July they had made no attempt to contest the port as expected, although they did control its water supply.

General Younghusband's 28th (Frontier Force) Brigade arrived soon after, taking the Ottomans at Sheikh Othman by surprise. The water supply of Aden and local commerce therefore resumed and Younghusband decided to fortify Sheikh Othman rather than advance into the interior to take Lahej. He reasoned, correctly, that to do so would tie up an entire brigade for no useful strategic purpose. The only penalty was that the Ottomans retained

Lahej which damaged the standing of the British as 'protectors'. It was not until October 1918 that a counter-offensive was contemplated. Nevertheless, the Ottoman commander, Ali Said Pasha, was entirely dependent on the Yemenis for his supplies. He was unable to either advance or retire and his brigade remained fixed for the entire war. Indeed, it was later revealed that his communications with Istanbul were so poor that he was unaware of the Armistice in November 1918 and it took lengthy negotiations to persuade him to capitulate.[42]

Two other clan leaders of the Arabian peninsula had the power to alter the strategic plans of the Ottomans and the British, and represented another form of limitation on the major powers' strategic plans. Ibn Rashid, emir of Hail, was aligned to the Ottomans, but Abdulaziz Ibn Saud, who was emir of Riyadh and the dominant leader in the Nejd, the vast desert region of the interior of southern Arabia, held sway over the clans affiliated with the doctrine of Wahabism. Ibn Saud thought that better relations with the British offered a greater chance of more autonomy than anything the Ottomans and their revolutionary secularists in Istanbul could offer—and perhaps even control of Mecca and Medina. When it was suggested that a caliphate might replace the sultan's Ottoman regime, he expressed strong approval and even accepted the idea that the existing sharif of Mecca would be the most suitable leader.[43] The British political officer working closely with him thought that an alliance was required, but sadly the officer, Captain William Shakespeare, was killed on 24 January 1915 during the Battle of Jarrab between Ibn Rashid's forces and those of Ibn Saud. No agreement was concluded.[44] Sharif Hussein of Mecca was more troubled by his rival from the Saudi clan. His own adherents were attracted to the idea of Wahabism, and to the arms and largesse distributed by Ibn Saud, which made him appear a far stronger leader, with great prestige.[45]

The German Strategy of Revolution

The first phase of the German Zimmermann plan, namely to get Turkey into the war, had been completed successfully, but there had been little strategic thinking in the Foreign Ministry before the war about action against Britain. It was elements within the German administration, and in the Ottoman consulates, who were eager to fulfil the idea of 'Gott strafe England!' ('God punish England!') They took their lead from Kaiser Wilhelm who believed that he would be regarded as the leader of the Muslim world, and that his rise would be achieved through the destruction of the British and French colonial world. On 30 July 1914, he exclaimed: 'Our consuls in Turkey and India, our agents, etcetera, must inflame the whole Mohammedan world to wild revolt against this hateful, lying, conscienceless people of hagglers; for if we are bled to death [by their encirclement policy], at least England shall lose India.'[46]

The sultan, as the spokesman of Muslims everywhere, dutifully declared his jihad on his enemies. Specially prepared inflammatory literature was then despatched from Berlin and Istanbul, and Ottoman agitators, primarily radical preachers and scholars, set out for the east. However, with some reluctance, the Ottoman triumvirate agreed to support a simultaneous German-led strategy, largely because they wanted to maintain control of its consequences. They were suspicious of German motives. For their part, the Germans were dependent not only on the Ottomans, but on a handful of experts, mainly men who had served in consulates in the region in the past, and academics.[47] The joint Turco-German mission to Persia and then Afghanistan, which was intended to stir up the local tribes and persuade the rulers of the two states to declare holy war on the British and Russians, therefore got underway quite late in 1914.[48] Nevertheless, festooned with volumes of propaganda and replete with arms and gold, German 'consuls' (without any recognized status from the government at Teheran but accompanied by heavily armed escorts), prepared to march into Persia.[49]

Wilhelm Wassmuss, who had an intimate knowledge of southern Persia from before the war, detached himself from the delayed main body after disagreements with the expedition's commander, Oskar von Niedermayer, and he proceeded towards the Gulf coast. British intelligence knew he was on his way. He was ambushed and captured on 5 March 1915 by Persian tribesmen working for Major Sir Frederick O'Connor, the British consul at Shiraz. O'Connor's men had been tipped off by a network of Persian informers paid by Sir Percy Cox. However, Wassmuss gave his captors the slip before he could be interned, although he lost all his propaganda literature, and, concealed within his baggage, a diplomatic codebook.[50] This proved to be of immense strategic value in deciphering German codes in 1917.[51]

Enver did his best to delay the rest of the German mission lest it interfere with his own plans to dominate the region, and he was keen to give his Turkish envoys a head start. The Germans' selected Persian puppet was to be

Salar ud-Daula, a man who had intrigued against the shah and had been exiled. The Ottomans were concerned about this legitimate claimant to the Persian throne and imprisoned him. However, in July 1915, Otto von Hentig's mission finally set out accompanied by German troops, Indian Army deserters, Mohammed Baraktullah, a Muslim radical, and Raja Kunwar Mahendra Pratap, an anti-British prince who had spent years in exile in Switzerland and who entertained fantasies about becoming India's next head of state.[52]

The Persian government was desperate to maintain its neutrality, and the presence of Russian troops in Persian Azerbaijan in November 1914 elicited a diplomatic rebuke.[53] The Russians asked, if their troops were withdrawn, what security the Persians would offer against an Ottoman incursion into the same region. It was a question that drew attention to the fundamental weakness of the Persian state. In December, during elections, the Persian Democrats argued that it would be safer to align the country with Germany, as the Russians, British, and now the Ottomans, appeared to have designs to occupy the state. Russian troops at Qazvin, just 93 miles north-west of the capital, alarmed by the pro-German sympathies expressed by this faction, immediately marched on Tehran. The thirty Democrat deputies fled to the Shi'a holy city of Qom, about 80 miles south-west of Tehran, and formed their own provisional government known as the Komiteh-e Defa'-e Melli (Committee of National Defence). Hounded from Qom, they remained on the move until they established themselves at Kermanshah, but, even here, they were ousted and dispersed by the Russians in 1916.

In January 1915, the Russians had driven off local irregulars and established a presence at Tabriz in Persian Azerbaijan. From there, planners considered the possibility that, swinging south-westwards, a large Russian force could cut across the headwaters of the Tigris and sever Ottoman communications with Mesopotamia. Yet the supply routes were problematic, as they would cross mountains and cover hundreds of miles of potentially hostile territory.[54] Consequently, the Russians were content to stabilize the front, make limited attacks against the Ottomans, but otherwise remain on the defensive. However, Halil Pasha, commanding the Ottoman 36th Division, was skirting the southern shore of Lake Van, heading towards the Persian frontier. At Dilman in May 1915, this Ottoman thrust was defeated.[55] The arrival of thousands of Cossack cavalry in the area checked any prospect of another Ottoman advance, suppressed Kurdish irregular resistance, and overawed the Persians.

The situation changed in late 1915 when the British and imperial forces offensive on Gallipoli stalled and there seemed every likelihood the Mediterranean Expeditionary Force would be evacuated, freeing at least twenty Ottoman divisions for service on other fronts, including Persian Azerbaijan. The Russians anticipated a large offensive into Persia. To pre-empt the possible collapse of Persian resistance, in December 1915 General Baratov of the 1st Caucasian Cossack Division at Qazvin, on his own initiative, dispatched a mounted brigade to Hamadan, 200 miles south-west of Tehran, and then to Qom, where they managed to defeat the Persian gendarmerie and their Democrat leaders. Qom remained under Russian control, with a regiment guarding the approaches to Kashan, in central Persia, where local resistance continued.

To counter the Russian move, the German commander in Mesopotamia, General von der Goltz, sent a battalion of Ottoman infantry and a mountain battery to Kermanshah, near the western border of Persia, to support the pro-German Persian politicians.[56] At the village of Asadabad, close to Hamadan, on 25 December 1915 and then again at the nearby Kangavar on 13 January 1916, this force was intercepted by the Cossacks and was eventually broken. Nevertheless, the Ottomans sent further reinforcements to Kermanshah until the garrison was made up of four regular infantry battalions, supported by some 6,000 Persian gendarmes and irregulars. Yet, in late January, even this composite force proved no match for Baratov's Cossacks and Kermanshah was captured.

Meanwhile, British intelligence was kept informed of the movements of the German mission to Afghanistan.[57] There were sufficient numbers of Persians with little sympathy for the Ottomans and their German allies to provide information, while neutral consuls within the Ottoman Empire, particularly the Americans, relayed announcements by the government in Istanbul to the world.[58] At a more clandestine level, wireless intercepts—or 'SIGINT'—proved valuable in determining the objectives of the German mission. Niedermayer and Hentig made a punishing ride across central Persia to try and outpace the British informers. Alerted by Cox's network of Persian spies, the viceroy of India, Lord Hardinge, authorized the consulates at Meshed and Kirman to use money liberally in order to obstruct and delay the German mission. Meanwhile, British Indian troops were ordered to set up a screen of troops known as the East Persian Cordon to prevent the Germans from reaching neutral Afghanistan.[59]

Nevertheless, there were several major problems to overcome. First, the Cordon required troops to travel all the way from Quetta on the Indian border and to be spread across a frontier of several hundred miles. Given the harsh climate and the lack of infrastructure, this was a considerable undertaking. Secondly, Persia was still theoretically neutral and the blatant deployment of troops could push Teheran further into the German sphere. Already Prince Henry of Reuss, the German minister at Teheran, was making substantial efforts to win over the shah. Reuss even tried to convince the shah that the Russians were intending to overthrow him and that his only hope lay in making a *hejira* (a flight in emulation of Mohammed to the safety of the holy city of Qom), a move likely to ignite the passions of many young Shi'a Muslims and thus mobilize the country against the British.[60] The third problem the British faced was the paucity of troops available to man the Cordon. Even if patrols covered vast distances each day, inevitably there would be gaps. As a solution, the government of India sought Russian help from the north, but the Cossacks, now extended across western Persia, could not redeploy in time and the Russians objected when Lieutenant Colonel Wolseley Haig, the British Consul General at Meshed in the north of the country, tried to raise volunteers amongst the local Hazara clans in 'their' sphere of influence.

As a result, the Germans successfully slipped past the East Persian Cordon and reached Afghanistan in July 1915. Accompanied by news of stalemate in Gallipoli, the bottling-up of a British and Indian force at Kut al Amara in Mesopotamia, the assassination of British officials in Persia, and the robberies of seven out of seventeen British banks in that country, the outlook was bleak. However, Hardinge believed that the Afghans could be relied upon to resist German inducements to support the Central Powers. In the meantime, further efforts were made to strengthen the Cordon and to discover the whereabouts of other Ottoman and German parties.[61] In particular, the aim was to prevent any sizeable forces or munitions arriving in Afghanistan.

The Persian government was concerned about growing lawlessness in the country and refused to recognize the status of the new German 'consuls', especially Lieutenants Zugmayer and Griesinger, who had established themselves in Kirman, deep in the south-east of the country. Using bribes and assassinations, they seized control of the town through their nationalist Persian allies. The two officers then pressed on to Baluchistan, hoping to rouse the tribes to join a jihad. Like so many of the Persians, the Baluchis were more than willing to relieve the Germans of their funds and arms without any further commitments. Indeed, information about them was regularly passed to Quetta by British sympathizers until Brigadier General

Reginald Dyer was sent out with just 100 men to take on the Germans, and the Persians and Baluchis they had recruited. Carefully spreading the idea that his force was just the advance guard of a whole brigade, the irregulars had no wish to take on a British expeditionary force and the Germans were forced back towards Kirman to avoid capture.

Another German officer, Lieutenant Seiler, the former German consul at Isfahan, had tried to lead a second force into Afghanistan, but he was intercepted by the East Persian Cordon. After a long pursuit and four casualties amongst the Germans' escort, Seiler escaped eastwards. Calling for reinforcements, the British cavalry patrol then set up an ambush for the main body which they expected at any moment, but the German party had scattered. Seiler and Zugmayer both tried to link up with Wassmuss in southern Persia, but they were attacked by local brigands and forced to withdraw.

The only successful operations conducted by the Germans were those of Wassmuss in the south. He had recruited a guerrilla force that made raids on isolated British posts and in November 1915 they overran the Residency at Bushehr on the Persian Gulf.[62] Qashqai and Tangistani tribes were particularly antagonistic towards the British, and resented the subsidies the British paid to the Bakhtiari clans of the south-west to protect their oil interests. The greatest appeal of Wassmuss though was his promise that, by aligning with Germany, there was loot to be acquired from British-owned properties. The growing brigandage of Persia, which had plagued the country before the war, was now affecting everything. Rising wartime prices added to the hardships of the rural poor, and raiding any commercial enterprise was the last hope for desperate people. Even before the war, the 'police' and local officials had been in league with the bandits, and the decision to create a foreign-trained gendarmerie had been the antidote, but now not only corruption, but active sedition was destroying the last vestiges of law and order. By early 1916 Persia was, to use a modern expression, a 'failed state'.

The British preference was to work for stability through tribal leaders. In 1911 they had enjoyed some success in persuading the governor of Shiraz, Qavam ul-molk, the leader of the Khamseh clan, to counter-attack his kinsmen who were engaged in repeated raids. The situation was made more critical in January 1915 because two Ottoman regiments and Arab irregulars had crossed into Persian Arabistan, urging the locals to join their jihad.[63] On 5 February, oil pipelines to the south were cut. The local Bakhtiari and the sheikh of Muhammarah remained 'true to their salt' and prevented further incursion into the oil fields, and British reinforcements were sent in to assist them. In March, however, further attacks were made on the pipelines leading from the oil fields. It took until June to make the necessary repairs, but, by then, the Ottomans had been defeated in southern Mesopotamia and the threat was reduced. Moreover, the behaviour of Ottoman troops against Persian villagers had turned local sympathy into anger against the so-called liberators.[64] There were violent demonstrations against the Turks in Karbala and Najaf in Mesopotamia too, suggesting that, far from waiting for the call to revolt against the British, it was the sultan and the government in Istanbul that were detested by the Shia populations of the region.

By the end of 1915, the Persian government was in disarray and had lost control of the country. That December, Prime Minister Mostowfi ul-Mamalik authorized an increase in the Russian Cossack force to suppress pro-German agitation, but the British government argued that this was not enough, particularly as the gendarmerie was in the hands of the Germans as far as they were concerned. Worse, when Kut al Amara fell to the Ottoman Army in Mesopotamia, 18,000 fresh soldiers of the sultan were released to occupy parts of north-eastern Persia.

Under the pretence of reinforcing the East Persia Cordon, to which the Persian government had agreed, the British government intended to establish a new force to counter the Ottoman threat.[65] Cox, the Resident of the Persian Gulf with the most experience of the region, recommended Sir Percy Sykes to be the political officer of a British-led contingent, and the government of India agreed, but the authorities in London could not wait for the normal peacetime arrangements to be established: they needed a man with experience of Persia to act right away and they wanted Sykes to operate, not as a political officer, but as a military commander. The situation was critical: although German funds to the Democrats had ebbed away, there was still a great deal of civil unrest, and the Democrats tried to ensure that local authorities took their instructions from their Committee of National Defence. To augment their legitimacy, the secularist Democrats also tried to recruit mullahs to support their cause. There was a strong possibility that the Democrats, the Persian gendarmerie, the Germans, and Ottoman divisions might find common cause after all and march right through the country.

The government of India, who saw the Persian question only as one of internal unrest, instructed Sykes to recruit a police force that could march into Kirman in the far south-east and restore order. The local Persian governor had tired of the overbearing Germans and the anarchy they had created. He actively encouraged Sykes in the request for the restoration of law and order.[66] The problem Sykes faced was that the strategic plans of the Foreign Office and the War Office in London were at odds with the government of India. London demanded that Sykes move to Bandar Abbas to support Qavam ul-Molk, the leader of the Khamseh clansmen, while at the same time raising a local military force entitled the South Persia Rifles. Unfortunately, in Farsi, the translation *Qoshun-i Jenub* sounded like an army of occupation.[67] The Persian government expected the British to pay for the new force, but the British argued that its financing would form part of a loan, which the Persians never acknowledged. Nevertheless, with fifty-one officers and Indian troops, they set about recruiting. Initially the Persians were afraid they would be sent to Mesopotamia, but when fears were allayed and elders endorsed the honesty of their village men, the force began to swell. Rumours of the growth of the South Persia Rifles spread throughout the south, and stories were exaggerated en route. In no time at all, the 300 men of the actual force were being estimated at a strength of 20,000 by their rivals.[68]

The rumours had a useful effect. Not only was the pro-British Qavam ul-Molk encouraged to advance on Shiraz, but his rivals, the formerly hostile Qashqai, joined forces with him. Sykes took two companies of the 124th Baluchi Regiment and two squadrons of the 15th Lancers of the Indian Army to Kirman, forcing the German consuls to flee. The Imperial Bank reopened, telegraphic communications were restored, and commerce flourished. Recruitment to the South Persia Rifles accelerated, reaching 8,000 by mid-1916.[69] The news was applauded in London but condemned in India, which had no wish to see Persians trained and armed lest there be trouble across the frontier later.

Regardless of the success of the South Persia Rifles, it was clear that, all over Persia, the German efforts to raise a holy war were beginning to unravel.[70] When the German minister to Tehran, Heinrich Reuss, tried to induce the shah to abandon his capital, the shah allowed the Germans to depart but, on the advice of his courtiers, he himself hesitated before settling a deal with the Russians. Isolated at Qom, the Germans declared that there had been a revolution and the shah was overthrown. For a while, attacks on British and Russian posts took place, but they died away when the truth was revealed. The defeat of the German plan to raise a jihad was achieved in the nick of time: the fall of the British and Indian garrison at Kut al Amara was interpreted as a blow to prestige which might have encouraged Muslims, both Sunni and Shi'a, to resist the British Empire, although news of the disaster was skilfully concealed at the time.[71]

Neidermayer's mission in Kabul was still a cause for concern in India. Reports of the cordial reception offered to the Germans were passed by a British engineer who had been working in Kabul, but the Amir Habibullah initially refused to meet the Germans personally. Niedermayer and his colleagues used the unorthodox threat of hunger strike to shame the Afghans into a more cooperative attitude, and Habibullah was compelled to grant Niedermayer an audience. Negotiations were protracted. Habibullah deliberately delayed in an effort to avoid any commitment that might elicit a military response from the British and the Russians. It was difficult for the British to be sure what was actually happening in Kabul. Indian intelligence was still reliant on the official Muslim envoy and a handful of 'newswriters', local men paid to gather information, but the system was unreliable; Sir George Roos-Keppel, the chief commissioner of the North West Frontier Province, admitted that: 'News from Afghanistan is scanty.'[72] The situation improved slightly with the despatch of an Indian agent known only as 'X'.[73] But the amir eventually disclosed the truth. Transmitting secret correspondence to the viceroy through trusted couriers, he indicated that he had no wish to jeopardize his relationship with (or his generous subsidy from) the British authorities in India.

To strengthen the amir's hand against anti-British factions who would have willingly accepted German support, Sir Charles Cleveland, the head of Indian intelligence, suggested that a letter from George V, congratulating the amir for his loyalty and neutrality in the war, and written in the king's own hand, would provide a useful counterweight to the expressions of friendship now being proffered by the kaiser's agents. The letter was eventually delivered to the Afghan border with great ceremony and the amir was delighted. Nevertheless, there was still a strong possibility that the amir would be overthrown by more radical elements. Encouraged by the Indian Army deserter Mohammed Baraktullah's taunts that Habibullah was not defending Islam, there were many Afghans who would have been only too willing to fight the British if supplied with German arms. However, a coded message from the Germans that was intended for their minister at Tehran, concerning a coup against the amir, was despatched by a courier who had formerly been in Russian service. He took the message to the Russian consulate in Meshed, and the Russians passed a copy to the British ambassador at St Petersburg, Sir George Buchanan. Unaware of the intercept, the Germans mistakenly believed they had 1,000 armed men on their way from Tehran. The amir was forewarned, and the coup was thwarted.

Even though Afghanistan had so far resisted the temptation to join a German-inspired holy war against Britain, the threat to India through subversion remained. In October 1915, Maulvi Obeidullah, a radical Muslim, had made his way to Afghanistan in secret with a group of loyal followers. Joining Pratap and Baraktullah, the three men formed an Indian 'Government in Exile'.[74] They declared the formation of an 'Army of God', and, encouraged by news of a mutiny by the 5th Light Infantry at Singapore in 1915, and by stories of desertions from some Indian frontier units, they expected thousands of Pathans from the North West Frontier to join it.[75] Acting on the intelligence about the formation of the 'Government in Exile', Colonel Roos-Keppel, the governor of the North West Frontier Province, called together 3,000 tribal leaders from across the frontier to his headquarters at Peshawar. In the presence of thousands of onlookers, he announced an increase of subsidies to all the clans.[76] Then, to the astonishment of the tribesmen, the Royal Flying Corps gave a demonstration of how accurately they could bomb and strafe targets from the air. This timely display of force had a salutary effect and the tribal districts were quiet for months. A militant Islamic faction called the 'Hindustani Fanatics' were also kept under close observation after the interception of two letters written on yellow silk that announced a revolution, and twenty of their leaders were arrested in 1916.[77] Another conspiracy inspired by the Germans, known as the Ghadr, had emerged within India which meant there was still a possibility that unrest could spread from Afghanistan.

Having effectively delayed any deal with Hentig, Habibullah concluded a vacuous Treaty of Friendship with the Germans and then promptly refused to ratify it, arguing that he could not do so until material support arrived to prepare for operations against Britain. The Germans at last realized they had been deceived. Hentig decided to strike out for Kashgar, hoping to raise Muslim guerrillas there to tie up British and Russian troops. However, after much wrangling, the British and Russian consuls managed to persuade the Chinese to arrest him and he was eventually repatriated. Niedermayer wanted to return to Persia to stir up anti-Russian feeling, but he was attacked by Turcoman bandits and was forced to return to Germany months later. The main body of the German mission under Lieutenant Wagner was also attacked by tribesmen as it withdrew past the East Persian Cordon and many of its personnel were taken prisoner. They were subsequently handed over to the Russians in the north. All this marked the collapse of the German attempt to stir revolution in the Middle East. In contrast, Sykes marched into Shiraz and Isfahan unopposed, and ensured that he demonstrated to the Persians that the British and the Russians were firm allies, acting together against the Ottomans.[78]

The German plan for war by revolution had failed, with every scheme between Libya and India thwarted or defeated. The Ottoman aspiration to carve out their own sphere of control in Persian Azerbaijan and Arabistan had been checked. In these set-backs, the Central Powers had exhibited an astonishing lack of strategic thinking. The ends had been confused with ways: raising revolution was all very well, but to what purpose? What were the local actors supposed to do after the revolution—were they expected to accept German or Ottoman imperial dominion instead of the British, or the Russians? The Germans had failed to coordinate their subversive campaigns and at times the Ottoman authorities were actively working against their partners. Nevertheless, the strategic factor in all these endeavours was the power and presence of the local actors themselves. Their alignment with the Great Powers was often instrumental and certainly not sentimental. Ideologies of jihad appealed to a minority, but it is striking that so few ever responded to its call. Indeed, it is this which revealed just how fundamentally flawed the faith in a universal response to such a call really was.

4

Eastern Strategy

The Dardanelles and Gallipoli, 1915

For many in the Anglophone world, Gallipoli is synonymous with defeat, futility, and incompetence. Along with the battles of the Somme (1916) and Passchendaele (1917), it is an operation that has come to symbolize the very worst aspects of the First World War. The execution of the Gallipoli campaign, and the milestones towards the humiliating Allied evacuation, are often held up as the epitome of disaster through bad planning, poor judgement, and hubristic overconfidence. One historian, in a recent narrative of the fighting, opens his work with the trenchant remark: 'It was a lunacy that could never have succeeded, an idiocy generated by muddled thinking.'[1] Another described the campaign as an 'agony', which carried a message of 'eternal reproach'.[2]

The litany of criticism is so unrelenting it might seem impossible to give the sort of reasonable analysis that would be offered to any other historical episode. Nevertheless, there are some grounds for doubting the damning orthodoxy. There is considerable evidence to show that the command and decision-making process was not suffering from 'lunacy' or 'idiocy'. Plans may have been ambitious, even over-optimistic, but this characterizes many campaigns and conflicts. What is striking is that British senior officers are thought to have sole responsibility for the high casualties and mission failures, part of a general approach towards the study of the First World War. This is in spite of the overwhelming evidence that specific changes in the character of war, not least the increased defensive power of new weapons technologies, had a far greater effect on operational outcomes than individual command decisions. Moreover, at the strategic level, the power of mass, logistics, and materiel was very influential, certainly far more so than single battles or short campaigns. It is noticeable that the Ottoman Empire lost the

First World War, despite its victory at Gallipoli, because it could produce no solution to its lack of industrial capacity or its infrastructural weaknesses.[3]

It is striking that strategic analysis of the campaign is downplayed in favour of the condemnation of the tactical and operational failures of the Allies or praise for the individual heroism of the participants. Yet, such a selective approach renders contemporaries' decisions devoid of context. Without acknowledgement of the pressures on the decision-makers and calculations of commanders, the phases of operations appear to be no more than purposeless and hopeless efforts. This is as true of the various tactical assaults on Krithia or Chunuk Bair as it of the strategic decision to make the initial landings at Gallipoli in the spring of 1915.

The impetus for the Allied invasion was not, as is so often asserted, due to the ambitions of British politicians and commanders: it was provoked by the weaknesses of Russia. Initial Ottoman success in the Caucasus prompted a Russian appeal for Allied assistance on 1 January 1915. From the outset, the Russian war machine had been exposed as inefficient and incompetent. It had lost the opening battles of 1914 against Germany. Despite its fearsome reputation as the 'steamroller', it had failed to make headway against the Habsburg armies of Austria-Hungary. It had failed to relieve its Slavic allies in Serbia. Now, in the Caucasus, on its own territory, and despite grandiose ideas of seizing Constantinople to realize its historical destiny, it was being defeated.[4] In December 1914, the Russian Chief of Staff, Yanushkevich, despaired that the tsar's armies might not be able to sustain resistance because of a lack of munitions: 'Many men have no boots and their legs are frostbitten. They have no sheepskin ... mass surrenders to the enemy have been developing, sometimes on the initiative of wartime officers [who ask] "Why should we die from hunger and exposure, without boots? The artillery keeps silent, and we are shot down like partridges."'[5] Despite increasing production in its heavy industries before the war, and indeed, during it, they struggled to convert this into resourcing the armies: only one-fifth of its requirement of shells was delivered to the artillery in the field.[6]

The British and the French had taken catastrophic losses in the first few months of the war in Western Europe and their own resources were stretched. Any operation to relieve Russia would, therefore, have to be primarily naval in nature, and, if landings were required, they would have to have a disproportionate strategic effect; that is, they would have to achieve significant outcomes at the lowest cost in terms of manpower and munitions commitments. Kitchener, the British Secretary of State for War, did not believe that

Figure 4.1 Lord H. H. Kitchener, Secretary of State for War, 1914–16, who envisaged a caliphate alongside British Arabian interests

resources could be spared in early 1915, but, if an operation was imperative, only a thrust at the Dardanelles would have any strategic value.

There were several advantages to operations through the Dardanelles, and they were articulated as such by the First Lord of the Admiralty, Winston Churchill; the Chancellor of the Exchequer, David Lloyd George; and also, of course, Kitchener.[7] The strategic reasoning was that an Allied victory could achieve many of the Western allies' 'ends' in the Eastern Mediterranean. It could reopen a merchant-shipping route to Russia, equipping this vast imperial army with the materiel of industrialized warfare. It could undermine the Central Powers by driving the Ottomans out of the war. Bulgaria would not fight on alone in the Balkans, and the Allies would be able to make a concerted and united effort against the vulnerable fronts of Austria-Hungary. In essence, the Dardanelles offered a chance to fulfil the common purpose against Germany by 'knocking the props from under her'.[8] Indeed, victory over the Ottomans held out the possibility of developing a larger alliance against the Central Powers, including bringing Greece, Romania, and possibly Bulgaria into the Entente. Operations against the Ottoman Empire would provide a much needed alternative to the developing stalemate on the Western Front.

From the imperial perspective, the British hoped that a naval blockade and a direct menace to the Turkish capital, leading to the Ottomans' surrender, would neutralize any sympathy for the Ottoman cause amongst Muslim subjects of the empire. They also hoped to assert British pre-eminence in Ottoman territories, including Syria, which France believed might provide a convenient colony. Crucially, the defeat of the Ottoman Empire would cut off German intrigue which was directed against British interests in the Middle East and India.[9] Given the need to find alternatives to the Western Front, it was not surprising that there were few voices urging caution or consideration of the consequences of a set-back.

There were several problems with the assumptions underpinning the Dardanelles enterprise. The British hoped that any operations would not only defeat the Ottoman Empire but would bring in neutral nations, such as Italy and Greece.[10] It would also, along with the securing of the Suez Canal and landings at Basra, reassure the littoral Arabs and Gulf Sheikhdoms who were sympathetic to the British cause. Nevertheless, in the winter of 1914–15 there was, as yet, no coordination of the strategy of the Entente powers. It was not until December 1915, a year later, that simultaneous offensives were agreed upon. There was no settlement of war aims either, which was crucial for the Dardanelles. The Greeks and the Italians wanted security and territorial compensation. According to the Constantinople Agreement, the Russians would acquire the Straits and Istanbul, but it was unlikely that the Ottomans would ever agree to give up their capital, and so the conflict would have to be fought to an unconditional surrender, rather than, as Churchill had hoped, to 'get into parley with them'.[11] The British wanted to ensure that, after the war, neither the French nor the Russians acquired possessions in the Middle East that would pose a threat to its own national interests, particularly the prosperity and security of the British Empire. Ironically, it was the Germans who offered the Russians a compromise settlement of the Dardanelles: Bethmann Hollweg, the chancellor, made a secret offer to the tsar in the summer of 1915, when German armies were driving back the Russian forces in Eastern Europe, for a joint Russo-German condominium over the Straits. The Russian Cabinet rejected the proposals.[12]

To demonstrate British intentions and to protest at the Ottoman hostilities against Russia, the Royal Navy bombarded Aqaba, sank an Ottoman vessel in the port of Smyrna, and, on 3 November 1914, shelled the Ottoman fortifications at the mouth of the Dardanelles. In the ten-minute bombardment against the tip of the Gallipoli peninsula, at a range of around 7 miles, two British battlecruisers and two French battleships severely damaged the fort at Sedd el-Bahr, killing over 100 Ottoman gunners. The action had not in fact been approved by the Cabinet, despite its strategic significance, and, at that point, the Foreign Secretary had not yet had the opportunity to issue a declaration of war.[13] The issue was not contested in government, however, because of the actions of the Ottomans in the previous few months.

The success of this limited operation raised British expectations, but the Ottomans, who had already realized the vulnerability of the fortifications, redoubled their efforts to prepare for further naval attack.[14] Until then, the focus of their defensive arrangements had been Bulair, on the northern coast of the Gallipoli peninsula, and the prospects of a Greek naval assault. The possibility of a major attack by the world's largest navy, rather than the limited threat posed by the Greeks, galvanized the Ottoman General Staff.[15] Reinforcements poured in, including artillery, and the new forces rehearsed their anti-invasion drills, anti-ship gunnery, command, and communications. Crucially, sea mines were sown in sectors across the Straits.

The Royal Navy's initial response to the call for ideas of how to wage war against the Ottoman Empire ranged from multinational operations on several axes to a limited British naval bombardment of Alexandretta. Churchill sought the specific comment of Vice Admiral Sackville Carden, commander of the East Mediterranean Fleet, who noted that mines were a significant problem but that minesweepers and battleships with 'mine buffers', might, with 'extended operations and a large number of ships', force a passage.[16] Naval gunfire was supposed to silence the shore batteries, allowing smaller vessels to get close inshore and clear the mines. A British 1908 plan concluded that Ottoman fortifications were not mutually supporting and 'not strong enough at the crucial point'.[17] In the late nineteenth century, the feasibility of an amphibious operation had been discussed and the former Commander-in-Chief of the British Army, Sir Garnet Wolseley, had been among those who had considered a *coup de main* at the Dardanelles.[18] In common with many strategic plans of the period, it was expected that forcing the Straits would compel the Ottomans to sue for peace. Churchill thought a bombardment of Istanbul would provoke a *coup d'état*.[19] Above all, opening the Dardanelles would restore the supply route to Russia and neutralize the pan-Islamic threat to British imperial prestige and security.[20] The only disappointment was that Greece did not join the Entente: although the Greek Prime Minister had offered naval and military support, perhaps even an invasion of Gallipoli, he was overruled by the king.[21]

The Russian request for diversionary action in January 1915, coming after a gruelling autumn campaign, the absence of any realistic Balkan offensives to relieve pressure on the tsarist armies, and a winter stalemate in Europe, prompted the British government to consider an alternative, predominantly naval strategy proposed by Churchill.[22] A Continental war had given the Royal Navy only rare opportunities to engage in the conflict. Its role was more strategic, confining the Central Powers to Europe and applying a slow stranglehold on the economies of Germany and Austria-Hungary. Churchill initially considered operations in the Baltic as the means to effect better cooperation with Russia.[23] Lloyd George favoured first the Balkans and then an amphibious landing in Syria. Maurice Hankey, the Secretary of the War Council, thought that Britain could not incite the Balkan nations to fight the Central Powers unless it participated in operations and the best way to do this was a combined operation, with Greece and Bulgaria, against Istanbul.[24] Seizing on a solution to the question of the future of the Dardanelles, he suggested the Straits might easily be distributed in any post-war settlement by offering the northern shores to their allies while the Ottomans retained the southern coast. To achieve this objective, he thought that three army corps would be needed.[25]

In order to give local commanders the freedom of action they required, the government ordered the Royal Navy to 'bombard and take the Gallipoli Peninsula, with Constantinople as its objective'.[26] Opinions were nevertheless divided. Kitchener hoped the Ottoman garrison on the peninsula would give way without even landing British forces, but there was no evidence to support this assumption.[27] Admiral of the Fleet, 'Jacky' Fisher, mindful perhaps of more recent assessments of mines, torpedoes, and shore batteries' effectiveness against ships, thought the naval operation 'hazardous'.[28] He later tried to dissuade Asquith by a tirade of objections and claimed that he had gone 'totus porcus' (the whole hog) against the Dardanelles scheme.[29] Richard Haldane, the former Secretary of State for War, believed a set-back at Gallipoli might actually provoke the Muslim unrest in the empire so many feared.[30]

Sir John French, commanding the British forces on the Western Front, had been asked by Kitchener for his opinion on the war strategy that was causing so much disagreement in London. His response was to point out how critical the situation in France and Flanders still was, but he summed up the dilemma perfectly: 'I consider the Eastern theatre of war is one in which a success on the part of the Allies would have the most decisive results. On the other hand a great German success in the West would be fatal.'[31]

The debate therefore continued. Lloyd George pondered whether two simultaneous operations in the Balkans and the Dardanelles would be the ideal.[32] When the Greeks refused to countenance a Balkans offensive, the War Council was thrown back on the Dardanelles option.[33] Fisher argued that if the plan was to go ahead it must be a joint operation, with both naval and land forces, but there was too little manpower available—the crucial means—for a joint operation to be an option. Only one regular division, the 29th, remained available for deployment, which made the debate about its use all the more intense. Balfour and others therefore dismissed Fisher's demands as 'altogether absurd'.[34] Troops would be available later, it was thought, and these would simply occupy Gallipoli and Istanbul as a garrison force.[35] It was suggested that Territorial Force troops would be suitable for such a task, and given their limited role, they would not require the heavy artillery assigned to divisions operating on the Western Front. This verdict stood in direct violation of a War Office appreciation drawn up in 1906. This had stated clearly that a joint operation was essential and warned that, if opposed, one could expect 'heavy losses'.[36] Asquith only read this report *after* the decision to launch the operation.

Yet, in the final analysis, despite all the criticism of the execution of the subsequent campaign, these decision-makers, like all strategists, faced a significant dilemma: how to evaluate risks and costs against the imperative to tackle a threat. The critics have the luxury of hindsight. It is conceivable that *operational* failure at Gallipoli has become conflated with the contemporary strategic assessment. The strategic options for the Allies included sustained land-based campaigns on multiple axes, but in early 1915, the resources were simply not available as priorities lay elsewhere. The Allies had not yet mobilized the manpower and materiel that would characterize the operations of 1917–18. Reducing the Ottoman economy through blockade, another option, would take months, if not years, and the Russian war effort might, in the intervening time, be crippled. Raising local Muslim forces against Ottoman rule, a third option, presupposed Britain could command such loyalty against the lingering authority of the caliph, which was far from certain. A threat at Gallipoli would have 'strategic effect'. Hew Strachan notes that 'the Germans thought the Gallipoli Campaign the most important in 1915'.[37] Perhaps, then, the strategic failure of 1915 was not that the campaign went ahead, but that the Allies didn't realize the sheer importance of it, and, consequently, that it was never properly resourced.

Naval Operations

The Straits presented the Allies with a significant operational problem. With strong currents, abundantly mined and narrow waters overlooked by fortified gun batteries, and no landing forces yet prepared or assembled, the obstacles were considerable. Nevertheless, the British and French had concentrated a flotilla consisting of one Dreadnought-class battleship, sixteen pre-Dreadnought battleships, one battlecruiser, twenty destroyers, and thirty-five minesweepers. The Ottoman defenders were drawn from the Fifth Army, under the energetic direction of General Liman von Sanders, which, at 84,000 men, was more numerous than the initial Allied landing force. The Fifth Army was overwhelmingly Turkish in its ethnic composition, giving it a homogeneity exceptional to the Ottoman forces. It consisted of a significant number of men seasoned by the Balkan Wars, practised in the small-unit tactics they would need to meet any invasion. They were well-rehearsed, spending weeks preparing their trenches, their fighting drills, and their communications. The army's five infantry divisions, with a sixth in reserve co-located with a brigade of cavalry, were distributed to cover the most vulnerable points: two divisions on the southern coast of the Straits, the 9th Division along the western coast of Gallipoli, the 19th Division concentrated at Chanak, and the 7th Division guarding Bulair, the narrow 'neck' of the peninsula.[38]

On 19 February 1915, two British battleships and two destroyers shelled the forts and dummy positions on the tip of the Gallipoli peninsula. There were subsequent bombardments, but, despite evident damage, Ottoman guns in the narrowest section of the Straits remained in action. Howitzers and mobile field artillery proved particularly hard to locate.[39] Silencing the guns was crucial to afford protection to the minesweepers. To secure the batteries, and augment the effect of naval gunfire, Kitchener and the War Council began to assemble a landing force at Lemnos, the Greek Aegean Island off the Turkish coast, consisting of the Royal Naval Division and the newly arrived ANZACs. Initially the Royal Navy enjoyed some success against the outer forts which encouraged the planners to consider extending the naval operation. One officer aboard HMS *Triumph* was 'surprised at the poor shooting they [the Ottomans] made... the next day we closed the range and a close inspection showed the defences had been abandoned'.[40] Parties of marines landed at Sedd el-Bahr and Kum Kale and met little resistance. They put out of action several guns. Yet the guns of the inner forts were better protected and field-gun batteries were moved between positions, making targeting more difficult. Admiral Sir Sackville Carden, the naval commander of Britain's East Mediterranean Force, was methodical in his approach. He insisted on taking his time, and aimed to protect his ships, especially the *Queen Elizabeth*, his latest Dreadnought, from concealed batteries. Night-time minesweeping was made impossible by Turkish searchlights while air reconnaissance for the naval guns was made hazardous by small-arms fire.[41] Nevertheless, this was interpreted as a 'lack of vigour' in London, and pressure was building for a more comprehensive, all-out attack.

The drive was to have a daylight assault that would 'rush' the Narrows. Commander Worsely Gibson on HMS *Albion* wrote: 'Everyone [believed] it would be madness to try and rush them . . . Personally, I feel sure that it is pressure from our cursed politicians which is making him [Carden] consider such a thing—A large army of 60 or 70 thousand is collecting for purposes of cooperation, the only way to tackle this job, and [so] why not wait for them.'[42]

Carden, compelled to act when faced with a problem beyond the capability of the force at his disposal, fell sick. The second-in-command, Vice-Admiral John de Robeck, who was dismissive of Churchill's pressure to attack, nevertheless proceeded with the plan to push through the Narrows.[43] There were to be three waves in the assault. Six modern British battleships would bombard the forts while four older French ships and six British ships would follow up, anchor close inshore and pulverize the Turkish guns at close quarters. Once the guns had been silenced, minesweepers would be able to complete their work and the entire fleet would sail on into the Sea of Marmora to regroup.

As the action began, the French commander of the battleship *Bouvet*, who believed he was having some success in his close-quarter bombardment, refused to push on up the Straits and when finally on the move, hit a floating mine and sank in under two minutes, losing over 600 crewmen. HMS *Irresistible* also hit a floating mine, drifted and was subjected to intense fire from the shore. HMS *Ocean*, in attempting to draw fire from the stricken ship, collided with another mine. Three more vessels were damaged critically by Ottoman guns, many of which simply could not be located from the water. The minesweepers failed to make headway when the shore batteries were intact.[44] Admiral de Robeck called off the operation.

There has been speculation since that, had the attack been resumed, there might have been greater success. This was certainly Churchill's preference.[45] Damage inflicted on Ottoman shore positions was presented as evidence of 'what might have been'. The fact that the shore batteries had run low on ammunition, and the poignant set-backs of the subsequent land campaign, seemed to reinforce the idea that one more determined effort might have provided a breakthrough. It is striking how much emphasis was placed on neutralizing forts when the most significant threat to the shipping was from mines.

On 22 March on HMS *Queen Elizabeth* de Robeck could see for himself that only a combined sea–land operation could have any chance of pushing through to Istanbul. Furthermore, at the Admiralty, the 'War Group' defied Churchill and refused to agree to continuing naval operations.[46] There seemed to be some evidence of strategic effect in that the Ottoman government was preparing to decamp from the capital, having already removed its treasury to a safer point in Anatolia.[47] They only stopped when the news of the 'victory of 18 March' was received in Istanbul. Nevertheless, the Ottoman gunners and their commanders all expected the Allies to renew their naval offensive.[48]

General Ian Hamilton, veteran of the South African War, was appointed the new commander of the amphibious Mediterranean Expeditionary Force (MEF). He had arrived on 17 March, in time to observe the naval attack, and it was evident that only the ability to control the Narrows from the water, combined with domination of the Kilid Bahr plateau on the Gallipoli peninsula itself, could secure the Straits.[49] A second naval assault, without a significant and sustained operation, would clearly have cost a number of ships, and even if the Narrows had been passed by some vessels, they would have been harassed by fresh Ottoman artillery and reinforcements from the north and south. Hamilton was nevertheless surprised that he was not tasked to make an assault against Bulair, the slim neck of the peninsula that lay much closer to Istanbul, and that planning was so short term. In London, in a meeting with Kitchener, Sir Archibald Murray, then Chief of the Imperial General Staff, and General Callwell, the Director of Military Operations, the most recent appreciation was dated 1912 and was based on the Greek plan devised during the Balkan Wars.[50] Callwell noted that the Greeks assessed that 150,000 troops would be needed to take and hold Gallipoli. The British still had only half that number in 1915.

Fisher and Hankey both demanded that further study be conducted before launching an amphibious attack, but the War Council never met to discuss the matter: events in the Eastern Mediterranean were running ahead of the decision-makers.[51] Kitchener was already concentrating on the Western Front and demanded the allocation of two divisions there. Hamilton was too loyal to his former commander from his service in South Africa to argue for more men for Gallipoli. He understood the constraints that

Kitchener faced and knew that manpower was in short supply.[52] The Russians, by contrast, had plenty of men, but Sir Edward Grey refused a Russian offer of support, which would have involved landing at the Bulgarian port of Burgas prior to an advance on Istanbul from the north.[53] Grey's reasoning was that the Bulgarians might be brought into the war on the side of the Entente, and a Russian landing would almost certainly push them into the arms of the Central Powers. The decision was fateful and certainly provokes fascinating counter-factual speculation about the outcome of the Gallipoli campaign if there had been a dual thrust against the Ottoman capital. A Russian corps remained readied for operations but in May 1915, with an offensive out of Galicia by the Austro-Hungarian army, it was diverted to Eastern Europe. The Foreign Office hopes that other neutrals would join the Entente on account of the 'Mediterranean strategy' also evaporated. Italy did not enter the war as expected in May 1915 and the Bulgarians too refused to be drawn in.

The amphibious operation would require far more men than the contingents of Royal Marines could provide. Only one regular British division, the 29th, was as yet uncommitted to the war, a force grouped together from scattered imperial garrisons. It had been concentrated in Egypt, as had the fresh, if untrained, volunteers from Australia and New Zealand. The latter had been bound for Europe, but this contingent, the Australian 1st Division and the amalgamated New Zealand and Australian Division, collectively known as the ANZAC Corps, was re-tasked for Gallipoli. The Royal Naval Division was a third hastily composed force of naval personnel, but they too lacked any experience of tactical land operations, higher-formation command, or staff work, and they possessed no artillery or land-based logistics. The fourth and final landing force was the French 1st Division of the Corps Expéditionnaire d'Orient, but this had no experience of multinational cooperation. The entire amphibious force numbered 75,000 men, fewer than the Ottomans, and it faced the prospect of landing on a defended shoreline, without prior rehearsal, topographical intelligence, and without the element of surprise.[54]

The Ottoman 19th Division held high ground overlooking all the landing sites, was dug in and well-prepared. The period between the naval attack on 18 March and the beach assault of 25 April was crucial for the final adjustments to their defensive plans. There was only one significant dilemma: Liman von Sanders, in overall command, sought to reinforce the beaches only when he could be certain of the location of the main Allied attack.

He therefore retained an operational reserve at the centre of the peninsula, while concentrating on the most threatened locations at Cape Helles, Bulair, and Besika Bay.[55] In contrast, Colonel Mustapha Kemal, who served in the 19th Division, thought the British would concentrate their attacks only at Helles and at Gaba Tepe, and, as a result, reserves should be placed closer to these points of vulnerability.

Hamilton was aware of the obstacles before him, but there was little time for the preparations that characterized the D-Day operations some twenty years later. To ensure a broad front, reduce congestion, and create multiple axes of attack, as well as deceiving the Ottomans as to the direction of the assault, Hamilton selected six simultaneous landings between the headland Arnı Burnu (sheltering what was subsequently nicknamed Anzac Cove) and Cape Helles. The southern beaches could be covered by naval gunfire and the Ottoman positions there formed a salient that could be 'pinched out'. To get as many men ashore as fast as possible, he agreed with the suggestion made by Commander E. Unwin to convert the collier *River Clyde* into a landing craft that would be run ashore, disgorging troops from its sides.[56]

Yet the disadvantage of the assault locations was that the hills beyond the beaches, dissected by deep gullies, perfect for small numbers of defenders to hold, would make it far more difficult to break out. The beaches designated for the ANZACs were similarly overlooked by steep and forbidding bluffs. Unless they could secure these high features swiftly, they too risked being hemmed in on the coast. Hamilton's solution was for the ANZACs to make a landing at night, try to secure the high ground at Maltepe as quickly as possible, and then, in the days that followed, make a more deliberate advance across the Peninsula. Subsequently, the entire landing force would be able to seize the shore batteries lining the Dardanelles from the rear. As in all amphibious operations, the first twenty-four hours of progress were vital, but even if a beachhead could be seized, everything depended on the ability to reinforce and supply the troops ashore, to build up reserves rapidly, and maintain the momentum of a break-out.

The Landings

On 25 April 1915, from 05.00 hours, the leading files of the invasion forces rowed ashore under cover of a naval bombardment and dashed onto the beaches under intense fire. At Cape Helles, the British and Irish troops leading the attack took heavy casualties as they tried to get through the surf or navigate the barbed wire. Of the first 200 Dublin Fusiliers soldiers who tried to get ashore at V Beach, only twenty-one survived.[57] The *River Clyde* was run aground into the beach but, as soon as the Munsters and Essex troops emerged from the improvised sally-ports in its side, they were cut down by fire from the bluffs above. When General H. E. Napier arrived with the main body to renew the beach assault at 08.30 hours, he was killed along with all his staff. Approximately forty men from the first wave survived. The soldiers of the Lancashire Fusiliers, who famously won 'six VCs before breakfast', and who faced the same murderous conditions at W Beach, were later given the opportunity to nominate who would receive the gallantry awards in their regiment. Of the nominees, three men were selected who had shown exceptional courage in breaking through the wire, much of it hidden beneath the water, showing just how problematic the initial landings had been.[58] Despite a significant naval bombardment, the company of Ottoman troops had maintained their defence there and only evacuated once their position became untenable. They had inflicted losses of 533 on the Lancashires, out of an original strength of 950.

By contrast, the landings at Y Beach had been a success. The Royal Marines and Scottish Borderers, having secured the shoreline, moved inland only tentatively, even making a reconnaissance as far as Krithia, but they waited for further orders which took hours to arrive.[59] The chief problem they faced was that their maps had not revealed the presence of the massive Gully Ravine, and, from its opposite slopes, the Ottomans started to pour fire into the rear of the British troops. There were 700 casualties, and the entire attack in this sector stalled.[60]

Despite setting off at 04.25 hours, some of the Australian and New Zealand forces, due to strong currents and misinterpretation of orders, landed in batches at the wrong locations which delayed their advance. Many units clustered in the north of the beachhead, adding to the confusion. Nevertheless, after intense fighting, they struggled up through the gullies above the beach, and, from 06.00 began to secure the higher ground.[61] Kemal, realizing the seriousness of the situation, pushed his reserves into the gaps with great energy, rallying his troops in such an inspirational way that he has become immortalized as the most decisive Ottoman leader that day.[62] The Ottoman soldiers' achievement in this phase of opposing the landings is also rightly praised. It epitomized their dogged courage throughout the campaign which has become so admired in Western writing both at the time and subsequently. It has also provided an explanation for the subsequent failures of the ANZACs, and has overshadowed the fact that large numbers of shocked Australian soldiers demanded to be re-embarked on the ships. Inexperienced, stunned by the effectiveness of the Ottoman fire, and exhausted by the fighting, it is clear that, for some, morale had collapsed.[63] The Royal Navy refused to evacuate them, arguing that the risks and complications were too great, not least because it would take two days to get the wounded off the beaches. Hamilton recommended that the ANZACs dig in, in order to stabilize the situation. Fresh advances further south by the British, he promised, would 'divert pressure' and he urged his subordinates to make 'a personal appeal to your men... to make a supreme effort to hold their ground'.[64]

Meanwhile a French attack at Kum Kale on the Anatolian coast, which had not got underway until 10.00 hours, had also been checked. Gunfire from across the Straits had added to the casualty toll on this force. At Liman von Sanders' headquarters, the arrival of reinforcements which had stopped several Allied attacks was a cause of some satisfaction, but it had been a near-run thing.

Within days, Allied troops were exhausted, short of water, and depleted by significant casualties. On 28 April, a major attempt to break out from Cape Helles, the first large-scale assault on Krithia, which overlooked much of the surrounding landscape, was checked. The Ottomans themselves tried a massive night-time offensive against Cape Helles on 1–2 May but it was stopped dead and the *Mehmetçik* (Ottoman soldiers) suffered 6,000 casualties. They tried again on 3–4 May taking losses of a similar magnitude with no gains to show for it. A second British attack on 6 May against the village of Krithia failed. The third attempt on 4 June fared no better. There was no break-out in this crucial first phase.

The Ottomans made another bid to drive the ANZACs into the sea on 18 May. Assembling 50,000 troops, they committed wave after wave to the assault, but the Allies knew they were coming and they cut them down in their thousands. After a seven-hour engagement through the night, over 10,000 Ottoman soldiers were killed or wounded.[65]

There were therefore two strategic options for the British: the first was to overwhelm the defences with 'mass'. The Allies would have to use greater numbers and heavier fire from their confined beachheads if they were to secure the plateau. The only other option was to open new fronts with fresh landings elsewhere on the peninsula, in order to envelop the Ottoman defences.[66] Neither of these options proved successful. By July, while the Allies increased the number of divisions in the theatre of operations to twelve, the Turks had amassed fifteen.[67] The idea of withdrawal was dismissed, although Kitchener had threatened to do so if the Royal Navy did not support the land operations adequately. Fisher was convinced that sending more vessels to the Dardanelles was a waste of resources and resigned on the issue.[68]

Despite the enduring tendency to criticize the plans and the commanders, the landings had above all revealed the fundamental character of the First World War and the reason why success while on the offensive was so elusive. The rate of fire, accuracy, and range of new weaponry meant that it was far more difficult to cross open ground. The machine gun, magazine-fed breach-loading rifle, and field artillery could lay down such a weight of fire, that survival, unless dug-in, was precarious. A Maxim machine gun and a company of riflemen, firing steadily for a quarter of an hour—the minimum time taken to disembark and cross a beach or traverse 'No Man's Land'—could together fire over 16,000 rounds. Modern field obstacles, especially light-weight barbed wire, could channel and impede troops, delaying them in designated zones of fire. Field telephones enabled a defender to alert reserves to the direction of any attack, so even the loss of forward positions could be sealed off, and, if necessary, counter-attacked before fresh waves of attackers could secure any location. To make matters worse, in 1915 no means had yet been developed for crossing ground other than infantry and cavalry. In the broken terrain of Gallipoli, toiling foot soldiers could rarely advance very far or at speed, further adding to the advantages of the defenders. Communications were dependent on quite vulnerable and slow systems, and ship-to-shore messaging was always difficult. There were frequent episodes of indecision because orders took so long to formulate and arrive. Accusing commanders of idiocy, and criticizing their operational plans, is to ignore the fundamental character of war in this period. Had the invasion of Gallipoli occurred either twenty years before or twenty years later, its conduct would have been quite different. The outcome of this campaign can only really be understood in the context of its time.

Stalemate

The situation by early May was one of strategic stalemate: the Allies could sustain themselves on the shore and Ottoman forces, despite determined efforts, could not drive them out. The Ottomans had contained the landings, but this did not yet constitute a victory. Having established their lodgement on the coast, the Allies attempted to build up their resources for further break-outs, the aim being to envelop the Khilid Bair plateau from the beaches in the north and south. The 52nd Territorial Army Division arrived in May but the Ottomans also reinforced their defences. In June, the Ottoman 2nd Division deployed against the beachhead trenches, so the stalemate was reinforced.

The Allies were at a particular disadvantage in having to convey all their logistical support from Egypt via the small port of Mudros on the isle of Lemnos. However, the nearest suitable port was at Alexandria, some 650 miles distant. All the stores, ammunition, guns, and reinforcements had to be brought up, painstakingly disembarked on beaches or improvised piers and jetties which were subjected to constant, if desultory, Ottoman shelling. The lack of fresh water was a significant and at times acute problem. Wounded personnel also had to be conveyed along the long and hazardous lines of communication, and they suffered from the heat, flies, and inevitable delays in their treatment. The losses of the first few weeks overwhelmed the arrangements that had been prepared. Hamilton was especially frustrated by the lack of lighters to serve the larger transport ships and bring the wounded out and supplies ashore. He wrote in July: 'Ships arrive carrying things urgently required, and then, before they can be unloaded, sail away again.' In one case, ships containing engineering equipment arrived and were forced to depart no less than five times.[69]

In comparison with the Western Front, Gallipoli was not a strategic priority for the Allies. Joffre, the Commander of the French Army, was desperate for more men to mount offensives in France. Britain too could ill-afford to release men for the Dardanelles. Yet it was in munitions that the situation became most acute. The scandalous shell shortage in Britain, which made such high-profile news in 1915 in the European theatre, affected the troops on Gallipoli just as badly. Field guns found themselves with only three rounds to fire each day, and, on some occasions, with only one. There were too few 60-pdr heavy guns, barely a handful on the whole peninsula, and a shortage of grenades considered essential for trench fighting. Troops took to improvising explosive devices from jam tins, attached periscopes to sniper rifles and dreamt up their own deception plans.

The second attack on Krithia on 8 May suffered from this evident lack of fire support. Despite the heroic efforts of each of the formations involved, infantry assaulting uphill into well-prepared positions could only prevail with the heaviest of casualties. The 2nd Australian Brigade, led by Brigadier General William McKay, went in with 2,900 men and lost 1,056 in their efforts to take 1,000 lateral yards of Ottoman defences. That evening, Hamilton informed Kitchener that: 'The result of the operation has been a failure . . . the fortifications and their machine guns were . . . too strongly held to be rushed . . . Our troops have done all that flesh and blood can do against semi-permanent works and they are not able to carry them. More and more munitions will be needed to do so.' Shortages in Britain meant that only 25,000 shells could be sent, a quarter of the amount that had been expended in a single action at Festubert in France.

To make matters worse, a small German U-boat squadron sent to the Dardanelles torpedoed and sank two British battleships, HMS *Triumph* and HMS *Majestic*.[70] The submarine attacks transformed the operational situation, since, as the capital ships were withdrawn, it deprived the troops ashore of crucial naval fire support. Subsequently, a British transport ship was sunk, causing further consternation about the precarious supply line.

Much of the fighting across the beachheads through the summer was inconclusive, if bloody. Hamilton believed that Russian intervention against the Ottoman Empire might draw their attention away sufficiently to allow him to seize the heights at Achi Baba and secure the coast. His troops were making some limited progress, trenches and dugouts made the Allies' fortifications stronger, and raiding was bringing in valuable intelligence. At Gully Ravine, at Cape Helles, continuous fighting between 28 June and 5 July inched the Allied line deeper into Ottoman territory. The Ottoman standing procedure of counter-attacking immediately after each Allied attack cost them significant losses. Estimates for the Battle of Gully Ravine vary between 13,000 and 16,000 casualties. On the ANZACs front, relatively small topographical features such as Quinn's Post, Steele's Post, and Courtney's Post became the scene of intense struggles. Sniper fire in the congested lines was feared by both sides for its lethal effectiveness, and those sharpshooters who were captured were sometimes executed. Trenches and outposts in certain places were separated by just a few yards of ground, close enough to hear the other side.

Troops began to suffer from the stultifying conditions as the summer wore on, and there were more casualties from the environment than combat: 'The trenches were like ovens; the grass had long since withered and vanished, and the hot wind stirred up the dust . . . loathsome green flies

[were] feasting on the corpses in No Man's Land, swarming hideously in the latrines, filling every trench and dug-out and covering the food...'[71] There was an epidemic of dysentery and enteric fever. British casualties from sicknesses are estimated to have been 145,000; more than two-thirds of the casualties of the campaign. The only relief in such conditions was the opportunity in rare armistices to bury the dead, or, if close to the sea, to have the opportunity to swim and cool off, although safety from shelling was never guaranteed.

The War Council of the government in London, retitled as the Dardanelles Committee, argued about the way forward. Hamilton had requested four divisions 'to finish the task'.[72] Kitchener believed the Mediterranean Expeditionary Force should persevere without reinforcements, given the priorities elsewhere. The verdict seemed to be that Hamilton should 'get on' in order to 'get out', and Kitchener threatened to resign if the Dardanelles Committee refused to support a continuation of the operations.[73] The committee members fell into line, concerned that withdrawal implied a loss of prestige that would be too great and terminate all hopes of persuading the neutral powers to join the Entente. Moreover, there was reassurance from Hamilton that he was confident that he could secure the Khilid Bair plateau. There were other imperatives too. The first was scope. U-boat activity made it too risky to consider operations as far as Bulair and so any new operations had to be in or close to the existing beachheads.

A second imperative was the fate of Russia and Eastern Europe. News of Russian defeats in Poland lent a sense of urgency to the Gallipoli campaign as ways had to be found to divert the pressure of the Central Powers by making attacks on other fronts. On 4 August Warsaw fell to the Germans and it was possible that, in the late summer of 1915, Russia and perhaps France might seek a separate peace.[74] The British government needed to ensure it had achieved sufficient gains to take to the negotiating table. In September, Bulgaria joined the Central Powers, which meant that it was only a matter of time before German war materiel flooded into the Ottoman Empire, and perhaps German reinforcements. Time was running out.

Hamilton resolved to make a fresh landing with new reinforcements at Suvla, 5 miles to the north of Anzac Cove, as part of a concerted assault on the Sari Bair ridge. The War Office in London encouraged Hamilton's plan to seize the summit at Chunuk Bair, although to take such a position would require the forming of a vulnerable salient, and risk taking fire from the flanks, if they were strongly held.[75] The new offensive at Suvla was to be carried out by three 'New Army' Divisions (10th, 11th, and 13th), made up of enthusiastic if barely trained volunteers, under the command of Lieutenant-General Sir Frederick Stopford, who, like Hamilton, was a veteran of the South African War. While the landings were made to outflank the Ottoman defences to the north, the ANZAC Corps and the British 13th Division were to break out from Anzac Cove and envelop the Sari Bair ridge. However, the Ottoman Fifth Army had also been reinforced and was sixteen divisions strong.[76] Once again, the lack of experience of the Allied troops was a serious handicap. The 10th and 11th Divisions had never seen action before and were pitched straight into the battle from training. Stopford was blamed for his dilatory performance immediately after the landings, but he had little faith that his untried troops could move other than in a methodical manner.[77] Moreover, there is some evidence to suggest that Hamilton had regarded the Suvla landings as a supplementary arm of the more significant assault on Sari Bair by the ANZACs and existing British units, and that he only insisted the Suvla landings were the main effort once the Sari Bair attack had miscarried. That said, Stopford was less than energetic in his pursuit of his objectives and he was fortunate in being able to argue, after the campaign, that his instructions were vague. Despite the controversy, the Suvla operations were an attempt to reassert a strategic solution to the operational stalemate.

On 6 August, the offensive began with attacks at Cape Helles and Anzac Cove prior to the landings at Suvla Bay. At Helles, three battalions belonging to the British 29th and 42nd Divisions, intending to divert the Ottomans to the southern sectors, gradually required the support of their brigades and the fighting escalated to involve the two divisions. The fighting intensified and also drew in four Ottoman divisions. Counter-attacks over three days and nights prevented any substantial Allied gains until the assaults subsided on 13 August with heavy losses.[78] The second axis of Hamilton's offensive was made by the Australian 1st Infantry Brigade at Lone Pine ridge. The detail of the planning process had impressed some Australian officers.[79] They succeeded in carrying the Ottoman trenches, and, thanks to the configuration of the ground, they defeated every counter-attack. The Australians inflicted over 7,500 casualties for a loss of 1,700 of their own. Nevertheless, their advance was also contained and Ottoman reinforcements were free to switch their effort towards Suvla Bay.

The most poignant episode of the entire campaign was the fate of the Wellington Battalion of the New Zealand Brigade, which broke through to the summit of Chunuk Bair ridge on 8 August. Exposed on every side, the defenders clung to its slopes while neighbouring units tried in vain to secure their flanks. Kemal led the counter-attack with three divisions. It took two days of close-quarter battle, but, by 10 August, Kemal was able to recover the entire line. Some 711 of the 760 men of the Wellington Battalion were casualties. The ANZAC Corps lost a third of the entire force in four days. The proportion of British losses was similar: the British 13th Division lost 5,500 men.

At Suvla Bay on the night of 6–7 August 1915, the 10th and 11th British Divisions had made their way ashore. They outnumbered the three Ottoman battalions who contested the assault, but General Stopford believed he was only supporting the main effort elsewhere. His troops, unfamiliar with the terrain or even their precise objectives, did not execute the manoeuvres Hamilton later claimed was his intent and which Stopford, with rather more success, subsequently maintained he was unaware of. The two divisions suffered losses of 1,700 on the first day, and matters deteriorated when Ottoman forces, now alerted to the strength and dispositions of the British, launched their counter-attacks. Another thrust was therefore hemmed in on the coast, with the high ground in Ottoman possession.[80] Landing fresh forces on 9–10 August, Stopford pushed the 53rd and 54th Divisions into action, but these formations could not fight their way up onto the high features in the teeth of stiffening resistance. On 15 August, Stopford, much-criticized for his failure to act more energetically or to use his initiative, was dismissed. His successor, Major General Beauvoir de Lisle, made an attempt to cut through to the high ground beyond the beaches a week later, in order to complete the pincer movement originally intended. The attempted breakthrough failed.

Evacuation

There was no immediate withdrawal from Gallipoli, despite the failure to break out that August. Various options remained open, but evacuation was considered to be too damaging to Britain's imperial prestige. If shown to be defeated by the Ottoman Empire, how, the imperial governors pondered, might such news be greeted in the various colonies and dominions? The functioning of the British Empire had always been dependent on a small number of British administrators and troops supported by vast numbers of 'sub-imperialists', locals co-opted, paid, and otherwise loyal to Britain's rule.[81] If British military prowess was damaged, the imperial garrisons, already stripped out for the duration of the Great War, might be overwhelmed by agitation and unrest. The fact that the withdrawal from Gallipoli did not spark a general collapse of British imperial rule indicates either that their fears were exaggerated or, perhaps, that concealing this strategic vulnerability was the most profound success of the entire Dardanelles Campaign.

The British were certainly concerned. The viceroy of India, Sir Charles Hardinge, feared that 'defeat, or the necessity of cutting our losses in the Dardanelles, would be absolutely fatal in this country'. He concluded that a set-back at the hands of a Muslim power would mean that 'Pan-Islamism would become a very serious danger.'[82] In India, there was rigorous censorship, and, amid fears of new conspiracies, an increase in surveillance. At least two genuine anti-British plots were uncovered, and two German attempts to reach India, one involving the smuggling of arms, were detected and neutralized.[83] Nevertheless, the Foreign Secretary, Sir Edward Grey, informed the Cabinet that: 'At present we are practically bankrupt of prestige in the East, and our position could hardly be worse.'[84] Efforts were made to drive forward in Mesopotamia in order to capture Baghdad and thus strike a blow at Ottoman prestige.[85] The small force available reached Ctesiphon before being besieged at Kut al Amara. Attempts to relieve that beleaguered garrison cost the lives of 23,000 men, but the relief force faced the same problems that beset the assaulting troops in Gallipoli and on the Western Front. The weight and lethality of fire was too great for men or horses to prevail without taking severe losses.

On the Gallipoli peninsula, desultory fighting continued from August into the winter. Bad weather worsened the plight of the troops. A three-day rainstorm in late November flooded trenches, turning gullies into torrents, taking the living and the dead with them down into the sea. By December, snow, freezing winds and the cold led to hypothermia and frostbite.

The most important strategic issue that had arisen, however, was Bulgaria's decision to join the Central Powers in October. Serbia and Greece requested that they be sent reinforcements, and that meant drawing down formations in Gallipoli with some urgency. Hamilton wanted more men to stabilize his lines, now depleted by disease and casualties, before resuming his offensive, but he was forced to release his own men to shore up the less valuable deployment at Salonika. Worse, Bulgaria's entry into the war made the rail link between Berlin and Istanbul a realistic possibility, and that would mean that artillery, munitions and men could flood into the Middle East, and overwhelm the beachheads at Gallipoli.

Evacuation had been considered even before the Suvla landings, but the failure to make progress in the autumn reinforced the idea. In October 1915 Kitchener asked Hamilton to consider what the cost of withdrawal might be. Initially, both hoped that the perimeter might be held through the winter and that fresh forces could acquire vital ground before the Ottomans could be reinforced, but Britain needed the manpower elsewhere, not least for the operations planned against Germany on the Western Front in the summer of 1916.

When Hamilton was dismissed soon after, General Sir Charles Munro, his replacement, was confronted with the same question. On arrival, Munro carried out a thorough three-day survey of the situation, visiting the key sites and consulting the various commanders at each point. On 31 October, he passed Kitchener a memorandum advising evacuation, but warned that the casualties of such an operation might total one-third of the entire expeditionary force.[86] He wrote:

> The position occupied by our troops presented a military situation unique in history. The mere fringe of the coast line had been secured. The beaches and piers upon which they depended for all requirements in personnel and materiel were exposed to registered and observed artillery fire. Our entrenchments were dominated almost throughout by the Turks ... The position was without depth, the communications were insecure and dependent on the weather.

Despite the potential losses, Munro believed that evacuation was preferable because a forward movement was impossible and the logistical chain could not support an advance. Kitchener left London to come and form his own verdict.[87] At first, he considered another naval operation to open the Straits, but Munro disabused him of that, and once Kitchener had toured the beachhead front line for himself, he too concluded that a renewed offensive would not succeed.[88]

At a November 1915 conference at Mudros for the commanders-in-chief in Egypt, Gallipoli, and the new deployment in Salonika, the conclusion was that operations from Egypt and in Mesopotamia would have to be stepped up. Kitchener thought that only the forces at Suvla Bay and Anzac Cove needed to be pulled out, while Cape Helles might be held, but the War Committee in London would consider only a complete withdrawal. At the Joint Staff Conference in France on 8 December 1915, the decision was taken to evacuate Gallipoli in order to strengthen the forces at Salonika. Suvla Bay and Anzac Cove were thus evacuated successfully on the night of 19–20 December 1915 and the Allies left Cape Helles on 8 January 1916. These evacuations are often praised as model efforts in deception and organization, as there were none of the losses anticipated by Munro. However, Hew Strachan notes that it was hardly in the interests of the Ottomans to contest the Allied withdrawal and incur unnecessary losses which would not change the outcome of the campaign.[89]

Strategically, the Allies had failed to align their 'ends, ways, and means', and their operational set-backs stemmed from their inability to coordinate naval and land operations. That said, the British naval attacks on Ottoman shipping in the region were so comprehensive that by 1918 overland routes were the only reliable ones left. More importantly, however, the tactical disadvantages the Allies suffered prevented operational plans from being realized. The power of defensive technologies overmatched the ability of infantry to cross open ground. Broken terrain added to the advantages of defence. The determination of the Ottoman defenders must also be taken into account, although no army on the peninsula monopolized courage and resolution.

Churchill concluded that the Gallipoli landings had failed because they were never fully resourced. It is true that the Western Front was always the priority and that Gallipoli became a sideshow.[90] Typically, like every imperial operation, commanders had been forced to improvise and find their own solutions for operations outside of Europe. Moreover the parlous state of artillery ammunition and absence of heavy guns was a major problem, although naval gunnery offset this to some extent.[91] Churchill was also correct in his estimation that withdrawal from Gallipoli reinvigorated Ottoman resistance. He argued that, as a result, the subsequent campaigns in Salonika, Palestine, and Mesopotamia were far more difficult for the Allies. The conclusion of the Gallipoli campaign certainly enabled the Ottoman Army to redeploy reserves to other theatres. Yet Churchill was wrong in his belief that another naval attack might have forced the Narrows, after 18 March, if sufficient resolve had been shown. He had not, unlike Kitchener, been able to visit the key sites, and it is noticeable that all the senior officers who did so reached the same conclusion.

The consequences of the Gallipoli campaign were felt politically. Such was the level of criticism from the opposition that Asquith was compelled to form a coalition government. Churchill lost his post and shortly after joined the army on the Western Front. Fisher had already resigned. Lloyd George, having argued for more munitions for the campaign, got a new ministry established. Kitchener was thought far too prestigious to be forced out, but his reputation was badly damaged amongst the political elite. He considered a new appointment as a centralizing commander-in-chief of all the armed forces, but there was no precedent or agreement for such a move.[92] Such had been the importance of the campaign, that the War Council had been restyled as the Dardanelles Committee, and this title continued for some time after.

Turkish national confidence, rather than a profoundly Ottoman imperial one, was boosted by the campaign, although there were mixed reactions at the time.[93] The historian Edward Erickson remarked that victory had been achieved because 'the Turks fielded a very well-trained, well-led and highly-motivated army'.[94] The infrastructure of Gallipoli gave them a strategic central position on the peninsula from which to deploy their reserves and thus meet each threat as it emerged. Nevertheless, it was a campaign victory that came at an enormous cost. It is estimated that there were 230,000 Allied casualties but possibly 300,000 Ottoman losses.[95] Some 86,692 Ottoman soldiers died at Gallipoli, and, despite the successful outcome of the campaign, it has to be said that they were no more able to dislodge the Allies than the Allies were able to get off the coast and into the interior.

Gallipoli is thus a paradox. While being held up as an example of folly, waste, and incompetent execution, it made no material difference to the outcome of the war, which was an Allied victory. The perspective in Turkey today is no less contradictory: Turkish writers regard the campaign only as an operational triumph and tend to ignore the strategic defeat of the Ottoman Empire. Moreover, while praising the dedication and sacrifice of Muslim soldiers in the defence of an Islamic empire, the most significant development was in fact the political apotheosis of Kemal Atatürk, the architect of a modern, secular Turkish nation. The contradictions of the campaign are, perhaps, appropriate. The Gallipoli battlefields, still preserved today, are haunting and disturbing; they bear mute testimony to a bitter struggle of such intensity that it almost defies meaning. Every visitor is left with uncomfortable questions about the assumptions that lay behind the decision to engage in this grim theatre of war. Nevertheless, while Gallipoli imposed great hardships on the belligerents of both sides, the conditions that were experienced in the unfolding drama of the Sinai were perhaps even more severe.

5

Strategy of Forward Defence

Sinai and Palestine, 1915–16

To divert the Entente powers from their Gallipoli and Mesopotamian fronts, the Ottomans looked to apply pressure elsewhere. There was still hope that progress might be made with the Senussi or with operations against Russo-British influence in northern Persia, but the most promising option was to attack through the Sinai. As the Gallipoli campaign reached stalemate, it was noted that the Ottomans had accelerated the pace of their railway construction into Syria and Palestine. When complete, the Ottomans would be able to transfer large numbers of men and supplies to the Sinai and mount a bigger offensive than those of February and March 1915. There were still gaps in the lines and tunnels to complete in Asia Minor, but concurrent road construction made it a significant development. In Palestine itself, a line now extended from Jerusalem to Lydda, and, in 1915 it was pushed on to Beersheba. Kitchener enquired of Maxwell how a defence of the Canal might be now be mounted and his revised plan consisted of the same linear defence but with provision for a more vigorous and large-scale counter-offensive.[1]

Kitchener visited Gallipoli and Egypt soon after, and gave consideration to a new plan to land forces in the Gulf of Iskanderun in order to seize the nodal city of Alexandretta. The idea had resurfaced because, with Bulgaria in the war, it was now possible for Germany to provide additional armaments and munitions to their Turkish allies. In October 1915, Enver Pasha had addressed the Ottoman parliament and promised that, despite the initial set-back of the 'reconnaissance' to Egypt, a large-scale operation would be forthcoming. Moreover, there were concerns that, unless Britain could show it was still able to make aggressive offensives against the Ottoman Empire, its forthcoming evacuation from Gallipoli would be regarded as evidence of British weakness in the eyes of its imperial subjects. On a more positive note, the success that Major General Charles Townshend had achieved at Kut in September and his advance on Baghdad seemed to reinforce the idea that the Turkish leadership could be severed from their Syrian, Arabian, and Mesopotamian possessions. Kitchener's first reaction to Maxwell's suggestion for landings at Alexandretta was to emphasize the German submarine threat, which had already caused considerable problems to the supply and reinforcement of the Gallipoli campaign. Above all he was concerned about yet more manpower requirements. Moreover, as operations in France and the Dardanelles had demonstrated, Britain was still struggling to meet the munitions requirements for the developing war effort.

That same month, the General Staff and the Admiralty considered jointly the idea of landings at Alexandretta (Iskanderun), comparing them with alternatives, such as sustaining the Gallipoli campaign or holding the existing line in Sinai. At Mudros, on Lemnos, Kitchener met with Maxwell, Sir Henry McMahon, and Sir Chares Munro (who had just relieved Sir Ian Hamilton as commander of the Mediterranean Expeditionary Force), his interim commander, General Birdwood, and Admiral de Robeck, who controlled all naval operations. On the basis of avoiding a loss of prestige and risking widespread unrest, Maxwell, McMahon, and Munro were in favour of the Iskanderun landings. They had estimated the mission would require 100,000 men, and Kitchener requested two divisions, knowing that four were already destined for Salonika and two for Egypt. Kitchener proposed that, if approved, two divisions from Egypt would make the attack at Ayas Bay, where the Anatolian coast and the Levantine shore meets, and two divisions from Gallipoli would be used as a second wave. The total force would therefore consist of six divisions, with a cavalry brigade, and would hold the area around Misis (Mopsuestia), on the Turkish shore. Robeck believed the naval aspect of the operation was entirely feasible. Kitchener asked the General Staff to examine the strategic plan and make their own critical judgement.

The General Staff were not in favour. They pointed out that the nodal point of Alexandretta particularly favoured Ottoman troop concentrations, and if the landing force got ashore, it would be forced to hold a position some 25 miles inland and defend a perimeter of 50 miles, for which it would require 160,000 men. With experience of the wastage in lives through disease and exposure that troops had endured at Gallipoli, the General Staff estimated the losses would be 20 per cent a month in the first three months of acclimatization, with some 15 per cent a month thereafter.

There were objections too in terms of the balance of force and the weight of effort. The General Staff felt that to have three simultaneous operations underway in the Eastern Mediterranean risked 'a dangerous dispersion of military and naval force'. Moreover, the expenditure of effort held out no prospect of weakening Germany in the 'main theatre'. Against a background of pessimism about withdrawing from Gallipoli without significant losses, an almost universal expectation that November, the planners felt that an 'eventual withdrawal would be difficult, perhaps impossible'. It is striking how the failure of Gallipoli was having such a significant impact on the planners' thinking. There was no sense that the Iskanderun landings would be a springboard to further operations. They were being considered, in light of the Gallipoli campaign, as an inevitable stalemate. Crucially, the General Staff argued that they had rejected the plan on the basis of strategic thinking: 'the scheme offended against a fundamental principle of strategy: to retain the power of concentrating strength for a great offensive in a decisive theatre of war'.[2] The Admiralty also returned a similar verdict, citing concern about protecting another sea route of 400 miles from Alexandria to Iskanderun. But the context was crucial. The objections were really part of a wider debate about an Eastern Strategy or a Western Strategy.

Sir Charles Munro was asked to respond to the objections. His recent experience of the Western Front would, it was reasoned, give him a neutral perspective. While Munro agreed with the substance of the military objections, he argued that this was a strategy that required a political, rather than a military, priority. Egypt should not, he argued, be defended from the Canal, but away from its actual borders and whatever scheme was adopted there must be, from a political point of view, a 'counterpoise to the evacuation of Gallipoli'. The Intelligence Section in Cairo had estimated that a landing, if achieving surprise, would be opposed by no more than 5,000 men, and it would take the Ottomans a week to assemble a division there. As the garrison of Gallipoli was evacuated, more men would be available to the British effort in Iskanderun. No mention was made of the corresponding release of Ottoman divisions from Gallipoli which presumably would neutralize this advantage. Munro continued that a perimeter would be only 40 miles, and by use of a major river, only the crossing points need be held in strength. He therefore concluded that only 80,000–100,000 men would be required. He pointed out that the wastage figures were the same across the Near East, and he saw no reason to contemplate an evacuation.[3]

The discussion was concluded when the French raised their own objections. They argued that secrecy would be vital and yet the assembly of such a large force would be almost impossible, especially with Egypt as the primary base of operations. The result would be an opposed landing, which, as Gallipoli had demonstrated, was likely to be a costly undertaking. Nevertheless, it was on political grounds that the strategy was most strongly resisted. Colonel le Vicomte de la Panouse, the military attaché in London, noted that any operations at Alexandretta would have to consider French economic interests and their political and moral position. Panouse pointed out that 'French public opinion could not be indifferent to any operations attempted in a country which it considers as destined to form a part of the future Syrian state ... and, should such action be taken, the greater part of the task should be entrusted to French troops and French generals commanding them'. The British Prime Minister, who convened a joint Anglo-French conference on the military and naval situation, informed Kitchener on 19 November that, since France was not in a position to mount any operations to Ayas Bay, the plan had to be abandoned. It was a reminder that imperial considerations in this war were paramount.

The defence of the Suez Canal remained the strategic priority for Britain. Throughout the Gallipoli campaign, and subsequently for the expeditionary force in Salonika, Egypt had demonstrated its strategic value as a conduit for manpower and supplies for the British imperial war effort. Domestically, Egypt provided foodstuffs and cotton, exporting such vast quantities that the country became dependent on maize and wheat imports from India to sustain its own population.[4] Given the unsuitability of the island of Lemnos to support the large formations required on the peninsula, Alexandria and Port Said were vital to the campaign. The only difficulty was in the chain of command and the supplies that had to procured locally, as Brigadier General C. R. McGrigor, commanding the Mediterranean Expeditionary Force's logistics in Alexandria, found himself competing with Sir John Maxwell's Egyptian force for the same resources.[5] The dilemma was resolved by the creation of a Resources Board. The return of the Mediterranean Expeditionary Force from Gallipoli in the winter of 1915–16 led to a dramatic increase in Indian supplies to Egypt in order to avoid a crisis of shortages and high prices, underscoring the importance of resources management to the entire strategy of the war. New regulations were imposed to restrict cotton production in favour of food crops, and controlling agencies evolved from moderate influence under the Supplies Commission to full direction under the Supplies Control Board.[6]

The development of the Gallipoli operations increased the demands on the manpower available in Egypt. Deducting the sick and wounded, and those in training, the total available manpower for the defence of Suez in July 1915 was reduced to 40,000, with 28,000 reserves of the Mediterranean Expeditionary Force. By the late summer, that strength had fallen still further as the 28th Indian Brigade was despatched to Aden and the opening of new fronts in Gallipoli drew away more manpower. Part of the growing concern was that the Ottomans were making fresh attempts to raid the Canal and to mine its approaches. Eight mines were recovered from the Red Sea on 9 March at a time when much of the naval force was being stripped out for the Dardanelles operations. On 22 March, a Gurkha patrol discovered part of a brigade-strength Ottoman force entrenching some 10 miles east of the Canal. A flying column was assembled and, during a wild storm that night, they surprised the Ottoman force and routed it, with a loss of just three men. In late April, more mining attempts were made and a second Ottoman force was intercepted, and another in May. These raids underscored the importance of a defence in depth, extending out into the Sinai, but the weakening of the Ottoman attacks, which petered out entirely in May, signalled the Turkish prioritization of Gallipoli. The Dardanelles campaign had drawn off the best regular units from Sinai and forced the Ottomans to rebalance their defences elsewhere.[7] Egypt was secure.

There were changes too in the Arab position regarding the war. An Ottoman force had been surprised and destroyed in November, its Turkish camel-mounted unit retreating behind a Bedouin rearguard. Crucially, among the killed, was Sheikh Ridalla Selim Dadur, a local leader who had participated in several raids. His death ended the Bedouin participation in anti-British operations in the Sinai.

Sir John Maxwell, who now faced the Senussi revolt on the western border of Egypt and the prospect of Egyptian unrest as news of the Gallipoli evacuation got out, and a future Ottoman offensive across Sinai, advocated a much stronger defence of the Suez Canal. He called for twelve infantry divisions, a cavalry division, and twenty batteries of heavy artillery. For internal security, he required two divisions, while the western borders would need three infantry brigades with detachments of artillery and cavalry, the latter a vital component in mobile desert warfare. The War Office thought the estimates too high, but Maxwell's scheme of defence now envisaged not a linear defence of the Canal, but a series of overlapping lines some 8–10 miles into Sinai. He advocated a light railway should be constructed to Qatiya some 28 miles east of the Suez Canal in order to dominate the water supplies that existed there, and thus deprive any attacking force a crucial resource.

Kitchener reinforced the request with his typical engineering approach, detailing the great quantities of wire, telegraphic equipment, Egyptian labourers, water pumping facilities, transport, aircraft, aerodrome facilities, heavy guns, and reserves.[8] The War Office revised the figures but agreed with the conclusion that a renewed Ottoman offensive could not be ruled out, perhaps as early as February 1916. They increased the numbers of mounted forces thought to be required, but scaled down the rest. They concluded that eight infantry divisions and five mounted divisions would be needed to protect the Canal, adding aircraft, armoured cars, and heavy guns to the inventory. While these deliberations went on, the set-backs in Mesopotamia required the despatch of the 28th Indian brigade from Aden, and not back to Egypt, with other battalions sent on to Basra. The Egyptian garrison was reduced to 60,000, many of whom were undergoing training.

When the Mediterranean Expeditionary Force returned, there were eleven divisions to manage. Between March and June 1916, ten infantry divisions were reorganized and sent to France, while one was dispatched to Mesopotamia. Four Territorial Divisions remained in Egypt to defend the Canal.[9] To rationalize the defence, the chain of command was also altered. On 9 January 1916, General Archibald Murray replaced Munro as Commander-in-Chief of the Mediterranean Expeditionary Force and was given responsibility for the Canal Zone while Maxwell retained control of internal security and Egypt's Western Frontier. However, concerned that in the event of an Ottoman offensive, the two systems might not work smoothly, Maxwell informed the War Office that a single chain of command was required, under Murray.[10] As a result, Murray was appointed the commander of a unified Egyptian Expeditionary Force (EEF), and Maxwell, by far the most experienced officer in Egyptian matters, returned to Britain.

The 'expeditionary' in Egyptian Expeditionary Force hinted at its offensive outlook. The Chief of the Imperial General Staff (CIGS), Sir William Robertson, regarded the EEF as the Imperial Strategic Reserve.[11] While it remained unclear which direction the Ottoman Empire might drive its next offensive—in the Balkans, Mesopotamia, or Sinai—Robertson wanted to retain no more troops in Egypt than absolutely necessary, as he saw

France as the primary theatre of operations. But he was in agreement that the divisions that were stationed there should be brought up to a war establishment, making good the losses suffered in Gallipoli. From there, they could be despatched to the various fronts as required. Nevertheless, on 15 February 1916, Murray explained to Robertson that Egypt should be defended by a forward position, and he suggested advancing across the Sinai Peninsula to the town of El Arish, 75 miles east of the Canal.[12] This would prevent the Sinai being used as a springboard for attacks on the Canal.[13] It would also deprive the Ottomans of the major water supply required to mount operations against Egypt. Crucially, El Arish would provide a base of future British operations into southern Palestine.[14] His concern was that it would be perfectly possible for the Ottoman army to bring a force of 250,000 to Beersheba and cross the Sinai. Yet there was a window of opportunity because, while the Turks were 'anxious to undertake the invasion of Egypt', their 'German military advisers in Turkey are averse at the moment to this undertaking'. Murray felt that remaining passive would simply invite an attack, and some 80,000 Ottoman troops could make the crossing of Sinai even in the hot weather of spring if they were in possession of El Arish and Qatiya.

Approval for the scheme arrived in March, and Murray was as meticulous as Kitchener in preparing the forward move. As Maxwell had foreseen, a light railway was constructed from Kantara on the Canal, with a water pipeline, and the target was to construct the first part of the link to Qatiya, some 28 miles to the east, and Romani, a cluster of oases just to the north. Murray felt that two divisions on the Canal and a division forward, accompanied by three mobile cavalry brigades, would be sufficient for the task, demonstrating his awareness of the manpower issues in the war. One of his officers described Murray's attribute as 'thinking imperially', that is 'taking the wide view that his responsibilities were for the whole empire and not for Egypt alone'.[15] Referring to Egyptian and Muslim opinion, Lord Kitchener had warned Sir John Maxwell not 'to risk a reverse, which would have far reaching effects'.[16] This warning was not lost on Murray. Robertson permitted the extension forward but he was not yet ready to permit an advance as far as El Arish. He doubted the Ottomans' capacity to bring 100,000 men through the Sinai, although he conceded that it was perfectly possible to expect 30,000. The headquarters at Cairo nevertheless maintained that up to 250,000 could make an attack on Egypt.

The difficulty was in knowing precisely what Ottoman intentions were. Despite the public histrionics of Enver in Istanbul, there was clearly some

Figure 5.1 Kress von Kressenstein, the advisor to Djemal in the Sinai and Palestine campaigns 1914–16, and the 'saviour' of Georgia in 1918

division of opinion between the Germans and the Turkish leadership. Kress von Kressenstein noted in his memoirs that 'Eine grössere Expedition' was anticipated, while the Turkish General Staff considered an offensive with seven divisions, specifically 100,000 men in fifty-seven battalions with twenty-three batteries of guns.[17] The operations had been postponed by Gallipoli and then by operations in the Caucasus, so the plan was to return to an offensive in the Sinai in October 1916. The Historical Section of the Turkish General Staff later noted that 'patience was not exercised... for some urgent reasons'. The explanation was that the Ottoman Fourth Army needed to act quickly to disrupt the forward moves of Murray lest they were permanently deprived of a base for operations against the Canal. The British Official History also noted that the availability of food in southern Palestine limited the number of troops that could be concentrated for operations against Sinai. Reflecting on the ragged and half-starved nature of the Ottoman troops holding Gaza in 1917, the verdict was that while all supplies, manpower, and munitions could be brought from Anatolia or northern Syria, it was broadly correct that sustaining them in the Sinai or southern Palestine was more difficult.

Nor can we neglect the Herculean British efforts that were made to construct the railway and defences to Qatiya, and subsequently on across the

Sinai. In hot weather, an 8-mile trek, equipped in full marching order, was considered to be the limit of endurance for troops. Every day required excavation of defensive works, and even the construction of a trench meant digging 15 feet of ground, revetting with batten and canvas sheets, and then the back-filling of sand and soil. The *khamseen* wind would invariably fill a line of trenches with soft sand in a night, forcing the diggers to start over. Temperatures of 120°F (50°C) scorched the workforce, while high winds could pull down tents and reduce visibility to a few yards. But the railway was constructed, relentlessly, at a rate of 4 miles a week. Permanent posts were constructed along its length to protect labourers from marauding Bedouin. Around Qatiya, raids and counter-raids followed, as British Yeomanry collided with the mounted patrols of the Ottoman cavalry. However, on 23 April Kress von Kressenstein orchestrated an attack in brigade strength on the 5th Mounted Brigade at Qatiya, in an attempt to destroy the railhead. Their approach was covered by dense fog and despite a spirited resistance, the outpost garrison was overwhelmed.[18] From a tactical point of view, the Ottoman attack raised the confidence of their own forces, but it had no operational benefit.[19] The railway continued to be built, the British continued to advance across Sinai. Moreover, alerted to the new threat of raiding in larger numbers, the British defences were strengthened.

The Ottomans were prompted to make a second attack on the railhead when news arrived of the outbreak of the Arab revolt in June 1916. Djemal believed that a successful attack would reduce British prestige and cause wavering Arabs to abandon the nascent uprising. This second assault was thus far greater in scale, and it was conducted by the 3rd (Anatolian) Infantry Division, the German Pasha I Group, and supporting machine guns and artillery units. Traversing the desert with wheeled guns, in the full heat of July and August, the Ottoman formation attempted another surprise attack on the British cavalry outposts at Romani. However, despite losing air superiority to German aircraft, Murray's patrols were able to obtain sufficient warning. Around Romani's defences, some 14,000 men were assembled. The Ottoman forces entrenched themselves a few miles away, which puzzled Murray and his headquarters, but this was assumed to be an attempt simply to delay any further forward movement.[20] In fact, the Ottomans had to wait until their artillery could be brought up through miles of soft sand. Murray considered pinning the Ottomans in their advanced position, and making an amphibious attack against El Arish in order to cut their lines of communications. Vice Admiral Sir Reginald Wemyss and Robertson approved the

Figure 5.2 Lieutenant General Sir Archibald Murray, who saved Suez and Egypt in 1915, fostered the Hashemite Revolt, but faltered at Gaza

plan, but while arrangements were being made, they were overtaken by events at Romani.

Murray anticipated that the Ottomans would avoid an assault on the main defences of Romani, and would instead focus on the area south of the highest ground at Katib Gannit, a vast dune in a range of sand uplands. Murray deliberately deployed a skeleton line at this point, hoping to draw the Ottomans into a prepared defence zone, and then use his cavalry and mounted infantry to take the attackers in the flank. As expected, the Ottomans used the cover of darkness to get as close to the British fortifications as possible, opened an artillery barrage on the main defences and then, while making a feint against these positions, advanced south of Katib Gannit. The Australians held their outpost line for an hour, inflicting severe casualties on the Ottoman infantry toiling up the sandy slopes. Gradually, they gained possession, and the Australians disengaged in order to fall back on a second prepared line. By daybreak this too was under pressure, so the line fell back again. Although the British encampment below the sand range was under fire, a combination of sustained British shelling and fresh reserves drove the Ottomans off the crests. The fighting had now continued for some hours. The Australian and New Zealand Mounted Division resistance had been resolute, and with the Ottoman forces everywhere committed and their exhausted soldiers running out of water, the remaining British mounted units swung into action. Mount Royston was taken in a charge by the Gloucester Hussars and Worcester Yeomanry, and when they dismounted on the summit ridge, they were able to fire on the Ottoman batteries below. A weak counter-attack fell apart and the Ottoman troops, their position now hopeless, started to surrender. British infantry regiments also began to move into the fight from the main position, pinning the Ottomans in their salient. The following day, 5 August, the Ottomans were in retreat pursued relentlessly by both mounted and infantry units. The Ottoman defeat became a rout, and some 1,500 were killed and 4,000 taken prisoner. The remainder fell back to a defensive position at Oghratina, and Murray called a halt to the operations.

The Battle of Romani, in contrast to the Ottoman raid at Qatiya, had strategic significance. It was to be the last Ottoman offensive towards Egypt, and it demonstrated that British forces had the momentum of the advance and could not now be stopped from reaching El Arish. The concurrent outbreak of the Arab revolt meant that Robertson was now willing to endorse another forward move, which put the initiative back in British hands. The Ottomans, moreover, had failed in their strategic objective of halting the British progress across Sinai and could not now establish a strong position opposite Kantara, as planned, in order to shell and interdict British shipping in the Canal.[21] The only criticism on the British side had been the apparent failure to capitalize on this significant Ottoman set-back. Kressenstein's force withdrew with all its artillery, the traditional measure of military victory, and discipline was maintained, largely because the troops knew they were falling back on strong entrenchments, abundant water supplies, and fresh rations.[22]

The British forces were unable to keep pace with the Ottoman retreat, partly through inexperience, and once again, water supplies dominated the avenues of manoeuvre. To some extent, the British follow-up reflected not only the physical difficulties of operating in the Sinai, but also the methodical approach of Murray as a commander, which was resonant in his subordinates. The trait was manifest in his conduct of operations. Murray's anticipation of the Ottoman attack plan at Romani was accurate in all but one respect: the speed of the attack on his outpost line. He had expected, perhaps, an offensive that he himself would have conducted: one that was more deliberate, securing all the high ground first, running the gauntlet of his artillery fire plan and ensuring all orders were strictly adhered to. That said, he correctly delegated authority to the local commanders, allowing them to conduct the fighting as the situation developed, which created flexibility in defence.

Murray's systematic approach to the campaign paid off. In December 1916, he had extended the railway and water pipeline as far as El Arish, accumulated his stores, constructed large canvas tanks filled with water pumped or carried by rail from Egypt, built up a vast herd of baggage camels (all duly treated for disease before being issued to their respective units), stockpiled his munitions and deployed his acclimatized brigades. It was a method of which Kitchener would have approved, copying exactly his advance into Sudan between 1896 and 1898. The Ottoman forces did not even attempt to deny El Arish, and they evacuated it without resistance.

At Magdhaba, an Ottoman garrison was surrounded and 1,300 were captured by the rapid movements of General Sir Harry Chauvel's Australian and New Zealand Mounted Division and their supporting artillery. Although there was great anxiety that such a remote position would be devoid of sufficient water, which might limit the operations, Lieutenant General Philip Chetwode, commanding the 'Desert Column', had pre-positioned parties of camels with fodder and water.[23] The whole operation was regarded as a complete success. Indeed, there was now considerable pride within the Egyptian Expeditionary Force in their achievements as a composite imperial force. The Hong Kong and Singapore Artillery 'came up smiling' after the action at Magdhaba. There were enthusiastic soldiers from the Princely State of Bikaner and Indian Imperial Service Troops too, while Australian Light Horsemen referred affectionately to the Lowlanders who had fought alongside them at Romani as 'their Scotties'; Yeomanry troopers were accepted as seasoned cavalry by their regular counterparts, and Chetwode impressed the Australians with his 'absence of stiffness or formality' which they had expected from British senior officers: one Australian subaltern, tasked with a reconnaissance, was so struck by the general's willingness to devolve command that 'I left HQ Camp wondering whether I was not the General and the General the Captain.'[24]

Confidence and cohesion increased further when General Chauvel's ANZACs and the Imperial Camel Corps, supported by British artillery, captured Rafa on 9 January 1917.[25] The taking of the settlement, again by envelopment, swept the coastal road of Ottoman forces and produced another batch of prisoners. Advanced patrols now entered grasslands, orchards, and a more verdant landscape. The unrelenting sands of the Sinai were behind them, and almost all ranks, brought up on biblical stories, referred in letters and diaries to their arrival in 'The Promised Land'.[26]

Success attracted attention in London. In December 1916, David Lloyd George outmanoeuvred Herbert Asquith to become Prime Minister with Conservative Party support. Asquith's approach to the war had been characterized by a desire to remain true to Liberal Party principles: retrenchment—and thus economies in spending on the war effort; respect for the rights of the individual—and hence resistance to the idea of conscription; and an unwillingness to interfere directly in military operations. Lloyd George had grown increasingly frustrated with Asquith's conduct, and advocated a more vigorous prosecution of the war. He had been an advocate of a Levant strategy, to sever Ottoman Turkey from its Arabian domains and prevent any offensive against Egypt. He had also advocated more active support for the Entente partners in the Balkans, but in 1915 he had accepted a compromise by attacking the Dardanelles. He never doubted the Ottomans' resolve to defend the Gallipoli peninsula and he had to accept that the operations were a strategic failure.

On taking up the office of Prime Minister, Lloyd George was aware that the situation for the United Kingdom was far from secure. Germany's submarine campaign threatened British food supplies; America was not yet in the war, and Ireland's republicans had made a failed attempt to revolt for independence. What Lloyd George brought to the war effort immediately was energy. The newspapers had already nicknamed his select team at the Ministry of Munitions as 'Men of Push and Go', and Lloyd George made it his priority to start with a reinvigoration of the strategic direction of the war. He assembled a War Cabinet, selecting men from all parties but with an emphasis on trusted old imperial hands: Lord Alfred Milner, the former high commissioner of South Africa with experience of running the civil administration of the South African War; Lord George Curzon, the former viceroy of India, again with considerable administrative experience; Arthur Henderson, representing the Labour Party and the Trades Unions; Andrew Bonar Law, the leader of the Conservative Party and the Chancellor of the Exchequer; and Lloyd George himself. Bonar Law and the Secretary of the War Cabinet, the indefatigable administrator, Sir Maurice Hankey, recognized the value of Lloyd George's energy and creativity, but they provided the essential critical judgement of his ideas. The result was an executive that combined experience, unlimited authority, determination, and self-criticism. Lloyd George himself described the effect as 'exhilarating', praising his colleagues' 'practical criticism', the force of which was sometimes so severe as to be 'insuperable [while] at other times I found it necessary to alter or modify the idea in order to meet some obstacle which I had not foreseen'.[27] To augment its expertise, the War Cabinet occasionally called in the service chiefs and Sir Edward Carson, the permanent Under Secretary of the Foreign Office, or Sir Austen Chamberlain, the Secretary of State for India. Shipping matters were placed in the hands of Joseph Maclay, a business magnate, and an early decision of the first war Cabinet was to convene an inter-Allied conference to coordinate the war efforts of the Entente and its partners.[28]

The first War Cabinet also discussed the possibility of despatching troops to Rabegh to support the Arab rebels in the Hejaz against an Ottoman counter-offensive. The War Cabinet debated whether Murray could despatch a brigade, but Robertson advised that such a force was too small to make a difference. Curzon and Chamberlain insisted that the Arab cause, which was at a vulnerable early stage, must not be extinguished. Nonetheless, over December 1916, far more consideration was given to the forthcoming options for 1917. Lloyd George and Hankey drafted a memorandum, advocating an Italian offensive, a coordinated action by Russia, and support for an attack on the Western Front by the confident new French Commander-in-Chief, General Nivelle.[29] At the subsequent conference in Rome, there was no resolution of the ambiguous position of the Salonika campaign. While taking place on Greek territory, Greece was not yet officially in the war and the government was divided over its possible full participation. Until that was resolved, no moves could be made further into the Balkans.

Lloyd George was also eager to assert his authority over the British Army, the leadership of which he blamed for the significant losses of 1916 on the Western Front. Upon becoming Prime Minister, he tried to replace Kitchener, but knew that the field marshal's popularity prevented a public sacking, so he contented himself with working with Sir William Robertson as CIGS, with powers given him by Order in Council, in December 1915. Kitchener, as Secretary of State for War, did not object, and when he was lost at sea on HMS *Hampshire* in 1916, it was Lloyd George who assumed Kitchener's position himself. The Commander-in-Chief, Sir Douglas Haig, enjoyed the backing of the Conservatives, and Lloyd George was dependent on them for his position in government. However, since Robertson reported directly to the War Council, a committee of the War Cabinet, Lloyd George believed he had the means to overrule Haig.

Initially, 'Wully' Robertson was an appealing figure to Lloyd George, given his background as a Lincolnshire working-class man who had risen from trooper to general, but Robertson, who had served alongside Haig in 1914, remained loyal to his former comrade, particularly in prioritizing the Western Front.[30] His position, honest and plainly spoken, gradually turned Lloyd George against him.[31] Robertson came to regard Lloyd George as an interfering civilian with no qualifications to form a judgement on strategy.[32] Yet, while asserting that the Western Front would be the place where the war would be decided, he acknowledged that, if coordinated, offensives from other fronts could contribute to victory by absorbing German reserves. That at least gave some room for compromise on Middle Eastern strategy, although, for the time being, the EEF was to ordered to limit itself to the possession of Sinai as a bulwark for Suez.

The priority given to the Western Front had already drawn away the divisions of the Mediterranean Expeditionary Force and following Murray's victory at Rafa, which secured Sinai, another Division, the 42nd, was taken from him. The Ottomans, alarmed by the British advance, despatched reinforcements to hold an entrenched 20-mile front from Gaza to Beersheba. But there was no British offensive. Murray had been ordered to remain where he was until the autumn at the earliest, and, deprived of a division, he was in no position to dispute his instructions. The delay merely gave the Ottoman army time to develop their defences.[33]

At the Entente military commanders' conference at Calais on 26 February 1917, there was a strong desire to coordinate attacks on all fronts, including Mesopotamia, where General Stanley Maude had already achieved considerable success using the same methodical approach as Murray, although accompanied by a much greater weight of artillery fire. In March 1917, Baghdad fell to the British Army. Encouraged by this progress, Murray anticipated orders for a further advance on his front. He had prepared accordingly. His railhead was now just 15 miles from Gaza, and he had already absorbed the settlement of Khan Yunis. Everyone in the Egyptian Expeditionary Force had expected to make an advance as early as the end of March, and there was an eagerness amongst the 11,000 cavalry, 12,000 infantry and the reserve of 8,000 to 'get to it'. The Ottoman defenders on the Gaza line numbered some 4,000, with a reserve of 15,000 in depth.[34]

The value of taking Gaza lay in the water and food supply.[35] At that time, the Egyptian Expeditionary Force was sustained at the end of a long line of communication, and while a degree of support could be offered from shipping off the coast, securing a base at Gaza would provide grazing and fresh rations. The War Cabinet, while at that time debating the relative merits of a primarily Western Front or multi-front strategy, finally endorsed the idea of the EEF taking southern Palestine. From a political perspective, it would also augment the gains made in Mesopotamia and provide the British government with a record of achievements to match the widely anticipated French successes on the Chemin des Dames in north-eastern France, the forthcoming so-called 'Nivelle Offensive'. In Arabia too, the taking of southern Palestine could have an important effect. It would demoralize and isolate the Ottoman forces in the Hejaz, encourage the Arab revolt, and persuade Arab opinion that British military supremacy was unquestionable. From the grand strategic perspective, it would also give Britain a better negotiating position in any post-war settlement.

Criticism has been made of Murray for attacking Gaza in March 1917, on the basis that 'he was not under any pressure from London to attack'.[36] Yet this judgement is based largely on hindsight, when the attacks at Gaza failed to produce the expected results. There were several reasons for Murray's decision to go on: first, the possibility of another Ottoman offensive to recover El Arish could not be ruled out. Secondly, there was a strong imperative to support the unfolding Arab revolt, not least because of the fate of the Armenians, who had been killed in their thousands due to Ottoman suspicions of treachery. Thirdly, Murray was getting indications from the CIGS that all offensive action was desirable in the context of the Entente's strategy of pressuring the Central Powers on *all* fronts. Murray informed Robertson that he intended to 'clear the Turks out of southern Palestine and relieve pressure on the Sherif'.[37] In response, Robertson stated that, for the new government and its War Cabinet facing heavy losses on the Western Front, Murray's 'success was . . . all the more welcome'. He then explicitly encouraged Murray to continue to Gaza, invoking the spirit of the French revolutionary leader Danton:

> We have had many changes here owing to the change of Government . . . The desire was to get a business government and the result is I think we have got one which makes bustle for business . . . I am looking forward to your reaching the Egyptian frontier and giving the Turks a jolly good fright as well as inflicting upon them a blow which they will never easily forget . . . I am inclined to think it is a case of *l'audace* for you.[38]

The operational plan followed the pattern of Magdhaba and Rafa, with the ANZAC mounted division making an envelopment of the long Ottoman front to take the town of Gaza from the rear. In previous engagements, Murray had been criticized for either allowing the Ottomans to withdraw, or for not anticipating this manoeuvre. At Magdhaba, the flight of Arab troops had been interpreted at the time as a general withdrawal, and this news had caused consternation in the various headquarters. A similar report had accompanied the operations against Rafa. Murray was determined this should not be the case at Gaza, particularly as deserters brought news of the intended evacuation of precious Ottoman stores in the event of a British attack.[39] However, it was also clear that his mounted envelopment needed to secure Gaza in a single day. Failure to do so risked having the men and horses without water, and so it was expected that, if the town had not been reached, there would have to be a withdrawal. The main infantry assault was to be made frontally, from the south. This was expected to pin the Ottomans to their line and prevent their escape.

In the event, a thick fog delayed the infantry advance, largely because the commanders needed to reconnoitre the ground in front of the Ottoman positions, but it provided concealment for the cavalry envelopment.[40] By around 10.30, the Australian and New Zealand Mounted Division, the Imperial Mounted Division, and the Camel Brigade were all in position,

Figure 5.3 First Battle of Gaza: 5th Suffolks advancing at noon on 19 April 1917

behind the Turkish lines.[41] Their manoeuvre had achieved complete surprise, with a Turkish commander of the Ottoman 53rd Division taken prisoner. Yet still the infantry took far longer to get into range of the Ottoman lines than expected, as orders had to be issued to conform to the new intelligence about the ground to their front, and the artillery was having trouble getting across the broken terrain to get within range.[42] It was not until midday that the toiling foot soldiers could commence their skirmishing against the Ottoman trenches. Although subjected to intense fire, and hindered by swathes of cactus, two brigades pressed on. Meanwhile, Chetwode used his initiative and pressed the Australians to attack the northern outskirts of Gaza.[43] By 16.00 they were in action and, shortly after, they started taking possession of the buildings on the edge of the town. Meanwhile much of the infantry of the 53rd Division had secured their objectives. The battle seemed to be over, but for the question of the advancing Ottoman reserves and how to defeat them.

Yet, war is the realm of friction and chance. Faced with a significant threat from the north and with riders and horses deprived of water, Chetwode withdrew his mounted screen.[44] To bring the army back into a defensible line, infantry brigades were also ordered to change their positions, but this led to the abandonment of the high ground at Ali Muntar, which, when reoccupied by the Ottomans, left the remaining brigades exposed to attack.[45] As a result these too were withdrawn. In some confusion, the EEF found itself back on its start lines. The situation was not much better on the Ottoman side. The defensive lines had been overwhelmed, Gaza penetrated and the reserve regiments had been stopped short of making a counter-attack because they had been too far away and Kress von Kressenstein had no faith in maintaining control of his Ottoman units in a night attack. He resolved to wait until the following day. Djemal overruled him, arguing the counter-attack must go ahead.

Murray believed, or at least claimed, the assault to have inflicted perhaps some 7,000 casualties on the Ottomans, but despite having got miles into the rear of the Ottoman positions, there was no disguising the fact that the First Battle of Gaza had not succeeded, largely through communication errors.[46] There had been some fundamental problems in training and experience too: infantry and artillery had not rehearsed their coordination; there was no developed artillery fire plan and observers were forced to ride from the front to the batteries with requests for fire support that were soon out of date.[47] Battalion commanders lost control of their units when their subalterns advanced at different rates, were killed or wounded, or, as casualties mounted, could not maintain communications through runners.[48]

Nevertheless, acting on Murray's optimistic report, which implied success, Robertson ordered Murray to press on from Gaza to Jerusalem.[49] Murray replied that Ottoman defences still lay ahead, he expected considerable losses in taking them and that the progress of the railway, at 20 miles a month, would dictate the rate of his advance. Congratulations had been pouring in from all quarters for Murray, as there had been a general interpretation that this was a victory, but it gradually dawned that the Battle of Gaza had not succeeded. The War Cabinet demanded a longer and more comprehensive account of what had happened. To be charitable to Murray, he may not himself have realized the extent of the set-back after the initial reports of progress—after all, by dusk Gaza had been surrounded and the Gaza line occupied in several places. He was also not responsible for the interpretation placed on his initial report by the government and the CIGS. At home there was such an appetite for good news that Murray's report was only seen in a positive light. But on the front line at Gaza, the troops were actually falling back.

Robertson told Murray that the 'War Cabinet have given careful consideration' to his report 'and ask me to tell you that they think you may not fully realize the great importance of your operations'.[50] He continued: 'The strain of war is now being felt by everyone [and] therefore the moral effect of success is of great importance in strengthening hands of the Government.' Robertson concluded with an injunction that the War Cabinet was 'anxious that your operations should be pushed with all energy'.[51] General Maude's occupation of Baghdad in March 1917, and the capture of some 9,000 Ottoman prisoners of war, increased Lloyd George's expectations of the Palestinian campaign.[52]

The troops of the EEF were bitter at the failure to take Gaza and incensed at the subsequent withdrawal after such a resolute if costly attack. They felt their comrades had fallen in vain and there was surprise that they had not been ordered to hold on to their gains. The Ottoman *Mehmetçik* were equally astonished and lost no time in recovering all their former lines. Kress von Kressenstein had been aware of the advance of the British divisions, all of which were reported on by his air reconnaissance, but Djemal, while permitting one regiment to reinforce Gaza, had held back the bulk of the reserves to face a possible landing on the Levantine coast. Although Gallipoli is subjected to endless criticism as a campaign, the prospect of further British landings against any of the shores of the Near East was a constant anxiety for the Ottoman authorities.[53] Djemal nevertheless believed that Murray would be determined to take Gaza and the amphibious threat was not the highest priority. He wrote: 'I decided to hold that front and prevent the English from breaking through at any cost by concentrating all the Turkish forces there.'[54] The Gaza–Beersheba line was reinforced, new trenches and fresh earthworks constructed. New detachments of machine guns were deployed, encased in strong points. The artillery registered targets on the approaches to the positions, and fields of fire were cleared.

Murray knew, through air reconnaissance, that the Ottomans had strengthened their defences. There was no prospect of a *coup de main*, or surprise assault. The extension of the Ottoman lines to the east also meant that any envelopment manoeuvre would have to push so far out into the desert interior that water supply would, once again, limit the range or timing of offensive action. What was required was a deliberate attack, and Murray needed a tactical edge to overcome the formidable defences being built to his front. The solution was either a greater weight of artillery, or poison gas, with an attack led by armoured vehicles, followed by much greater numbers of infantry to exploit the devastation. Naval fire could also be added to the battle plan. Murray's problem was that he had too little of these assets. There were only six heavy 60-pdr guns, and a handful of heavy howitzers; he had some reserves of gas but just eight first-generation tanks. He did not have anything like the textbook requirement of a 3:1 ratio in assaulting infantry; indeed, the three divisions were each on average 1,500 below establishment.[55] Murray had twenty-five aircraft to provide reconnaissance and spotting for artillery but his machines were outclassed by the German variants.

Major General Charles Dobell was tasked with devising the operational plan to take the Ottoman positions, and he advised that three divisions should make the assault rather the one used in the First Battle of Gaza. Two divisions were to seize the high ground at Ali Muntar, and then swing westwards to roll up the Ottoman lines, while the third would assault towards Gaza through the sand dunes on the coastal side. The Desert Column of mounted forces would protect the right flank of the main assault, delaying or pinning down any attempt by the Ottomans to counter-attack from the north. Once this manoeuvre was completed, the town would be cleared and two divisions would establish a defensive line to the north of Gaza. The first phase of the operation was to secure the Es Sire ridge before making the main attack on Ali Muntar, and a full day would be set aside to construct strong points, entrenched and wired in, as a secure jumping-off point for the subsequent assault. The intervening day would give more time for the artillery and the naval guns offshore to smash the Ottoman defences.

New aerial intelligence obtained on 10 April forced Dobell to modify his plan: he realized that the strength of the Ottomans in depth made a swing to the west impossible. Intelligence estimates placed the Ottoman garrison at Gaza as 8,500 strong, with another 26,000 in the defensive lines and in depth.[56] He therefore altered the operational plan to ensure that, having seized Ali Muntar, the two assaulting divisions would now press on to the north-east, and establish their line there, while Gaza, which would be relatively isolated, would be attacked by just one division. Murray concurred with the plan and its alteration.

At dawn on the 17 April 1917, the infantry crossed the start lines, preceded by their eight tanks. The Ottoman outposts were soon overwhelmed, but one tank and 300 men were lost to artillery fire in the preliminary stages. Nevertheless, by 07.00 the first objectives had been carried and there was no counter-attack, since it seemed to the defenders that this was a probing attack, like several that had occurred over the preceding days. Consolidation of the morning's gains got underway, subjected to a steady bombardment from Ottoman artillery around Ali Muntar. The Mounted Division was also successful in establishing an outpost line out to the east, cutting telegraph lines in the process. On the 18 April, the planned British bombardment got underway, and from his more advanced position Dobell made the adjustments to the plan for the main attack. Murray had established his own headquarters in a rail carriage at a nodal point in the communications just behind the lines.

The next morning, the full weight of the British bombardment commenced at 05.30, including the first employment of the gas shells, and two hours later, the infantry rose from their improvised trenches. Almost immediately it became apparent that the gas had failed and the artillery barrage was of insufficient weight to suppress the Ottoman defences. Machine guns opened up along the line, their mechanical rhythm punctuated only by the scream of shells and the ear-splitting detonations of the Ottoman guns. The British Official History recorded, with great understatement: 'The attack was carried out with admirable steadiness, the leading battalions moving straight on their objectives, despite heavy casualties.'[57] The 4th Norfolks had lost two-thirds of their strength and were pinned down 500 yards short of the Ottoman lines; the 5th Norfolks managed to get into a strong point, until the tank they were following was destroyed by artillery fire. Registering all the local guns on this lost position, the Ottoman gunners pulverized the Norfolk men, then lifted the barrage to drive the stunned survivors back out of the position. In their brigade, every company commander was killed and two of the three battalion commanders were dead. Lieutenant Colonel V. L. N. Pearson, the commanding officer of the 2/10th Middlesex wrote: 'my loss in officers is as bad as anything in France—70 per cent'.[58]

To the left, a party of Lewis gunners of the 4th Northamptons were the only ones to reach the Ottoman trenches where they established themselves for some minutes, pouring fire into the surprised defenders, but, shortly after, they were wiped out to a man. The 10th Londons did well, reaching their objectives too, but they were driven back by twice their number in a counter-attack and only survived the onslaught when British machine gunners caught the Ottoman infantry in the open. The pattern was repeated along the entire line. In places, the British managed to secure a foothold, only to be driven out. The King's Own Scottish Borderers contested a lunette shaped position several times, until casualties, especially amongst the officers, made it impossible to continue.

The Mounted Division were initially successful, taking a number of small positions on the Ottoman flank, but counter-attacks were halted with considerable difficulty, and it was decided to withdraw their exposed line once darkness fell. At dusk, after an intense day of fighting, Murray urged his units not to concede ground and to renew the assault on Ali Muntar the next day; Dobell also wanted to press on, using the darkness to consolidate, but, having received the reports of the casualties sustained and the ammunition expended, he called for the attack to be postponed for twenty-four hours. He reported to Murray that he felt another attack would not succeed. Murray was also now fully aware of the situation and informed the War Office that he was calling off the attack.

The Official History recorded that: 'it needs no comment, save that it illustrates once more the high quality of Turkish troops in prepared positions and emphasizes the advantages of defence by areas as opposed to linear defence, at least by day and in clear weather'.[59] The German and Ottoman accounts tended to agree, noting that the British naval and artillery bombardments had had little effect on their defences. Haze and dust, raised by the bombardment, made accurate artillery spotting difficult as the battle progressed. The gas 'had some effect' but clearly not as much as had been intended, possibly because of the heat which caused the vapour to rise rapidly.

Murray's report to the War Office was far more detailed and sanguine than his report on the First Battle of Gaza. He pointed out that only local successes could be contemplated and no advance towards Jerusalem could be considered without five fresh divisions and a considerable complement of artillery, especially heavy guns that could destroy Ottoman trenches.[60] Robertson explained that the strategic situation had changed again. The planned Russian offensive through the Caucasus, with which Murray in Palestine and Maude in Mesopotamia were to have linked up, had been postponed indefinitely. As a result, Jerusalem was no longer the primary objective of the Egyptian Expeditionary Force. Instead its task was 'to defeat the Turkish forces south of Jerusalem'. He went on to state that it was not possible to send on more divisions, but heavy guns would be forthcoming. Murray responded in May that the Ottomans had further reinforced their positions, and there was now an estimated strength of 45,000 south of Damascus, dwarfing his own depleted divisions. He argued that the reason for his failure at Second Gaza was insufficient manpower, and he advocated the abandonment of the invasion of Palestine if more reinforcements could not be found. The War Cabinet would not contemplate withdrawal: Lloyd George regarded the set-backs of the two battles of Gaza as 'spurs to new endeavour'.[61] Strategically, the Prime Minister felt that there were great opportunities in Palestine at a relatively small expenditure in means, and a relentless pressure against a weakened Ottoman Empire could ensure its collapse.

There was in fact considerable concern in the Ottoman Empire about its ability to sustain the war through 1917. The Levant was suffering the combined effects of the Allied naval blockade, severed trading routes, and the after-effects of a plague of locusts that had scoured the region in early 1915. The resulting famine killed between 100,000 and 200,000 civilians in 1916.[62] A German newspaper listed the shortages this created for the army in acquiring supplies, 'ammunition, foodstuffs, commodities like petrol, coal, cloth, drugs, fodder, sugar, leather, spirits, or preserves: all had grown scarce'.[63] The home front too was under pressure.

Germany considered that the Ottoman Empire was in need of stiffening, and despatched a contingent to form the core of the new Ottoman Seventh Army, a task codenamed *Yıldırım* ('Lightning'). Its purpose was to reinforce the depleted Sixth Army in Mesopotamia and stop the withdrawal that General Maude had induced. As events turned out, it never got the chance.

6

The Lure of Quick Victory

The Mesopotamia Campaign, 1914–16

At the outbreak of war, the government of India despatched overseas more formations than it had planned for, and expressed some reluctance to land forces in East Africa as well as furnish divisions for France and Egypt. Its preference was to secure the Gulf, and therefore the approaches to the subcontinent, and it had to be forced by the Cabinet in September 1914 to extend its operations to Tanga, the port on the coast of German East Africa (Tanzania). The imperial strategy being expressed in London was more offensive than India's. The War Office and Admiralty wanted to knock out German wireless communications, and therefore their ability to coordinate German shipping, by seizing Germany's African colonies. Depriving Germany of ports would also prevent the re-coaling of her surface raiders. The Foreign Office also believed that possession of African territory would give it a stronger bargaining position in the event of a negotiated settlement.[1] The Tanga expedition failed, and the War Office assumed responsibility for Africa thereafter, which permitted the government of India to return to what it believed were its own priorities.

General Sir Edmund Barrow, the Military Secretary to the India Office, urged the government to send an expedition to land on Persian soil in order to secure the oil installations at Abadan and in southern Persia. The motive for the subsequent landings was also to maintain British prestige among the local sheikhs of the Gulf, including Sheikh Mubarak al-Sabah of Kuwait and Ibn Saud of Riyadh, who enjoyed British protection in return for an allegiance that gave British hegemony in the region.[2] The two drivers of this strategy were combined too. Oil had been located in Ahwaz in 1901 and a refinery established on the island of Abadan in 1912, which was owned by pro-British Sheikh Khazal of Muhammerah. This local leader commanded

20,000 irregular cavalry, but both Britain and Sheikh Khazal were interdependent for their security. With shipping converting to oil-fired engines, these assets were located within striking distance of the Ottomans, who were already showing signs of belligerence. The British Cabinet therefore approved the landings on 2 October 1914, and a force, known as Indian Expeditionary Force D, had been assembled in the Gulf within two weeks.

The government of India believed the invasion of Ottoman domains would be 'provocative' and might precipitate belligerence, but, urged on by the India Office, the 16th Infantry Brigade of 6th (Quetta) Division was diverted from Force B bound for East Africa.[3] Initially the objective for Force D was simply to assert a military presence at the Shatt al-Arab at the head of the Gulf and it landed at Fao on 6 November 1914.[4] However, once war had been declared by the Ottoman Empire, following its actions against Russia, Force D was ordered to advance northward toward the town of Basra, which it captured on 21 November. There were subsequent operations as far as the junction of the Tigris and Euphrates in order to control the approaches to the town. However, once the position had been consolidated, the Mesopotamian expedition had achieved its strategic purpose.[5]

The population of Basra were reported as being generally antagonistic towards Britain, but they were dependent on commerce in and out of the Ottoman Empire and many predicted that a war with the British would lead to economic collapse.[6] The British had therefore preceded the invasion with a political strategy, offering the governor of Basra the opportunity to administer his city with complete autonomy. There had also been active support from the emir of Kuwait, urging his fellow Arabs to join the British in the liberation from Ottoman rule. Sir Percy Cox, the British Resident in the Gulf, issued a proclamation ahead of the landings, reassuring the Arabs of Britain's intent: 'to protect commerce and friends and expel the hostile Turkish troops'.[7] The Ottomans made their own efforts to recruit the Gulf sheikhs and approached Ibn Saud for backing. Ibn Saud made a show of support, but withdrew his men when Basra fell to the British forces: he had no intention of waging war on a more powerful force in the Gulf.

To cover its expanding area of control, the 16th Infantry Brigade was soon augmented by the arrival of the 18th Brigade, while a third brigade arrived in January 1915. In due course another infantry division would be deployed, as proposals were made for an advance up the River Tigris toward Baghdad, particularly when operations in the Dardanelles stalled in the summer of 1915.[8]

In late 1914, the Indian Army had proceeded with some caution. A single brigade of 4,182 men did not have the firepower to seize Basra in a *coup de main* and it was estimated that the defences of the area might be considerable, including the blocking of the river on which all substantial movements depended. The surprising success of the 16th Brigade in enveloping the Ottoman defences at Saihan, and their hurried evacuation of Basra, led to a collapse of law and order and widespread looting, which drew Force D forward. Order was restored by the British and Indian troops, and economic activity resumed, boosted by the presence of the soldiers. Nevertheless, it proved harder to find the manpower for a local police force, so Indian personnel were recruited and shipped in. In addition, the lack of camping grounds, caused by seasonal flooding, meant that troops had to be billeted in the city, which, in turn, compelled the thorough reorganization of the system of water supply and sewerage.

On the Ottoman side, there was little strategic interest in the headwaters of the Gulf, particularly when their priorities lay elsewhere. The Royal Navy had attacked the entrance of the Dardanelles in November 1914, close to the Ottoman imperial capital, and that had required the lion's share of reinforcements. The initial Ottoman assault across Sinai to capture the Suez Canal and the route through Palestine was also a greater priority than the Gulf. Above all, there seemed to be better opportunities to strike against the Russians to secure the strategically important Caucasus routes, than in the backwaters of the Tigris and Euphrates, and it was to Erzurum that the most significant Ottoman offensive was launched. The defence of Mesopotamia was left to a local garrison, a mere remnant of Fourth Army, whose main task was to maintain internal security against Arab populations.[9] There were some forward elements at the Shatt al-Arab, with the rest held in reserve at Basra, but Lieutenant Colonel Suleyman Askeri Bey, who commanded there, did not even have maps of the area he was expected to hold. Just 350 men and four guns were available to oppose the British landing at Fao. Days later, the Sheikh Mubarak al-Sabah of Kuwait led a force to expel the Ottomans, and their presence, in combination with the British landings, compelled Suleyman Bey to withdraw. His commander, Khalil Pasha, was in no position to support him: the nearest reinforcements were 275 miles to the north near Baghdad. The governor of Basra, commanding 1,000 men, offered token resistance and then abandoned the city.

When suggestions were first made for a British advance on Baghdad, almost 300 miles up-river against an estimated enemy force of two Ottoman divisions, the India Office wanted to limit the objective to Qurna, 45 miles north-west of Basra, a position that would continue to cover the Persian oilfields but not overextend the forces available. It was also the limit for ocean-going vessels on the river. Lieutenant General Sir Arthur Barrett, the divisional commander, had curtailed operations with the taking of Shaiba, 30 miles from Qurna. His first attempt, while successful, could not be sustained, and so an outflanking operation was required the following day. Qurna then surrendered. Yet, as the seasonal flooding got underway, Barrett was compelled to remain in place until the waters had subsided.

This gave the Ottoman forces the opportunity to recover and counter-attack the British. Suleyman Bey had concentrated some 4,000 Ottoman regulars and summoned approximately 14,000 Arab and Kurdish irregulars to support him. At Shaiba, where the advanced British entrenched encampment lay, the Ottomans attempted a dawn attack. At 05.00 on 12 April 1915, a surprise preliminary bombardment covered the approach and the Turko–Arab infantry tried to locate and then pass through the gaps in the British wire. Here they were repulsed by the sustained fire of the garrison. Two days later, they tried again, attempting to by-pass Shaiba in a wide arc. The British deployed a small mounted contingent with the 104th Wellesley's Rifles to intercept them, but this time it was the British Indian force that was repulsed. General Melliss, in command at Shaiba, then made a second attempt using the 2nd Dorsets and 24th Punjabis, this time with field guns as fire support. The attack was a complete success. The Arab force, unfamiliar with the relentless assault of trained troops, was routed and 400 were taken prisoner. The remaining Arab formations refused to engage the British and Colonel Suleyman Bey had no choice but to pull his Ottoman regulars back to their assembly area at Barjisiyeh.

Here, the British again attacked in force on 14 April. Locating the Ottomans proved difficult and several adjustments had to be made to the dispositions during the action, which lasted all day. By late afternoon, the British attack had stalled, but, with ammunition running low and their water exhausted, the Dorsets made a bayonet charge. The Indian units, sensing the opportunity, also dashed forward and the Ottoman position was overrun, the remainder pulling back out of range. Suleyman Bey, embittered by the failure of the Arabs to stand their ground, and fearing the humiliating consequences of failure, subsequently killed himself.

In defeating all Ottoman forces in southern Mesopotamia, the British had achieved a considerable victory, which earned the epithet the 'Miracle of Shaiba', although it had come at some cost. Nevertheless, what a small number of determined men could accomplish led to optimism about the future successes that might be achieved on this front. Perhaps more importantly the Arab populations had seen that the Ottomans could be defeated and ejected. Basra was effectively liberated, and there were popular revolts against Ottoman rule at Najaf in May and Karbala in June. The Turkish authorities were driven out and new local administrations were created. The Ottomans made desperate attempts to conscript local men, but those who had already deserted put up considerable resistance.[10] Several towns and settlements rose in sympathetic revolt including al-Kufa, Al-Shamiyya, al-Hilla, al-Samawa, and Tuwayrji. This internal revolt had a significant weakening effect on the Ottomans' ability to hold Mesopotamia, which greatly facilitated the British advance.

Throughout 1915, the Indian Army extended its control of Mesopotamia by capturing Amara, Kut, and Nasiriya. Justifications were made that inaction might damage prestige but also that military victories were achieved with relatively low casualties and so further possibilities had opened up. However, insufficient attention was paid to the overstretched supply and transport network, the lack of boats, the paucity of medical personnel and equipment, or the absence of river port facilities able to handle the mass of materiel, men, and munitions now arriving from India.[11] Set-backs at Gallipoli were adding to the pressure to march on and achieve a significant military victory. Baghdad seemed to be within reach, and offered the opportunity to deal a decisive blow against Ottoman–German standing in the Middle East, to interdict enemy efforts in Persia, and to enhance the reputation of the Indian Army and the Allies, at a time when operations in Europe had degenerated into a stalemate.[12] The early successes in Mesopotamia were regarded as 'the one bright spot' in the Allies' fortunes in 1915, and on 23 October London informed the government of India that General Sir John Nixon and the Basra force were permitted to move on Baghdad.[13] The result was an advance up-river to Ctesiphon, with the promise that two more divisions would follow on from Egypt. Kitchener opposed the idea, believing that there were insufficient troops to hold Baghdad and its extended lines of communications. Nevertheless, given the concern about Muslim opinion in the event of a withdrawal from Gallipoli, the policy was set.

To by-pass the defences near Qurna, Major General Charles Townshend had created a riverine force that May, and it had chased the retreating Ottomans up the River Tigris in a flotilla of river boats known as 'Townshend's

Regatta'. Arab civilians cheered and waved them on from the banks, and the Ottoman resistance began to collapse. At Amara, an Ottoman garrison surrendered to Townshend's little advance party without the main body having reached the town. The British government in India had originally approved the penetration of Mesopotamia on the basis that it protected the approaches to Basra, and therefore increased the security of British possessions. Now the defensive strategy looked completely redundant. Townshend's advance seemed irresistible. For a period of a few weeks it looked as though he would pursue the remnants of the Ottomans all the way to Baghdad. This would represent a spectacular and daring triumph for Britain, and assist in the diminishing of the prestige of the Ottoman sultan.

Yet the river was falling. The lower Tigris had dropped from a navigable 5-feet deep in June to a barely passable shallow flow in August. This had the effect of delaying the passage of troops up-river, and when the Ottomans dug new positions at Nasiriya, the British had to make do with the forces they had. Yet, crucially, the Arab troops were not content to face the British guns and opened fire on the Ottomans instead.[14] The resistance of the Ottoman forces was nevertheless stubborn and losses were heavy on both sides. The result, though, was that the Ottomans were once again ejected from their defences and the local Arabs surrendered to the British.

The government of India was eager now to press on while it was achieving victories and within reach of securing the entirety of Mesopotamia. There were concerns that the manpower requirements would grow, and representations were made to London to prevail on the government to release Indian troops sent elsewhere. The solution was the despatch of the 28th Brigade from Egypt, but the situation in Yemen required them there instead. Townshend also had doubts about manpower and logistical needs but got reassurance from General Sir Beauchamp Duff, the Commander-in-Chief in India, that he would not be required to move north of Kut unless he was reinforced.[15]

Colonel Nurud'din Bey, the commander of the Ottoman forces and a veteran of several conflicts, conducted a more determined defence of the approaches to Kut, at Al-Sinn. Here, lines of trenches extended on either side of the river until they abutted marshland. The operational choices for the British were stark—a long outflanking march into uncertain terrain, or a frontal assault. In late September, in an effort to combine the two, some units lost direction in their attack. Consequently too many troops found themselves in the open right in front of the Ottoman positions as dawn broke. The result was a bitter engagement lasting all day.[16] As night fell, the Ottomans once again fell back.

Nurud'din had been buying time for reinforcements to make their way into Mesopotamia, and every step back further stretched the British lines of communication. In other words, this was a strategy of defence in depth. Falling back on Baghdad also ensured that the various Ottoman contingents could be reorganized as a single force, Sixth Army, and it came under the command of the aged Prussian Field Marshal Colmar von der Goltz. There were popular demonstrations of support in Baghdad, and it was resolved to stop the British before they reached this iconic city.

At Ctesiphon, the Ottomans had spent fifty-five days digging and wiring in. Taking advantage of the flat terrain and the configuration of the Tigris, which formed a 6-mile loop, Nurud'din knew that he would be able to sweep the ground in front with fire. Reinforced from Anatolia with the seasoned 51st Division, which he held in reserve, he placed the 38th Division in the main line and the newly arrived 45th Division in trenches that formed another line perpendicular to the first, a configuration that created a cross-fire to the front. Behind the first trench line, a second system was dug, to provide support to any threatened point. The 35th Division was placed across the river to the east to cover the flank. Twelve strong points were built at intervals along the first line, while fifty-two guns, far more than the British could muster, covered the entire defence. Pitted against these formidable defences, manned by 18,000 troops, General Townshend had only 11,000 men. Some of the units were under-strength, having been depleted by casualties and disease, but there was confidence in the physical fitness they had acquired, as well as their ability to assert themselves over every defence so far thrown in their path, and the prize was near.[17] The only other blots to Townshend's prospects were the difficulty of obtaining reliable intelligence on Ottoman troop numbers, even by air reconnaissance, and the handful of desertions of Indian Muslim troops who were unwilling to launch an assault on Salman Pak, the last resting place of one of the Prophet's companions.[18]

Townshend formed four columns to attack Ctesiphon: three of infantry to pierce the defences and a cavalry wing that would envelop the Ottoman left flank. A small flotilla of river boats were to provide fire support. The attacking units set out after dark on 21 November, planning to open the attack in the early hours of the next day. The first problem they encountered was that the ground made the going difficult. Secondly, the river boats were unable to navigate a heavily mined waterway, especially when they came under fire from Ottoman guns to the west. 'C' Column, closest to the river, came under intense fire and was unable to reach the first line of Ottoman trenches. Column 'A', in the centre, was also pinned down. On the left, 'B' Column nevertheless got up to the first Ottoman line, ejected the defenders in a close-quarter battle, and drove them back into their second line. Nurud'din immediately counter-attacked with the reserve regiments of the 45th Division and brought the 35th Division back into the centre to provide more depth. Townshend also reorganized. Withdrawing 'C' column, he pushed them around to support the success of 'B', although they were subjected to enfilade fire throughout the manoeuvre. Nurud'din now deployed his 51st Division, counter-attacking 'C' Column. By the close of the day, the British had taken possession of the Ottoman first line, but had been checked at every point thereafter. Fighting continued into the night, with rushes of infantrymen cut down by small arms fire and the battering of the field artillery. Eyewitnesses referred to the ground being strewn with the dead and dying.

The following day, Townshend renewed the attack, with an attempt to envelop the Ottoman flank. The attack was checked, but the Ottoman counter-attack, using all their reserves, was also held in a series of tooth-and-nail, close-quarter engagements. By the close of the second day, the Ottoman casualties were severe: some 6,188, a third of the force, were killed and wounded. The 45th Division had taken losses of 65 per cent. Nurud'din decided to withdraw towards Baghdad, leading to subsequent speculation that, had the British had more men, they might have been able to invest the city. Yet Townshend had taken losses of 4,600, some 40 per cent of his force, and he made the decision that, with only 8,000 effectives left, he was no longer strong enough to take Baghdad as ordered. There was no reserve. As he withdrew, the Ottomans halted and then turned in pursuit. With further reinforcements available, and close to their lines of communication, the Ottomans were in a much stronger position strategically.

Ctesiphon was a largely pyrrhic victory for Townshend that led to an inevitable withdrawal to a stronger position—in this case, Kut al Amara.[19] In doing so, however, he handed the initiative to the Ottoman forces. The siege of Kut was a particularly harrowing episode much downplayed at the time. Initially there was optimism. Defences were constructed swiftly in a series of trench lines with bastions overlooking them. At first there was also a plentiful supply of food. Yet conditions deteriorated over time and the need for a breakthrough by the relief force became more pressing. The rations of the

Indian Sepoys, who made up the majority of the garrison, were so meagre by the end that, to ameliorate their hunger, some had taken to gnawing their leather equipment. The weather was particularly hard to endure with frequent storms of rain, flooding, and cold. Casualties had been heavy in the battles that had pitched them back from Ctesiphon, but the fetid conditions and lack of medical supplies now made death by disease even more prevalent than through combat. The Royal Flying Corps had managed to drop a few cases of supplies, but there was too little to sustain a force of 11,000. Even more heartbreaking was the fact that for several days a relief force had been heard battling its way to the town up the Tigris. They had been checked on several occasions, losing a staggering 23,000 men in the attempt to reach the beleaguered garrison. In late March, it appeared that the relieving troops might even break through the Ottoman lines, but even where they managed to get into their enemies' trenches, they were thrown back by determined counter-attacks.

At Ali Gharbi, south of Kut, Lieutenant General Fenton Aylmer had been tasked with collecting the relief force. The only available troops at this point in the campaign were the 6th Indian Cavalry Brigade, the 35th Indian Infantry Brigade, and the 28th Indian Infantry Brigade. Aylmer wanted to wait until the 7th (Meerut) Division had arrived before launching his attack against the Ottomans, but Townshend in Kut and General Nixon at Basra insisted that the relief force set out immediately. Consequently, Aylmer could only wait until the lead elements of the 7th Division were mustered. His force was therefore made up of 9,900 infantry, 1,340 cavalry, and forty-two guns. Set against him and now firmly dug in, there were 9,000 Ottoman infantry, the cavalry brigade, and some twenty guns. Setting aside Lanchester's law of attack, namely that attacks rarely succeed unless they enjoy a 3:1 ratio in the attackers' favour, the defenders possessed the advantage of an unusually flat terrain that increased the effectiveness of rifles, artillery, and machine guns. Moreover, while the Ottomans had difficulty supplying their formations around Kut, the British were in an even more precarious position with regard to logistics.

In fact, the British had a number of important disadvantages. While the majority of the Indian army units were now acclimatized, the Meerut Division had only recently been withdrawn from France where it had suffered significant casualties. Many of the reserves who replaced them were not well-trained. Officer replacements were even more difficult to find because of the need for language skills in order to command the various

Indian Army ethnicities. Indian Army formations possessed insufficient artillery compared with British divisions, and while the units in France had been equipped with new weapons for trench warfare, much of this equipment had to be left behind when they were withdrawn. There were still deficiencies in casualty evacuation facilities and the lack of infrastructure in Mesopotamia meant that Aylmer's force was entirely dependent on the River Tigris for its transport. He had insufficient numbers of staff officers for such a complex operation, just three in total, and the Meerut Division, led by Major General Sir George Younghusband, had no staff at all.

The Ottoman forces were well-prepared to meet the British relief attempts. Having failed to overwhelm the defences of Kut by storm on two occasions, the newly appointed German commander of the Sixth Army, von der Goltz, overruled his Ottoman subordinates and insisted that Kut be besieged. The besieging forces, XVIII Corps, were commanded by Colonel Kazime Pasha. Meanwhile, XIII Corps, under Colonel Khalil Pasha, formed the blocking force where the Tigris loops to the east of the city. XIII Corps consisted of the 52nd Division, which had taken part in the battle of Ctesiphon, and the 35th Division (which consisted of the units that had garrisoned Baghdad and the survivors of the 38th Division that had taken significant casualties the previous year). A large number of the 35th Division could be categorized as 'unreliable'; the largest complement consisted of Arab and Kurdish troops who were indifferent to Ottoman leadership and had little faith in being able to defeat the British. An Ottoman cavalry brigade was supported by Arab irregular horsemen, but these were no more reliable than the infantry.

At Sheikh Sa'ad, however, the Sixth Army had the advantage of not having to manoeuvre beyond their series of trench lines, constructed between the river and the marshy terrain that lay to the north and east. The river was blocked with obstructions, and beyond the Ottoman trench systems there were other extensive areas of waterlogged ground. South of the river, there were further Ottoman trenches and redoubts. To prevent any wide envelopment to the north, more trenches, posts, and strong points had been built, and Ottoman cavalry were in strength to the far south.

Uncertain as to the exact layout of the Ottoman positions, Aylmer sent forward Younghusband on 3 January 1916 with three brigades to reconnoitre. Bad weather prevented the use of the handful of aircraft for reconnaissance and the going was made difficult by heavy rains that turned the landscape into a sea of mud and slush. Local Arabs gave Younghusband some indication of the general location of the Ottoman defences; nevertheless, he admitted that the flat topography and the Ottomans' ability to conceal their trenches meant that the only certain way of locating each system was 'to march on, 'til we bumped into them'.[20] At 10.30 on 6 January, Younghusband was alerted to the first collisions which had occurred simultaneously as his troops marched up both banks of the river in the mist: he ordered the 19th and 35th Brigades, to the north of the river, to attack immediately, while the 28th Brigade launched a probing operation south of the river. The soaked, cold, and outnumbered Ottoman defenders resisted stubbornly at first, but north of the river they began to fall back into their reserve lines. To the south they were able to hold their positions. By mid-afternoon, the British occupied the Ottoman front line to the north of the river, but any hope of outflanking the remaining defences was lost when the Indian cavalry were delayed by the marshes and the myriad irrigation ditches. Younghusband, mindful of Aylmer's instruction not to engage the Ottoman positions determinedly until the rest of the Tigris Corps had come up, decided to break off the engagement. The captured front-line trenches were abandoned and the division regrouped.

Alarmed by the relative success of the initial attack, the Ottomans committed their reserves from the 35th Division, and the bulk of 52nd Division, to the defences. Aylmer came up with the newly formed 9th Infantry Brigade, the 6th Cavalry Brigade and more guns, although, being unable to locate the Ottoman positions precisely, their effectiveness was in reality much reduced. A more deliberate attack was planned for 7 January: the 35th Brigade would pin the Ottomans to the north of the river with a 'demonstration', while to the south, the 19th and 21st Brigades would make an assault on the other trenches. At dawn, these brigades had to make a long march through fog which caused significant delays. By midday the fog began to burn off and the day turned unusually hot. Alerted now to the presence of the British, who had temporarily halted to realign themselves for the offensive, the Ottomans made a brief counter-attack to the north of the river. The skirmishing developed into a sustained firefight, but the 35th Brigade could not get further forward under heavy fire. Attempts by the infantry to advance were soon cut down. The only option left was to dig in hastily just 300 yards from the Ottoman trenches.

Nevertheless, the 28th Brigade under Major General George Kemball enjoyed greater success. Having advanced under cover of the mist, and taken advantage of the temporary distraction afforded by the engagement north of

Figure 6.1 British troops in the trenches during the attempted relief of Kut in 1916

the river, the British and Indian troops seized the Ottoman strong points. The 92nd Punjabis penetrated the main defence line, and were soon reinforced by the 1st Leicestershires and the 51st Sikhs. The Ottoman forces began to fall back, which then enabled the 28th Brigade to bring enfilade fire against the remaining defenders on the north bank. Overnight, the Ottomans withdrew, retreating to a new position 7 miles up-river at the Wadi, a fortified position.

The operations at Sheikh Sa'ad had achieved their objective although the power of modern weapons in defence was evident in the cost to the British and Indian forces: some 1,962 were killed and a further 2,300 were wounded—more than a quarter of Aylmer's force. There was to be significant controversy about the situation later. The Tigris Corps had facilities for only 250 casualties at the time of the Battle of Sheikh Sa'ad because of the urgent need to march to the relief of Townshend at Kut. Townshend himself was subsequently criticized for his overconfidence in being relieved in a short period, his failure to manage the available rations, and his reluctance to break out. A combined attack, with Aylmer, had a far greater chance of success. Despite his losses, Aylmer felt compelled to push on again, and believed he could not await further reinforcements if he was to save the garrison at Kut.

The relative success of Sheikh Sa'ad was also manifest in the manoeuvres made by the Ottoman commanders. Colonel E.A.E. Lethbridge, who formed part of the garrison at Kut, observed on 18 January: 'the Turkish forces in front of the northern defences of Kut withdrew from immediate contact with our troops and fell back for about 2,000 yards to some redoubts which they had thrown up all round our northern defences'. Lethbridge surmised this was to 'hold and pen in the garrison of Kut-el-Amara with as few troops as possible and thus release the bulk... for opposing the advance of the relieving force'.[21]

Aylmer observed that the Ottomans held the new Wadi positions with a line of trenches behind a large waterway, and this was supported by several redoubts. Beyond, and up-river towards Kut, there was a narrow defile of dry ground between the Tigris (to the south) and the Suwada Marsh (to the north) which was defended by a position known as the Hanna. To take these positions, Aylmer would attempt to pin the Ottoman front line with the 28th Brigade and outflank the whole position with the rest of his force. There were, however, several obstacles to the execution of the operation. The first problem was the need to act quickly and so any deliberate preparations were out of the question. This meant that, without maps and the time to conduct a proper reconnaissance, formations would have to gather information as they advanced.

The second problem was the weather. Not only did thick mists make navigation more difficult but torrential rain turned the soft ground into a morass. Soon, infantrymen, artillery, and horses were struggling to get through the glutinous mud. Moving a few hundred yards took hours. Consequently, the Ottomans could detect the flanking manoeuvre the British attempted to execute and rapidly improvised a new trench line perpendicular to the original front. The attacks, when they eventually came, were soon halted. The 28th Brigade's pinning action became a series of frontal assaults that could not break into the original Ottoman lines. The troops were drenched, exhausted, and had suffered a further 1,600 casualties: the general assessment was that the attacks on the Wadi had been a failure. In fact, the real success came after the engagement, when Aylmer moved much of his force to the south of the river where it could outflank the Wadi defences on the northern bank. The Ottomans were again forced to withdraw and Aylmer prepared to advance again against the Hanna position.

The weather conditions and the nature of the soft ground meant that any encircling movement around or through the Suwada Marsh was out of the question. It would be a journey of over 50 miles to circumnavigate the worst of the waterlogged ground, but at the time, the extent of this waterlogged terrain was in any case not known. An extensive manoeuvre to the south seemed equally doomed to failure. With time ebbing away for the troops in Kut and with painfully few rations and stores available up the riverine line of communication, Aylmer opted to pit his more determined men against what he hoped were demoralized and exhausted defenders in a frontal attack. To support them, units were to be ferried across to the right bank, in the south, from where they could offer enfilade fire. A handful of gunboats on the river itself would add to the artillery bombardment set to precede the attack.

The assault on the Hanna position, known as Felahiye Muharebesi to the Ottomans, began well for the British. The fire was directed onto the Ottoman trenches and although a morning mist had again caused delays, the infantry of the Black Watch and Jats managed to cross the exposed open ground and seized part of the first trench line. The rest of the brigade was not so fortunate. Struggling across the mud, they were cut down. The Ottomans then counter-attacked the Jats and Black Watch, gradually enveloping and recovering the entire section. The survivors of the attack drew back. Younghusband ordered that a second attempt be made after a short bombardment of ten minutes but by now the weather had deteriorated into a howling gale. The rain lashed down and the churned ground took on the consistency of a quagmire. The situation in the Ottoman defences was just as chaotic. A rising tide of floodwater and the torrential rain was filling the trenches, and the defenders were clinging to the melting walls amidst the dead and wounded from the previous hours of fighting. The British second wave attempted to wade forwards, but Younghusband realized the outcome was obvious. He authorized a withdrawal to the start line.

Stiffened with cold, the survivors could only endure the freezing rains. The wounded who had not been able to get out of the killing zone largely died of exposure, and the handful of those who got through the night were rescued when a truce was arranged to collect them. The same day, at Kut, the floodwaters of the Tigris arrived, filling the trenches of British and Ottoman soldiers alike. As the Ottoman soldiers evacuated from their forward positions, they were shelled on their way, but the environmental situation now made any break-out much less feasible. The city was surrounded by a moat, but that was little consolation to the garrison, now reduced by sickness to 8,356 effectives. As garrison eyewitnesses put it, in the first phase of the siege, until the Battle of Hanna, there had been sufficient food, work, and action to keep morale high. After that engagement, as hopes of immediate relief passed and rations dwindled, the inaction and onset of sickness reduced the fighting capacity of the defenders.

The operational situation had changed dramatically in other ways. Although a further 10,000 British Indian Army reinforcements had arrived at Basra, there was too little transport to get them up-river to Aylmer and the arrival of the annual floodwaters made movement across the plains on foot a painfully slow process. By contrast, General Khalil Pasha had arrived at Kut with over 20,000 fresh troops.

It was not until March 1916 that General Aylmer was strong enough to make another attempt to break through to Kut. An attack was made on the Dujaila Redoubt, south-east of the River Tigris, but, after initial successes, the assaulting troops were ejected from all their gains. The failure of the assault and the onset of the storms and floods, which last until May, marked the end of the relief attempts.

The Siege of Kut

The siege of Kut al Amara had begun on 7 December 1915 and the initial situation appeared positive for the British. The Ottoman Sixth Army, despite investing Townshend's force, was unable to operate elsewhere: the garrison was sufficiently large to threaten any attempt to by-pass the town. Townshend had managed to evacuate the wounded prior to the Ottoman investment, and he had rations sufficient for sixty days, the first thirty-four of which would be meat-rich. There was fodder for the draft animals too. In fighting strength, Townshend could depend on almost 9,000 combatant defenders, although the 6,000 inhabitants and the 3,000 civilian camp followers were a significant burden on supplies. He had forty-three guns of various calibres, and a gunboat, the *Sumana*, to provide fire support.

The settlement of Kut in the winter of 1915 had some defences, but they were for the exclusion of Arab raiders rather than fortifications to resist an army equipped with modern weapons. Hasty preparations were made by the exhausted garrison, linking an old mud fort with barbed wire and an outpost line of four blockhouses inside the loop of the River Tigris. This system covered a middle defence line, and a second or inner cordon that protected Kut on the river. Outside of the river loop, on the western side, lay the village of Yakasub, known to the British as the Woolpress, which not only provided cover for any assaulting force, but also a significant store of grain that could not be moved prior to the siege.

The initial Ottoman objective was not to invest the settlement at all, but to take it by storm. The advantage of numbers, with over 12,000 men, and in firepower, seemed to suggest that they could pin and defeat the apparently demoralized British force. Consequently, on 9 December, a major attack was launched from the north-west. The Ottomans, advancing in extended order after a short but intense bombardment, were soon shot down and forced to withdraw. Colonel Lethbridge, the commanding officer of the 1st Battalion, The Oxfordshire and Buckinghamshire Light Infantry, noted that the Ottoman guns did 'little material damage' at this stage of the siege due to a lack of heavy calibre pieces that could throw high-explosive shells.[22] Later in the operations, there was a steady improvement in Ottoman shell-fire, with much larger guns brought to bear.

Overnight the Ottoman forces dug in close to the British lines. On 10 December, a second assault was made, with further shelling, but it met with the same result. A third attempt was made the next day, but, despite pushing their own lines closer, they had not carried the defences at any point. Townshend's force had nevertheless sustained 531 casualties and expended tens of thousands of rounds of ammunition.

Nurud'din now switched tactics, ordering his men to commence the construction of saps that would create jumping-off points closer to the British defences. The British believed this change of approach to be the result of advice from Colmar von der Goltz, the presence of the German advisor being confirmed by prisoner reports. But ten days passed in which defences could be improved. A raid against the Ottoman sap closest to the old fort was a great success and lifted morale. On 23 December, Nurud'din ordered the Turkish guns to bombard the town and the defences throughout the night, and on into the following morning. At noon, the gunners focused their fire on the old fort, and assaulting infantry sped across the open ground to the deteriorating ramparts. Inside, two field guns were knocked out, but the remnant of the three Indian battalions held the defences in a close-quarter battle, while the medium guns and enfilade fire of the 119th Infantry Regiment, in a trench adjacent to the fort, cut down a number of the assailants. The Ottomans drew back, hastily improvised defences were erected, and reinforcements fed into the fort.

The most vulnerable position was a rapidly constructed stockade in the north-east section, and at 20.00 hrs, this point was subjected to a renewed Ottoman attack by 52nd Division. The assaulting wave was preceded by lines of bombing parties. Once again the attackers were held off with great difficulty, but were thrown back by the promptness of a counter-attack by the 48th Pioneers. It was now clear that Nurud'din regarded the fort as a piece of vital ground, which, if he could wrest it from the defenders, would give him a platform from which to assault the second line. The first night assault having stalled, the Ottomans regrouped and made another attempt at 02.30 hrs. It proved impossible to drive the Indians out, and with casualties of over 2,000, the Ottoman attack petered out. The defenders had suffered losses of 382, which brought the total casualties from the start of the siege to 1,625. At this rate of attrition, Townshend's force could be practically wiped out in a month.

The operational situation was changed by new factors. First, General Aylmer had commenced his relief march which compelled Nurud'din to invest Kut, suspend assaults, and to concentrate on opposing the British relieving force. Secondly, the British and Allied forces were in the process of evacuating Gallipoli, and, as a result, it would be a matter of time before Ottoman reinforcements were available. The Ottoman posture thus changed temporarily from offensive to defensive.

The hazards for the Kut garrison were now primarily shelling, sometimes directed by Arab fifth columnists, and sniping, which took a small but steady and unnerving toll. Nevertheless, the worsening weather conditions and unsanitary nature of the settlement meant that sickness was on the rise, especially dysentery.

January in Kut was a misery. Floodwater had inundated trenches, mud hampered all movement, and firewood was at a premium. Critically, only thirty days food supplies remained, or so it was thought: a supply of barley, previously unaccounted for, and the destruction of the 3,000 draft animals, offered the prospect of further resistance, and might, it was thought, offer more time for the relief force.[23] Townshend even communicated his willingness to make a sortie in conjunction with a breakthrough by the relief column. The breakthrough at the Redoubt, south of Kut, was briefly achieved on 6 March 1916, but Townshend judged that it was not sufficient to risk the defenders. General Khalil, estimating that the British were running out of time to make the breakthrough before the flooding got too serious for any manoeuvre, offered terms of surrender to Townshend.[24] He rejected them.

Recent research shows that the situation in the Ottoman lines was also ominous. There were insufficient tents, greatcoats, uniforms, shoes, and crucially food as the weather got worse. While in theory every division had a medical company and a mobile hospital, the reality was deficiency in every area.[25] The Turkish military archives estimate that of the 10,000 deaths on the 'Iraqi Front' at this time, half were from diseases.[26] Dysentery was the most significant problem and the transfer of troops from Syria and the Caucasus, later in the campaign, proved to be the vectors of other infections. Moreover, when British and Indian sick patients were encountered and transferred, these too moved the diseases with them. Baghdad, Kut, and Mosul were particularly badly affected. Nevertheless, the more lethal problem after April 1916 was malaria. Cases increased in number rapidly, from ten in the first month to almost 8,000 by the autumn. The death rate rose from 6 per cent to 11 per cent, as logistics and food supply came under increasing pressure and personnel were weakened.[27]

On 14 March, trenches were now constantly flooded by the rising river, but it had the added advantage of driving back Ottoman snipers and sappers too. The Woolpress fortification, which had been in danger of being overrun, was saved by the floods as a large lake appeared around it. Yet the relief was temporary. The food supply of Kut soon ebbed away.[28] Indian troops initially refused to eat horsemeat, despite the permission of religious authorities, and were thus more susceptible to infections. In mid-March, British soldiers were issued just 8 ounces of bread a day. Sikhs, eager to ward off scurvy, took to eating grass. Scarcity had a way of driving its own economy: there was a thriving trade in improvised cigarettes to suppress gnawing hunger. The food shortages had more tragic effects. Kut civilians who tried to escape were shot by the Ottoman troops, and only Indian deserters were permitted to pass over to the Ottoman lines.

The imminence of Kut's surrender prompted debate in the War Cabinet. Kitchener advocated two alternatives. One was to send agents provocateurs into Najaf and Karbala and raise a Shi'a revolt, which, if encouraged to spread, might draw sufficient numbers of Ottoman troops into a counter-insurgency role and away from the Tigris front. The other was to offer a significant sum of gold to the Ottoman commander besieging Kut, to be delivered by an officer of the Arab Bureau. The young lieutenant selected by Cairo to achieve either or both these tasks was T. E. Lawrence.[29] Lawrence did his best to persuade prominent Arab leaders to consider the first option, but they saw no prospect of success and were fearful of what the British would demand from them after the war. Lawrence concluded that Suleiman Feizi (Faydi), who had led a pre-war secret society, was 'too nervous' to lead a revolution. The British relief forces resorted to airdrops to reach Kut, delivering about 2,500 pounds of foodstuffs a day, but it was insufficient to feed such a large garrison.

The final relief attempts were made in April, but the ground, now limited by what was traversable, channelled the attackers into obvious and predictable routes, which the Ottomans could defend. Fresh attempts were made to supply the Kut garrison by air, but the raw mathematics of numbers to be fed, and the available machines, pilots, and payloads, meant that the failure of this approach on its own was inevitable. The last desperate gamble by the crew of the *Julnar*, which made a valiant attempt to reach Kut by river, marked the end of the siege. Packed with 240 tons of food, the crew tried to force a passage up the river. It got to within a few miles, stuck on a sand bar, and its courageous volunteers were cut down by machine gun fire from the banks. Those that were captured were executed.

Townshend tried to negotiate terms, but Enver wanted his military victory. Lawrence and Captain Herbert were ordered forward and reiterated the offer of £1 million, expecting to secure the safety of the population as well as the garrison. Halil Pasha had already been instructed to refuse the offer and he was irritated that the British garrison had been ordered to destroy all their arms and equipment on 29 April. Halil wanted the guns as trophies and he was uninterested in the offer of largesse.

As they marched into captivity, the British and Indian garrison left behind 1,025 dead from the fighting, and a further 721 who had perished from disease. Some 68 per cent of the British survivors, and 33 per cent of the Indian troops, died in the brutal conditions subsequently imposed by their Turkish, Kurdish, and Arab guards. Many of the wounded and the sick, who were not transferred by river, died or were beaten to death on the march north from Kut.

Townshend was much criticized for the fate of the garrison, a sentiment reinforced by his apparent lack of interest in the welfare of his men once they were held by the Ottoman authorities. Their situation contrasted with his own comfortable treatment. Historian Paul Davis is less critical, acknowledging that, after Ctesiphon, Kut was the only viable defensive position and Townshend's options to save the garrison were limited.[30] When informed by Nixon that relief might take two months, Townshend had offered to break out and move south. Nixon insisted he stay. By the time the General Staff advised the War Committee that Townshend should indeed withdraw further south, the garrison had already been cut off for a week.[31] The Commander-in-Chief in India, General Sir Beauchamp Duff, was eager for Townshend to stay as the means to place a British force in the Turko-German rear as it attempted to advance across Persia to India. The viceroy thought such a threat was unlikely and, while arguing that 'the war will not be decided in Mesopotamia', he thought that Townshend might break out whenever he chose.[32] Overtures to the Russians, to make a relief attempt, were given a positive response, but only as a joint campaign into Persia, before marching together onto Baghdad. The British had not the luxury of time for such a scheme, which was therefore quickly dropped.

Timing played a crucial role. Ottoman strength increased after the siege began, but before the relieving forces were fully prepared. This fact, and the nature of the ground, served to neutralize the advantages Aylmer might otherwise have possessed. Yet, once again, the logic of mathematics was the decisive factor: forces on the offensive were frequently unable to prevail against the volume of rifle, machine-gun, and artillery fire that swept across open ground. Just as the Turkish 52nd Division failed to carry the fort at Kut, so too the relief force could not get forward at the Hanna or the Wadi.

The fall of Kut was the worst military defeat suffered by British arms until the fall of Singapore in 1942, and the prisoners of the affair were treated little better than the hapless Allied troops of South-East Asia a generation later. It demonstrated above all else the twin perils of believing in a quick victory and inadequate resourcing; for all sound strategy depends the 'sinews of war': adequate logistics and resources.

The Strategic Effects of the Fall of Kut

In January 1915, there had been several concerns about the campaign on the Tigris. There was the possibility that an advance this far into the Ottoman Empire would arouse resistance in Muslim peoples that might, perhaps, also affect Muslim subjects in India. It was clear that the Ottomans were invoking the call to jihad in Syria and Mesopotamia. Moreover, the Turks and the Germans had launched a diplomatic mission towards Afghanistan with the specific purpose of igniting a holy war against British India. A German spy seized in Bahrein was found to have been passing details of British and Indian units arriving in the Gulf, which added to anxiety about the degree of subterfuge not yet detected elsewhere.[33] The Ottomans made a conscious effort to win over the Shi'a Muslims too by claiming that a holy banner of Imam Ali, raised above their troops, had been the cause of victory in Mesopotamia.[34]

British fears about Shi'a Muslim allegiances were magnified when Wilhelm Wassmuss, a member of the German intelligence mission, arrived in southern Persia and began to raise local auxiliary forces amongst the Tangistani clans for operations against the British. This prompted a punitive expedition of Royal Marines and Indian troops to land at Bushire, although that did not prevent the British Residency at Shiraz from being overrun by Persians under German command. Indeed, the situation in Persia began to deteriorate throughout 1915, with seven out of seventeen British-owned Imperial Bank of Persia offices raided, telegraph offices seized, and the oil pipeline in the south breached by a raiding force consisting of Shi'ite tribesmen, Persian mercenaries, and Indian Army deserters.[35] In Persian Baluchistan, German intelligence operatives were active against the British. However, the government of India made concerted efforts to counter the new threats. In southern Persia, the British raised the first of 11,000 auxiliaries known as the South Persia Rifles which, along with the Russians, would be instrumental in securing the country.[36]

In London, news of the fall of Kut had a significant political effect. Asquith was forced to convene an enquiry, alongside another on the Gallipoli campaign. After ten months of deliberations, the commission's report was so damning that Curzon thought it the worst 'exposure of blundering' since the Crimean War.[37] When published, Austen Chamberlain, the Secretary of State for India, resigned. In Cairo, there was a new imperative to engage the sharif of Mecca to counter the inevitable deluge of Ottoman pan-Islamic propaganda. But with that would have to come assurances to the Arabs about their future. In other words, an operational set-back was now dictating the wider constraints on British strategy.

In Mesopotamia, the defeat at Kut forced the British to remain largely on the defensive for the remainder of 1916. General Gorringe was recalled and Sir William Robertson made it clear that the War Office and the British government would take over responsibility for the theatre. He was insistent that the strategic posture would be entirely defensive.[38] Baghdad and Mesopotamia were judged to be of little strategic significance to the war.

General Lake, Gorringe's successor, was told to exploit opportunities on his front if the Ottomans were weakening but he was not to risk heavy losses either through unhealthy conditions or enemy action.[39] In a faint glimmer of hope there was some tactical success in a raid against the Ottoman defences on the Tigris below Kut, known as the Sanniyat position, but it was General Stanley Maude, appointed to command the Tigris Corps in July 1916, who pressed for a return to the offensive. This was then authorized following a decisive shift in the strategic situation in the Caucasus and northern Persia.

7

The Decisive Battle

The Caucasus and Sarıkamış, 1915–16

At the outbreak of war, the Russian Foreign Minister had announced:

> Russia's historical mission—the emancipation of the Christian peoples of the Balkan peninsula from the Turkish yoke—was almost fulfilled by the beginning of the twentieth century... The ultimate aim of Russian policy was to obtain free access to the Mediterranean, and to be in a position to defend her Black Sea coasts against the threat of irruption of hostile naval forces through the Bosphorus.[1]

The tsarist strategic plan, which was practically an article of faith for successive rulers, was the control of the Straits around Istanbul. The Russian Empire's geography was both its strength and its weakness. While Russia possessed a vast hinterland and therefore great strategic depth, its climate limited the number of viable ports and therefore its commercial wealth. Despite an enormous taxable population, which could be mobilized for war on a grand scale, its people were impoverished, its agriculture and industry were relatively weak and undeveloped, and there were significant fissures between the different social classes and ethnic groups of the empire. While Russia had a large and relatively modern iron industry, a vast reserve of coal and other raw materials, it lacked the technical and organizational requirements to manufacture and supply on a large scale at a consistently high quality.[2] Russian industry was concentrated into certain areas but did not have the diversity or levels of modernization to cope with the demands of the Great War. There were large blast furnaces, for example, but not the high-grade technical engineering plants for steel production and weapons manufacturing. In the first months of the war, the size of the Russian Army produced a requirement for 1.5 million shells a month, but at peak production its industries could generate only 360,000. The Russian government had placed significant orders with Britain at the outbreak of war, but British demands outstripped their own capacity, which relegated Russian needs still further. Worse, Germany, which had supplied about one-third of Russia's pre-war imports of manufactured goods, was now in a position to severely weaken Russian industry.

The Russians, realizing that Britain and France were not in a position to supply their requirements, were forced to compete with their Entente partners for American supplies. But access was the critical problem. At the outbreak of war, the Baltic was sealed off by a German blockade and Sweden refused to allow war materials to cross its territory. Then the Dardanelles were closed by the Ottoman Empire. The remaining access points were Murmansk, which was ice-bound in winter and served only by a single rail line, or Vladivostok, which required a transcontinental rail shipment—the difficulties of which had already been proven by the ill-fated Russo-Japanese War (1904–5). By the early months of 1915, the industrial crisis in Russia was already acute, and munitions, guns, and equipment remained in short supply through the war.

The Russian appeal for the Entente powers to assist, by clearing the Dardanelles, was therefore desperate. Of all the powers, it was probably Russia that most needed a rapid victory. Faced with massive wartime demands, the Russian government dramatically increased taxation, exhausted all domestic loan options, borrowed heavily from overseas, and abandoned the gold standard. Despite these efforts, the economy of the Russian Empire was undermined by a fourfold rise in inflation. Drawing on the manpower reserves of Russia deprived the agricultural sector of a large proportion of its workforce, and produced a decline in overall food production. Shortages fostered hoarding, further increasing prices in staple goods. The railway network also broke down. Foreign stocks could not be moved from their railheads, lines were blocked by disabled locomotives or coal shortages. The distribution of food had started to break down by 1916. Then there were the casualties. Some 4 million Russian soldiers are estimated to have been killed or wounded in the first year of the war. Some units were sent into the line without rifles, but there seemed to be a universal shortage of boots, greatcoats, and ammunition. What incensed officers and soldiers alike was that Russia was perfectly capable of greater levels of production and sacrifice, but that the war effort was so disorganized.

Manpower reserves, enthusiasm, and boldness were the hallmarks of the massive early Russian offensive into East Prussia in 1914, an enterprise that ended in disaster at Tannenberg and the Masurian Lakes, but there was a more cautious approach in the south against the Ottoman Empire.[3]

In the Caucasus Military District, contingency plans had been considered and prepared.[4] There were three possible situations: one, that the Ottoman Empire fought Russia alone; two, that the Ottoman Empire fought alongside the Central Powers and, three, that the Ottoman Empire remained neutral. In the period August–October 1914, it was scenario three that prevailed, but under these circumstances large numbers of Russian troops should have been despatched to the fronts against Austria-Hungary and Germany. Nevertheless, the strong likelihood of the Ottoman Empire joining the Central Powers meant that the Caucasus forces had to consider the second scenario. Accordingly, the strategic posture was to be one of 'active defence'. Some local offensive was envisaged but the overall scheme was to remain in place, using the topography to the Russian advantage. As they became available reserves would be sent to the other fronts or, in more limited numbers, augment the existing divisions.

The Russians were fortunate that the Turkestan frontiers and provinces were quiet, which permitted the transfer of forces into the Caucasus. As a result, three Caucasus Army Corps were joined by two Turkestan Army Corps and they covered all the avenues of approach across the border. The total strength available was 100 battalions, 117 *sotni* (squadrons), and 256 guns of various calibres. Most battalions were some 25–30 per cent over their peacetime establishments of 1,000 men, and by the end of November, Caucasian volunteers had also joined the Russian Army.[5] The Russian view of the Ottomans was rather different. They knew that the Ottoman IX and XI Corps would be mobilized and concentrated at Erzurum in eastern Anatolia some time after the Russians were fully prepared. Indeed, even if the Ottoman government decided on an offensive in the Caucasus, the Russian Army estimated it would not materialize until December 1914, and by then the winter conditions in the mountains made such an attack unlikely. Indeed the threat was assumed to be so remote that no effort was made to coordinate future army operations with the Russian Black Sea Fleet or with the British who had made landings near Basra and defeated the Ottoman 38th Division there.

The Ottoman position was initially chaotic. The understrength Ottoman Third Army, led by General Hasan Izzet Pasha, based at Erzurum, was not informed of the Ottoman naval operations against Odessa in October 1914 and therefore he had not anticipated war. The X Army Corps was based between Sivas and the Black Sea coast and so too distant to be of any practical support for some time. His defence of the frontier region was therefore dependent on four infantry divisions and a division of cavalry, a force totalling approximately 80,000 men with 160 guns. Although Hasan Izzet did not expect any immediate Russian offensive, he had confidence in the defences that lay on the approaches to Erzurum.

On 2 November 1914, in an effort to find a more easily defended line, General Georgi Bergmann led a Russian force in the direction of Erzurum. Having penetrated 15 miles, the Russians dug in on the high ground above the Pasin Valley. Without any resistance or any orders to the contrary, Bergmann felt emboldened to resume the advance towards the village of Köprüköy and its bridge across the Aras River. Like so many of his nineteenth-century forebears in the tsarist army he was determined to demonstrate his strength over local races by audacious offensive action. But as he occupied the Aras crossing on 6/7 November, in the teeth of strengthening resistance, he realized the position was overlooked by high ground beyond, known as the Badicivan Heights. There, as they approached, his leading six battalions were confronted by the combined firepower of two Ottoman divisions. The result was carnage. On 8 November, Bergmann made a second frontal assault, uphill, against superior numbers. As the fighting went on, so Ottoman battalions were beginning to filter to the left and right of Bergmann's smaller force. Then Köprüköy village was recaptured and the Russians were forced back. By 14 November, not only were Ottoman forces pressing on both flanks and centre, they were threatening to envelop Bergmann's lines of communication to the rear. The Russian commander was saved by the arrival of reinforcements, and Hassan Izzet, unwilling to engage the full strength of the Russian army on the border itself, drew back. By 19 November, both attacks and counter-attacks had petered out. Bergmann's contingent was decimated: he had lost 7,000 killed, and some units had suffered losses of 30–40 per cent. What the Russians did not know was that Ottoman casualties were estimated to be over 8,000.[6]

At Batum, the isolated Russian garrison were confronted by an entirely different threat. The Ottomans mobilized 6,000 hill fighters from the local Laz and Acars, and these successfully ambushed a Russian column on 15 November, wiping out a battalion and a half.[7] Two characteristics of the Caucasus campaign had therefore been established in the first weeks of the war: the adverse influence of the topography, and the presence of local irregular fighters.

Enver interpreted the successes of Hasan Izzet and the guerrillas as evidence that the Caucasus was the weakest point of the Russian Empire. He calculated that, with the bulk of the tsarist forces engaged in Eastern Europe, there was a golden opportunity to wrest the Caucasus from Russia, and establish a new Turkic empire in its place, or at the very least a buffer zone of colonies to protect the Ottoman Empire. Despite Hassan Izzet's misgivings, Enver was set on a major offensive without delay.[8] By contrast, General Yudenich, the Chief of Staff to the deputy commander of the Russian Caucasus Military District, had regained control of Bergmann. His advice to the Russian imperial viceroy, Count Vorontsov-Dashkov, was to restrain Bergmann, remain on the defensive and prevent Ottoman victories until such time as a more substantial offensive could be launched. The strategic posture of both powers was thus reversed from the position of October 1914, but the consequences were to be far more significant.

Enver reasoned that Ottoman soldiers would fight more determinedly for the irredentist cause of the *Elviye-i Selâse* (the three lost provinces of Ardahan, Kars, and Batum) which had been annexed by Russia in the 1870s.[9] The recovery of these lands would, he and his colleagues believed, unite Muslims behind the Ottoman cause and set off a mighty pan-Islamic revolution.[10] Determined to claim the credit for such an ambitious project, he had already sent a delegation of agents ahead to Persia and Afghanistan, and then set off to lead the operations in the Caucasus himself. His plan was to use XI Corps to pin the Russians, and then take the IX and X Corps over the mountains to envelop the Russian forces in the vicinity of Sarıkamış. From here, the Ottomans would march on the city of Kars, in the far north-east of Anatolia. Liman von Sanders, the German advisor, had pointed out the risks of traversing poor mountain routes in the depths of winter, but Enver dismissed his objections, arguing that everything had been considered and the routes reconnoitred.[11] Historian Eugene Rogan suggests that Enver's hope to emulate the German success in enveloping large Russian forces may have been reinforced by the presence of two German advisors in his headquarters.[12] Nevertheless, Enver was a man who favoured action and audacity at the tactical and operational level throughout his career. He believed his strategic vision justified the risk and had faith that operational successes would guarantee the strategic outcome he desired.

The harsh reality was that Enver's Third Army was going to have to outmanoeuvre the Russians without the benefit of railways or proper roads. They were going to have to cross mountain passes of over 3,000 metres in altitude, in winter, with snows averaging 1.5 metres in depth and temperatures at −5 °F (−20 °C). The conditions made the traffic of wheeled transport and artillery almost impossible. General Hassan Izzet supported his superior officer but pointed out that the men required winter clothing, winter ration scales, and more ammunition. Enver responded by pointing out that mountain artillery would be sufficient and the roads would be cleared. He informed the troops that all that they required was waiting for them in the Caucasus, and announced 'our supply base is in front of us'.[13] Hassan Izzet, a man never on good terms with Enver, resigned. Enver assumed command of Third Army directly, and initiated the offensive without further delay.

Approximately 100,000 Ottoman soldiers were on the move into the mountains, with a further 50,000 deployed to guard the rest of the 300-mile frontier. Against them were 80,000 Russian forces, many more units having been sent to fight Germany and Austria-Hungary for the winter months. If he had numbers, Enver also needed speed: he ordered his troops to abandon their tents and their marching order packs with bedding and cooking equipment. They were to live off the Russian villages they overran. Fortunately for the Ottomans, the Russians had concentrated much of their force in the occupied salient taken in November 1914 and the main supply base at Sarıkamış was defended only by railway crews, sentries, and militia.

The first engagements began on 22 December amid heavy snowfall. The Ottoman XI Corps tried to pin the Russians along the Aras River. The situation deteriorated and in places the Ottomans were thrown back beyond their start lines. Some Armenian soldiers of the Ottoman army deserted, and it became a popular rumour that all Armenian deserters provided intelligence to the Russians. Murders of Armenian soldiers increased steadily.

Meanwhile, the Ottoman X Corps had managed to skirt around the Russian right flank and took Oltu, an important road junction in the avenues of communication in these mountains. The Ottoman success came in spite of a costly accidental four-hour firefight between their own units that resulted in 1,000 casualties. The settlement was sacked for its provisions, and then X Corps set off in pursuit of the retreating Russians. No attempt was made by its commander, Hafiz Hakki Bey, to coordinate the manoeuvre with the other corps, with the result that he drew further and further away from any support. Meanwhile, the troops of IX Corps, accompanied by Enver himself, hauled themselves through narrow defiles and deep drifts towards Sarıkamış. Without tents, fuel, or firewood, thousands of men died of exposure. Fully one-third of the corps died in the snows of the mountains. On 24 December, on the edge of Sarıkamış, the survivors regrouped and were heartened by intelligence that the town was weakly guarded.[14] Better still, there was news that the Muslim populations between Batum and Ardahan, districts to the north of the Ottoman offensive, had risen in revolt against the Russians. The Ottomans still enjoyed a numerical advantage locally and the most hazardous initial phase appeared to be over, with the Russians apparently taken by surprise.[15]

Russian patrols had in fact kept their commanders informed of periodic observations of the Ottoman advance, across the Top Yol plateau, a snow-swept mountain in the complex of the Caucasus mountains, that lay above the Oltu Valley. General Bergmann, alerted to insurgent activities, initially dismissed these reports as exaggerations until more concrete evidence, including intelligence from an Armenian agent, confirmed the details of the Ottoman offensive. General Yudenich and the deputy commander of the Caucasus, General Myshlayevski, now arrived to take control of the situation. The Russian officers on the front line, sensing that their line of retreat to Kars was about to be cut, were particularly anxious for a solution. Bergmann insisted on a general offensive on the Aras River, where the Ottoman attacks had stalled. Yudenich argued that saving Sarıkamış was the priority. Myshlayevski compromised—initially permitting Bergmann to launch his attack but drawing some of the reserve regiments to strengthen the approaches to Sarıkamış. He then changed his mind and cancelled Bergmann's attack as he was influenced by the stream of reports coming in about the size and direction of the Ottoman offensive. Meanwhile, Yudenich had taken temporary command of the four brigades at Sarıkamış, believing that the largest force the Ottomans could bring to bear might be six divisions. These, he reasoned, would attempt to envelop the town, attacking along certain axes. However, Myshlayevski, who had been shot at by an Ottoman patrol as he motored north-west, ordered a general retreat to avoid his front-line brigades being cut off.[16] Bergmann passed this on to his own command and the entire force started to march northwards along the available routes. But Yudenich remained, as did the little garrison of Sarıkamış.

Enver, realizing that Hafiz Hakki Bey, the commander of the Ottoman X Corps, was miles off-course, demanded that his X Corps change direction to conform to the envelopment plan of Sarıkamış. Hakki Bey complied, but faced the prospect of a 30-mile march in rapidly deteriorating weather conditions. The 3,000 metre Allahuekbar range astride his route was an obstacle in itself but blizzards reduced visibility and severed all communications. Groups of men were cut off, some collapsed in the snow, while frost killed the others. Almost half of the column perished on the ridges and slopes of the mountains.[17] The survivors were struggling on as best they could but contact with Enver's headquarters was lost. Enver, frustrated by the slow progress of all of his commanders, and anxious about the prospect of Russian reinforcements arriving at Sarıkamış, refused to wait until the envelopment was complete. Calculating that the capture of the town would, in itself, cut off the retreating Russians and lead to a general collapse, he ignored the cautionary words of his subordinates and his German advisors. Furthermore, having witnessed for himself the conditions on the mountains and the steady attrition of his troops, he reasoned that taking Sarıkamış would provide his suffering soldiers with the fuel, shelter, and rations they so desperately needed. His officers were less charitable: they believed that he could not risk Hafiz Hakki Bey seizing the town and all the glory, and therefore rushed the operation.

Enver's plan failed. The one regiment allocated to take Ardahan did so, but was driven out soon after. Hafiz Hakki Bey and his survivors emerged from the mountains and briefly held the line of communication from Sarıkamış, until overwhelmed by the Russians marching down from Kars. The surviving 1,000 men were surrounded and forced to surrender. The leading division of IX Corps, the only one available on 26 December 1914, made its attack, but was driven off with heavy casualties. It had started the campaign with 8,000 riflemen and yet it commenced the attack at Sarıkamış with just 4,000. Opposing them were a collection of armed railwaymen, militia, officer cadets, two companies of untrained infantrymen, two field guns, and eight machine guns.[18] The remnants of two more Ottoman divisions arrived during the day and were thrown straight into the assault, with the same pitiful results. By contrast, Russian reinforcements began to stream in to augment the garrison, including a Cossack regiment with horse artillery, and four battalions of infantry. Enver paused for three days, trying to consolidate and realign his formations for a second attempt. In the interval, cold and exhaustion claimed more lives.

Figure 7.1 Nikolai Yudenich, the victor of Sarıkamış, Erzurum, and Trebizond who fell foul of the Bolsheviks in 1919

Chance was to affect strategy on this front in so many ways. Not only had the exceptional weather conditions significantly reduced the strength of the Ottoman forces and interrupted their communications, but another chance event gave the Russians access to the entire Ottoman plan of operations. An Ottoman staff officer was captured on the night of 26 December and consequently all of Enver's orders were available to General Myshlayevski. It located the Ottoman forces at Ardahan, gave details of the planned envelopment of Sarıkamış, and illustrated the availability of the XI Corps along the Aras. Myshlayevski did not yet know the shocking state of the Ottoman forces and so it was understandable that he assumed the threat to Sarıkamış to be particularly grave. Ordering a brigade to abandon the Aras line and concentrate at Sarıkamış, he urged his remaining forces to continue the retreat in order to save them from the envelopment. At the same time, he reallocated forces to the gap between Ardahan and Sarıkamış, in the hope of preventing any further encirclement of his army. Yudenich argued that to commit to a retreat in the face of the Ottoman offensive courted disaster and urged Myshlayevski to halt and fight. Myshlayevski eventually agreed but was so demoralized that he informed the city administration of Tiflis (Tblisi) that an Ottoman attack was imminent, causing widespread panic.[19]

On 29 December, the Ottoman final assault began. With just 18,000 effectives left from two corps, the Ottomans were facing 14,000 Russians, dug in, with reinforced contingents of artillery, and machine guns. The daylight attacks were cut down although the Ottomans managed to halt all the Russian counter-attacks and inflicted significant losses with their own machine guns mounted on a high feature known as the Turnagel. Enver made a last ditch attempt to take the town with a night attack. To everyone's surprise there was some initial success. They recovered the high ground overlooking Sarıkamış; they burst across a bridge and entered the settlement itself, with one contingent seizing a barrack block in the centre. The fighting then degenerated into a series of small-scale firefights and close-quarter battles with bayonets in the dark. At dawn, handfuls of Ottoman survivors had surrendered and the barrack block contingent were blasted with close range artillery until they too capitulated. The streets and the approaches to Sarıkamış were littered with the dead and dying. The 17th Division of IX Corps had ceased to exist; of the other two divisions, just 3,000 could be mustered.

The challenge for the Russians was how to capitalize on the blunting of the Ottoman offensive. Bergmann, having previously been an advocate of going on the offensive, now insisted on continuing with a retreat, despite Yudenich's entreaties for him to halt. Yudenich, for his part, made a limited counter-offensive on the settlement of Bardiz from which he was able to bring shell-fire onto the Ottoman line of communication to Sarıkamış. Indeed, an opportunity arose to encircle the exhausted Ottoman force but Bergmann again frustrated operations by insisting on trying to manage it himself. Nevertheless, the Ottoman IX Corps was cut off and the survivors surrendered. The remnants of X Corps only narrowly escaped complete destruction. Just 3,000 men returned across the Ottoman border. Enver also avoided capture by the narrowest of margins, keeping just ahead of Cossack patrols to reach the relative safety of XI Corps headquarters. This corps had suffered 50 per cent casualties.

Of the whole of Third Army, originally 100,000 strong, just 18,000 exhausted and frostbitten men had survived. Even by the standards of the Great War, the Ottoman defeat at Sarıkamış was catastrophic. The topography and harsh winter conditions had made the entire plan hazardous. Enver had insisted that the element of surprise could be sustained, but this was predicated on men being able to march across broken and frozen mountainous terrain faster than the Russians' ability to move troops south from Kars on their rail network and assumed the Russians would be unable to detect the advance of the Ottoman corps until it was too late. The attrition effect of the sub-zero temperatures, desertions, and combat casualties, along with the inadequate logistical support, including winter equipment, made the success of the Ottoman plans unlikely. General Fevzi Pasha, Enver's most experienced officer in the Caucasus region, had resigned in protest at the plan.

Enver had rejected the option of having another corps transported from Istanbul to support the offensive, arguing that delay would sacrifice the element of surprise. An additional corps, according to historians Allen and Muratoff, might have enabled the Ottomans to push on as far as Kars, but even this seems over-optimistic.[20] An additional corps could not have been supported along a line of communication that crossed the high plateau of Top Yol and the road network was already impossibly congested and snowbound. It is reasonable to suppose that the commitment of another corps would merely have increased the statistics of the butcher's bill.[21]

The response in Istanbul, when the full extent of the disaster was realized, was denial. The destruction of the Third Army was not acknowledged, although Enver was much diminished as a political figure. The full strategic implications were only gradually understood. The first was that there were too few forces left in Eastern Anatolia to resist a full-scale Russian offensive in the spring.[22] The sense of vulnerability and widespread rumours of Armenian or Kurdish betrayal made brutal incidents against them more common, which, in turn, sparked resistance.

There was a strong sense of failure too surrounding the expected response to jihad: apart from some isolated examples of voluntarism, the call for a pan-Islamic revolution against the Entente powers had not roused the masses. The defeat of Djemal Pasha's 'invasion of Egypt' and the stubborn refusal of the Egyptians to join the Ottomans in January 1915 added to the despondency of the imperial leadership. Pan-Islamism had proved an Ottoman fantasy of no strategic validity.[23] In April, after a series of naval attacks on the Straits, the British and French landed the Mediterranean Expeditionary Force at Gallipoli, threatening the capital itself. The reaction was to extract the best units for the defence of the heartland, leaving forces in Mesopotamia and in Sinai just sufficient to delay or confound the British. Gendarmerie were mobilized, larger numbers were conscripted, and local militia were formed from any loyal Ottoman subjects that could be found.

These efforts were even more pressing when epidemics swept through the Ottoman Army. The war and the resulting transfers of populations were acting as new vectors for infection and contagion. By May 1915, 150,000 died of diseases in north-eastern Turkey. Typhoid and dysentery, from contaminated rations and water, were the biggest killers, just as they were for the British and imperial troops at Gallipoli. Typhus from lice infestations was just as lethal. In Erzurum, hospitals were overwhelmed and the food supply broke down. Rations failed to reach the healthy or the sick, further weakening both. Many patients died of starvation or the cold, as the logistics chain collapsed,[24] and the death toll was abnormally high amongst the survivors of Third Army. One Ottoman doctor noted that 'Many villages... as well as on the plains of Painsler and Erzurum were full of ill and wounded soldiers.'[25] In the spring of 1915, when the threat on all fronts was at its greatest, some 45 per cent of the personnel of Third Army, including the replacements, were incapacitated by disease.[26] One in four of those infected subsequently died, including the impetuous Hakki Pasha, commander of X Corps, who had led his force into disaster on the Alluakbar Range.

The Ottoman authorities had already considered mass civilian deportations to relieve the pressure on their national resources. Thousands of Christian subjects had been driven out of the empire into Greece so as to free up property, land, and resources in the Balkans.[27] Those who resisted the forced moves were beaten and in some cases killed. There was also a new fear of the Armenians, and of the possibility that they might assist the Russians over the Caucasus frontier, or commence sabotage and insurgency within the Ottoman borders. The vulnerability of the Third Army, the sense of foreboding about a Russian offensive and the latent distrust of the Armenians in the feverish atmosphere of war produced anxiety and a demand for pre-emptive action. When the chief of operations of the Ottoman secret service, Dr Bahaed-din Şakir, returned from the Caucasus front and met the Interior Minister Talaat Pasha and Dr Mehmed Nazım of the ruling Committee of Union and Progress Party, they reviewed the conditions in that region and proposed a mass deportation policy that would neutralize the Armenian threat.[28] They first authorized the forced ejection of Armenians from the area around Alexandretta where a British landing was anticipated.

When Armenians began to organize to resist their deportation in February 1915, fearing reprisals, the Ottomans' concerns seemed to be justified. Ambushes of Ottoman gendarmes crossed the threshold of violence. In eastern Anatolia, anticipating resistance, the Ottoman armed police took no chances, arresting and executing potential Armenian insurgent leaders.

Far from snuffing out any nascent organization, it fuelled it. The Armenians were convinced the Ottomans intended to massacre them, and on 20 April they had taken up arms. The result was a further escalation: Ottoman gendarmerie and locally raised irregulars began systematically killing men of fighting age around the city of Van. In Van itself, the insurgents took control of everything except the citadel which remained in Ottoman hands.

Russian forces that were deployed into northern Persia to prevent an Ottoman manoeuvre to the south of their frontier, now marched to the relief of the Armenians in the hope of exploiting the unrest. When they arrived at Van on 19 May 1915, the Ottomans had evacuated the city and Armenian militias were brought under the control of a local administration. Once regrouped, the Ottomans launched a counter-offensive, and the Russians found themselves on an extended and precarious line of communication. By the end of July, unable to sustain the defence against Ottoman counter-attacks, the Russians were preparing to withdraw. The civilian population, fearing reprisals, moved out *en masse*, and the city was left to the contending armies. The focus of intense fighting throughout the summer, it changed hands three times.

Facing a crisis on all fronts, the Ottoman government was convinced that the Armenian revolt at Van was part of a coordinated fifth-column campaign of revolution. The sense of desperation merely accentuated the fear of internal betrayal. The result was a set of instructions that would besmirch the reputation of the Ottoman Empire irredeemably. While ostensibly a plan of mass deportation from areas deemed to be sensitive from a security point of view, new research suggests that there were secret and verbal instructions to annihilate the Armenians.[29]

The strategic role of the massacres and deportations, leaving aside for a moment its moral and legal repugnance, was to remove the Armenians from provinces where they might attain a majority and thus threaten the integrity of the Ottoman Empire. From a counter-insurgency perspective, the objective was to remove all civilian support for the guerrillas operating from the hills and mountains. Without sufficient rail transport, the deportations were to be made on foot, and all signs of resistance were to be dealt with by methods of terror. The result was that men and boys were often murdered in order to wipe out the part of the population that was of fighting age, while the survivors were robbed, starved, or died of neglect. Making the Armenians, and then the Assyrian Christians, the focus of popular anger also bonded the population behind a cause. Ottoman citizens could affirm their allegiance and identity against 'traitors' in a public and direct way. The war was no longer distant or remote, and brutality against Armenians provided a visceral outlet for participation in the war. Others claimed it was a religious duty and an opportunity to enter into the jihad against infidels. Approximately 250,000 Assyrians died in the murders, representing almost half of their pre-war population.[30] Conservative figures estimate 800,000 Armenians were killed, but others suggest the figure may have been as high as 1 million.[31] The results, from a strategic perspective, were nevertheless limited: while Armenian insurgency was suppressed, it was not extinguished and certainly became more embittered and determined. Moreover, the Russians overran Erzurum in February 1916 and marched into the Black Sea coast area without any assistance from Armenian collaborators. Indeed, internal security units and armed forces that could have been used for other tasks were unable to play their part in the defence of the eastern frontier because of their actions against the Armenians and other Christians.

The Russians had their own strategic internal security dilemmas. The precipitate withdrawal in the winter of 1914 from the frontier districts had encouraged Muslim and Kurdish Russian subjects to seize the opportunity to raid and loot at will. Pre-war secret organizations saw an opportunity to achieve their long-cherished political objectives. The Azeri underground Musavat (Equality) Party aimed to unite all Muslims in the region under its leadership.[32] Christian populations packed and fled, further encouraging disorder. In Azerbaijan, local auxiliary cavalry had been raised to overawe neighbouring Turkish Kurds, but these had become unreliable. Two of the four local *aşiret* cavalry divisions had been disbanded, but these men had joined local marauding bands. With the defeat of the Ottoman offensive at Sarıkamış, General Yudenich set about restoring control. Throughout the winter, larger groups were dispersed and with spring approaching there was a good chance of mopping up the remainder. Pre-war railway construction enabled the Russians to move troops efficiently against these threatened border regions.[33] Nevertheless, constant demands for more men on the fronts against Austria-Hungary and Germany drew away much needed manpower. Troops were also required to oppose a possible Ottoman offensive from Van towards Persian Azerbaijan.

On the other hand, the Entente powers were sustaining their assault on the Gallipoli peninsula which was pulling Ottoman reserves from all *vilayets* for the defence of their capital. British forces were also still on the offensive in Mesopotamia. Despite some unrest in Muslim districts of Caucasian Russia, the population had not risen up in revolutionary insurrection.[34] There was therefore an opportunity to exploit the temporary Ottoman weakness by making a large enveloping movement through northern Persia. A march towards the Tigris, taking control of Diyarbekir and then the entire region of Tabriz, offered the chance to outflank the Ottomans, relieve Van, pre-empt the planned Ottoman offensive led by General Halil Bey, and encourage Armenians, Kurds, and possibly even the Syrians to abandon the Ottoman cause.

This ambitious plan was only scaled down because of the manpower requirements. Yudenich believed that the two Ottoman divisions at Van were still being reconstituted, and, with a much reduced flanking attack, the main effort should be made against these formations with his own IV Caucasian Corps, concentrating at the settlements of Malazgirt and Muş.[35] The more modest plan also shortened lines of communication in the difficult, mountainous country and was more certain in its establishment of strategically valuable starting points for any subsequent offensive.

The decision was a sound one. General Halil Bey made a premature offensive on 1–2 May towards the Russians south of Van and after initial successes, his conglomerate force of regulars and Kurdish mounted irregulars was defeated. Hopes of reviving a pan-Islamic wave of support once again withered with Ottoman military defeats.[36] The Kurdish units deserted and Halil withdrew in the expectation of a serious counter-attack. Yudenich now moved to exploit the growing Armenian resistance to the Ottomans around Van. He transported the entire Caucasian Cavalry Division and the 3rd Transbaikal Cossack Brigade by rail and deployed them in a swift march through Kurdish districts. As he anticipated, this had the effect of quelling Kurdish raiding immediately. The sight of vast hordes of horsemen made a significant impression on the irregulars. Persian Azerbaijan was pacified with hardly a shot fired.

On the Ottoman side, the regeneration of the X and XI Corps had been achieved on paper, although the troops were of variable quality and levels of training. The 36th Division arrived from Mesopotamia and was deployed near Lake Van, the cavalry was consolidated into a single 3rd Reserve Cavalry Division, and the remnants of IX Corps were moved to the rear to await replacements. Gendarmerie and the 1st Expeditionary Force covered the southern flank. On 6 May, the Russians had advanced towards Erzurum but were checked after seizing 9 miles of territory. To envelop this salient, the Ottomans counter-attacked on 11 June and recovered their lost ground. However, by then the Russians had taken Van and with it the town of

Malazgirt, and then they captured the territory north of Lake Van. To take back the entire area lost to the Russians required an even greater Ottoman effort.[37] The unreconstructed IX Corps, irregular horsemen, and the consolidated 3rd Reserve Cavalry Division made a movement to the south-east, entirely in secret, and their attacks caused the Russian offensive to be checked by 16 July 1915.

Yudenich's staff had believed that the Ottoman IX Corps was still to the rear of Erzurum and in need of reinforcements and training. They calculated that they faced only four divisions, when, in fact, the Ottomans had eight at their disposal, with a total strength of 70,000. These miscalculations were the direct result of failing to use information available from the Armenians or the large body of cavalry available for reconnaissance, but it also indicates the over-optimism on the Russian side about the consequences of the Sarıkamış campaign. At the operational level, the Ottoman infantry dug in and enjoyed a tactical advantage against assaulting Russian infantry and cavalry. The Russians were also guilty of pursuing too many objectives at the same time with the result that they achieved not one of them.[38] Some units lost up to 40 per cent of their strength in the fighting during the first half of 1915 and commanders began to lose touch with their formations when the Ottomans counter-attacked. Roads were crowded with retreating Russian and Cossack troops and thousands of terrified Armenians.

Having stopped the long-awaited and much feared Russian spring offensive, it was now assumed the Ottomans could continue to drive the Russians back. Optimism returned when Malazgirt was retaken on 26 July and Ottoman forces reached the Eliskirt Valley. Enver's hopes for a pan-Turanian victory were revived, and, amid the gloom of continued Allied offensives on every front, and mounting casualties at Gallipoli, the Battle of Malazgirt assumed a significance out of all proportion to its actual importance.[39] General Mahmut Kâmil Pasha, the commander of the Third Army, was effectively overruled by the enthusiastic Abdul Kerim, who commanded the right flank of the Ottoman forces but who had a direct line of reporting to the government in Istanbul. Kerim could command nine understrength divisions and there was strong support for him to pursue the Russians while they were still retreating from Malazgirt. However, the Russians could summon between 10,000 and 15,000 fresh troops to augment their defences along the high ground that ran astride any Ottoman line of advance. Confronted by the intelligence coming in, Abdul Kerim's ardour soon cooled and his advance became more cautious.

Yudenich picked up on the Ottoman commander's caution, and planned to implement an operation he had considered in advance. He would have the Ottomans thrown back by Russian counter-attacks, and with the over-extended Ottoman formations committed to battle, he would encircle them.[40] Instead of reinforcing the depleted Russian divisions, Yudenich prepared a striking force of twenty battalions of infantry, thirty-six *sotni*, with thirty-six guns, under the command of General Baratov. Operational secrecy was essential and none of Yudenich's subordinate officers was informed of the presence of the strike force. To all appearances, the Russians appeared to be continuing their retreat. Yudenich was assailed by reports of panic at the presence of Kurdish insurgents in the rear and alarm on the line of march, but remained unmoved. Instead he watched to see in which direction the Ottomans would move: he wanted to be certain before unleashing his operational reserve. The risk was that the Ottomans would have dispersed their forces along a fairly wide front, which would enable them to blunt any counter-offensive. The risk seemed even greater given the limited number of passes and roads in the Eliskirt Valley, a factor which would channel the Russians into particular routes or approaches. In fact, the Ottomans were trying to concentrate but had to move by echelons because of difficulties with their logistics.

Yudenich launched his counter-offensive on the 4 August 1915, and while the Ottomans were driven back, the stubborn defence of hill tops and their local counter-attacks slowed down the Russians, which, in turn, permitted some consolidation. Abdul Kerim was able to extract his units before being completely enveloped. Yet when ordered to fall back, the Ottoman withdrawal degenerated into a rout. Stores and guns were abandoned. Some 6,000 were taken prisoner and 10,000 lay dead and wounded in the hills and valleys. Soon after, both sides consolidated. A combination of losses and logistical constraints made operations into the autumn impractical for the Russians and the Ottomans.

The 'means', especially a shortage of trained troops, was the critical issue. News of the British offensive in Mesopotamia forced the Ottomans to despatch the 51st and 52nd Divisions in an effort to halt General Townshend there. The battles on Gallipoli were also taking reserves that would otherwise be available to regenerate the units in the Caucasus. After the summer of 1915, Ottoman divisions in Third Army were on average only 6,000 strong—that is, less than half of their expected wartime strength.[41]

For the Russians, the success of the Caucasus Army, especially after the set-back at Malazgirt in the spring, was welcomed as a relief from a summer of defeats on the Eastern European Front: Warsaw and all of Poland had been lost to German offensives. But Yudenich knew his army was not strong enough to continue against the Ottomans until reinforced. When local recruits became available he did not dilute his best formations but made use of them as guards for lines of communication. He preserved the quality of his hand-picked border guard regiments, ensured he had strong reserves in depth, and did not neglect the provision of better rations, winter clothing, equipment, and munitions. Over the winter he built up three army corps and a strategic reserve of corps strength.

The Grand Duke Nicholas had been assigned to replace the viceroy, Count Vorontsov-Dashkov, in September 1915 and he ordered that Yudenich should prepare a new expeditionary force to operate in northern Persia. The Germans had despatched agents to orchestrate a pan-Islamic revolt in Persia and Afghanistan which might have implications for the Muslim population in Russian Turkestan. Moreover, the German military attaché in Tehran was organizing a coup using German and Austrian civilians, escaped prisoners of war, and sympathetic Persian gendarmes. Persian militias were also being formed and trained by the Germans. The only pro-Russian unit in the Persian capital was the shah's Cossack bodyguard but they were in danger of being outnumbered and outgunned by a national insurrection. Yudenich duly despatched his 1st Cossack Division, two border guard regiments, and two militia regiments, with supporting guns, via the Caspian to the Persian coast.

Alerted to the move by spies, the Germans implemented their putsch, which failed. Loyalists spirited Shah Ahmet to the Russian embassy, while the pro-German militias, some 3,000 strong, regrouped at the holy city of Qom. Despite the chaos, Russia had achieved one strategic objective, namely to thwart pro-German elements and assert its control of Tehran. Nevertheless, it was imperative to neutralize the threat from Qom or countless Russian troops would be tied down in suppressing a Persian insurgency, and these were troops that were badly needed on other fronts. There were other strategic reasons for urgent action. Bulgaria had joined the war on the side of the Central Powers and that meant that German arms and supplies transiting through that country would soon reinvigorate the Ottoman war effort. Moreover, the British offensive at Gallipoli was to be withdrawn, which would free up some twenty-two Ottoman divisions for other fronts, including the Caucasus.

In fact, in December 1915, Enver tried to persuade General von Falkenhayn, the German Chief of Staff, that the Ottoman divisions from Gallipoli could make a significant contribution to the European theatre, such as the Italian front. Falkenhayn suspected the Ottomans were trying to prevent any possibility of German control of their imperial strategy by shifting the centre of gravity to southern Europe, and he did not rate the offensive capabilities of the Ottoman Army, unless it was supplied and equipped by Germany. Falkenhayn therefore countered Enver's plan by suggesting there should be either an Ottoman offensive in the Caucasus, or against the British in southern Mesopotamia, or perhaps even towards Suez. Enver concurred and began planning the redistribution of Ottoman divisions. But he was, in effect, too late. Yudenich had carefully prepared his own surprise offensive in the winter of 1915–16. Despite the need to despatch the Cossacks to northern Persia, he had diligently organized an offensive to catch the Ottomans off-balance and disrupt their strategy.

The Ottomans had excavated strong defences on the eastern approaches to Erzurum, but their system of interlocking fortifications was less dense to the north of the city.[42] Yudenich planned to use this relative weakness as the avenue for his attack. Creating a deception plan by spreading ideas of an attack into northern Persia, stores were accumulated over time both on the apparent and actual lines of advance. Messages designed to be intercepted reinforced the fabrication. Details of the offensive were kept secret, and troops were issued with their winter equipment as if they were to settle down for the entire season.[43] Movement into assembly areas was conducted at night, with daylight marches apparently being made to the rear. The Grand Duke Nicholas had some misgivings about a winter offensive but he was reluctant to lose more divisions to the European theatre if an opportunity was not taken to inflict a significant defeat on the Ottomans. The expected arrival of the divisions formerly in Gallipoli would end any other chance of conducting an offensive in this sector.

Consequently, on 10 January 1916, Yudenich launched his offensive, starting with a two-pronged assault north of Köprüköy and on the River Aras, attacking the junctions between Ottoman formations.[44] Four days later, with the Ottomans reeling and committed, he made the main attack on Köprüköy itself. Almost encircled, the Ottomans extracted their garrison with difficulty and the settlement was captured on 16 January.[45] Ottoman casualties were heavy, and the Russians were at their heels, advancing on Erzurum.[46] Here, the Ottoman defences were at their strongest, and so there was some confidence in now being able to hold the line.[47] Enver, alerted to this unexpected Russian onslaught, ordered seven divisions from Istanbul to reinforce the Third Army at Erzurum.[48] The Grand Duke Nicholas was concerned that with the Ottomans now alerted to the offensive and faced with strong defences, the attack should not continue. Above all, he was concerned that to attack without sufficient siege guns was against the accepted rules of war. Yudenich nevertheless made further careful preparations. He had the approach roads improved so that motor vehicles and artillery could be brought up. Rail lines were extended right up to the border and air reconnaissance provided better intelligence on Ottoman dispositions.[49] Then, with the Ottomans' attention focused on the eastern approaches, Yudenich launched the second phase of his offensive against the fortresses to the north of Erzurum.

On 11 February, an artillery barrage preceded a night attack by infantry, led by a regiment of Bakinskis who had distinguished themselves in several previous operations. Close-quarter fighting followed, but, by midday on the 12th, two fortresses and their outlying posts were in Russian hands. The intense struggle continued for several days and nights, until, with four forts taken and the route to the city open to attack, the Ottomans began their evacuation. On 16 February, the Cossacks broke into Erzurum and immediately took 5,000 prisoners.[50] Some 327 guns were captured. Stores and equipment also fell into their hands. With over 10,000 killed and wounded, and thousands more missing, the Ottoman Third Army could muster only 25,000 troops and these were now in full retreat.[51] There was little hope of them holding any defensive line and Yudenich pressed on to take Muş and Bitlis around Lake Van.[52] He also seized Rize on the Black Sea and then the strategically important port of Trabzon (Trebizond).[53] By the time Enver's fresh divisions reached the Caucasus front, they were in no position to drive into Russian territory. Instead, they were compelled to stabilize the line as best they could. Despite terrible weather conditions and bitter fighting, some of it hand to hand, Yudenich's strategy had been a complete success.

The Entente struggled to coordinate its offensives in the Middle East, but the evacuation of Gallipoli and the loss of Kut al Amara were offset by the Russian victory in eastern Anatolia. Moreover, the British had plans of their own for an offensive that would break through in Palestine, and, in a move that would turn the tables on Ottoman plans for a pan-Islamic jihad, the British Empire would now act in support of an Arab revolt.

8

The Arab Revolt in the Hejaz and Palestine, 1916–17

German and Ottoman efforts to raise a pan-Islamic jihad against the Entente powers had been orchestrated from the outbreak of war, but the Muslim world was far from united and the Ottoman Empire itself was divided on its response to the caliph's call to arms. In the early operations in Mesopotamia, while some Arabs had expressed enthusiasm for the Ottoman Empire's war, and while local military formations had fought the British incursion, others had proved unwilling to stand their ground and a few had turned on the retreating Ottoman regulars. By mid-1915, several areas were in revolt against the sultan's authorities. Syrian opposition was also evident, but the repression and deportations were severe and any chance of resistance was extinguished. In Sinai, some Bedouin had joined Djemal's march on Egypt, but once the tide of war turned, and Sinai fell into British hands, Bedu resistance ebbed away.

The mixed reaction to the call to jihad revealed not only the immediate operational situation, confirming British and French assumptions that the Muslim world would follow the European power that appeared to be the strongest, but the experience of living under Ottoman rule. The pre-war coup of the Committee of Union and Progress had caused particular anxiety about the future. The war also brought new and painful demands, including requisitioning and rising prices. Coupled with a new authoritarianism from Istanbul, resentment increased.

The sharif of Mecca exemplified the complexity of Arab concerns. Before the war, Sharif Hussein had been detained in Istanbul until the caliph, Sultan Abdül Hamid II, hastily conferred on him the title of emir of the holiest cities of Mecca and Medina in the Hejaz in order to prevent the Committee of Union and Progress from appointing its own crony. In 1909 the sultan was overthrown, and Istanbul's relationship with the sharif deteriorated. The revolutionary triumvirate was eager to assert political control over the Hejaz and extend the rail links into the Emirate, largely to be able to deploy troops more rapidly there if required. The sharif opposed the changes, ostensibly to protect the incomes of camel drovers who carried the pilgrims to the holy places, but his motives were revealed in a secret meeting in the spring of 1914 between his son, Abdullah, and the Consul General of Egypt, Lord Kitchener and his secretary, Ronald Storrs.[1] The sharif and his sons, while eager to resist Istanbul, by force if necessary, needed British intervention. Kitchener refused, arguing that, at that time, before the war, Great Britain had no sovereign powers of intervention in an internal matter of the Ottoman Empire, although, as Abdullah knew, the British had arranged to become a protector of the Emirate of Kuwait in 1899, had asserted their influence over the other Gulf States in 1903 with a series of high-profile diplomatic overtures, and, ultimately, had made the military intervention against Egypt in 1882 which had led to the long-term occupation of what was still, ostensibly, an Ottoman domain.

When the war with the Ottomans was imminent that autumn in 1914, Storrs and Kitchener advocated restarting the negotiations, asking the sharif to declare any Ottoman fatwa of jihad against the Entente to be illegitimate.[2] At the same time, the Ottomans sought the sharif's endorsement for their declaration of holy war. Sharif Hussein hesitated: he gave his personal endorsement to the Ottoman cause, but refused a public declaration on the grounds that it would invite aggression by the Entente powers against Muslims. Moreover, if the British Royal Navy imposed a blockade on the Red Sea then the peoples of the Hejaz, who were dependent on imports of food, would be moved to rebellion. The disappointing response prompted the government in Istanbul to claim the sharif had approved of the call to jihad anyway, but they now sought ways to neutralize the sharif and his Hashemite family.

Meanwhile Storrs offered an alliance with the sharif if he would promise to support the British war effort. In return, Kitchener, as newly appointed Secretary of State for War, was prepared to offer 'independence' to the Arabs of the Hejaz. While ensuring their safety and freedom from the Ottomans, what Kitchener had in mind was a caliphate that was spiritual in nature, not political.[3] Hussein delayed, knowing that he could not yet guarantee that many Arabs would follow him and also that the Ottoman forces in the region were strong enough to crush any premature revolt. Moreover, his ambitions were initially unclear. It was only later, once the British had begun to secure their position in Palestine, that Hussein began to consider a role as leader of the entirety of Arabia and, perhaps, of the Muslim world.[4] Far from being a proto-nationalist struggle for the sake of Arabism, this was a bid for dynastic security and an opportunity to replace the secularists in Istanbul with a genuine caliphate. Hussein could claim descent from the Prophet, and, as keeper of the holy places, was the most prestigious leader of the Umma. The war was opening up the opportunity to fulfil a long-cherished ideal.

Concurrently with Sharif Hussein's planning was the conspiracy of Syrian nationalists centred on the secret organization Al Fatat, which had been founded one year before the war. Al Fatat approached Hussein to enquire whether he would lead the movement against the government in Istanbul, despite the presence of Ottoman Army officers in the ranks of the secret movement who might themselves have been candidates for a *coup d'état*. Hussein again hesitated, but the discovery in February 1915 of Ottoman plans to have him arrested and executed compelled the sharif to act. He sent his son Feisal to gather intelligence in Damascus and Istanbul about the strength and readiness of the Syrians and other Arab factions to unite behind him.

Meeting the conspirators, Feisal discovered that the nationalists were concerned that, if the Ottomans were defeated, the French would make a bid to take over Syria. Yet they were reassured by news of the secret talks between Abdullah and Kitchener that seemed to suggest the British favoured independent Arab states under British protection. The defeat of Djemal at Suez in early 1915 and the Ottoman disaster in the Caucasus reinforced the nationalists' optimism. In Istanbul in May, Feisal met with the triumvirate in an attempt to ascertain the degree of threat to his father's position: the government, facing the invasion force on Gallipoli, demanded that the sharif give his full and unequivocal support to the Ottoman regime, and that he should mobilize the Arab populations of the Sinai and Hejaz against the British.

The nationalists drew up their own plans, defined in the Damascus Protocol, for a territorial empire encompassing Syria, Mesopotamia, and Arabia, but excluding the British port of Aden. They desired an alliance with Great Britain, to provide military and naval protection, and accepted the principle of economic preference for the British Empire. In June 1915, these plans and the Ottoman demands were considered by Hussein and his sons, before being presented as terms for cooperation with the British at Cairo. In the exchange of letters with the British, known as the Hussein–McMahon correspondence, the Hashemites claimed to represent 'the whole of the Arab nation'.[5]

The British reaction was to dismiss this extensive claim to represent the Arab 'nation', but there was some sympathy for the idea of an Arab revolt which might potentially tie down thousands of Ottoman troops. Sir Henry McMahon, the British high commissioner in Egypt, therefore reiterated his support for the idea of a caliphate, the association with Great Britain, and support for a revolution, but he refused to give any backing to a final territorial settlement, which, he perceived, would change as the war progressed. Hussein tried to press the British on the basis that this was a claim substantiated not by his clan, the Hashemites, but by the Arab people. Arab defectors and deserters confirmed the aspiration for a caliphate, free of Ottoman control, led by Sharif Hussein. It was not until October, as British fortunes in the Dardanelles began to falter, that McMahon would confirm the details of any territorial settlement. He insisted, understandably, that Britain's allies and partners in the Gulf, namely the rulers of Kuwait, Oman, the Arabian coast, the Trucial States, Qatar, and Bahrein, were to remain under British supervision due to long-standing treaties. McMahon, conscious of the efforts made by the government of India to secure Basra and Baghdad in the military operations of 1914–15, also claimed that 'special administrative arrangements' would have to prevail in Mesopotamia. Reflecting the lack of faith in the strength of a tribal alliance of Arabs against the Ottoman Empire in the future, McMahon argued that the British would have to remain in control of Mesopotamia to prevent 'foreign aggression'. As events turned out, the British were right: the Hashemites were not strong enough to rule Arabia against their rivals in the region.

Britain had acknowledged French aspirations for Syria in March 1915 in the Sykes–Picot Agreement. This secret wartime pact between the British and French governments to allocate defined spheres of influence across the Middle East once the Ottoman Empire had been defeated was not disclosed to Hussein. The agreement was only revealed when Russia collapsed in revolution in 1917 and the new Bolshevik regime published it. By its terms, France was to control southern Turkey, Syria, the northern Levant, and part of northern Iraq; Britain was to administer the *vilayets* of Palestine, Jordan, and Iraq; for its part Russia would acquire Istanbul and Armenia.[6] The exact boundaries were not determined and the agreement was a contingency document designed to coordinate war aims, but it was later regarded as a conspiratorial imperialist agenda and seen as evidence of betrayal by Arab nationalists. They argued, subsequently, that Britain and France were insincere about an independent national homeland for the Arabs.

In fact the British were concerned from the outset that the French did not intend to permit any form of self-determination in Syria and Lebanon, where they would rule through selected intermediaries. This conflicted with the British assurance offered by Sir Henry McMahon to Hussein that Damascus and part of Syria would come under Arab jurisdiction. The British government envisaged a far greater degree of autonomy and sovereignty in their provinces, even to the extent of granting the Jews a homeland of their own within an autonomous region of Palestine, as they made clear in 1917. They saw no contradiction in these arrangements, as 'federation' plans had succeeded in Canada and South Africa where communal differences were stark. Sir Mark Sykes (Kitchener's Middle East Advisor) and François Georges-Picot (the former French Consul General of Beirut) had also assiduously set aside the entire interior of their demarcated zones for Arab autonomy, and, once the agreement was published by the Bolsheviks and the idea of a Jewish homeland had been articulated, they discussed this matter with Hussein in 1917.[7] Nevertheless, when the war came to an end, there were other intervening factors. The United States had asserted more strongly the idea of national self-determination and Britain and France agreed in a Declaration, in November 1918, to the establishment of 'national governments and administrations'. They insisted that this declaration superseded the Sykes–Picot Agreement. In addition, the new League of Nations was to be the governing body that would supervise the occupied territories administered by Britain and France in the Middle East. The so-called Mandate territories, territorial units administered by Britain and France on behalf of the Arabs, nevertheless left ambiguity in the question of sovereignty, and suited no one.

Back in March 1916, the McMahon–Hussein correspondence was concluded with an agreement that the Arabs would be able to administer their own territories, subject to later adjustments, and, in return for supporting this project, the Arabs would join the British war effort as allies. This would ignite the anticipated revolt. The agreement was reached at a critical strategic moment in the war: that winter, British forces had been compelled to abandon the Gallipoli offensive and had lost the garrison at Kut al Amara in Mesopotamia. Sharif Hussein, sensing his opportunity, insisted the British recognize him as the monarch of an 'Arab Kingdom', and while he was prepared to tolerate a temporary British occupation of Mesopotamia, even after the war, he expected to be compensated. Hussein also demanded that, after the war, French claims to Syria must be dropped. But the British had secured an important strategic advantage. Hussein had agreed to launch an Arab revolt and to lead fellow Arabs in alliance with Britain. Hussein had acknowledged British claims and rejected entirely his association with the Ottomans. Whatever disagreements were to follow, the British had succeeded in mobilizing a portion of the Ottoman population against their own regime.

Nevertheless, in the spring of 1916, the Ottomans maintained their insistence that the Hejaz and Sinai should provide tribal militias to resist the British. There was deep suspicion when Hussein had failed to provide substantial forces, despite the British advance across Sinai. Moreover, the discovery of Syrian nationalist conspiracies after the French consulates in Beirut and Damascus were seized indicated that many Arabs were planning some form of insurrection, supported by foreign enemies. Some leading nationalists and community leaders, including Christians, had been deported from their homes, or tried and hanged, and small groups had been 'ethnically cleansed', to use a modern expression, although there was nothing on the scale of the Armenian and Assyrian persecution. This was because the Ottomans still needed Arab men to fill the ranks of the army, and, indeed, some of the more senior posts in the staff. Nevertheless, Djemal's reprisals had the effect of breaking the Syrian nationalist movement.

The combination of deportations, executions, conscription, rising prices, and the exhaustion of the population was severe, but in Syria, which in 1915–16 included Palestine and Lebanon, worse was to follow: a plague of locusts. In Jerusalem, the waves of insects poured across the city for seven days, but they lingered longer in the countryside. The available crops, already diminished by manpower shortages, were consumed by the locusts, leading to famine conditions across the region. In the winter of 1915–16, there were already wartime shortages of fuel, rice, and sugar, but now there was a complete absence of bread. By the spring there was mass starvation, and estimates of the death toll vary between 300,000 and 500,000.[8] Enver blamed the British naval blockade, arguing that the Entente was trying to encourage revolt against the Ottoman authorities. Locals blamed the war itself.[9]

In January 1916, Feisal was in Damascus and became aware of the extent of the disasters that had befallen the Arab nationalist cause. It was clear the

Syrians were in no position to launch a coordinated revolt, and, with the imminent outbreak of revolution further south, Feisal attempted to secure the release of the leading nationalist and local leaders who were imprisoned by 'cooperating' with the Ottoman authorities. The following month, intent on exploiting this willingness to support the Istanbul government, Enver and Djemal travelled through Syria to the Hejaz to review security arrangements, drum up support, and raise auxiliary 'mujahideen' units of Arab volunteers. Hussein made his own demands: insisting on the release of nationalist leaders, hereditary governance of the holy places, and autonomy for the Hejaz. Enver countered with the warning that the sharif was in no position to make such claims, threatened to hold Feisal hostage, and reminded him that, in wartime, his allegiances meant he was obliged to furnish the forces the Ottomans required.[10] The immediate task was to find the manpower for the projected second invasion of Egypt. Hangings of prominent leaders persuaded the Syrians to remain loyal, despite all the hardships, and there was now no question of revolt there. Sharif Hussein and the Hejaz were isolated, and it was clear that the Ottoman authorities would not tolerate any conspirators. The Hashemites would now have to act, or wait to be destroyed.

As Feisal travelled south to rejoin his family, and, as far as the Ottoman authorities were concerned, produce the required mujahideen, Djemal took the precaution of appointing a loyal Ottoman officer, General Hamid Fakhreddin 'Fakhri', as Pasha, to keep watch on the Hashemites and, if there was unrest, to assume command in Medina. This would effectively replace the theocratic local government with martial law and snuff out the flames of revolt. Djemal knew the Arabs were divided along clan lines and undisciplined in military matters. Although Fakhri possessed only a relatively small garrison, some 11,000 strong, his presence would in all likelihood deter the revolutionaries. In fact, Ali, another son of Hussein, could muster only 1,500 fighters at Medina and with this small force he hoped only to detain the Ottoman troops while his father launched the revolt in Mecca. Ali issued an ultimatum to the garrison commander on 9 June 1916, and Sharif Hussein announced the outbreak of war between Arabs and Ottomans the next day with a single gunshot from his balcony.

The Ottoman garrison in Mecca numbered only 1,500 and was divided into three locations. While one of these was overwhelmed on the first day of street fighting, the other two used artillery and machine-gun fire to halt the Arab attacks. The result was stalemate, but with the Ottoman advantage in artillery, they could not be dislodged. It took until July for an Egyptian formation and some light guns to assist in the little siege. Finally, short of water, the garrison capitulated on 9 July 1916. Meanwhile, at Medina, Ali's forces had attempted to seize a railway junction at Muhit but were driven off. Fakhri then counter-attacked with two brigades, pursuing the Arabs southwards and establishing strong points along his main communications routes. At Taif, south-west of Mecca, Abdullah's initial attempt to take the town also ended in failure. The Ottoman troops were determined in their resistance and even when the Egyptian guns arrived from Mecca, the garrison held out until September.

At this point, while strategic surprise had been achieved, the Arab fighters lacked the heavy weapons necessary to capture towns and rail junctions. Without these in their possession, there was nothing to prevent the arrival of Ottoman reinforcements. Early assessments therefore suggested that the revolt was doomed to failure unless they could secure British assistance urgently.[11] This required the capture of the Red Sea ports, where the Royal Navy could land arms, especially artillery, supplies, and munitions.

The subsequent seizure of the ports of Jeddah, Yanbu, and Rabegh, along the Red Sea coast, transformed the operational situation. As well as the Egyptian troops and guns, a battalion of 700 Arab regulars, mainly Iraqis who had become prisoners of war of the British but agreed to serve now against the Ottomans, landed in the Hejaz. British officers coordinated the new operations and their complex logistics.[12] Jeddah was under the command of Colonel Cyril Wilson, the former governor of the Sudan, and Colonel Pierce Joyce assumed control of Rabegh in December. Colonel Stewart Newcombe, a Royal Engineer, took a keen interest in the Hejaz railway as the most operationally important feature of the region, and planned to disrupt all its traffic with a series of raids.

By the autumn, French officers had joined the campaign, focusing largely on the area around Mecca and Medina. The opportunity to 'escort' pilgrims using Muslim North African troops offered the chance to establish a French presence in the Arab cause in order to fulfil the aspirations of the Sykes–Picot Agreement, but the British regarded this as an enterprise in colonial rivalry.[13] Colonel Edouard Brémond was the liaison officer to Hussein and Abdullah, while the Muslim officers of French North African regiments, Colonel Cadi and Capitaine Ould Raho, worked alongside Arab raiding parties.[14] Capitaine Rosario Pisani, a French officer attached to what became the Arab Northern Army, was one of the most successful raiders of all.

There was also a steady increase in the numbers of regular Arab troops available, some 2,000 strong, and these came under the command of Major Ali Al-Masri with the title of the 'Sharifian Army'. The British and the French did their best to limit the presence of non-Muslims, being eager not to offend the religious sensitivities of the Arabs so close to the holiest sites of their faith. There were other, more prosaic considerations too. Since the Arab forces were abandoning pastoralism or agriculture, and often refused to operate far from their homelands, the fighters had to be paid, usually in gold, to serve on a continuous basis.

The Agayl, who made up the majority of fighters, considered themselves to be inherent warriors, but British assessments of their fighting styles considered them unsuitable for anything other than raids. Without modern weapons or training, they could not be used to assault defended positions. Heavy weapons would also compromise their mobility, which was their chief defence until the Ottomans increased the number of aircraft operating against them. Later in the campaign, it became essential to equip the Arab Northern Army with aircraft, armoured cars, and anti-aircraft guns and to augment their regular and irregular contingents with British Imperial Yeomanry and units of the Indian Army.

With these 'means', and with a limited number of 'ways', the Arab 'ends' were to liberate the Hejaz by defeating the Ottoman forces. To gain legitimacy as the true leaders of the Muslim world, which was perhaps Hussein's real ambition, it was vital to secure Medina as they had done Mecca, and, concurrently, they had to keep open the sea ports on the coast through which came all their essential supplies. At the same time, if the Ottoman line of communication and reinforcement, the Hejaz railway, could be cut, there was a chance they could prevent large Ottoman formations from concentrating against them, and perhaps, starve the garrison of Medina into submission. Despite Hussein's plans, his son Feisal had another agenda: aware that he was unlikely to gain any significant position in the post-war dispensation in the Hejaz, Feisal looked to Greater Syria as a potential source of future power. It was this factor which drew the forces under his command northwards.

The British 'ends' were more limited. General Murray, the commander in Egypt, believed the Arab revolt was capable only of drawing a proportion of Ottoman forces into the strategically insignificant Hejaz, and away from the more important theatre of operations in Sinai and Palestine. Murray therefore practised an economy of effort in supporting the Hashemites, and he was certainly not prepared to divide his forces and take on a secondary theatre, especially given his experience of having to suppress the Senussi on Egypt's western borders at the same time as fighting the Ottomans and their Bedouin allies in Sinai. Robertson, as Chief of the Imperial General Staff (CIGS), was even more trenchant: 'My sole object is to win the war, and we shall not do that in the Hijaz or in the Sudan.'[15] The British concerns were, from a political perspective, that there would be anger at the deployment of non-Muslims, and, from a military point of view, that there would be yet more demands for troops in another theatre when manpower was in short supply on every front.[16] General Allenby was more supportive when he assumed command because of the Arab capture of Aqaba in July 1917—a factor which demonstrated the value of Arab forces operating behind or on the flanks of Ottoman regular formations. Nevertheless, the British in Cairo and London were not impressed with Hussein's claim to be the 'King of Arab Lands' from the outbreak of the revolt. They knew that his success was dependent on them, and they signalled their conditional support for his territorial claims by referring to Hussein as 'King of the Hejaz'.[17] What was worrying was that Indian Muslims in the subcontinent condemned the revolt and its British backing, arguing that it was not legitimate to fight the caliph. Anxious signals were conveyed to Sir Henry McMahon that the revolt was proving counter-productive.

The Ottoman response to the revolt was unequivocal. They intended to recover the lost territory, crush the insurgency, and de-legitimize Hussein and his sons. They moved to install a new sharif, Ali Haider, in Medina, and began reinforcing the garrison there. The intention was to secure the major towns before despatching expeditions to hunt down the elusive raiders. The crucial task, however, was to keep open the Hejaz railway. This was vital not only for the garrison of Medina; it was also important to be able to move troops against the rear of any British army that attempted to drive into Palestine. The Hejaz railway was the link in the strategic lateral communications that connected Syria and the Anatolian heartland on a north–south axis, and it was this railway that could thwart British advances against the Ottoman Empire from Sinai or the coast of Alexandretta.

In the Ottoman Army, the Arab revolt produced disquiet, but no mass defection. Some Turkish officers openly criticized their Arab comrades and refused to dine or pray with them, associating them all with Hussein and the Syrian nationalists. Most Arab personnel remained steadfast, at least initially. They hoped for greater concessions in the future by demonstrating loyalty, and, in any case, for soldiers, disobedience doesn't come easily. The extreme conditions of campaign were still, for them, the key determinants of loyalty or desertion in 1916. If there was demoralization amongst Arabs, it was not confined to the ranks of the Ottoman Army. British intelligence revealed that their own Arab fighters were hungry and downcast, while the Egyptian gunners sent to their aid were equally disenchanted, believing the Arab revolt was a lost cause.

The Ottoman forces of Fakhri Pasha had been built up over the autumn and in December he was able to make his first thrust against the Arab fighters at Yanbu. He intended to retake the port and then march down the coast, crushing all resistance along the way. Arab contingents could not hold the Ottoman regulars, and just when it seemed the port would fall, the arrival of a Royal Navy flotilla tipped the balance.[18] Air attacks launched from the ships and naval gunfire deterred a full-scale assault. Fakhri turned instead against Rabegh, but was again subjected to air attack by the Royal Flying Corps, and

Figure 8.1 Emir Feisal, the ill-fated royal revolutionary, king of Syria, and king of Iraq

while he could defeat Arab fighters sent against him, he could not stop their raids on his supply lines back to Medina. The crucial factor though was a new Arab attack towards Wejh, the last Ottoman-controlled port in the Hejaz.

Feisal led a core of 1,200 Agayl, supported by other clans and factions numbering 7,000, in an expedition to draw Ottoman forces away from Medina and thereby relieve pressure on Arab fighters elsewhere. Operations against Wejh would also force the Ottomans to reinforce garrisons in areas to the north against possible Arab raids. The plan was that while Feisal made a landward attack on the port, the Royal Navy would bombard and land 600 regular Arab troops there. On 23 January 1917, the amphibious assault, under Major Charles Vickery, went in, but Feisal and the Arab irregulars did not appear. The port was taken in bitter street fighting by the outnumbered attackers, and the Arab Northern Army eventually reached the port two days later. The strategic objective was achieved, but it was necessary to attribute the significance of the offensive to the *existence* of a united Arab force, rather than to its operational effectiveness.

More was being achieved by raids on the Hejaz railway in 1917. Murray was eager to ensure Fakhri was prevented from moving a significant proportion of his army northwards against his flank as he pushed into southern Palestine. Raiding parties set out consisting of small groups led by British, French, and Arab regular officers with explosives. These railway attacks served their purpose: the capacity of the Ottomans to launch offensives was hamstrung by a lack of supplies and while new Ottoman sweeps were made in the spring and summer of 1917, there was something of a stalemate: Fakhri could not take back the ports and the Arabs could not capture Medina. Ottoman repair teams did their best to keep the lines open, although more audacious raids targeted trains, bent long sections of track, and demolished bridges. At Al 'Ula (a railway junction 236 miles north of Medina, in today's Saudi Arabia), a strong raiding force, augmented by Egyptian and Indian troops and supported by aircraft, severed the Hejaz line for three days.

Nevertheless, from a strategic perspective, the raids were no more than harassment. The raiders did not threaten Ottoman control of Medina and while there might be a localized and temporary loss of control of parts of the railway, they possessed sufficient force to retake and repair any section. The Ottomans could remain in the Hejaz, continue to supply their detachments as far south as Yemen, and maintain contact with the armies in Palestine.

The strategic breakthrough was the unexpected Arab capture of Aqaba on 6 July 1917. In many ways it was a strategic plan as bold as the Dardanelles in its conception, but with fewer resources and potentially less chance of success. The 'means', the Arab Northern Army, was reduced in strength after the capture of Wejh as southern fighters, far from their homelands, began to leave the force. Fortunately, at the same time, it was being augmented with the handfuls of volunteers from Greater Syria, northern Hejaz, and the interior, including the clans of Howeitat, Shararat, Bani 'Atiya, and Rwalla. Unsurprisingly, these men looked to the north, hoping that operations against the Ottomans would be conducted there. The 'ends' were not only the 'liberation' of these lands, but the more ambitious idea of seizing all of Syria and Palestine. The driving force of this plan was the rumour that the French intended to land an expeditionary force in Beirut while the British would hold on to Palestine and southern Arabia. The details of the Sykes–Picot Agreement were now public, and it was therefore imperative to take possession of these territories before the British and French could. Nevertheless Feisal knew that he was dependent on the British and cooperation was essential to avoid destruction at the hands of the Ottomans. Auda abu Tiya, of the Howeitat, and the British advisor, Captain Thomas Edward Lawrence, therefore devised a daring plan that would put Feisal in a much stronger position.

Figure 8.2 T. E. Lawrence, the enigmatic if troubled Oxford scholar who articulated the essence of desert warfare

Aqaba was the last Red Sea port in Ottoman hands but was strongly defended from the seaward side, making any landing like the one conducted at Wejh far too costly. However, with Arab forces approaching from the rear, there was a chance the port could be taken, opening up a new supply route for the Egyptian Expeditionary Force (EEF), and, crucially, a reconstituted independent Arab Army. Lawrence collaborated with the Arabs to the extent that he misled Colonel Joyce, who commanded operations in the area, suggesting that he was coordinating an Arab mission against Ma'an (a town with an important railway junction in today's southern Jordan) to divert Ottoman attention from the mission of Colonel Newcombe against the railway junction at Al 'Ula. The contingent that left Wejh was only seventeen strong and it intended to cross the waterless desert tracts known as Al Houl, travel over 600 miles, and then recruit fighters from among local men en route with generous handouts of gold. The chances of survival were marginal, but by May 1917, they had started their recruitment campaign in the interior, eventually creating a force of 650 men. Lawrence then travelled further north into Syria on reconnaissance, raiding rail lines, and communicating with the Metawila clans. By July, Lawrence had rejoined the main party and carried out an attack on the Ottoman fort at Fuweilah. Learning of the massacre of local Arabs by the garrison, the fighters gave no quarter. An Ottoman relief operation was interdicted and the battalion concerned was defeated.[19] Other outposts were captured, often by negotiation rather than fighting. As the Arabs approached Aqaba, new volunteer fighters came forward, which tipped the relative strengths of the two sides.[20] The Ottoman commander, realizing he was cut off without hope of relief, offered to surrender the port, and Aqaba was taken on 6 July 1917.

The importance of the action at Aqaba was not the operation in itself, despite the dramatic image of a charge in to the port (after it had already surrendered), but its strategic effect. Lawrence reported the capture in person to GHQ Cairo, where General Sir Edmund Allenby had just taken command. Allenby agreed to support the Arab force at Aqaba, realizing that it could provide a new flank against the Ottoman forces dug in at Gaza in Palestine.

The strategic significance of Aqaba was not lost on the Ottomans. Knowing that the Arab clans were often enemies, they offered financial incentives to various groups to abandon the Allies. Inactivity also fuelled the old resentments, and there were disagreements between Feisal and Hussein about the leadership and direction of the revolt. The Ottomans made air attacks against the port, hoping to disrupt any build-up of logistics, which further demoralized the Arab rebels.

The solution to the possible fragmentation of the Arab force was to conduct more raiding against Ottoman lines of communication, and consequently there were more tactical successes against railways. It was clear the strength of the 'revolt' lay in a strategy of guerrilla warfare. By contrast, the momentum towards the liberation of Syria was lost entirely, making it patently clear that, for all its later legendary status and bravado, it was not the Arab revolt that mattered in this theatre, but the relentless pressure exerted by the EEF under Allenby.

Allenby had listened to Captain Lawrence's ideas for a general uprising in Syria and the potential of the Arab Northern Army. While committing some resources to support the Arabs, and reinforcing Aqaba against counterattack, Allenby also insisted on bringing the Sharifian forces under his own command.[21] Only then, he argued, could he achieve the necessary coordination of effort. Appealing to London with the possibilities that the joint EEF–Arab forces might open up, he requested two new divisions, reversing the trend that Murray had faced where formations had constantly been drawn away to other theatres.

Meanwhile, the Ottomans were also trying to augment their forces by recruiting local Arab irregulars. In particular they appealed for men from the Jordan Valley.[22] The initial attempts were a failure, most of the men being too old for active service conditions, and it was far more effective to conscript younger men into the existing regular units. The exception were the Circassians, men who had migrated from the Caucasus since the nineteenth century, who serviced a volunteer cavalry force of two squadrons that proved valuable in mobile patrolling against the Arab raiders. The settlements of Karak, a mixed Muslim and Christian community, fielded a volunteer militia. More success was achieved with the generous funding of Howeitat, Rwalla, Billi, and Bani 'Atiyya clansmen. With assurances of more money, generous rationing, regular artillery, and air support, the Ottomans prepared for the recapture of Aqaba using these Arab volunteer formations. Yet it was evident from the outset that no regular Ottoman army support was to be provided: the intention was rather to set off blood feuds and rivalries amongst the Arabs that would ensure that the sharif's cause would collapse. When the first attack was made towards Aqaba, the Howeitat and Bani clansmen stood by, while the volunteers of Karak drove off the Sharifian outposts and seized livestock and supplies for themselves.

No further progress was made and Aqaba was not threatened, but division had been sown.

The situation to the east of Gaza, where there had been stalemate, was more fluid not just because of local allegiances but also geography: the EEF was limited in the range it could traverse eastwards, even with mounted forces, by the availability of water. The Ottomans, who possessed Beersheba, had an advantage in controlling the local supplies. Lieutenant General Sir Philip Chetwode, who had command of this sector, was determined to protect the limited water he possessed, but also to keep his mounted forces in action and threaten the Ottoman left flank. In a line extending from the sea, trenches were improved on both sides, and wire entanglements were used to consolidate the lines. The constant labour to excavate drifting sand, high temperatures, and *khamsin* winds added their own trials to the entrenched infantry. On the Ottoman side, trench systems were, in places south of Beersheba, blasted into the solid rock, and instead of keeping a strong reserve which had almost led to disaster at the Second Battle of Gaza, the lines were reinforced with two divisions.

Yet the chief killer was neither heat nor combat but disease. The EEF imposed strict health regimes to combat malaria, but also had to tackle scabies, diphtheria, and sand-fly fever.[23] On the Ottoman side, the biggest causes of death and sickness were cholera, typhoid, and typhus. Malaria and dysentery were recurrent problems, but the shortages in trained medical staff, bad battlefield hygiene, a steady reduction in rations, and the lack of medical support increased the wastage of the Ottoman forces through 1917.[24] Even the Ottoman General Staff, with a sense of tragic understatement, recorded: 'the treatment of the ill and wounded was far from satisfactory'.[25] According to Djemal Pasha, the food supply problems that were contributing to the epidemics, which had begun to have an effect in the spring of 1916, reached serious proportions in 1917. Shortages were related to the demands of war, especially the prioritizing of the army, but also the Royal Navy's blockade. Where the Hejaz, in Arab hands, was supplied with food, Syria and Palestine under Ottoman control were starving.[26]

The relative weaknesses of the Ottoman forces were not the immediate concern of the British War Cabinet, or of the CIGS. Robertson informed Cairo that the request for two divisions would be denied and that, while 'every opportunity should be taken' to defeat the forces to their front, the EEF would not be required to conduct major offensive operations for the time being.[27] However, the Prime Minister, given the grave situation in

Russia and on the Western Front, could not permit inactivity, and more mounted troops were despatched. The whole mobile contingent of the EEF was then reorganized as three distinct divisions, with their supporting artillery.[28] Moreover, the two infantry divisions requested were eventually despatched. Rail and water supply lines were extended to support the EEF's lines and the troops were subjected to intensive training, incorporating lessons derived from operations on the Western Front.

The only bleak aspect of the preparations was the need to retain sufficient forces in Egypt to deal with any popular unrest. Martial law was resented, especially as the threat to Egypt appeared to have receded, but there was more concern that conscription of labourers was being imposed in an arbitrary and draconian fashion, largely due to the attitude of the local *mudir* (intermediaries). In addition, high-handed treatment by British and ANZAC personnel, fuelled by racism, embittered the population. Wartime prices, the departure of more experienced and sympathetic British officials, and the death of the pro-British Sultan Hussein of Egypt in October 1917 caused further deterioration in the mood towards the authorities.

The Ottomans had their own plans to consolidate their empire, while guarding against internal unrest. By thorough reorganization, significant redeployments, and the realization of military victory, the Committee of Union and Progress intended to recover the lost territories and drive the British out of the Middle East. The objective was to recapture Baghdad, lost in the spring of 1917, and then, when Mesopotamia was retaken, push the British back into the Sinai desert, and clear the Russians from the Caucasus. It was perhaps an indication that in Istanbul, strategy was still, to borrow the words of historian Hew Strachan, 'shaped disproportionately by political factors rather than by operational considerations'.[29]

Germany, realizing that Russia was faltering after a revolution against the tsar in February, offered a contingent of experienced troops, staff, ammunition, the latest arms, and motor transport to keep the Ottomans in the war. This Asia Corps, also known as Pasha II, consisted of three battalions with a larger-than-normal establishment of machine guns and trench mortars, and was supported by artillery, aircraft, signals units, and 400 vehicles. Inspired by the German offer, Enver argued that seven divisions should be withdrawn from the Balkans and assigned to the retaking of Baghdad. The combined Turco-German force was entitled the *Yıldırım* (Lightning) Army Group, or Army Group F, and was placed under the command of General Erich von Falkenhayn, the former German Army Chief of Staff who had enjoyed success in Romania.[30] He and the government in Istanbul directed that the Sixth Army, in Mesopotamia, would be reorganized, while a new Seventh Army was formed up. The final contingent was the Ninth Army, made up of the formations previously deployed in south-east Europe.

The plan did not meet with the approval of Djemal, or his advisor Kress von Kressenstein. They believed that the preparations being made by General Edmund Allenby of the EEF indicated that the greater threat to the Ottoman Empire was in Palestine, from the joint British and imperial divisions and their Arab confederates. Enver dismissed the complaints of his peer, who insisted that the Seventh Army would concentrate at Aleppo in Syria before making the epic march 540 miles on to Baghdad. Success in retaking Baghdad would give popular impetus to his projected advance into Persia and central Asia in order to realize his ideal of a pan-Turanian dominion. The Ottoman front commanders were stunned by the boldness of the plan at a time when the husbanding of resources across all fronts was the priority.[31] Djemal demanded that at least one division of the Seventh Army be diverted south of Damascus to act as a strategic reserve for Gaza. Privately he did not want the German-led *Yıldırım* Group in his area of responsibility, and he was supported by Mustapha Kemal, the commander of the Second Army who had been reassigned to the Seventh Army. Falkenhayn made his own reconnaissance to the Palestine front, and, partly to resolve the dispute, agreed to release the Seventh Army to enable a counter-offensive against the EEF. Yet, Djemal was also removed: his Fourth Army was to be broken up and he himself reappointed to govern Greater Syria, although he was offered the token gesture of maintaining his command of the Ottoman units in southern Arabia. Meanwhile, Pasha II was moved from Germany to take up its billets in Istanbul. The fact that German forces were arriving to bolster the Ottoman fronts should perhaps have been a cause for celebration, but Ottoman and Turkish officers resented the assumed seniority of the German officers. Kress von Kressenstein and Liman von Sanders warned that the relationship between German and Ottoman commanders might be jeopardized, but no action was taken, largely because the British were able to dictate events soon after.

The British EEF now had the 'means' to achieve its 'ends'. It had been expanded to ten infantry divisions and four mounted divisions, and possessed 116 heavy guns. This force was supported by new aircraft, particularly the Bristol Fighter plane, which gave the EEF a technological advantage on their front. The EEF was grouped into three corps: the XXI Corps of three infantry divisions, facing Gaza and its south-eastern approaches, was commanded by Lieutenant General Edward Bulfin. Opposite Beersheba, Lieutenant General Chetwode commanded the XX Corps, with three infantry divisions with an attached Yeomanry division, while Lieutenant General Harry Chauvel's Desert Mounted Corps faced Beersheba's south-eastern approaches.

Allenby insisted on visiting every part of the front, and news of his appointment produced a positive effect on the troops. His arrival seemed to herald the end of the stasis of trench warfare, with all its hardships, and there was every likelihood of an advance into the more temperate landscape of Palestine. His physical presence, his experience, his willingness to talk to soldiers, and his unwillingness to tolerate oversights amongst his officers had a positive and energizing effect across the army.[32] Chetwode, who had conducted an appreciation of the Ottoman defences, and the possible avenues of attack, presented his findings to Allenby, who approved strongly. Both had considered the possibility of an Ottoman counter-offensive and how it should be defeated. Both also believed there could be no half measures in any offensive.

The key to the Gaza defences, according to Chetwode, was the 'hinge' at Hareira and Tell el Sheria. The fortifications in front of Gaza would only be passable if there were overwhelming artillery concentrations, and even then it was thought that the Ottoman Army would merely regroup in one of several parallel lines of defences further back. The centre of the Ottoman lines, at Atawine, were protected by large waterless tracts and an open plain over which assaulting troops would have to endure withering fire. On the extreme right of the line, some 40 miles from the coast, the Ottomans had built strong points which offered mutual support: an attack on one would invite retaliatory cross-fire from neighbouring posts. However, at Beersheba, the gaps between strong points were larger and here there was a possibility of effecting a wide flanking manoeuvre. Chetwode had cautioned: 'it would be fatal . . . to make a half-bite at the cherry' which allowed the Ottomans to remain intact.[33] He advocated 'rapidity of action' and an effective deception plan that diverted Ottoman reserves to particular points. Allenby concurred, and noted that a frontal attack on Gaza would be too costly.[34] He insisted on taking personal charge of the preparations and the operations, placing his headquarters behind the front line. Correspondingly he delegated responsibility for Egypt to Sir Reginald Wingate, the former governor of Sudan, and thus concentrated all his effort on the Gaza front.[35] He also redeployed the units that had held the Suez–Sinai lines and reallocated them to Egypt and his own front.

Allenby's requests for troops and munitions from Britain could not be met in full measure. The opening of the Third Battle of Ypres in July 1917 was absorbing available reserves, and the CIGS recommended instead that three Territorial divisions should be brought from India to augment Allenby's army.[36] Two further divisions were to be spared from Salonika, although there had to be protracted negotiations with the French to get Allied approval. In artillery, Allenby was also short, and he received half to two-thirds of his requests. Despite the shortfalls, the War Cabinet insisted that, by the autumn, Allenby should 'strike the Turks as hard as possible'.[37] The Official History offered the reasoning that 'A big victory in Palestine would tend to strengthen the confidence and staying power of the people at a season when a like success in Europe was improbable.'[38]

Allenby had been dispatched by the Prime Minister to Palestine to capture Jerusalem 'as a Christmas present for the British nation'.[39] The regional context was nevertheless more pressing. There was concern that, with the situation in Russia deteriorating, it was unclear whether more Ottoman troops might be released from the Caucasus front. According to Lloyd George, Allenby was expected to defeat and then pursue the enemy 'to the limit of his resources'. Yet, Allenby's intelligence seemed to suggest that the Ottoman and German force at Aleppo, and forces drawn from Mesopotamia, could bring the available enemy army in Palestine to twenty divisions. The scale seemed unbelievable, although Allenby noted that logistical constraints meant the force against him could not exceed twelve divisions.[40] Lloyd George claimed the War Office had invented the numbers in order to prevent any offensive against Gaza and thus preserve the strength of the army for the Western Front in France.[41]

The disagreements between Lloyd George and Robertson over future strategy seemed to embroil Allenby in intrigue. Lloyd George's first choice for command in Palestine had been Jan Smuts, who had carried on successful operations in Africa, but Smuts had turned down the offer. Allenby, who did not get on with General Sir Douglas Haig, was far more willing to engage in independent operations against the Ottomans, provided there were sufficient resources. Robertson, facing genuine difficulties in allocating manpower and munitions, was also keen to try to limit the grandiose ambitions of his Prime Minister. The government had again raised the possibility of an amphibious attack on Alexandretta, despite the paucity of manpower and shipping then available.[42] He wrote to Allenby that 'it will be a good thing to give the Turk in front of you a sound beating, but that the extent to which we shall be justified in following him by an advance into Northern and Central Palestine is a matter which for the moment must be left open'.[43] Referring to the Clausewitzian problem of a culminating point, he added: 'The further we go north the more Turks we shall meet; and the greater will be the strain upon our resources.' He added a 'P.S', in which he pointed out it was not so much going forward that he opposed, but how to 'maintain ourselves after going forward and to a useful purpose'.

Allenby replied that he understood Robertson's constraints.[44] The concern that the offensive could not go ahead if the Ottomans and Germans were able to significantly reinforce the Gaza front, if entertained at all, was short-lived. He merely wanted time to train, prepare, and accumulate as much materiel of war as possible. Robertson probably would have preferred to have had a limited offensive, and was prepared to approve any attack that did not demand more resources than he could supply. Lloyd George had his own agenda: to reduce the power and direction of Robertson and Haig, in whom he had no trust at all. The Prime Minister believed that 'side shows', while denigrated by 'professionals', were as important in the Great War as they had been in the Seven Years War, and with just as significant imperial consequences.[45]

For the German and Ottoman planners, the deployment of such a critical reserve as *Yıldırım* and the associated divisions was not easily decided upon. The debate about whether to emphasize the Mesopotamia theatre, or the Palestine one, or both, continued for months, which caused fatal delays in deployments. In Palestine itself, the Ottoman Eighth Army, commanded by Kress von Kressenstein, consisted of two corps, with a total strength of 40,000 infantry and some 1,500 cavalry. The XXII Corps, made up of two infantry divisions, held the entrenched positions at Gaza, while the XX Corps, also of two infantry divisions, held the line to the east of Gaza toward Beersheba. The Seventh Army, under General Fevzi Çakmak, held the area around Beersheba. An understrength formation, the 27th Infantry Division, with a mixture of supporting regiments, was based in the town itself and this force was made up of 4,400 troops armed with a generous supply of sixty machine guns and twenty-eight field guns.[46] Von Falkenhayn, expecting the British to concentrate on Gaza, held most of *Yıldırım*'s divisions in reserve. Çakmak too kept his strength to the rear, and, north-east of Beersheba, the experienced Ottoman 3rd Cavalry Division was concentrated several miles behind the lines. Holding these forces so far back meant that, if the British advanced rapidly, they might not reach the firing line in time to make an effective counter-stroke.

The German commander's reasoning was a response to the multiple threats to the defensive line at Gaza. Von Falkenhayn could not rule out the possibility of an amphibious landing to the north, which would cut off the Ottoman forces in Gaza. The British had created elaborate measures designed to give the impression of preparations in Cyprus, with wireless traffic, and the contracting of civilian dockers. The Ottomans did not take the preparations seriously for long and guessed it was a deception.[47] The biggest coup was in fact designed by Colonel Richard Meinertzhagen, the intelligence officer of the EEF, in dropping a satchel during an encounter with Ottoman cavalry.[48] The satchel contained faked documents and maps, as well as sentimental mementoes and 'official' correspondence, purporting to outline a planned attack on Gaza. Disused ciphers were also dropped and subsequently messages were sent in the 'lost' cypher asking if the satchel could be found. The Ottomans appeared to fall for the deception, with troops moved to Gaza and additional aircraft allocated to its defence. Colonel Ali Faud, of the Ottoman XX Corps confirmed the ruse had worked by issuing orders about the capture of the British plans and his formation's own operational security.[49]

In the final days before the battle, Ottoman cavalry had discovered the movements of British and imperial forces towards Beersheba, which was in actuality to be the main point of attack. However, neither Kress von Kressenstein and the Ottoman officers nor von Falkenhayn were prepared to diminish the defending forces around Gaza, which, logically, would be the most advantageous for the British in terms of naval fire support, water, roads, and troop concentrations. Moreover, while they contemplated withdrawing the extended line at Beersheba into the Judean Hills, they were reluctant to abandon the town's valuable corn supplies to the British.

The Third Battle of Gaza (31 October–8 November 1917) opened with a sustained artillery bombardment on the defences of the town, and was then extended by Chetwode's XX Corps against Beersheba. The infantry of the 60th and 74th Divisions approached methodically from the south-west, the troops following just 30 yards behind a curtain of explosions, but they suffered some casualties from Ottoman retaliatory fire. Significant features such as Hill 1070 were captured, but progress was slow because of the resistance shown by Ottoman units.[50] It was not until the evening that all their objectives were secured.

The Desert Mounted Corps used the cover of darkness overnight on 30–31 October to ride around to the east of Beersheba. As planned, the XX Corps' attack from the south-west and west had compelled the Ottoman III Corps commander, Colonel Ismet Bey, to push his reserves against Chetwode's infantry. As a result, Chauvel's Mounted Corps outnumbered the Ottomans. The Australian 7th and 5th Light Horse regiments drove back the Third Ottoman Cavalry Division north of Beersheba, while the 6th Light Horse acted as a reserve in support of the New Zealanders' attack on the hill at Tel es Sabe. An Ottoman battalion was dug-in on this high ground, whose commanding position gave it wide fields of fire across Beersheba's eastern approaches. It took the New Zealand Mounted Rifles brigade most of the day to assault and capture this tactically vital position.[51]

Clearing this feature made it possible for the Australian 4th and 12th Light Horse regiments that evening to charge through the twilight, 800 strong, towards the town. Under machine-gun and small-arms fire, the leading squadrons dismounted when they reached the Ottoman trenches and engaged in a close-quarter battle, mostly with bayonets.[52] The squadrons behind them continued to fight their way into the town on horseback. The result was the capture of Beersheba, its seventeen water wells, and a haul of Ottoman prisoners. Despite this success, owing to a lack of potable water across the front, and the level of Ottoman resistance which had caused such severe delays, the 53rd British Infantry Division and the Desert Mounted Corps were unable to envelop the Ottoman Seventh Army as hoped. Çakmak's units conducted a successful fighting withdrawal to the north, towards the Judean Hills via the Hebron road.[53] The EEF at Beersheba had not been able to convert tactical success into a broader operational achievement on the first day's action.

The Ottomans were critical of Kress von Kressenstein's deployments, not least when he himself admitted that Ismet Bey should not have accepted a decisive engagement at Beersheba and ought to have withdrawn, and then manoeuvred against the Desert Mounted Corps. The Ottomans' complaints were such that Falkenhayn was compelled later to relieve Kress von Kressenstein of his command. Nevertheless, all the while, there was still a widespread belief that Beersheba was a feint designed to mask the main attack against Gaza. The Turco-German command also suffered from the 'chance' factor of war: a German aircraft had managed to photograph the movements of the Desert Mounted Corps as it advanced towards Beersheba, but it was intercepted and shot down, with the result that Kress von Kressenstein estimated the British forces opposite Beersheba to be no more than two mounted brigades. By contrast, there were improvements in the

EEF's intelligence and counter-intelligence capacity, which produced accurate maps, strength assessments, and dispositions of the Ottoman forces.[54] Precise details of the Ottoman divisions arriving in Palestine allowed Allenby's staff to develop an appreciation of the strength of Falkenhayn's forces facing them. Part of the success can be attributed to decryption of Ottoman signals, although Arab and Jewish human sources were also used. The Nili intelligence ring, a Jewish group, provided information on the state of the wells at Beersheba, topographical assessments, as well as accurate data on Ottoman units in the area.

The attack on Gaza itself began on 1 November with Bulfin's XXI Corps artillery hammering the Ottoman defences, before mounting an infantry assault with the advancing troops keeping just behind an exploding '*tir de barrage*'. Attacks were made on the advanced strong points, and raids made against others, but the full weight of the offensive had not yet come.[55] Bulfin's artillery barrage was the largest outside Europe to date in the war, with 15,000 rounds smashing into the ground around the settlement before the infantry reached the position, but despite the staggering volume of fire, the Ottoman garrison defended their collapsing trenches with courage and determination.[56] Believing that the British would press home the attack, more Ottoman units were rushed into the defences, while the line beyond Hebron was stripped of manpower. Allenby had succeeded in weakening the Ottoman positions in their centre, at the hinge of Hareira and Tel el Sheria, two settlements at the heart of the Ottoman defences. On the 6 November, the main attack went in against this section, and the Ottoman line was cut.[57] A gap 7 miles wide was opened up, through which his reserves now marched. Yet, once again, the Ottomans had put up a tremendous fight. At Beersheba, the XXI Corps and Desert Mounted Corps were unable to exploit their success with an envelopment as they were being pinned down from new Ottoman positions in the rear; but to the west, Gaza was now no longer tenable for them, and the ruins of the town were evacuated on 7 November.[58]

The criticism of Allenby's plan, and the failure to encircle and destroy the Ottoman Eighth Army, began almost immediately. The 'Gaza School' posited that Allenby should have attacked the western end of the Ottoman line and not at Beersheba, or the 'hinge' at Hareira and Tel el Sheria.[59] The question is counter-factual: had Allenby succeeded in trapping the Ottomans in Gaza, the criticism would not have arisen. Moreover, the subsequent pursuit was such that Jerusalem, the strategic objective, was secured soon after. The ANZAC Mounted Division seized Ramla and Lidda in

Palestine, while the Australian Mounted Division captured Latrun and the New Zealand Brigade took Jaffa.[60] Faced with having isolated pockets picked off piecemeal, Falkenhayn pulled his entire force back north of the ancient holy city of Jerusalem, while delaying the pursuit as best he could.[61] Allenby had prioritized the strategic over the operational outcome by emphasizing speed and as few casualties as possible. Although the EEF had made a direct attack on the Ottoman lines, the enveloping manoeuvre had prevented the necessity of costly frontal assaults on the strongest section of the defences. He had subsequently taken considerable risks in the pursuit into the Judean Hills, where local counter-attacks and resistance from strong points in depth against mounted forces had been overcome with some difficulty. Yet, it is ironic that Allenby should be criticized for avoiding a frontal assault that would have incurred heavy casualties, precisely the cause of condemnation of senior commanders on the Western Front.

Allenby had succeeded where Murray had failed for a variety of reasons, but the scale and firepower of the EEF was perhaps the most significant. A number of commentators, both at the time and since, have instead emphasized his strong and inspiring leadership, and much is made of his reputation for a fiery temper that earned him the epithet 'the Bull'.[62] However, while his personality certainly galvanized, he won trust and influence with all ranks and his subordinate commanders by his attention to detail, a willingness to engage with all, and his ability to keep both the Prime Minister and the CIGS content: given the relations between the War Cabinet and Field Marshal Robertson, this was a significant achievement.[63] Allenby certainly had the political backing he needed, as Lloyd George was supportive of operations in Palestine. That support meant the heavy artillery, fresh divisions, and aircraft he requested were provided. It is in this sense that the issue of 'personality' has relevance.

Unlike Murray, Allenby had the 'means' but the EEF also benefited from the experience of the Western Front to overcome formidable defences. There were a raft of developments, including the use of artillery fire to create deception, new fuses, sound-ranging, the creeping barrage to protect infantry assaults; the detailed arrangement of fire plans and coordination of all arms, including armour; new training for the infantry; and larger and more experienced staffs able to support the larger divisional organization.[64] Allenby was willing to delegate responsibility for conducting the battle at corps and divisional level, allowing his commanders to respond to unexpected delays and developments, which achieved flexibility. His 'Force Order No. 54', distributed to the EEF's corps commanders on 22 October 1917, issued a series of operational tasks for each of the three corps, and a time limit within which they were to be accomplished. The freedom to improvise and exploit situations was transmitted down through the chain of command. Allenby was also prepared to intervene when necessary. The Desert Mounted Corps had advanced slowly on Beersheba towards the end of the 30 October, not least as the light was failing and German aircraft had forced many units to disperse. Allenby stepped in and gave a direct order for the prompt capture of Beersheba on horseback, which produced the famous charge of the Australian Light Horse. Crucially, despite the demands issued down through the chain of command, Allenby had refused to be pressured by London to attack before his forces were at full strength and prepared, delaying for a full eight weeks at a critical juncture in the war.

The contrast in the Ottoman strategic situation was stark. The *Yıldırım* force was still in the process of being deployed when the British struck at Gaza, because of the disagreements about where its full weight should be applied. Enver's ambition collided not only with his colleagues, but with the Germans too: their objective was to bolster the Middle Eastern Front in order to absorb British reserves and prevent them from reinforcing the Western Front. Enver, however, still believed that a decisive victory against the British in Mesopotamia would unite the Muslim world behind him, cause the Arab revolutionaries to lose faith in the British and French, and open the way to the annexation of the Caucasus, the liberation of Central Asia, and the colonization of Persia. Despite his promise of overwhelming numbers drawn from the Balkans, the infrastructural weaknesses of the empire caused a fatal delay in their redeployment. Palestine could be served only by a single narrow-gauge railway, and it took time to transport each formation. For Mesopotamia, it was even worse. The much vaunted Berlin-to-Baghdad route was still an aspiration rather than an established fact. The line was incomplete and reserves had to detrain and march between two sections, and then slog their way beyond the railheads. Tunnels through the Taurus Mountains were not completed until September 1918.

Strategically, the demands of war were placing unprecedented burdens on the agrarian economy of the Ottoman Empire, and it was a struggle to feed the armies when so many agriculturists were serving in the ranks. The British naval blockade was adding to the pressure. Just maintaining the forces in Palestine and Syria was a challenge as destructive diseases, worsened by malnutrition, continued their lethal course. The biggest killer though was the malarial *Anopheles* mosquito. Indeed, the problem was so acute that, after the war, the British concluded that parts of Palestine might be uninhabitable.[65] The combined effects of reduced rations, disease, and defeat had a deteriorating effect on the morale of the Ottoman troops. Edward Erickson, the historian of the Ottoman Army, noted that of the 10,000 men of the 20th Infantry Division, only 4,634 arrived at the front 'fit for duty'. Of the rest, 19 per cent were sick and 24 per cent were 'missing'.[66] The *Yıldırım* force had a deficit of almost 70,000 men through casualties, sickness, and desertion.[67] Instead of the decisive blow against Allenby's tired troops, the *Yıldırım* formations were only able to prevent the collapse of the front, and to cover the withdrawal.

What had really saved the Ottoman Eighth and Seventh armies was the concept of defence in depth. Holding an area rather than a line, with a zone studded with mutually supporting strong points and entrenchments, dispersed the effect of British artillery fire, and allowed Ottoman units to dominate ground with fire, rather than physically holding it. Every fourth infantry company was stiffened with machine-gun companies.[68] When the British XX Corps attacked on 31 October, they had to suppress, assault, and overwhelm each of the defences in the zone in turn. It was this defence in depth that made envelopment almost impossible.

After Third Gaza there was continuing debate between Robertson and Lloyd George over the ends and means of the Palestine campaign, and how the campaign fitted into the overall strategy of the war. Impatient with the CIGS, the Prime Minister forced Robertson out in February 1918. Robertson had believed that the Ottoman Empire could not be induced to abandon the Central Powers while fighting on its own territory; rather, Istanbul could only be forced to give way if Germany was defeated in the West. He was concerned that the EEF would overextend its logistics, and yet face stiffer resistance as it advanced. This, in turn, would increase the demands of the EEF, especially in shipping, munitions, and manpower when the priority remained to supply and support the Western Front theatre. Reporting to the War Cabinet in December 1917, Robertson stated: 'it is for serious consideration whether the advantages to be gained by an advance [in Palestine] are worth the cost and risk involved'. He added: 'The answer depends to some extent upon whether the conquest of Palestine would put Turkey out of the war.'[69] He implored Allenby 'not be drawn into a position which you can only hold with difficulty', urging him to 'economise shipping', and to allow infantry divisions to be dispatched to France.[70] The solution was to 'Indianize' the EEF, by replacing British formations with Indian Army ones.[71]

The urgency of obtaining divisions for France was prompted by the transformation of the strategic situation for the Allies in the winter of 1917 when it became clear that the Russian war effort had completely collapsed. This would mean that, with Russia out of the war, German divisions would be released from Eastern Europe, free to participate in a huge offensive against the depleted British and French armies in early 1918.

Nevertheless, on 9 December 1917, it was Allenby's entry into Jerusalem that mattered to the Prime Minister. It was strategically important, not least for Britain's information war. Lloyd George told the House of Commons: 'The capture of Jerusalem has made a most profound impression throughout the whole civilised world...the name of every hamlet and hill occupied by the British Army...thrills with sacred memories.'[72] The magazine *Punch* portrayed the event in a cartoon, with the ghost of Richard the Lionheart gazing on the city, with the words: 'My dream comes true.' But it was a more prosaic affair on the ground in Palestine. Allenby deliberately chose to contrast his entry into the city with the histrionics practised by the kaiser back

Figure 8.3 General Allenby's entry into Jerusalem in 1917

in 1898, who had entered the city on a white charger with all the pomp of a conqueror. Where the German emperor had adorned himself with full regalia and a white cloak as if he were some ancient potentate, Allenby walked in through the Jaffa gate on foot and in simple khaki service dress. He made a point of having guards of honour and representatives of each of the Allies and imperial partners present. Proclamations were read in all the local languages, promising to honour all faiths and not to interfere in any religious practices.[73] The simple ceremony over, Allenby got back to the war.

The capture of Jerusalem marked a significant turning point in the Great War in the Middle East. The Ottoman Empire would no longer be able to contemplate offensive operations into the holy lands: Baghdad and Mecca had been lost and were now beyond reach. The fall of Jerusalem represented the last of the most significant religious sites to be taken by the British and their allies. From this point on, the Ottoman Empire could only fight a rearguard action. It was to do so against a background of diminishing resources, demoralization and ever-more frequent defeats. The distance of time obscures the sense of profound shock that the Third Battle of Gaza and the fall of Jerusalem induced among Ottoman leaders: just one year after the British set-backs at Kut al Amara and Gaza, the strategic situation had been entirely reversed.

Figure 8.4 Field Marshal Sir Henry Wilson, Robertson's successor, who was murdered by Irish terrorists after the war

Allenby's success had other strategic effects in London. Sir Henry Wilson, the War Cabinet's appointee to the new Supreme Allied War Council, who had followed Lloyd George's line of argument over Palestine, was selected to replace Robertson as CIGS. The autumn of 1917 had given the Allied leaders considerable concern. The Third Battle of Ypres had stalled amid unseasonably wet weather at the edge of the salient; the Nivelle offensive had also failed to achieve the expected results; and French front-line troops went on strike against further offensive action along the Chemin de Dames. Worse was the Italian defeat at Caporetto, which required the hasty redeployment of British and French divisions, while the loss of Russia as an ally was accompanied by considerable gloom. The Supreme War Council, first proposed in November 1917, was designed to coordinate the Allies, enable American troops to flood into Europe, and prepare for offensives in the future. The Supreme War Council's publication of Joint Note 12 in January 1918 advocated a new offensive in the Near East to knock Turkey out of the war.[74]

Nevertheless, not all the War Cabinet members agreed: the minutes reveal that discussion of the Palestine campaign in the spring and summer of 1918 still prioritized the Western Front.[75] Lloyd George tried to by-pass his military advisors and set the agenda for Palestine, but Allenby brought some operational reality into the decision-making. Jan Smuts was sent to Palestine in February 1918 to implement Joint Note 12, urging a more aggressive policy, but Allenby was constrained by logistical and climatic considerations. To his credit, Smuts accepted Allenby's observations and his report to the War Cabinet confirmed the obstacles in the path of the EEF. He echoed Allenby's insistence on a methodical advance similar to Murray's over the Sinai and Maude's in Mesopotamia. There were constraints: the imminent German offensive on the Western Front meant that the EEF had to transfer some of its infantry divisions. In return, Allenby got assurances that he would be able to design and shape the campaign in Palestine when conditions on the Western Front allowed him to resume it. Allenby thus retained political support for a delayed offensive in Palestine and he could use this pause to prepare for the operations. The advantage was that, once he got permission, he would be able to conduct operations as he saw fit. Lloyd George's demand for immediate and extended operations to capitalize on the success of Jerusalem, in the hope of 'knocking the Ottomans out of the war', had been neutralized. In Mesopotamia hasty operations were also avoided. It was not panache but a methodical, steady, and relentless policy that led to Britain's eventual success.

9
Methodical Strategy
Mesopotamia, 1917–18

There is no doubt that the decision-making process for the Mesopotamia theatre makes more sense when assessed at the strategic level. Germany's *Ostpolitik* (Eastern policy), which attempted to carve out a new empire in the Middle East, by necessity drew in the resources and manpower of India and Britain's colonies.[1] The threat posed by the declaration of jihad by the Ottoman caliph, which the government of India could not ignore, indicates that we should measure the success or failure of the operations in Mesopotamia on the basis of how far German and Ottoman strategic plans, particularly the attempts to bring down the British Empire by conquest, subversion, and revolt, were frustrated.[2] The British were checked at Kut in 1916 but unlike Gallipoli, there was no retreat or evacuation of Mesopotamia. Indeed, the fact that the British went on to capture Baghdad, and then drove into the Kurdish north, suggests a successful strategic outcome. Despite the oft-repeated criticism that the British should never have embarked on the campaign up the Tigris and Euphrates, the government felt compelled to secure its 'national interests' in the region, which equated to resources and assets like the Imperial Bank of Persia and Anglo-Persian Oil. The British government of India saw its own interests as preserving its security. We should not underestimate the importance that was attached to maintaining the loyalty of Muslim subjects of the British Empire in India and Egypt and, consequently, how sensitive Britain was to upholding prestige as a factor in its imperial power.[3]

While upholding the indefatigable image of empire could be achieved partly through bluff, it also required a willingness to demonstrate raw power when this was called for.[4] It was not just a concern to retain reserves of oil that drove the British deep into Mesopotamia, but the far older, pre-war anxieties of regional and Great Power influence that Britain needed to forestall during the war and after.[5] The 'Great Game' had dominated British thinking about the region in the late nineteenth century and concerns about German schemes drove the campaign of 1914–18. The subsequent appearance of the Bolshevik threat ensured continuity in this area of policy.[6] What emerges from these observations is that the strategy the British developed was, in part, a reaction to the plans of the Central Powers, but combined the need to maintain the idea of imperial cohesion with some more pragmatic priorities about resources and security.

Unsurprisingly there was a deliberate attempt to play down the significance of the fall of Kut in 1916. The British authorities in India were anxious that this defeat in Mesopotamia might encourage Muslim soldiers (the most significant proportion of the Indian Army) to turn against their masters. The Singapore Mutiny of 1915, where the Indian 5th Light Infantry had murdered its British officers because they feared deployment against the caliph, was an indication that this was a serious and real danger. Perhaps, because of the attempt to reduce the importance of the fall of Kut, the subsequent assumption was that this theatre was relatively unimportant. Even though there had been a feeling in 1915 that the Central Powers of Germany, Austria-Hungary, Bulgaria, and the Ottoman Empire could be defeated by 'knocking away the props', by 1916, the prevailing strategic view was that the Allies should focus only on the war's centre of gravity—and that meant defeating the German Army in Europe.

Under-resourced, overextended and in too few numbers to achieve their objectives, it seems even more remarkable that the British and Indian troops still won most of their engagements in the first two years of the war. It is probably fair to say that the 6th Poona Division did not deserve the defeat at Kut in 1916, just as they did not deserve the terrible conditions of captivity they endured after their surrender. Some 70 per cent of the captured soldiers, British and Indian, died on the 'death marches', in labouring details, and in camps under the Ottomans. Sergeant Jerry Long recalled: 'we were beginning to think that the policy of the Turkish government was to have us marched around until we were all dead'.[7] Eye witnesses recorded how the survivors were reduced to skeletons, and how many were beaten to death. The same fate befell Arabs accused of collaboration: hundreds of the inhabitants of Kut had been hanged or summarily shot, and the trees of the city were 'dangling with corpses'.[8] Tripod gallows were erected to slowly strangle their victims. The Ottomans were clearly determined to make an example, through a policy of terror, that others would not dare to follow.

The official Mesopotamia Commission Report of 1917 stated that the fall of Kut had been the result of inadequate logistics, mismanagement in India, and bad decision-making by particular individuals, especially General Nixon who was in command at Basra and had permitted Townshend to go forward to Baghdad.[9] The judgements of the commission have influenced subsequent histories considerably.[10] In essence, the commission assisted in producing the orthodox explanation that bad leadership, rather than inadequate strategy, could explain the set-backs. Townshend was singled out as an overambitious general who had taken unacceptable risks with his logistics and the capabilities of his force in his headlong rush to take Baghdad. His arrangements over the casualties were singled out as particularly shocking. The dash up the Tigris meant that there were not enough casualty evacuation facilities and some wounded men were left untreated as they were sailed down-river for fourteen days to Basra. Other wounded men were not collected from the battlefields by the relief force, with the consequence that they either died of their wounds or were murdered by Arab irregulars sent out at night.

However, the offensive strategy was seriously handicapped by the particularly trying conditions endured by soldiers and commanders in Mesopotamia—to a far greater degree than the commission acknowledged. The viceroy of India, Lord Hardinge, had gone so far as to assert that with better leadership the relieving troops would have 'easily' broken through the Ottoman defences to reach Kut.[11] But the testimony of the soldiers, British and Indian, tells a very different story of floods, waterborne diseases, extreme temperatures, and long marches over terrain without any infrastructure at all and with limited riverine transport. Moreover, the high casualties bore testimony once again to the relentless mathematics of modern war.

After the war, as many struggled to come to terms with the sheer scale and cost of the conflict they had just endured, it was understandable that there was a search for scapegoats. Few seemed able to grasp that the war had occurred at a particular junction in military evolution. Whilst the range, rate of fire, and accuracy of weapon systems had developed rapidly after 1870, the means of manoeuvre on the battlefield, in Europe and in Mesopotamia, had not changed at all. It was still necessary to cross open ground to close with the enemy on foot or on horseback, which left the assaulting forces vulnerable to very high rates of fire. Telephones, barbed wire, high explosive, and other products of the industrial revolution, when they were available, further enhanced the power of troops in defensive positions. The configuration of rivers, marshes, and deserts in Mesopotamia canalized the Indian Army into a narrow axis of advance, intensifying the effectiveness of the Ottomans' defence.

Some criticisms do still seem valid however when it comes to the conditions the soldiers endured. Townshend chose to campaign in the very hottest part of the year, which meant that troops had to toil on foot for weeks in extreme heat to reach their enemies (that said, Mesopotamia was unforgiving at *any* time of year). The relief force for Kut had to wade through spring floods, had their trenches inundated, and were frozen or soaked in the cool season. Troops burdened with rifle and pack, broiled by the sun, could die of heatstroke. Flies were a constant menace, infecting food and personnel. Officers and men, expecting something better from such an ancient land, fabled for the Garden of Eden, were disappointed to find a dun-coloured, unrelenting monotony in the landscape and a sullen, suspicious, and often resentful local population.

Perhaps the chief criticism of the leadership is that the decision to launch an offensive up the Tigris in early 1915 was not the result of a clear and coherent plan, but a policy of 'drift', or, to use a modern expression, of 'mission-creep'. Instead of sticking to the defence of the coastal oil installations, close to the source of resupply and reinforcements, and also to intelligence sources and sympathetic local Arabs, the British allowed themselves to be drawn into the interior. This was not, as some suggest, a war for oil, because the British already possessed the Anglo-Persian Oil conglomerate, but rather a situation where the strategic imperative was badly defined or, where it was designed to exert a counter-balance against the Central Powers elsewhere, it was under-resourced.[12] Moreover, the acquisition of one position seemed to necessitate the protection of its approaches and therefore the seizure of another position further up-stream. As late as 1918, some advocates of a 'forward defence' still believed that Mesopotamia would only be safe if the headwaters of the Tigris and Euphrates were in British hands, a view that implied that Baku and Azerbaijan should also be annexed. It is still a matter of debate whether Mesopotamia was of any strategic value to the outcome of the war. Major General G. F. Gorringe, the former commander of the III Corps on the Tigris between 1915 and 1916, in giving evidence to the Mesopotamia Commission, felt that the campaign was 'a side show and nobody's child'.[13] The military historian Cyril Falls later echoed Basil Liddell Hart's assessment that the campaign had not contributed to winning the war, but, on the contrary, the diversion of resources had contributed to 'its dreary and bloody prolongation'.[14]

After their victory at Kut, Ottoman forces were initially too exhausted to consider an advance any further south, despite a local superiority of numbers. There was instead a general consolidation of positions and desultory shelling of the British lines. By the time Halil's forces had started to recover, in May 1916, news of Russian General Baratov's advance into Persia forced a realignment of the Ottoman strategy. The surprise was that Baratov's Cossacks had pushed south after the victory at Erzurum and occupied Qasr-i Shirin, a settlement on the Persian–Ottoman border, just 100 miles north-east of Baghdad. The Ottoman garrison at Khanaqin, within their own borders, was in danger of being by-passed by the Russians and there seemed a possibility that the tsar's forces, rather than the British, might actually seize the primary city of Mesopotamia. Halil therefore immediately diverted a portion of his command to reinforce Khanaqin and on 1 June 1916 he checked the Russian advance. Emboldened by the success, he ordered his men to counter-attack into Persia. They subsequently seized Kermanshah on 1 July, the same day the British began their offensive on the Somme, and then Hamadan on 10 August.

The Ottoman offensive into Persia and the men required for it reduced the Ottoman defenders on the Tigris to 20,000, although some estimates place their strength at no more than 10,500.[15] While a similar number were now in central Persia, their deployment placed them in an extended salient, the flanks of which were threatened by both British and Russian armies. Yet the experience of the fall of Kut had made the British particularly cautious about exploiting the Ottoman situation. The Chief of the Imperial General Staff (CIGS), Robertson, argued that Baghdad had no value from a strategic point of view, and no advance could be contemplated. The idea that British forces would risk a repeat of Townshend's fate was to be avoided, and the War Cabinet agreed. For the time being, the forces on the Tigris remained where they were.

The Second Battle of Kut and the Capture of Baghdad

General Stanley Maude was not prepared to accept the inactivity implied by his appointment to command in Mesopotamia in August 1916. He had fought at Gallipoli, and had seen action in France, where he had been wounded, so he was fully aware of the risks and implications of the conflict.

Figure 9.1 Lieutenant General Sir Stanley Maude, who broke the Ottoman resistance in Mesopotamia in 1916–17 with the methods of industrial warfare

He was no 'Chateau General' of the popular imagination, and his approach to operations mirrored the developing experience of the Western Front. He had the measure of the character of this war, and knew that it required overwhelming firepower, close coordination of all arms, and resolution throughout every level of the army. Training and preparation were crucial. Like Allenby in Palestine, he would not be hurried, but would proceed with methodical and relentless calculation towards his objectives in his own time. In short, Maude was one of the new scientific warriors.

Maude therefore proceeded systematically, reforming the medical and supply arrangements before attempting any fresh operations. There was a modernization of staff work, intelligence collection and processing, and air operations. Reinforcements were introduced, acclimatized, and trained, and formations rehearsed. His divisions would enjoy a stronger ratio of artillery to provide crucial fire support. Basra was redeveloped as a port, greatly increasing its capacity to handle large volumes of stores and munitions. A light railway was constructed up to the front lines, while new river boats and hundreds of Ford motor lorries were brought in to speed up the supply system. Depots were opened up along the route to the front, and a precise approach was adopted to the entire question of logistics.

Operational and administrative responsibility for the campaign was placed in the hands of the War Office in London in 1916, with India relegated to the role of supplying authority.[16] On 1 October 1916, General Charles Carmichael Monro, the Commander-in-Chief of the Army in India, assumed overall direction of the Mesopotamian theatre, integrating it into the strategy of the Middle East and the rest of the war effort against the Central Powers, which offered the opportunity for truly coordinated action against the Ottoman Empire. Monro was served by an experienced staff.[17] While the CIGS continued to insist that the theatre commanders make do with what they had, the Russian General Staff agreed in principle there should be coordination between the Army of the Caucasus and the British forces in the Middle East.[18]

By contrast, General Halil, now in command on the Mesopotamia front, was in a less favourable position by the end of 1916. The triumvirate of Djemal, Talaat, and Enver in Istanbul demanded that the Ottoman Sixth Army be divided into two, such that a contingent remained on the Tigris while the rest were sent against Hamadan, 250 miles from Baghdad, and deep inside Persia. This decision was critical from a strategic perspective. It meant that Halil could not control forces so widely dispersed, and this weakened the Tigris front significantly. As his army was depleted, the 38th Division was broken up and the remaining troops redistributed between the four remaining divisional formations. He also withdrew his most extended lines by 10 miles and consolidated in stronger positions, although the front was still 20 miles wide. His subordinate on the Tigris defensive line, Kazim Karabekir Bey, observing the British preparations, alerted Halil to the possibility of a renewed offensive, and called for reinforcements, but none were provided and the entire Ottoman force numbered less than 25,000.

By October 1916, Maude had under his command 150,000 troops, consisting of the original III Indian 'Tigris' Corps and the 13th (Western) Division of the British Army, but it took weeks to ensure that medical and transport arrangements were in place and permission had been given in London for the anticipated offensive. Maude got authorization for a limited, tactical operation in November 1916 against the Ottomans at Shatt al Hai, but, believing there could be no half measures, he informed London and his own subordinates that he was ready just three days before making a much larger offensive.

On the night of 13–14 December, the Ottoman sentries peered into the gloom towards the British lines during a heavy downpour, unaware of the

Leviathan about to be unleashed upon them. The first indications were a bright and intense flickering of light on the horizon, illuminating the sheets of rain around them. Within seconds, the air was filled with the dull thuds of the distant guns and then a blizzard of ear-splitting explosions in their midst. The British offensive had been anticipated, but the shock of the weight of fire was still profound. The scene would have very much resembled the memorable opening to *Desert Victory*, the classic Second World War film about El Alamein. Accompanied by the drum beat of the barrage, British and Indian troops emerged from their trenches and advanced with the bayonet across No Man's Land. And, just as at El Alamein, the opening bombardment, intense though it was, could not guarantee success. Some infantry units were pinned down by Ottoman machine-gun fire, others took heavy losses as they tried to get forward. In some locations, more fortunate bands penetrated the lines and started to consolidate. But this was a battle that would not be decided in one day. As had been found on the Western Front, engagements lasted days, weeks, and even months.

Maude had opened his assault with two corps advancing in parallel up both banks of the Tigris. Heavy rain had impeded progress but it was Maude's concern to minimize casualties and proceed methodically from one objective to the next that slowed the force. After two months of relentless pressure, Maude had secured the entire western bank below Kut including the strong points at Khadairi Bend on 19 January 1917, the Hai River position on 4 February, and the Dahra Bend, further up the river, some twelve days later.

On 23 February, Maude transferred part of his force across the Shumran Bend on a pontoon bridge and assaulted the right of the Ottoman line. Simultaneously, his corps attacked on the left, opposite the Ottomans' Sanniyat position. The manoeuvre, which enabled a force to cross the Tigris some 5 miles up-river from Kut, caught the Ottomans off-balance. The bridgehead was expanded quickly and the Ottomans were in danger of complete encirclement. Karabekir Bey had no option but to fall back, but he did so by fighting from prepared positions along the line of withdrawal. On 24 February he was clear of Kut, and, despite the potential for chaos in retreat, he maintained control. His massed machine-gun fire halted the attempts by British cavalry to outflank his force. The withdrawal was all the more remarkable when one considers that not only was he outnumbered three to one by the British, but his men were constantly harassed by opportunist raids by Arab irregulars. One British estimate was that barely 6,200

Ottoman troops escaped, which, even at conservative estimates, would imply that in resisting along the original defence line over two months they had taken losses of over 50 per cent.

The Ottoman withdrawal may have been conducted successfully, but it could not conceal the scale of the defeat, nor could it prevent the rout that followed. Captain W. Nunn of the Royal Navy led the pursuit with a flotilla of five British gunboats, seizing Kut without resistance and then steaming up-river. The Ottoman rearguard caught Nunn's little fleet in an intense cross-fire at point-blank range from the banks, but his crews pressed on regardless, ran the gauntlet and then steamed parallel to the main body of retreating Ottoman troops. His gunboats rained havoc on Halil's diminishing force. For miles, there were carcasses of animals, destroyed guns, blasted wagons, and corpses. The survivors surrendered although many of them, particularly the wounded, were murdered by vengeful Arabs. Nunn continued on up-river, overtaking the Ottoman steamers and lighters as they came across them. In the brief river battle, the Ottomans were again defeated and surrendered in order to protect the wounded. A total of 7,500 prisoners were taken. Maude had control of the river, complete air supremacy, and had broken all resistance on the Tigris.[19] Crucially, as far as the British were concerned, Kut was avenged and a union flag fluttered once more over it.

Once Maude had advanced 60 miles north of Kut, he ordered a pause in the offensive. He was not prepared to overstretch his vital lines of communication and thus repeat the error of 1915–16. He therefore consolidated at Aziziyeh, 40 miles south-east of Baghdad. Meanwhile, Halil, confronted by the British advance, was compelled to recall troops from western Persia which had been facing the Russians. The grandiose scheme to acquire Persia had to be abandoned entirely as Halil sought to shore up his defences on the Tigris.

The War Office and War Cabinet were divided about the next move. Robertson was adamant that there should be no further advance. While insisting the War Cabinet left the direction of the war to the military, he reasoned that if Baghdad was taken, how would it be held and to what end?[20] If the Ottomans reinforced the front, there was a risk that the British would merely repeat the siege of Kut but in the more exposed and extended location of Baghdad. He would permit raiding by cavalry, the extension of 'influence' into the province of Baghdad, but he cautioned against any situation that would compel a withdrawal of British forces because of the 'objectionable political effect' that might ensue.[21]

Monro in India took a diametrically different view. He urged Maude to press on and seize Baghdad while the Ottomans were broken on the Tigris. He argued that taking Baghdad would prevent the Ottomans from reforming at this nodal point and that it would provide an important prestige victory for the British amongst their colonial Muslim subjects.[22] Maude concurred with Monro, but the deciding factor was the prospect that the Russians might extend their own area of control from the Caucasus to Mosul and northern Mesopotamia.[23] A renewed Russian offensive toward Baghdad also could not be ruled out, particularly with Ottoman troops so significantly reduced. Robertson relented. He permitted an advance if Maude judged it prudent, with all his previous caveats.[24]

Maude therefore resumed his offensive on 5 March 1917 and it took just three days to reach the Diyala River where Halil had prepared defences on the confluence with the Tigris. On the 9 March, the initial British probing attacks were repulsed and Maude opted to outflank the river positions and threaten Baghdad directly. The city was 226 miles away but Halil could not protect it if Maude's force moved around his defences. The British manoeuvre forced Halil to readjust his line, and shift the bulk of his force to face the new threat and leave the defences in the hands of a single regiment. Maude's army then switched axis again, assaulted the Diyala River defences frontally and overwhelmed them. The outcome persuaded Halil to abandon Baghdad altogether and he prepared to withdraw his whole force. However, he had not anticipated the suddenness of Maude's next move, which was to chase the Ottoman troops closely. There were frantic efforts by the Germans and Ottomans to destroy anything of military value to the British, including radio transmitter towers and bridges, but the departure of Halil's force was chaotic and on the 11 March Maude was able to secure Baghdad without resistance. Some 9,000 Ottoman troops were captured in the confusion, while local residents, anticipating destruction, set about looting the city. Order had completely collapsed by the time the first British detachments arrived, but a few rounds fired over the heads of the mob were enough to restore some semblance of control.[25]

Maude issued a proclamation a week later, claiming that the British were not conquerors or occupiers but liberators. The text had been carefully crafted by Sir Mark Sykes, but the population of Baghdad were suspicious of British intentions and doubted their sincerity about 'independence'. Maude was, in essence, the military governor of the entire Tigris plain down to Baghdad and this gave him the authority, prompted by London, to prevent Sir Percy Cox, the political officer with the Indian Army, announcing that the government of India would now administer the occupied provinces. The bureaucratic contestation was only resolved by the creation of the Mesopotamian Administration Committee in London under Lord Curzon: the verdict was that Britain would govern the south and Baghdad would be placed in Arab hands.[26] Nevertheless, for the time being, Mesopotamia was 'Occupied Enemy Territory' and subject to martial law.

The 'liberation' therefore remained theoretical, not so much for ideological motives, as practical wartime necessity. Being so far up the Tigris with such a large force, the logistical strain on the available river transport was considerable. Moreover, the British were eager to extend control across the Mesopotamian clans to prevent a costly breakdown of order. As a result, military detachments accompanied by political officers radiated across the region, demanding supplies and local manpower, mainly for logistical work. Only the Shiite holy shrine towns of Najaf and Karbala were exempted from the comprehensive policy of extraction and flag marches, largely for reasons of political and religious sensitivity: these settlements were administered through local sheikhs, although they still came under British supervision. A new Directorate of Local Resources, and supply and transport officers, organized the labour flows.[27] Nevertheless, the process was something alien to many local tribes,

Figure 9.2 Baghdad: Indian Army camel transport on the move

who had little experience of centralized governance: if conditions were not maintained to their liking, resentment would surely stir.[28]

The ambiguity about the future of Baghdad could not however diminish the significance of the British military victory. By March 1917, the Ottomans had lost control of central Mesopotamia, Erzurum, Sinai, Mecca, and southern Palestine. In every theatre they were on the defensive. Moreover, the Ottoman Empire had passed the peak of its available manpower reserves, its food supply was under intense pressure, and it faced internal opposition from Arabs, Armenians, and other minorities. In other words, the strategic situation was dire and while continued resistance was possible, the opportunities for acquiring any strategic advantage were diminishing rapidly. In many respects, the defence of the Ottoman Empire was becoming more dependent on Germany and the fortunes of that nation, or the Central Powers that lay astride the vital supply route to Berlin. It was they who would determine the immediate future.

Maude's primary concern was to prevent the remainder of Halil's force north of Baghdad joining with the 15,000-strong corps led by Ali Ihsan Bey, a formation that was withdrawing from Persia under Russian pressure. The solution was to seize the rail junction at Samarrah, some 80 miles to the north. Marching out with 45,000 men, Maude planned four short attacks and his first objective was to prevent any attempt to flood the Euphrates plain and thus render further British operations impossible; the secondary objective was to conduct operations to secure the western approaches to Baghdad. The first thrust to the north was resisted strongly but the British drove the Ottomans back 22 miles to the Adhaim River. To the west of Baghdad, Maude took Fallujah on 19 March.

Nevertheless, an attempt to encircle Ihsan Bey on the Adhaim River was checked, and the Ottoman force looked as if it was about to be joined by 5,000 men under Halil's command. Maude attacked again at Dogameh, and, despite severe losses, the two Ottoman forces were prised apart. The Ottomans tried to consolidate their positions along the banks of the Adhaim, but the British drove them out of their positions on 18 April, relieving a cavalry contingent that had become pinned down at Shiala, near the confluence of the Adhaim and Tigris, at the same time.

Halil thus withdrew to a much stronger series of prepared defences at Istabulat, which lay between the Tigris and the Ali Jali Canal. Maude made a series of attacks along the defensive lines on 21 April, and some positions changed hands several times in close-quarter fighting. The Ottomans were eventually pushed out, and occupied a low ridge some 6 miles from the Samarrah railway junction. Maude kept up the pressure and when the Ottomans realized that their position could no longer be held, Maude's force secured the Samarrah junction. His offensive had been a complete success. Nevertheless, the operations had cost 18,000 casualties and a considerable number had succumbed to sickness. The toll necessitated another lull in the campaign, and once again there was pressure from Robertson to scale down the operations in Mesopotamia, not least as the situation in the European theatre was changing again.

Once more, Maude was confronted by the classic strategic dilemma of reaching a culminating point. Although he had begun the offensive in December 1916 with an overwhelming numerical advantage, the steady attrition of casualties through combat and sickness, the need to despatch columns to carry out pacification in central Mesopotamia, the requirement to garrison Baghdad and protect its western approaches, and the security needs of the long line of communications back to the coast had reduced the available forces in northern Mesopotamia to something approaching parity with the Ottomans. And the balance was tipping further out of his favour.

The German and Ottoman strategic dilemma in late 1917 was how to make best use of the new reserves that had been released from Europe and the Caucasus following the collapse of the Russian war effort. The divisions from south-east Europe gave Istanbul a strategic reserve, the *Yıldırım* Army Group, and this could be committed either to the recovery of Baghdad, which was the preference of Enver and his 'Turanian' supporters, or to bolster the Palestine front against an expected British offensive, which was the option supported by Djemal and the pan-Islamists. The German contribution was the Pasha II brigade, seasoned, well-equipped, and armed with a generous scale of machine guns and field artillery. This force was designed to bolster an Ottoman offensive to retake Baghdad, although Falkenhayn was conscious that any attack in that direction would first have to ensure the security of Jerusalem and Palestine, lest the Allies break through and threaten the Turco-German lines of communications in Syria.

Djemal, in common with many other Ottoman officers, was unwilling to accept German leadership in Palestine, and he refused to serve in a subordinate capacity to the Germans: the kaiser's officers were viewed as allies and advisors rather than superiors. Nevertheless, Falkenhayn succeeded in persuading Enver that Djemal should be made a nominal commander in Syria while the direction of operations in the Near East should be in German hands. In return, the Germans agreed to support the advance towards Baghdad. Enver still cherished the notion that the Caucasus, Russian Turkestan, Afghanistan, and Persia could be rendered subordinate to a Turkic empire or provide the necessary security buffers for a post-war settlement. The rest of the Arabian Peninsula was less significant, but could still be retained as colonial possessions. Pan-Turanianism lent the Ottoman enterprise cultural legitimacy in being the seat of Islam, but ultimately the people of the Middle East were regarded as subjects, not partners. Nevertheless, just as the leaders agreed on where the strategic weight of the Ottoman Empire would be committed, namely in Mesopotamia against Maude, Allenby commenced his operations in Palestine and the Ottoman *Yıldırım* Group had to be diverted. The strategic situation therefore altered again, and further operational successes for the British began to alter the balance irrevocably in their favour.

The first changes occurred along the Euphrates. In July 1917, an earlier attempt to defeat the Ottoman divisional garrison at Ramadi, 60 miles west of Baghdad, had ended in failure. In September, another attempt was made with a British force under the command of General H. T. Brooking. In the first phase, Brooking constructed a bridge and road on the north bank of the Euphrates, hoping to persuade the Ottomans that the British intended an assault from this direction. In fact, Brooking sent the 6th Cavalry Brigade in a wide arc to the south, and they launched their attack in conjunction with the 15th Indian Division on 28 September. The combined effects of surprise, the envelopment, and the rapid encirclement of the Ottomans by armoured car units, threw the defenders utterly off balance. An attempt to escape was cut off by the British cavalry and the remaining Ottoman forces were forced to surrender the following morning.

When operations were resumed in March 1918, the 15th Indian Division took Hit without resistance, as the Ottoman garrison gave way in its path. Brooking was determined to secure a decisive victory and he made use of 300 lorries to add mobility to his infantry for the next phase against Ramadi. He also ensured all the artillery had a surplus of horses, so that momentum could be maintained. Once combined with his 11th Cavalry Brigade and the armoured car squadrons of the 8th Light Motor Battery, Brooking could sweep around the Ottomans and establish cut-off groups that could be dug in along the anticipated line of withdrawal. As expected, the Ottomans offered some resistance to the conventional assault and then started to withdraw from Ramadi. However, they soon came under fire from the blocking groups and their cohesion collapsed. In a relatively short time, the entire Ottoman force of 5,000 men had surrendered. The victory was so complete that, in following up, the British mobile force overwhelmed the Ottoman supply base some 28 miles in their rear, and captured its personnel, including the astonished German advisors there.

The final phase of the Mesopotamia campaign, commanded by Maude's successor Sir William Marshall, was the result of the British government's direction that Mosul, and its valuable oil resources, should be in British hands at the end of the war. This was to be a vital diplomatic advantage for London in any peace negotiations, for it was anticipated that with Bulgaria now out of the war and an Ottoman peace overture imminent, the conflict would soon be at an end. However, Marshall's Tigris force had been denuded of some of its transport by the need to convey 'Dunsterforce', a detached contingent, to Baku, where it too could provide security against a final Ottoman attempt to control the oil resources of the Caucasus and Trans-Caspian region.[29] Resources also had to be diverted to Palestine for Allenby's final offensive, so the final push was made by a much diminished force.

Screening Mosul was the *Dicle Grubu* (Tigris Group), a remnant of the Ottoman Sixth Army, led by Ismail Hakki Bey which, despite nominally comprising two corps, had in fact been reduced by sickness and fighting to just five line regiments and a specialist rifle regiment. Confronted by Marshall's much stronger command of two divisions and two cavalry brigades, Hakki Bey withdrew a further 60 miles up-river. Nevertheless, the British 11th Cavalry Brigade caught and pinned the Ottomans while the 17th Infantry Division came up in support. Through numerous delays, the British cavalry came under sustained shelling and took the decision to mount their own attack on the high ground where the Ottoman guns were positioned. Arriving on horseback, the 13th Hussars dismounted and made an assault on the hill, capturing all the Ottoman guns. The action, subsequently known as the Battle of Sharqat, when combined with news that negotiations to end the war were already underway, convinced Hakki Bey to order a surrender. So, on the 30 October 1918, resistance came to an end. The British pressed on to Mosul, securing the city just after the announcement of the armistice.

Friction and Fog: Impact on Strategy

F. J. Moberly's official history of the campaign in Mesopotamia expressly avoided trying to apportion blame for errors during the first phase of the operations in 1914–16 and focused on the sequence of events as they unfolded.[30] Yet the operational orders of the campaign still allow us to uncover the differences between plans and policies in London and India, and how difficult it was to turn these into reality on the ground. Official records revealed the tendency of the British government in India to see the future political potential of Mesopotamia or the question of Muslim allegiance as more important than more immediate military considerations. Yet, when the approaches to Basra had been secured, it was in fact the British government in London, concerned by set-backs in Europe, which urged a deeper penetration of the country and the seizure of Baghdad. These aspirations faltered when the troops reached the limits of what could be achieved.

Analyses of the Mesopotamia campaign that are critical of the British leaders, their strategy, and the logistical arrangements, but which do not address the strategic perspective, present some problems.[31] First, such critiques rarely acknowledge the effects of strategic interaction or offer anything on the Ottoman side: the Ottomans are portrayed only as *reactive*. Yet, it was on the initiative of Khalil Pasha and his German advisor, von der Goltz, that the Ottomans immediately counter-attacked after Ctesiphon and besieged Kut successfully. It was the same Ottoman Army that held the British in Mesopotamia for four years, and generated an offensive into Persia which opened a new flank on the British in the region. Moreover, we should acknowledge that the British came within an ace of taking Baghdad in 1915: it was the arrival of Ottoman reinforcements from Anatolia and the Caucasus, especially the 51st Division, which forced the precipitate withdrawal.

It was not just the British who had failures in leadership and logistics. These were also a problem for the Ottoman Sixth Army. Rations and water were always limited. Medical facilities were inadequate. There were no metalled roads outside of urban areas, which hampered their transport arrangements. There was an acute shortage of riverine vessels which would have been the most efficient means of manoeuvre, and some reinforcements had to travel to Baghdad on improvised rafts. In essence, Mesopotamia was a backwater for the Ottoman Empire and its resources were allocated accordingly. Baghdad served as a propaganda icon, but its strategic value was otherwise limited. The reality was that Mesopotamia provided some strategic depth for the Anatolian heartland, and its manpower and resources were exploited ruthlessly by the regime in Istanbul for their war effort.

For the British, Mesopotamia lay at the junction of responsibilities of the governments in Britain and in India. London's indifference to the Persian Gulf before 1914 meant that responsibility for the region fell to the under-resourced

Indian authorities. The Indian Army suffered critical shortages in transport and medical provision, and the logistical arrangements remained inefficient until 1916. Having prepared before the war for the deployment of just three brigades, in 1914 the Indian authorities had to find three times that number and the demand continued to rise steeply throughout the conflict. Despite a mobilization plan, the expansion and the shortage of officers, particularly staff officers, meant that those who were given a staff appointment had little experience of their roles and had not served together. Intelligence personnel were too few in number to manage the workload required in Mesopotamia. Indian Army units lacked heavy artillery, and, whilst many units were adequate for frontier skirmishes and garrison duty, they lacked the training for sustained operations against a conventional army.

Remarkably, these shortcomings in the pre-war army were overcome from late 1916 onwards. There were increases in the manpower available, improvements in logistics and river transport, more artillery, improved staff work, increased intelligence collection, the development of combined arms operations (including integration of the new air arm), and the import of ideas from the Western Front.[32] General Stanley Maude commanded a very different army in 1917 to that available to Nixon and Townshend in 1915. More proficient in combat, more efficient in supply, and arguably more realistic about its capabilities and limits, the British and Indian forces in Mesopotamia, just one year after Kut, were far more effective.[33]

The fighting in the Mesopotamia campaign was just as 'modern' as that taking place on the Western Front in Europe and subject to many of the same problems. The inadequate artillery bombardments of the Kut relief force in 1916 resulted in the same difficulties that were encountered on the Somme that same year. Thick cloying mud was just as much an obstacle at the Hanna as it was at Ypres or Neuve Chapelle, leaving troops immobile and exposed to the high rates of fire of machine guns and field artillery. On 6 April 1916, in the attempt to relieve Kut, the 7th Meerut Division attacked in daylight on a narrow front hemmed in by marshes. They lost 1,200 men in twenty minutes. In contrast, when in 1917 Maude set out to retake Kut, his men dug saps and fought for each enemy trench exactly as the Allies did in Europe. Artillery was timed to drop a curtain of fire just in front of the advancing Indian infantry and air observation was vital for intelligence and surveillance. When mobile warfare returned in 1918, this too had its parallels in Europe and Mesopotamia. At Khan Baghdadi in March 1918, a mobile blocking force was deployed in the rear of the Ottoman Army by a fleet of

300 motor lorries, armoured cars, and a cavalry brigade: their success mirrored the achievements of similar motorized and cavalry forces on the Western Front later that year. In every respect, then, the fighting in Mesopotamia was as modern as any other.

On the other hand, this was a campaign that illustrated some continuities of warfare. Clausewitz had illustrated the problem of an attacking force that is compelled to advance far from its logistical bases: the gradual attrition of disease, casualties, and climate add to the difficulties of resupply until the attacking army reaches an often imperceptible culminating point. This is the moment at which the advantages switch decisively to the defending army. The concept certainly applied to Townshend's advance on Baghdad in the autumn of 1915. It was Maude's determination to avoid a repeat of this problem that led to his more methodical approach in 1917. However, it is always a temptation to focus on manoeuvre as the solution to successful campaigning when simply being able to concentrate and to resupply the right number of troops *en masse* is often just as important to the outcome. Townshend had 12,000 men for his task; Maude and his successors could command 150,000 for theirs. The Mesopotamia campaign shows that our frequent obsession with the new aspects of 'modern warfare' can obscure significant continuities. At the operational level, morale, mass, and appropriate tactics and training were just as important as new technology and firepower.

Events up to and including the siege of Kut have enjoyed the lion's share of scholars' attention, and significantly less work has been done on the operations afterwards. After Kut, the British strategy was to abandon all idea of taking Baghdad so as to focus resources elsewhere, and the posture remained defensive. It was not until late 1916 that General Stanley Maude, ably assisted by his logistician Sir George MacMunn, began a painstaking process of 'bite and hold' into the Ottoman trenches on the Tigris. He struck at the defences he had weakened and defeated the Ottomans at Kut. Once again success produced disagreements about the strategy to be adopted. Although the means were available and the ways successful, there was a difference of opinion over the 'ends'. Yet strategy is to some extent the consequence of new opportunities as much as constraints. Robertson lost the argument because he was still focused on the constraints and risks of the previous year. Maude was therefore given the approval he sought to press on while the Ottomans were still militarily weakened.

Before he could secure Baghdad, he had to mop up Ottoman detachments and contend with Arab attacks on his lines of communications.

Nevertheless, on 11 March 1917, he took Baghdad, raising Allied prestige after a year of set-backs. More importantly, he was able to break the back of the Ottoman counter-attacks that followed. The advance north was again limited by strategic priorities in Europe, but the collapse of Russian democracy in the autumn left the Caucasus and northern Persia open to Ottoman offensives. In late 1917, the strategic situation in Mesopotamia was far from optimistic, and despite further successes up the Tigris, a new threat emerged with a final Ottoman offensive across the Caucasus in 1918.

At the end of the war, British forces were authorized to secure Mosul, subsequently bringing this province into the new Iraq. Marshall was directed to take the town even after the Ottomans had begun their armistice negotiations. The official reason given was to disarm the Ottoman units there, but the real motive was to acquire as much of northern Mesopotamia as possible to adjust the Sykes–Picot Agreement and deprive both France and Russia of any access to Mesopotamia. In other words, new strategic 'ends' evolved with the success achieved at the operational level.

One factor that seems to attract relatively less emphasis is the posture of the Iraqi population. The Ottomans found that the majority of Arabs in Mesopotamia were quiescent, although they did have significant problems with certain groups. In the defence of Baghdad in 1917, for example, Halil Pasha had to spend much of his time quelling anti-Ottoman insurgents. Yet the Ottomans also employed a large number of Arab irregulars at the beginning of the campaign. At the Battle of Shaiba, there were 24,000 Arabs either in the line of battle or operating on the flanks and rear of the British. Maude had to tackle a number of villages from which insurgents were operating, and faced particular problems near Najaf when German and Ottoman funds had been distributed to encourage attacks on the British line of communication.

For their part, the British also employed local forces. The southern tribesmen and the Kuwaitis provided a great deal of useful intelligence on the Ottomans, including forewarning of the attack on Basra in 1914. When the tide of the campaign began to turn, more Arabs threw in their lot with Britain, but it was not always entirely clear what their motives were. Significantly, the Ottomans were unable to operate in Najaf and Karbala because of equally potent anti-Ottoman unrest there. After the Battle of Shaiba, a retreating Ottoman column was ambushed and massacred by Muntafiq tribesmen. When Halil's forces withdrew from Kut and were bombarded by the Royal Navy's flotilla, it was the Arabs who moved in to destroy the remnants of the army.

Despite the existence of intelligence officers and consular officials across the Gulf region, intelligence on the hinterland of Mesopotamia was limited. The predictions of Major General Sir Percy Cox, the Resident and chief political officer of southern Persia who had first been despatched to the area in 1904, to the effect that the Arabs would welcome British intervention against the Ottomans, proved only partially correct.[34] Many Arabs simply remained neutral, and a few thousand actively assisted the Ottomans. As a result, it proved more difficult to get information on the strength of Ottoman forces facing the British Indian advance on Baghdad than expected and the Allies were dependent on air reconnaissance to ascertain reliably the location of Ottoman formations.

It is a pity that all too often the history of the campaign in Mesopotamia is concluded in 1918 with the evacuation of British forces from the Caucasus, the seizure of Mosul, and the capitulation of the Ottoman Sixth Army at the armistice. From an Iraqi viewpoint, this was clearly not the end. Until 1920, the peoples of the Ottoman provinces of Basra, Baghdad, and Kurdish Mosul had believed they would gain their independence. Maude's proclamation of Baghdad in 1917 certainly indicated that Ottoman rule would not be reimposed. However, when it was announced that Britain would administer the new state of Iraq under a League of Nations Mandate, there was widespread rioting.[35] The fighting quickly got out of hand, and Indian reinforcements had to be deployed.[36] Many Iraqis were furious with the British suppression of the revolt and they had a sense that the promises of 1917 had not been fulfilled. Significantly, the wellspring of Iraqi nationalist resistance was the officer corps of the old Ottoman Army, suggesting a continuity not often acknowledged.

The campaign was marked by erroneous judgements as commanders on both sides struggled to understand the constantly changing operational and strategic environment. The Ottoman decision to detach a portion of the Sixth Army (which was dug in on the Tigris during 1916) to advance into Persia did little good and never managed to threaten the British control of the oilfields in the south. Its departure weakened the Tigris front just as General Maude began to push northwards at Sannaiyat, and Ottoman attempts to reunite with the main body in March 1917 prompted Maude to accelerate his attacks—defeating Halil Pasha before the junction between the two Ottoman forces could be effected. The Ottomans were just as prone as the British to making strategic errors. These included the pursuit of multiple objectives, inadequate resourcing of the priorities, and squandering the initiative.

Criticisms of military leadership seem more valid when the 'lessons' of previous operations are not learned. Armies require an ethos of 'operational learning', and some candour in appreciating what went wrong. Despite the orthodox criticism, the evidence in fact suggests that the British Indian Army did indeed recognize its structural and organizational weaknesses and, by and large, set them right whilst in direct conflict with the enemy. After the war a group of officers from the Indian Army Staff College at Quetta chose to produce a report following a tour of Iraq entitled the *Critical Study* (1925).[37] Their focus was the conduct of operations in 1915–17 and whilst perhaps failing to fully live up to its title, the work nevertheless analysed the tactical procedures that had been employed in this theatre. There was consequently considerable debate in India about the need to 'modernize' the Indian Army while, at the same time, being able to fulfil the demands of internal security and frontier policing. Central to this debate was the role of cavalry and light infantry, but the discussion about appropriate force structures, training, and tactics continued throughout the 1930s and 1940s.[38] There was a tendency to regard colonial warfare as an anachronism compared with the modern, industrial wars of Europe.[39] Colonial campaigners had tended to put more emphasis on traditional concepts of boldness and rapid offensive action, and frequently made do with ad hoc arrangements with their logistics. Townshend's drive up the Tigris fits this ethos exactly and this perhaps explains the key difference between his approach and Maude's in that transformative period in Mesopotamia between 1916 and 1917.

The context of the campaign in Mesopotamia is important, and the actions of the Russians made a significant difference to the changes that took place between 1915 and 1918. Baratov's thrust into Persia after their victory at Erzurum drew the Ottomans eastwards. Equally, the Russian Revolution had a dramatic effect. When Russian resistance collapsed in 1918, the idea of the Germans and Ottomans marching virtually unopposed across central Asia towards India looked entirely feasible. There was a chance that, encouraged by this apparent victory, the peoples of Persia, Afghanistan, and India might begin to doubt the ability of the British to win the war, and there were already signs of severe unrest in Persia. If internal security was challenged across the British Empire, then there would obviously be problems in sustaining further operations.

The Allied military victory in Mesopotamia in 1918 marked the culmination of four years of gruelling effort. Fighting up the Tigris and Euphrates had cost the lives of 92,000 British and imperial personnel, and inflicted casualties of a similar magnitude on the Ottoman forces. It was conducted under the most testing of conditions, where the climate and local diseases were twice as likely to take a life as combat.[40] Like all military operations there were set-backs as well as successes; confusion and uncertainty; vast logistical challenges; and, most memorable of all, on both sides, inspiring episodes of great courage, endurance, and dedication. From a strategic perspective, the campaign was supposed to serve a number of policies and imperial interests. The final shifting weight against the Ottoman Empire first became evident in Mesopotamia: it was soon to manifest itself in the other theatres of the Middle East.

10

The Defeat of the Ottoman Empire, 1918

Despite the set-backs of 1917 in Palestine and Mesopotamia, Enver had not lost his enthusiasm for bolstering the Bulgarian front and pursuing the disintegrating Russian forces in the Caucasus. The Treaty of Brest-Litovsk (3 March 1918), between the Central Powers and the new Bolshevik authorities in Russia, meant the return of the Caucasian provinces lost in 1878. Enver believed that with this springboard he could recover the entire Caucasus, without opposition, and drive on to the Caspian and deep into Persia. If the Ottoman Empire was to lose Arabia and Mesopotamia, then it could be reconstituted as a purely Turkic one astride the Anatolian and Caucasus mountains.[1]

On the Allied side, news that the people of Russia had overthrown Tsar Nicholas II in February 1917 and established a new Provisional Government had initially raised hopes of a revived war effort in the east. However, within days it was clear the situation on the ground was chaotic. Soldiers started to elect their own officers or 'executive committees', and improving conditions were prioritized over operational requirements. Workers' and soldiers' councils, the Soviets, began frantic communication across all fronts. In the Caucasus, rear units were more affected than those on the front line, and when orders actually got through, Russian units tended to continue to fight.[2] However, in April, changes in commanders started to interfere with operational planning and by the summer the army had begun to fall apart. Unlike the main Eastern European theatre, the process in the Caucasus was slow and piecemeal.[3] Some units moved out of the occupied territories but most remained. General Yudenich, the Chief-of-Staff of the Russian Army in the Caucasus, imposed upon by a variety of committees, resigned and was replaced by General Przevalski, but the decay continued. In October, when the Bolsheviks seized power in a *coup d'état*, units started to spontaneously demobilize. In the Russian heartland, there was no enthusiasm for fighting the Ottomans. Crowds in St Petersburg had shouted: 'We don't want the Dardanelles!' In Trebizond, Russian soldiers wanted to go home, and, short of supplies they took to looting, which only seemed to encourage lawlessness in the surrounding countryside.[4] An unofficial truce had come into effect along the Caucasus front when the revolution started. Now, the Russian formations just melted away.[5]

The only forces available for any resistance to the Ottomans were a few hundred officers and some local contingents of men, mainly Georgians, Armenians, and Azeris concerned about a possible invasion and subsequent reprisals. The Georgians took the view that they could negotiate with Germany to prevent Muslim massacres of their population, but the Armenians were under no illusion as to their fate. By January 1918 they had formed their own Armenian Corps, consisting of two experienced infantry divisions, three separate brigades and a cavalry brigade. Local militia were also mustered. Equipment was cannibalized from retreating Russian units, and there was a plentiful supply of machine guns, mountain artillery, and ammunition. Their ardour was not in doubt, but their chances of survival against the twelve Ottoman divisions that faced them were far less certain.[6] Vehip Pasha, who commanded the Ottoman Third Army, was ordered to remain in place until events in the Russian Caucasus were clearer, but by the autumn, preparations were made for a far-reaching offensive across the mountains.

In February 1918, despite negotiations with the 'Transcaucasian Federation', the Ottomans struck at Armenian posts and drove them back through winter snows for eleven days. The Armenians tried to position their units to protect centres of population, fully expecting that some deal would be concluded. There was some skirmishing but the results were inevitable: Ottoman troops swept into Erzurum on 12 March 1918, and soon after the Ottomans demanded that armed detachments evacuate all areas that had been assigned to the empire by the terms of the Treaty of Brest-Litovsk. The Armenians were compelled to fall back, but this placed them into two concentrated areas, at Kars and Erevan. Confused attempts were made to conclude an armistice, but the Ottoman commanders were under instructions to ignore all Armenian proposals.[7] Batum was taken from the Georgians and Kars was also seized, and the Third Army drove to the limit of what it could reasonably hold. Despite the deteriorating conditions on the Palestine front, Enver ensured that Vehip Pasha got more reinforcements from Romania in order to continue the advance across the Caucasus. He also despatched two loyalists to drive the operations: his half-brother, Nuri Pasha, and his uncle, Halil Pasha. To add a gesture of drama to the enterprise now unfolding, the Third Army was retitled 'The Army of Islam'.[8]

For the British, the ideological threat of pan-Islamism was augmented by the challenge of communist subversion. The British view of the Bolshevik revolutionaries, who had been working to take Russia out of the war, immediately raised suspicions that Lenin must have a German connection. Indeed, it seems that Lenin had accepted both German funds and the offer of a sealed train journey through Europe to reach Russia that spring on the understanding that the Bolsheviks opposed any further conflict with Germany and possibly would arrange to release German prisoners of war.[9] Members of the Russian Provisional Government certainly believed that Lenin was a German spy and raids on the Bolshevik headquarters in the late summer of 1917 apparently produced compromising documents.[10] The opening of the Soviet archives from 1990 has revealed that, in fact, millions of German marks were made available to the Bolshevik Party in order to promote peacemaking propaganda and support their newspapers. Lenin believed that, in time, Germany too would be overthrown and the matter of funding would be immaterial. In Lenin's mind the success of Bolshevism in Russia was but a prelude to a worldwide revolution. He predicted that the industrialized nations, including Britain, would be the first to be consumed by communist insurrection. What he opposed was imperialism (which he regarded as the latest manifestation of capitalism), and he predicted that the world war would soon be replaced with a class war.

In December 1917, Lenin had announced that the workers of Asia should follow the example of the Bolsheviks and throw off their oppressors. He believed that the momentum of 'world revolution' would come from the industrialized nations of Europe, but he saw that there could only be advantages for Russia if the Great Powers were deprived of their colonies. He described imperialism as an 'abscess' that provided the bourgeoisie with funds with which to 'bribe certain sections of the workers'.[11] If colonies were swept away, Lenin argued, then the workers would be able to bring down the weakened 'capitalist-imperialist' states.

Before Britain knew the extent of these ambitions, the journalist, diplomat, and British agent Robert Bruce Lockhart had been despatched to work with the new Bolshevik authority and encourage them to sustain the war effort against Germany. He quickly discovered that was a hopeless undertaking. By the spring of 1918 he was in contact with an anti-Bolshevik underground movement led by Boris Savinkov. The agent Sidney Reilly was also sent and he too made contact with the anti-Bolsheviks, as did his colleague Captain G. A. Hill. Felix Dzerzhinsky, the former Jesuit-educated tsarist secret policeman who became the head of the Bolshevik secret police, the Cheka, set up three *agents provocateurs*, Colonel Eduard Berzin, Jan Buikis, and Ian Sprogis, to mislead Lockhart, Reilly, Hill, and Captain Cromie, the British naval attaché.[12] Having exposed the conspiratorial nature of the British agents, the communists were subsequently even more incensed at their support for the Whites, the anti-communists, in Russia's escalating civil war. Moreover, the arrival of an Allied intervention force at Archangel in the summer of 1918 caused relations between the British and the Bolsheviks to break down entirely.[13] Against the background of a failed assassination attempt against Lenin by the socialist revolutionary Dora Kaplan on 30 August 1918, there was a crack-down against all dissidents. Hundreds of political prisoners were executed. In this atmosphere of fear and violence, Cromie was killed in a firefight when Red Guards stormed the British embassy in Petrograd. Lockhart and Boyce, Military Intelligence Station 1c head in Russia, were picked up and Berzin tried to entrap Reilly by suggesting he conduct another assassination attempt on Lenin. After the arrest of one of his mistresses, Reilly was smuggled out the country. Lockhart and Boyce were subsequently released in return for Soviet officials being held in London. In a political gesture, the Moscow Supreme Revolutionary Council sentenced Lockhart and Reilly to death *in absentia*.

The Bolsheviks now regarded the British as implacable enemies whose conspiracies should be fully exposed. In November 1917, the full details of the Sykes–Picot Agreement were published by the Bolsheviks as 'secret treaties' and reproduced by the world's press.[14] Djemal used the information to communicate with Emir Feisal and offer an amnesty for all the Arabs in revolt against the Ottoman Empire. He questioned why the Arabs would support the British if, as the agreement suggested, Syria would go to France, Iraq to Britain, and Palestine would be a religious settlement under international control. The latter was a reference to the statement made by Arthur Balfour, the British Foreign Secretary, in a letter (via the British banker Walter Rothschild) to the Zionist Federation of Great Britain and Ireland, that his government intended there to be a 'national home for the Jewish people' in Palestine—although Balfour had added the careful proviso, 'it being clearly understood that nothing shall be done which may prejudice the civil and religious rights of existing non-Jewish communities in Palestine'.[15] This letter was in time to become famous as the Balfour Declaration. Clearly Balfour's letter, written in February 1917, was motivated by a desire to encourage the Anglo-American Jews to support the war effort, the same month the United States joined the Allies.[16] It was not, as later posited, a blueprint for the creation of the state of Israel. Balfour had written only that the British government would help to 'facilitate' an entity they 'viewed with favour'. Like the vagueness of the 'spheres of influence' demarcated broadly as 'Zone A' and 'Zone B' on the map produced by the Sykes–Picot Agreement, this was not a concrete international agreement and did not determine borders.[17]

Djemal did not release details of the Sykes–Picot Agreement in his speech to assembled Ottoman officials in December 1917, for two reasons: one, he feared that Syrians and Lebanese might welcome the idea of French 'liberation' forces arriving in the region, and two, he was eager to win the Arabs back to the Ottoman cause.[18] He condemned the Arab revolt and the connivance of the British and French in trying to establish an Arab kingdom, under Sharif Hussein of Mecca, across the entire Middle East. In his correspondence with Feisal, he argued that the British intended to make slaves of the Arabs, rendering Mecca and Medina mere protectorates which would be cut off from the rest of the Middle East and therefore dependent on British supplies of food, fodder, and finance.[19] He offered full autonomy within the Ottoman Empire if Feisal now agreed to accept the amnesty on offer. Feisal and Hussein were aware of the Sykes–Picot plan, at least in outline, and had been in correspondence with McMahon over the future of Arabia. Far from accusing the British of betrayal, Feisal passed on the letter from Djemal to the Arab Bureau in Cairo.[20] Nevertheless, the Hashemites had understood that any British and French occupation of Arab lands would be temporary, in other words, wartime measures necessary for the liberation struggle against the Ottomans.

In Cairo, Commander D. G. Hogarth, the head of the Arab Bureau, reassured Sharif Hussein in January 1918 that the British were committed to giving the Arabs the 'opportunity once again of forming a nation in the world' and that there was no question of subjugation. Hogarth explained that Jewish opinion also had to be considered and their support could not be dismissed. The Foreign Office reiterated Hogarth's points and denounced the Ottoman attempt to sow discord, reaffirming the British government's willingness to liberate the Arabs.[21] Colonel Joyce and Major T. E. Lawrence also reassured Feisal at his headquarters that Djemal had distorted 'either from ignorance or malice' the original intent of the Sykes–Picot Agreement, deliberately omitting, for example, the British commitment to obtain the 'consent of native populations and safeguarding their interests'.[22] Lawrence later wrote that he had disclosed the essence of the Sykes–Picot Agreement in 1916 to the Arab leaders and felt a sense of shame. Yet this sentiment may well have come after the war, through his disappointment at the failure of the united Arab cause and the peace settlements.[23]

Part of the purpose of the Sykes–Picot Agreement had been to counter post-war Russian ambitions, and complete the containment of the tsarist state from the coasts of the Levant which had been a consistent line in British foreign policy for decades. The collapse of the Russian Empire rendered this strategic consideration redundant. In light of this, and subsequent negotiations with France about the future extent and status of Syria and Palestine, the original Sykes–Picot Agreement was declared 'dead'. Hussein was eager to see the end of the Sykes–Picot proposals, but he was reassured in any case by the previous McMahon negotiations. Moreover, as Hogarth discovered in visiting him in January 1918, Hussein's concern was to keep the British on side in order to diminish his Arab rival Ibn Saud. The sharif argued that the only reason the Ottoman General Hamid Fakhri Pasha was still in control of Medina was due to the support he was getting from Ibn Saud.[24] The British already knew this was not the case: Ibn Saud had ignored the requests for help from the Ottoman garrison, despite his declaration in October 1914 that he would back Istanbul. It was this inter-Arab rivalry, rather than the Sykes–Picot Agreement, that would damage irrevocably the idea of Arab nationalism and create divisions across the Middle East.

The chief dilemma for the Hashemites was their complete dependence on the British to sustain them. Reinforced at Aqaba, the Arab Northern Army possessed supporting British armoured cars, aircraft, and field artillery with which to renew the offensive. Their original objective was Ma'an, a railway junction held by 6,000 entrenched infantry, and mobile cavalry reserves. Lawrence correctly estimated that any assault by Arab forces on this strong position would be a costly failure. Instead, air raids and attacks on the rail lines to the north and south were launched to force the Ottoman troops onto the defensive. Reconnaissance missions were made along potential routes into Palestine which could provide water for advancing regular troops, and, after several successful minor operations, it was Lawrence who was tasked to sever the Damascus–Medina line in the Yarmuk Valley deep behind Ottoman lines. The mission was a disaster. The line was not cut, his force was scattered, and, although the train of the Ottoman commander of VII Corps was derailed, Lawrence claimed to have been briefly captured, although this claim, never substantiated, might simply suggest that he was trying to tell a story that compensated for his operational failure.[25] Still, there were sufficient numbers of small successes that otherwise convinced Allenby that the Arab Northern Army could be useful as a flanking formation during his proposed advance into Palestine. At the town of Tafila, an Ottoman force which had set out from Kerak to recover an area useful for grain and fodder were enveloped on 25 January 1918 by Arab fighters led by Sharif Nasir, accompanied by Lawrence. The Ottoman brigade, numbering around 1,000 men, was routed and part of the force defected. Although the Ottomans later recovered Tafila, it was lost again in the autumn.[26]

Allenby had been instructed to resume his offensive in February 1918 but he could not progress north into Syria until he had neutralized the 20,000 Ottoman troops on his eastern flank in Amman. His first manoeuvre, to take Jericho, was successful, with the town falling to Allied troops on 21 February. Next, Allenby seized the hills above Wadi Auja, which put Jericho and its line of communications beyond the reach of Ottoman artillery.

At that point, Lawrence returned to Cairo somewhat disillusioned with the Arab campaign, largely over the wasteful distribution of gold supplied by General Headquarters, but Lieutenant Colonel Alan Dawnay led the new Hejaz Operations Staff to improve coordination with the Sharifian Army. He explained that the plan was for a wing of the Arab Northern Army, under the Ottoman defector Jafar Pasha al-Askari, to take Ma'an, to cut the railway and all lateral communications, while Allenby's columns advanced on Amman. Lawrence was assigned to raise support amongst the local Bani Sakr clans nearby. Then, in March 1918, heavy rains made all movement arduous and prevented the deployment of field artillery. The Arab attack was called off. By contrast, the British advanced on Es Salt, en route to Amman, and found the Ottoman garrison had fled and the locals celebrating their liberation.[27]

Nevertheless, at Amman, General Liman von Sanders, now the commander of the *Yıldırım* Group, had called in his more exposed posts in order to concentrate his forces around the city. He knew that Amman represented the last rail link with the garrison in Medina, and therefore was a vital junction for the entire campaign theatre.[28] He called for further reinforcements from the north and despatched Ottoman cavalry to threaten the British lines of communication astride the Jordan River. Meanwhile, Allenby's force was struggling with the rain and mud, and a decision was made to transfer as much arms, equipment, and baggage as possible to camels and mules because of the difficulty in moving wheeled transport. Men and animals died of exposure on the wind-swept slopes of the valley. Consequently the British force that arrived in front of the Ottoman positions was exhausted before the fighting had even begun.[29] The Egyptian Expeditionary Force (EEF) brigade, with the ammunition and guns they could carry, launched four days of assaults against strong positions. Some 2,000 defenders were dug-in, armed with seventy machine guns and supported by field artillery which had been zeroed in on prearranged targets and beaten zones (areas that could be saturated with machine-gun fire). Further Ottoman reinforcements arrived during the fighting. Yet Liman von Sanders was so concerned about the mounting casualties and wavering resolve of the defenders that he ordered their positions to be held regardless of the cost.[30] The British and imperial forces could not, however, continue the attacks. On 30 March 1918, they commenced their withdrawal, accompanied by large numbers of refugees from Es Salt who feared Ottoman retribution.[31]

Britain's Official History explained the cause of failure clearly. The weather conditions which had imposed delays and prevented the movement of heavy artillery meant that the British troops did not have sufficient fire support to carry such a well-defended position. Armoured cars could not be brought beyond Es Salt, which limited manoeuvre and prevented any encirclement of the city. As a result, 'the main objects of the raid had not been achieved'.[32]

The Ottomans were now directed by Liman von Sanders to probe the defences north of Jerusalem and to try and recapture the bridgeheads over the Jordan, but despite heavy shelling, neither succeeded in changing the operational or strategic situation. The Arab Northern Army achieved some success in storming Ma'an railway station on 16–17 April, although subsequent efforts to take the town itself failed and the Ottomans managed to send a relief force of 3,000 men which forced the Arabs back to their start lines. Jafar al-Askari blamed the French artillery under Capitaine Pisani for failures in fire support. Pisani claimed he had too little ammunition, but the Arabs believed Pisani was under orders not to back the Arabs beyond Ma'an, the boundary of the Hejaz and Syria. The French officer had indeed stated he could not support any operations into Syria, which, of course, his leaders regarded as a future French colony.

Regardless of the gunnery, the Arabs could not, despite four days' fighting, dislodge the Ottoman garrison, and morale amongst the Northern Army began to fail. The set-back at Ma'an damaged the image of an invincible progress towards victory, underscoring the importance of actual and continued military success to any strategic narrative. Discredited by being in league with the British and French and their nefarious Sykes–Picot plans, accused of rebellion, criticized by other prominent Arabs, including Ibn Saud, and now militarily seen as ineffective without substantial British backing, the Hashemite cause was at its lowest ebb. The result was that the Arab forces returned to guerrilla warfare and continued their attacks on the railways, in the hope of keeping the revolt alive.

Allenby's own forces were also unable to secure the route to Amman on a second attempt, in part because divisions were still being withdrawn for service in France. The opening of the German Spring Offensive, or Operation Michael, on 21 March 1918 on the Western Front had dealt a severe blow to the British Army in France. With 38,000 casualties and 21,000 missing or made prisoner, the recall of British divisions was urgent and imperative. Dismissing the anodyne reports of the War Office, Lloyd George thought: 'It looked as if ... [the] tired army was giving way before the fierce onrush of German hordes.'[33] The Prime Minister blamed the military officers for spending their time engaged in 'arts and wiles' to outwit the political leaders, and of attempting to circumvent decisions he had taken. By contrast, he credited himself with an energetic response: despatching troops from Britain to France, insisting on the replacement of British with Indian troops in Mesopotamia, and the transfer of men from that theatre to Palestine.[34]

Allenby's second operation against Amman had involved the use of mounted forces to cut the routes into the city.[35] General Sir Harry Chauvel, commanding the Desert Mounted Corps, was concerned that one of these proposed cut-off contingents was to consist of the recently recruited Bani Sakhr, even though some, at least, were still loyal to the Ottomans. The suspicions proved correct: the clans did not appear, and almost certainly passed on details of the assault plan to Liman von Sanders' headquarters. The result was that the German and Ottoman defenders were able to intercept the advancing British mounted forces. Reinforcements had to be sent to extract units which were in danger of being encircled. By the beginning of May 1918, the raid had failed. Yet, despite the operational set-back, Allenby had succeeded in persuading Liman von Sanders to deploy more men in and around Amman, leaving the front north of Jerusalem with fewer reserves.

In the spring of 1918, the Germans seemed to be in their strongest position since 1914. The offensives in France were driving the British back and inflicting severe casualties. Russia was out of the war and had been forced to conclude a humiliating peace that effectively gave Germany control of huge expanses of wheat growing regions in Eastern Europe. The Italians had not yet recovered from their catastrophic defeat at Caporetto, and the Allies were confined to the southernmost portion of the Balkans, which shielded the ailing Austro-Hungarian Empire. The *Yıldırım* contingents, and their Pasha II units, had seemingly checked the British in Palestine, Trans-Jordan, and Mesopotamia, and, even without any offensive operations, they could tie down the EEF and Mesopotamian Expeditionary Force in the Middle East.

In London, Cairo, and Delhi, the set-backs to the EEF and the Hashemite revolt, and the total collapse of the Russian military presence in the Caucasus meant that it was possible that the Turco-German forces could muster for an offensive in Persia, towards Afghanistan, which could eventually threaten India. Lord Curzon told the War Cabinet that the focus of the Central Powers was swinging 'toward the east'. Allenby was ordered to resume an offensive after the summer so as to prevent any advance in that direction and to absorb the strategic *Yıldırım* reserves.

In the Caucasus, amidst a confusion of local ambitions—some pro-Ottoman, some pro-German, and others independent—the British were eager to provide some sort of front against Enver's projected onslaught towards Persia and India.[36] It was considered essential to prevent the precious oilfields of Baku from falling into the enemy's hands. Moreover, it was possible that the thousands of German and Austrian prisoners of war, who had been held in tsarist prisoner-of-war camps across Turkestan, might be able to join hands with the advance of the Central Powers, thus augmenting their forces significantly. As Russian resistance collapsed, the potential for the Germans and Ottomans to march virtually unopposed across the Caucasus and Central Asia was a serious and tangible threat. There was also the underlying fear that, encouraged by this apparent victory, the peoples of Egypt, Arabia, Persia, and India might begin to doubt the ability of the British to win the war, which in turn could lead to serious internal unrest. Already there were signs of disorder in Persia. Sir Percy Sykes' locally raised contingent of South Persia Rifles, for example, mutinied, while nationalist disturbances spread across the country in the spring of 1918.[37]

Until more troops could be spared to reach Baku, Major Aeneas Ranald MacDonell, a Foreign Office consul who was given a temporary military rank, was sent to persuade the collection of forces in the region to hold the Ottomans in check. By the time he arrived on the Caspian shore, MacDonell found that the situation was deteriorating rapidly. Each of the different groups in the beleaguered city refused to work with the others although all were eager to obtain British financial support. MacDonell found himself smuggling roubles to the Armenians, the only group really prepared to resist the imminent invasion, but the line of communication became impossible once the Azeris had seized part of the vital railway line from Tiflis (Tblisi). MacDonell was only able to get back to Baku when Bolshevik militia smashed their way through with armoured trains. In Baku itself, the provisional government collapsed and was replaced by an Armenian Bolshevik, Stepan Shaumian, and his communist clique, backed by thousands of Armenians who been driven out of their homelands to the west. This 'Baku Commune' of the Dashnak Party was nevertheless more concerned with attacking the Azeri population than preparing for Enver's projected offensive.[38] MacDonell was unable to persuade the Bolsheviks that the Ottoman Army posed an immediate threat, and communist reinforcements from Astrakhan numbered barely 1,000 men. The Ottoman Army of Islam was thought to be at least 14,000 strong but the militias at Baku were neither strong enough or sufficiently organized to offer effective resistance.

Enver seized the opportunity afforded by the persecution of the Muslim Azeris to announce a new forward move against the Bolsheviks which would mean the seizure of Baku, but his strategy was immediately criticized by the Germans in Istanbul, who wanted to acquire the oil fields of Baku themselves as a strategic asset for the kaiser.[39] Kress von Kressenstein was despatched to Georgia where he concluded an agreement with the new Caucasus state at Tiflis.[40] The Germans had established themselves in Sevastopol and were now, it seemed, in a position to make their own bid to control Baku. Erich von Ludendorff urged Enver to redeploy the Ottoman divisions available in the Caucasus to face the threat posed by the British in Palestine, but Enver was undeterred. His plan was to secure the Caucasus first before turning the army southwards into western Persia and thence on to recover Baghdad. He had some 60,000 troops and thousands of irregulars, mounted and dismounted, the latter ready to fall on any Armenian settlement for revenge or loot. South of the Caucasus, the Armenians, instead of conducting a partisan war, opted instead to try and halt this overwhelming force with just 20,000 men using conventional war techniques.[41] The Armenians were defeated in just three weeks with no appreciable strategic benefit.

The Ottomans nevertheless collided with the German-led Georgians on 10 June, after Vehip Pasha had issued an ultimatum against the Georgian declaration of independence. Skirmishes broke out and the German headquarters demanded an immediate halt to Vehip Pasha's offensive, threatening to terminate German assistance across the entire Ottoman Empire.[42] Officially, Enver halted the activities of the Ninth Army but his Army of Islam continued to press on towards Baku, with the claim that formations were needed to counter aggression by the British and the Bolsheviks in the eastern Caucasus.[43] It was therefore a reduced force of 6,000 regulars and 10,000 irregular cavalry that advanced on Baku in late June 1918.[44] On the German side, negotiations were conducted with the Soviets of Baku in order to secure the region, news of which reached Enver

Figure 10.1 Major General Lionel Dunsterville, Kipling's 'Stalky', who briefly held Baku against communists and Ottoman invaders

at the end of August. He reacted with indignation and immediately issued orders to Nuri Pasha to speed up the seizure of the port and its oil wells.[45]

The British expeditionary force destined for Baku was placed under the command of Major General Lionel Dunsterville, and, in the teeth of local guerrilla resistance and Russian intrigues, it assembled at Hamadan.[46] Despite the offer of British military assistance, the Armenian Bolshevik leader Stepan Shaumian was convinced that the British intended only to colonize the region for themselves. His condition for accepting any contingent at Baku was that it would have to serve under a communist committee and be subject to Red Army regulations. At the time this meant that British soldiers and NCOs would be able to elect their own officers and would be subject to the indoctrination of political commissars. MacDonell rejected this blatant attempt to spread revolutionary ideology to the British Army and tried to persuade the Bolsheviks to acknowledge the seriousness of the Ottoman advance.

Meanwhile, to secure the Turkestan coast of the Caspian, Major General Wilfred Malleson, a military intelligence officer, was sent to Meshed in northern Persia with a detachment of Indian troops. His mission was to keep abreast of developments in Trans-Caspia and Turkestan, and to resist the attacks of any Turco-German forces in the area. In the event of the Ottomans breaking through at Baku, he was to advance and cut the railway

Figure 10.2 Defence of Baku, 1918: a British officer and Armenian sentry await the final Ottoman offensive of the war

lines across Trans-Caspia in order to protect the approaches to Afghanistan and India.[47] It seems that MacDonell also had his contingency plans, namely to destroy the oil wells and sabotage the docks at Baku if the Ottomans approached. Some 1,200 Cossacks who had been assigned to Persia before the revolution also made their way to interdict the Ottoman offensive as the means to ensure their return to their homeland.[48]

However, in July 1918 Malleson had little real idea of what was happening across the Caspian or indeed of the location of the Army of Islam. He therefore sent Captain Reginald Teague Jones, another intelligence officer, disguised as an Armenian, to link up with MacDonell and inform him that he was to join forces with any anti-Bolshevik factions so that British troops could land at the threatened port. Teague Jones found German agents at Krasnovodsk frantically trying to purchase cotton, a vital resource for explosives. The impoverished Bolsheviks were naturally eager to sell it. Teague Jones managed to sabotage the supply.[49]

In Baku, despite the approaching Ottoman threat, there was disunity, intrigue, and disorder. A number of ex-tsarist officers were eager to get rid of Shaumian, but their attempt at a coup was bungled and MacDonell, who was associated with the plot, was forced to flee. Yet, the Bolsheviks were facing opposition from other quarters. On 12 July 1918, the Bolsheviks at Ashkabad had been overthrown by workers angry at communist repression. They had seized power and the Socialist Revolutionary Party was now in charge.[50] Then, on 1 August, another coup was launched against the Bolsheviks in Baku when the communists announced they would surrender to the Ottomans. A provisional authority calling itself the Centro-Caspian Dictatorship was established, and urgent appeals were now sent to the British for military assistance.[51]

General Dunsterville and his 'Dunsterforce' immediately set sail for Baku, but with only five battalions and a cavalry regiment, since the rest were still marching into northern Persia. By the time they arrived the Ottomans were already close to the line of hills that surrounded the port and Dunsterville knew that his small force, the first contingent of which numbered just seventy men, could do little without the active support of the local militias.[52] Forward detachments of the Armenians had put up strong resistance to the advancing Ottoman regulars but they could not hold their positions. Ironically, the most effective factor against the Army of Islam was not combat, but infection: dysentery decimated the ranks of Nuri Pasha's regulars and the Azeri militias.

On 2 August, the Cossacks helped the Baku defenders drive back a scouting force of the Ottoman army. The unfortunate effect of this was that it seemed to have convinced the entire population there would be no further fighting. On 5 August, the first major Ottoman attack was nevertheless checked, and severe casualties inflicted. Concerned by the rumours that a large force of the British Army was now present, two more Ottoman regiments were called up.[53] Having taken the brunt of subsequent Ottoman attacks, and suffering heavy casualties, the three British battalions, their guns, and three armoured cars were too heavily outnumbered to hold Baku and they fell back to Enzeli.[54] Without the British, resistance collapsed and Muslim irregulars set about massacring men, women, and children in revenge for the destruction of their co-religionists months before. The Ottoman troops put a stop to it when they reached Baku on 15 September and hanged the ringleaders. Order was restored, and Azerbaijan seemed to be the first of the new protectorates that Enver had envisaged.[55] From a British perspective, with Dunsterville's little army withdrawn, there was now no obstacle to the Army of Islam crossing the Caspian.

On the Turkestan side of the Caspian, an Indian Army detachment under Colonel Denis Knollys had become engaged in a battle with the Bolsheviks who were trying to retake Ashkabad from the east. Eager to retain control of the area against an Ottoman offensive, Knollys was able to drive off a Bolshevik attack at Kaakha, another railway junction 236 miles north of Medina, in today's Saudi Arabia, 90 miles south-east of Ashkabad on the Trans-Caspian Railway. The Bolsheviks, accompanied by Austrian ex-prisoners of war, had mounted a determined assault, but a company of the 16th Punjabis checked them and the Bolsheviks were forced to withdraw. What was even more disconcerting was the new Bolshevik way of war: they had been fired upon by Bolshevik sympathizers from behind, and had to endure a variety of ruses, including feigned surrenders and Bolshevik appeals to the Indians troops to kill their British officers. Despite being heavily outnumbered, Knollys' sepoys drove the Bolsheviks out of Dushak and occupied Merv. Ever alert to the importance of propaganda, the communists explained this defeat by multiplying the number of men in Knollys' command from the actual 400 to an imaginary 4,000.[56] However, to hold the region that was threatened now from both the east and the west, General Malleson knew he needed more troops. Yet, with operations underway in so many other theatres, his requests to pursue the Bolsheviks across Central Asia were refused by the government of India.

Nevertheless, the expected Ottoman landings on the eastern shores of the Caspian never came. Orders for the Caucasus Ninth Army to push deeper into Persian territory seemed to be beyond the capacity of the force to carry out. Not only were the troops at the limit of their endurance, but at that moment, the Ottoman Empire was being defeated decisively in Palestine and in Mesopotamia. As a result, Enver's adventurous plan to seize the entire Caucasus would be singularly condemned ever after as the most ill-conceived of his strategic decisions in the war.[57]

For the Ottoman and German commanders in Palestine and Trans-Jordan, the absence of reinforcements prompted more disagreement over the 'ends' being pursued. General Mustafa Kemal, reinstated as commander of the Seventh Army, argued that the *Yıldırım* reserve and the remaining Ottoman armies in Palestine should be withdrawn to southern Anatolia, creating a strategic reserve for the Ottoman Empire's southern fronts, and occupying topography that would favour the defender and put the EEF at a distinct disadvantage. Pulling out of the malaria-ridden parts of Palestine and Syria would also reduce the attrition of disease. Moreover, Ottoman lines of communication would be shorter, making it easier to supply troops on the front line. By contrast, the EEF would have faced a severe logistical problem of keeping the army supplied along extended lines of communication and would have had to confront the possibility of supporting the entire civilian population of Syria, at that time suffering the long-term effects of the naval blockade and wartime requisitioning.

Liman von Sanders had different strategic priorities. He intended to keep the *Yıldırım* force *in situ*, to delay the EEF and where possible prevent the despatch of Allied reinforcements to Europe. As a result, the Ottoman and German troops had to occupy a 60-mile-long line that was harder to hold than at Gaza, the strong defensive line that had held the EEF in check for months, with only 15 per cent of the numbers ordinarily deployed for zoned defence. The Ottoman operational level was subordinated to the strategic concerns of its high command, and its positions, just north of Jerusalem would depend now on the tactical effects that could be achieved by infantrymen, machine gunners, and artillerymen dug in along that line.

What Allenby could not see was the deterioration taking place amongst the ranks of the Ottoman Army. Supply shortages were increasing the levels of sickness and affecting the soldiers' morale.[58] Diseases such as cholera, typhus, and the appearance of the lethal Spanish flu affected the *Yıldırım* force in the weeks before the action which was to take place at Megiddo.

Although Turks later blamed Arab soldiers for the subsequent breakdown of morale and the inability to hold the line, it is clear that, after four years of war, there was a widespread sense of exhaustion in the Ottoman Army.[59] British military intelligence reports noted that the numbers surrendering were on the rise and, significantly, these were drawn from across the entire spectrum of Ottoman ethnicities.[60] From an operational perspective, Ottoman battalions were reduced in strength to somewhere between 150 and 200 men. The troops were tired, demoralized, and, faced with Allenby's more numerous and motivated force, they saw little chance of survival.

Allenby went to great lengths to conceal the direction of his long-awaited attack on the Ottoman lines. Some 15,000 wooden and canvas horses were built and dummy camps erected to persuade intrusive reconnaissance pilots that the EEF intended to attack from the Jordan Valley towards Amman. Units were moved at night, and camouflaged by day. Air patrols did their best to deny access over Allenby's formations. Bridges were built across the Jordan to give the impression of an impending thrust, and false wireless traffic was generated to support the idea of preparations. Jafar al-Askari and the Arab Northern Army played their part in creating the deception. With the bulk of the Arab force laying siege to Ma'an, one contingent advanced to within 50 miles of Amman. On 16 September, covered by aircraft of the

Figure 10.3 Field Marshal Sir Edmund Allenby, the victor of Megiddo, the final battle, in 1918

Royal Air Force, Colonel T. E. Lawrence's Arab irregulars conducted a series of guerilla actions on the railway line either side of the railway junction of Daraa. This inspired more local Arab tribes to join the revolt and drew in Ottoman reinforcements to defend the area. On the 17th, the Arab Northern Army made another attack on the line, north of Daraa.

Allenby's deception appeared to have worked although Liman von Sanders had already concentrated his artillery, including *Yıldırım*'s five heavy artillery battalions, with the Seventh and Eighth armies on the right and the centre of the Ottoman line. It has been argued that the concentration of heavy artillery tended to indicate where the main operations were to take place in the last phase of the war.[61] Moreover, as the Third Battle of Gaza had demonstrated, weakening any part of the line or sacrificing a strong reserve could have disastrous consequences. The German commander was evidently hoping to hold the EEF in place, inflicting heavy losses in front of his fortifications and trenches as he had done against the Jordan raids. Yet, Liman von Sanders' own account of the period before Allenby's offensive states that he reinforced the Jordan area, expecting a major attack to take place there.

The Battle of Megiddo, which opened at 04.00 hours on 19 September 1918 with a tremendous artillery barrage, was fought between the three corps of the EEF and the remnants of the Ottoman Fourth (near Amman) and the Seventh and Eighth armies of *Yıldırım*. Allenby had concentrated 35,000 infantry, 9,000 cavalry, and 400 heavy guns on a 15-mile front close to the Mediterranean coast, north of Jaffa. The shelling was the most intense delivered outside a European theatre, with 1,000 rounds a minute detonating on the Ottoman positions. Watching the barrage was Lieutenant General Bulfin's XXI Corps and behind them was Chauvel's Desert Mounted Corps which was poised to ride through the gap created by the infantry, where it would drive into depth. Lieutenant General Chetwode's XX Corps, with the ANZAC Mounted Division, were to pin the Ottoman Fourth Army in place and cut its line of retreat to the north, all the while giving the impression that they were the main assaulting force. The Ottomans could muster a total of 40,598 infantrymen in the front line, with 3,000 mounted troops, 402 guns, and 273 light and 679 heavy machine guns.[62] Facing them, the EEF across all its fronts totalled 57,000 infantry, 12,000 mounted troops, and 540 guns.

The Battle of Megiddo developed as Allenby had planned. The infantry assault of the XXI Corps carried the first two Ottoman lines and overcame the resistance of the third and fourth lines soon after. In just two and a half hours, they had penetrated 7,000 yards into the Ottoman positions, and broken open a wide gap in their lines. Chauvel's cavalry exploited the gap perfectly, chasing the routed Ottoman troops up to Tulkarm, which was captured. The cavalry pressed on with aircraft above them, seizing depots, rounding up prisoners, and destroying the telephone communications nodes on which the *Yıldırım* depended to allocate its reserves. Blinded to the location of the rapidly advancing British and ANZAC forces, Liman von Sanders himself was almost captured at his General Headquarters at Nazareth. Baisan and Afula were captured, and the speed of the advance seemed to exceed all expectations: the British 4th Cavalry Division covered 70 miles on 20 September, while the Australian Mounted Division in one bound advanced 11 miles in just sixty minutes. The Ottoman forces began to disintegrate in the confusion: entire Turkish battalions found themselves encircled or under relentless air attack. A key manoeuvre was the decision of the cavalry to switch to a new axis to the south-east, from Nazareth and Beth Shean, which cut off the retreat of the Ottoman Seventh Army. On 23 September, British and Indian cavalry took Acre and Haifa. Resistance from Ottoman forces in Palestine was ebbing away.

Allenby now turned to the securing of Trans-Jordan. The New Zealand Mounted Brigade recaptured Es Salt on the 23rd and Amman just two days later. The Ottoman garrison at Ma'an was unable to get back in time to assist: it was intercepted by the 2nd Australian Light Horse and surrendered. What was left of the Ottoman force fell back towards Damascus, but the British, imperial, and Arab armies kept a sword at their back: Deraa was assaulted by the Arab Northern Army on 26 September and, joined by the British, they set off immediately towards the Syrian capital. Meanwhile, British and Indian cavalry circled round to cut off Ottoman forces making for Beirut and Homs. By 30 September, the combined British and Arab force was on the edge of Damascus.

The entry to the city was an honour accorded by the British to the Emir Feisal's troops, although the 2nd Australian Light Horse was the first into the city for operational reasons. The population greeted the Arab Army as liberators but were angry when the sharif's men started looting. The British entry was more prosaic, but Feisal was accorded the honours of a conqueror for a short time before being informed, by Allenby, that the city was under British military occupation. Moreover, instructions had been received that the Arabs were not to administer either Palestine or Lebanon, the latter going to the French authorities. The rest of the former Ottoman dominions were Allenby's responsibility. For those who were critical of this decision by Britain to take responsibility for the security of the Ottoman *vilayets*, it is worth noting that it was the British and imperial forces that had borne the brunt of the fighting, and it was they who had defeated the Ottoman Army.[63] The Arab contribution had been valuable, but it was not militarily significant.

The Battle of Megiddo had broken the Ottoman forces in the Near East and created a situation that few could have anticipated. The pursuit continued and Aleppo was taken on 26 October, but resistance had almost ceased altogether by that stage. The British and imperial forces had lost 5,666 men in their advance, but, while Ottoman losses were not recorded, over 75,000 prisoners had been taken. Just four days after Aleppo was captured, on 30 October, the Ottomans concluded an armistice. Now, it was necessary to design the strategy for winning the peace, and, in many ways, this was to prove just as difficult as the war itself.

11

The Strategy of Negotiation

Peacemaking, 1919–23

The Ottoman Army had been defeated on the Mesopotamian and Palestine–Syria fronts, and the capitulation of Bulgaria on 30 September 1918 cut Istanbul off from the resources of the Central Powers. This rendered further resistance impossible. News that the Germans had submitted peace terms to the Americans, and that their armies were being driven out of France, increased the pressure on the Ottomans to seek terms themselves. On 8 October, the triumvirate and their Cabinet resigned, and, after a frantic search for a new government, Izzet Pasha, the commander of the Caucasus army, assumed control. The man delegated to negotiate with the Allies was General Townshend, who had lost Kut, and who had been held in captivity thereafter. Admiral Sir Somerset Gough-Calthorpe, the commander of the Royal Navy's Mediterranean Squadron, invited the Ottomans to submit to the terms of an armistice at Mudros on the island of Lesbos, lost to the Greeks in 1913 and the base of operations during the Gallipoli campaign. Mindful of the need to assert strategic priorities, Lloyd George had sent instructions to exclude the French at this crucial early stage as much as possible. The British government was also determined to use symbolism to effect. The armistice was signed on board HMS *Agamemnon*, one of the warships that had taken part in the naval attack on the Dardanelles in 1915. The terms were simple: they accepted the full surrender of Ottoman forces; the peace would be decided later.[1]

The reopening of the Dardanelles underscored the fact that Gallipoli had been a pyrrhic victory for the Ottomans in the classic sense. Their minefields were cleared. All Ottoman ships were handed over to the British. On 5 November 1918, British aircraft landed at the German-built airstrip above the Narrows. On the 9th, British soldiers came ashore at Gallipoli, marching past the scrubby and increasingly overgrown battlefield of 1915 to establish themselves with total control of the Ottomans' most strategic point. Having passed through the Straits, the Royal Navy anchored off Constantinople on 13 November determined to impose the conditions of the armistice. It was striking, and of course deliberate, that leading the flotilla was HMS *Agamemnon*.

The Royal Navy could claim, with some justification, that they had brought about a strategic victory despite their defeat in March 1915. The Allied naval blockade had taken its toll on the Ottoman war economy, for the empire was in a state of decomposition. Wheat and livestock production had fallen by almost 50 per cent, and inflation had risen inexorably.[2] If the war had continued it is likely that, in conditions similar to those prior to the revolution in Russia, the entire Ottoman system would have collapsed in a popular revolt. One Ottoman cavalry officer, observing his own troops, had noted: 'their stomachs are totally empty, like the imperial treasury... They have no shoes [and] you can see their whole bodies through their ragged clothes.'[3] According to the same eyewitness, desperate soldiers were being arrested for highway robbery and murder. There was a chance that widespread disorder would follow the outbreak of peace. Accordingly, every railway, telegraph, and telephone network came under British supervision and an army of occupation was despatched to Istanbul.[4]

The British had demonstrated that, even while they were engaged in a demanding European war, they had been able to mobilize the resources of their empire, recover from the setbacks at Gallipoli, Kut, and Palestine, and mount larger offensives each succeeding year. Maude's drive up the Tigris and Euphrates in 1917 had captured Baghdad. After the Third Battle of Gaza, the Allies began to assert their superiority over Ottoman forces in Palestine too. The fall of Jerusalem had been immensely symbolic in the Middle East, and at the Battle of Megiddo the British drove back Ottoman forces to such an extent that resistance on that front began to collapse long before the Allies took Damascus. A brief Ottoman counter-offensive in the Caucasus in 1918 against disorganized Russian revolutionaries could do nothing to alter Britain's domination of the Middle East.

The armistice terms had also specified that Ottoman forces were to be withdrawn from Cilicia (the southern coastal region of Asia Minor, corresponding to the modern region of Çukurova in Turkey). This suggested that territorial changes would follow in the peace treaty; furthermore, there were indications that the Armenian *vilayets* would not remain in the

Ottoman Empire and there would be a reckoning for the enormous numbers of Armenians who had died at the hands of the authorities during the war.[5] The Ottoman war veterans faced an uncertain future.

The Paris peace conferences in 1919 dealt with each of the Central Powers, but it was not until 10 August 1920 that the Treaty of Sèvres on the future of the Middle East was concluded. It produced bitter disagreements throughout its formulation. The initial meetings had taken place in Paris, but the lack of progress led to subsequent conferences in London in February 1920 and then at San Remo in April. The difficulty was not only satisfying French, British, Italian, Greek, and Arab aspirations but also managing a fluid situation, for local actors seized the initiative and forced significant adjustments in the peace planning. In theory, at least, France, Italy, and Greece were awarded territorial control of parts of Anatolia, and Greece took Thrace, which ended the Ottoman presence in the Balkans. Britain remained in control of all Ottoman territories that they had overrun and Istanbul too was placed under occupation, with no clear end date for military rule.

Angered by the humiliation of defeat and occupation, and fearful of the terms then under negotiation in Paris, Turkish representatives attended a series of emergency congresses in 1919. They designed their own manifesto, and then declared themselves independent of the Ottoman regime. The Turkish National Movement convened its own parliament, the Grand National Assembly, in Ankara, and met for the first time on 23 April 1920, just as the Allies were concluding the terms of the peace.[6] Mustapha Kemal rallied the Turks as a series of desperate conflicts broke out across Anatolia—the Armenians, Greeks, and French fought the emerging Turkish state separately. The fighting, and the first success against the Armenians in November 1920, had the effect of rendering the old Ottoman order irrelevant. Turkish ex-soldiers and volunteers flocked to the banner of a successful and dynamic new entity, abandoning the old regime that they now associated with defeat.

To settle the eastern border and free their forces for greater focus against their Western enemies, the Turkish nationalists concluded the Treaty of Moscow in March 1921: this awarded Armenia to the Soviets in return for Kars and Ardahan—two of the 'lost provinces' of Anatolia that had featured as war aims in 1914. France, exhausted by the world war and engaged in a conflict in the Cilician hills for which there seemed no end, withdrew the same year. This permitted Kemal and the nationalists to concentrate all their efforts on the Greeks in Smyrna (Izmir). Initially, the Greeks had the upper hand and they advanced towards Ankara. In actions that are celebrated in Turkish national histories as much as Gallipoli, Kemal led Turkish forces back to military victory. The battles of Afyonkarahisar-Eskishehir and Sarkayar were particularly hard fought, but the turning point came following the action at Dumlupinar, after which the Greeks retreated. It was in some ways an anachronistic struggle: cavalry was prevalent, but armour was absent; and most engagements were fought by men armed with rifles and machine guns. The Greek forces were finally driven back to the coast, and then compelled to evacuate, along with thousands of civilians.[7] The situation was chaotic.

Kemal then swung his attention to Istanbul and the Allied occupation forces. To halt the offensive, Lloyd George issued an ultimatum in September 1922 and demanded that the Allies stand together on the Chanak coast. He may have been prompted to take this line because of his success the previous year in facing down the Irish nationalists, where his threat of war had led to a partition treaty. His strategic objective was to ensure a strong Greece, an Allied partner, close to the Dardanelles and sufficiently pro-British to ensure lasting regional influence. Nevertheless, the demands for unity this time went unheeded: only New Zealand supported Lloyd George's action. France and Italy, unenthusiastic about intervention in the Turkish war of independence, declined. British forces were reinforced and the scene was set for a significant confrontation between the Turkish revisionists, on the one hand, and the British with their determination to uphold the terms of the Treaty of Sèvres, on the other.

At the eleventh hour, the 'Chanak Crisis' was resolved by local negotiations at Mudania between General Harrington and General Ismet 'Inönü'. The British agreed that Eastern Thrace and Adrianople would be returned to the Turks, while the Turks agreed to the 'neutralization' of the Dardanelles and the Bosporus. These terms formed the basis of the Treaty of Lausanne. Despite averting war, the Conservative Party were deeply alarmed that Lloyd George had taken Britain to the brink of war without consultation. They were already concerned by the Prime Minister's protracted intervention in Russia, and their '1922 Committee' in the Carlton Club in London plotted the removal of their dictatorial colleague. The resurgence of Turkey had therefore claimed an unexpected casualty: the political career of Lloyd George. The other significant departure was the Ottoman regime—abolished in November 1922. Within two years, the concept of the caliphate was also formally consigned to the dustbin of history, while Turkey embarked on a period of rapid and comprehensive modernization.[8]

In September 1923, after the conclusion of the Treaty of Lausanne, the Allies left Istanbul, obtaining from the Turks a renunciation of all non-Turkish territories that had formed part of the Ottoman Empire. On 29 October that year, the Turks formally established the republic. It is easy to assume that this was the inevitable outcome of the dismemberment of the Ottoman Empire, but the rump of Anatolia was, in 1919, just as likely to fall under the spheres of influence of France, Greece, Italy, and, in time, the Soviets. Despite criticism of the hagiography of Kemal 'Atatürk' in the decades that followed, there is no doubt that his foundation of a secular republic so soon after a catastrophic defeat was remarkable, achieved as it was in the face of opposition by several powers.

In Egypt, in November 1918, a delegation (*wafd*) of nationalist representatives had approached Sir Reginald Wingate to demand to be able to present their case for independence to the British government in London. There was a strong expectation that, like the Arabs, they would be permitted to send a party to the Paris peace conference, not least because of the economic contribution, especially in terms of conscripted labour, that Egypt had made to the war effort.[9] The British government refused, arguing that the *wafd* was not representative of the people and that Britain had a responsibility to govern under the terms of the wartime protectorate. One officer in the high commission at Cairo believed the British government was overwhelmed with the tasks of peacemaking in Europe, and it simply did not have the time to entertain a group of doubtful legitimacy.[10] The rejection was keenly felt in Egypt. The Prime Minister, Husayn Rashidi, resigned. Egyptians, embittered by the wartime inflation and depressed economy, began to organize in political groups. Some favoured a national republic, while others considered a greater Arab state led by secularists and modernists.

The prospect of disorder prompted a standard crisis response by the British authorities: the arrest of the ringleaders including the prominent nationalist advocate Saad Zughlul. The *wafd* delegates were deported to Malta, and Wingate hoped that this action would overawe the trouble-makers and create a 'temporary reaction' in Britain's favour.[11] It didn't. The deportation proved to be the spark of a widespread campaign of disobedience and rioting. The political administration came to a stand-still when any officials working with the British were threatened with murder by conspirators.[12] Allenby believed that the *wafd* delegates were actually relieved to have gone, because they feared the nationalist rank and file.[13]

Order had broken down. The courts were not functioning because Egyptian lawyers joined the demonstrations. The second standard British response to this sort of civil disorder was therefore to reinforce the police with detachments of the army and impose martial law.[14] The problem was that the men of the Egyptian Expeditionary Force (EEF) were eager to go home. Demobilization was proceeding slowly and there had been soldiers' strikes on Easter Day, 20 April 1919. Allenby wrote to the Chief of the Imperial General Staff (CIGS), Sir Henry Wilson, that there was 'great unrest in the army' in Egypt and that administrative services were verging on 'mutiny'.[15] The result was that rioting spread across the country from the epicentre of Cairo, and seat of the unrest at the Al-Azar mosque. Nationalists tried to secure communications, including telegraph and railways, to deprive the British the ability to move against them. Support for the revolt increased but significant elites, including landowners and businessmen, even if they showed sympathy for the national cause, condemned the disorder and violence. Over 1,000 died in the fighting in the first six days of the unrest, and seventy-five British and Indian soldiers were killed, most of the victims being assaulted by gangs armed with knives and clubs.

To neutralize the revolt, the British government recalled Wingate, and appointed Allenby as special high commissioner. Allenby combined political concessions, including the promise of a commission of enquiry into local grievances, with the imposition of force. By mid-May, Allenby reported that 'Egypt is quiet', although he was concerned that nationalists were attempting to whip up a press campaign against British troops, accusing them of atrocities.[16] The commission, led by Sir Alfred Milner, struggled to get much purchase on the nationalists, who refused to participate. Milner's conclusion, presented in February 1921, was that the protectorate was unsustainable. Egypt was to be granted its independence, subject to certain conditions, including a treaty of alliance, protection of all foreign interests, and the retention of control of the Suez Canal. In addition, Britain pledged to defend Egypt against all foreign aggression, and insisted on the protection of minorities and the control of Sudan.

The greatest collision between the competing interests in the post-war Middle East took place in Syria. In the final days of the war, Allenby had permitted the Arab Northern Army under Feisal to enter Damascus once it had been cleared by the Australians, but the entry was symbolic and in no way represented the distribution of power in the region. Britain held the balance through the existence of the EEF. There was some incredulity when

Feisal claimed Damascus by right of conquest, since the occupation had been enabled by the British. Allenby told the War Office that the Arabs had raised their flag the moment they entered the city, and they quickly established a provisional government.[17] Allenby demanded that while the war continued, he must retain supreme control of the administration of Syria. Balfour, as Foreign Secretary, insisted that France would be granted control as soon as it was possible for them to take over. The reaction was shock, disbelief, and anger, and there were scenes of 'frenzied and despairing Arabs' in the Syrian capital.[18] In the immediate post-war period, Allenby compromised, giving the Arabs control of the city and the French a coastal strip in Lebanon, an arrangement that was in no way intended to be permanent. Lawrence departed for London to plead the Arab case, and soon after conceived of taking an Arab delegation to the Paris peace conference to demonstrate that the Arabs had to be taken seriously. Allenby had some sympathy for Feisal and pointed out to his government that the Arabs had, to that point, not been notified officially of Foreign Office plans for the region.[19] Whatever the sincerity or otherwise of the British, it was France that now determined the future of Syria.

The arrival of French forces increased local tensions. There were skirmishes, the first in December 1918 and with increasing in frequency thereafter, especially in Damascus and in Aleppo. In Lebanon, an administrative council was formed under the supervision of the French military occupation, but it was opposed immediately by pro-Syrian factions and nationalists. Some twenty-two delegates were to be sent to Paris, drawn from Palestine, Lebanon, and Syria, to plead the united greater Syrian cause.[20] Feisal supported the delegation, hoping to reinforce his case as leader of the Arab people.

Allenby struggled to placate the French and the Arabs. Noting that the French military governor had little conception of local politics, and that the Arabs were concerned with French control of the coast, which confined them to 'a house with no door', he continued to insist that his was a temporary administration of enemy-occupied territory.[21] There was concern that Feisal might resign, leading to 'blood, fire and ruin throughout all Arabia and Syria'.[22] Sir Henry Wilson sympathized, and intended that the remnants of the Sykes–Picot Agreement 'must be torn up, somehow'.[23] Allenby also had to resist the arrival of stronger French detachments, including Algerians who were detested for their conduct.[24] This necessitated retaining a substantial British garrison in Syria, despite the unrest in Egypt. Allenby reported

Figure 11.1 David Lloyd George, Britain's energetic Prime Minister 1917–22

that, if the British withdrew, the Arabs would immediately declare independence and fight the French. In May, he noted that demonstrations included armed men and Feisal had made it clear he intended to resist the French takeover in Syria.[25] Allenby was also concerned that a military withdrawal under such circumstances would damage British prestige, especially in the eyes of Egyptians.

In London, in December 1918, Lloyd George and Clemenceau held a meeting in private to revise and replace the Sykes–Picot Agreement. Lloyd George, aware that northern Mesopotamia in British hands would ensure control of the headwaters of the Tigris and seal off Persia, and its oilfields, from the Turks and the French, stated baldly: 'I want Mosul.' Clemenceau agreed to that. Lloyd George then asked for Jerusalem. Again Clemenceau agreed. In return, the French would keep Syria, although Clemenceau admitted he had little interest in the matter personally—the concession was to placate the political right in France.[26] The meeting was informal, and nothing was recorded, which was to cause considerable debate and confusion later. But the assurance gave Britain what it had wanted throughout the war: security zones that would protect its strategically important interests—Suez, the Persian oilfields, navigation of the Straits, and the reduction of the Ottoman-Turkish and German threats. For the French, however, the British appeared to be an obstacle to their long cherished idea of controlling the Levantine coast and therefore establishing a presence in the eastern as well as the western Mediterranean. Britain had retained control of Palestine and Mosul, and now they witnessed the British officer, Colonel Lawrence, accompanying the Arab delegation that was disputing the French claim to Syria. The fact that Feisal was dependent on a subsidy from the British government only made the suspicions and antagonism more keenly felt.

By December 1919, the situation had changed. The steady demobilization of the British armed forces and the costs of maintaining the occupation of Syria meant that withdrawal was inevitable. Along with the draw-down of forces was the reduction of Feisal's contentious subsidy. Both elements had been essential to the propping-up of the Arab cause in Syria. There seemed only one remaining hope for the Syrians, and that was the findings of the American King–Crane Commission which was to determine the viability of Syria as a self-governing state. The results were that the Syrians wanted a US Mandate administration. President Wilson could not sustain the request, not least because Congress was eager to distance American policy from Europe and the war. In Paris, Alexandre Millerand, the former Minister of War, became Prime Minister, and he was determined to settle the Syrian question in favour of France, by force if necessary. Clemenceau met Feisal in private in January 1920 and offered a way out: Feisal would accept French mandatory control in return for economic relief and a commitment to eventual independence. The proposal was rejected by nationalists in Damascus.[27] The time for compromise had passed.

The Syrian Congress declared independence on 7 March 1920, which prompted the British and French governments to convene a conference at San Remo where the declaration was condemned. With Italian participation, the Allies agreed on the establishment of Mandate authorities across the former Ottoman territories. Endorsement was given by the new League of Nations, and the legitimacy of the Mandate authorities was to reside in this international institution. Britain and France would have control on the ground, but they would be accountable to the League, which, it was hoped, would come to represent international and universal interests. The Allies' declarations made no difference to the Syrians, and the French prepared to enforce their control with an expeditionary force. On 23 July 1920, at the Battle of Maysalun, the French 24th Division routed Feisal's army, and he was sent into exile.

The Hashemite clan were in retreat elsewhere. In May 1919, the forces of Ibn Saud had clashed with Abdullah's army in the Hejaz and defeated the

Figure 11.2 Ibn Saud, king of Saudi Arabia (full name: Abdulaziz ibn Abdul Rahman ibn Faisal ibn Turki ibn Abdullah ibn Muhammad Saud)

Sharifian cause at the Battle of Turaba. The following year, Ibn Saud's forces overran Asir, north of Yemen. In 1921, Ibn Saud crushed his main rival Ibn Rashid, and then pressed on deeper into the Hejaz. Mecca and Medina were captured in 1924, and access to the sea was secured with the seizing of Jeddah. In 1926, with the Sharifians driven out of southern Arabia, the British recognized Ibn Saud as the new king of the Hejaz.[28]

In Palestine, there were changes of a different character. In the first three years after the war, some 19,000 Jewish migrants arrived, enthused by the Balfour declaration or driven out of Europe and Russia by unrest in their home countries. Local Arabs protested to the King–Crane Commission and then to the British, and, repudiating the Balfour Declaration, which promised a Jewish national homeland, an Arab delegation from Syria argued in favour of Palestine's inclusion in a Greater Syria. There was considerable disappointment when Britain prevented a Palestinian delegation from attending the Paris peace conferences. The British announced they were eager to protect the rights of all communities, but they also recognized the enterprise and industry the Jewish brought in, which seemed to hold out the possibility of economic development in the province. Jewish businesses and lobby groups were keen to purchase Palestinian land, and impoverished peasants were often just as eager to sell. At the annual Palestinian Arab Congress there were protests, and these turned to violence in Jerusalem in

1920 and Jaffa in 1921. Forced to reduce costs, there was concern amongst the first Mandate authorities that there were insufficient funds to develop infrastructure or the port facilities at Haifa. The Colonial Office even insisted that the high commissioner, Herbert Samuel, find savings of £1 million in the first few years of the Mandate. Samuel, although himself Jewish, did much to reassure both communities that Britain intended to govern in the interests of all: he even advised the Jewish settlers that the Balfour Declaration was no longer valid, since what mattered was the reconstruction of Palestine. Field Marshal Lord Plumer, an affable veteran of the Western Front, took over from Samuel and continued the work of conciliation, such that the Mandate, while never fully accepted, became an established government throughout the inter-war years.

Despite its pre-eminence in Palestine, Britain could not find a solution to the dilemma of having promised a national home to the Jews and Arab self-government. Inadvertently, it had encouraged some speculation that a pan-Arab state could be established in the Middle East. Britain believed that these two aspirations could be incorporated in a regional federation: the concept of a Jewish homeland did not automatically mean a separate Jewish state. Britain had enjoyed success with schemes of federation in the past, where distinct ethnic and communal groups could unite for the sake of economic development, such as Canada and South Africa. Rivalries within the Arab world meant that separate Arab states were likely, but Britain still hoped and trusted that federations, cooperation, and diplomacy was the best course.

Britain's plans for a post-war settlement had not included consideration of a steady increase in immigration of Jewish settlers, fostered by the World Zionist Organization. Despite unrest in 1921 between settlers and Arabs, and increasing anger among Arab inhabitants, as exemplified by the meetings of the Palestine Arab Congress, the government in London did not believe the immigration issue would create serious problems in the future—an initial surge was to be anticipated perhaps, but there was every expectation it would abate. The new Jewish settlements continued to be the most industrious, and offered the possibility of significant economic development. Arresting the flow entirely was therefore not in Britain's interests. There were good relations between the British government, local Jewish agencies, and the World Zionist Organization, but it was of course especially important, for an empire that ruled over several million Muslims, to respect Arab interests too. As a result, many Ottoman regulations that favoured the Arabs were retained, particularly their privileges over the Holy Places.

The reduction in the size of the British and imperial armed forces after the First World War, a preference for the use of cheaper methods of 'air policing', and the demand for further cuts and economies in the inter-war years, added to the pressure to curb local unrest before it got out of hand. Moreover, the supervision of the League of Nations meant there would be greater legal and international scrutiny of the actions taken by a relatively small number of administrators and service personnel, who consequently came under immense pressure.

Nationalists on both sides had their own agendas. Zionists envisaged an independent state of Israel and believed working with the British offered the best chance of its fulfilment—that is, until the rioting of 1929. In that year, a wave of lethal unrest in Palestine was caused by a combination of several problems: a legacy of communal antagonism, worsened by the coincidence of holy days at religious sites that lay in close proximity to one another; a breakdown of trust in the British authorities and their impartiality; and the insufficient numbers of security forces in the Mandate territories.[29] Low investment, long-standing disputes over land ownership, a drought, and an earthquake in 1927 increased the pressure in Palestine, and Plumer's departure due to ill-health signalled a change in mood. The outbreak of the fighting in 1929 was a combination of unfortunate timing, bad-tempered demonstrations, defiance of the police, fearful reaction, and escalating 'tit-for-tat' violence.

The sheer death toll from the fighting that summer convinced some, including Chaim Weizmann of the World Zionist Organization, that Britain simply could not and would not protect Jewish interests. The Jewish Agency of Palestine criticized the British authorities and the British issued a rebuttal of their claims, but the Zionists terminated their cooperation.[30] Some intellectuals on the Arab side also believed that a pan-Arab state might still be possible, but there was a mixture of reactions towards the British: some felt that cooperation would preserve their position against Jewish interests, while others believed the British were too pro-Zionist and that London had essentially reneged on the promises it had made during the First World War. Ironically, intelligence records reveal that the British selected Amin al-Husayni as the grand mufti of Jerusalem at this time, even though they knew he was opposed to British interests, because he was the least radical of the local Muslim leaders and offered some opportunity for dialogue.[31] Yet the nationalists were far from reaching any compromise. There would be further trouble ahead.

The Mandate for Palestine had been formally established in 1922, but territories that lay beyond the eastern bank were separated and became Transjordan, largely because Winston Churchill favoured the division of the city of Amman and the jurisdiction there of Abdullah bin Hussein, as a distinct polity that would be uncontaminated by the politics of Palestine, and, moreover, would provide a cordon against French influence in southern Arabia. Abdullah had fought to secure the Hejaz from the Ottomans but the Hashemite cause was in disarray, and Transjordan was created as Abdullah's kingdom and a secure Hashemite territory. Despite the overturning of all the governments and states created in the period 1919–20, it was Jordan, the last to be arranged, that would emerge unscathed. Indeed, arguably Jordan and Saudi Arabia have been the most stable of the entire region, an exception to the tumultuous changes of the twentieth century. They are really the only ones that can trace a direct line of continuity from the Great War.

In southern Arabia, preserving stability was far more difficult despite Britain's backing of the Idrisid clans against the former pro-Ottoman ruler Imam Yahya. His offensive from the Yemeni highlands in 1919 was halted by British air-policing methods: air power proved highly effective against the Yemeni tribal forces. Yahya made a second attempt to expand his area of control against the Idrisids in 1922, but, once again, British air control proved decisive against him. In 1925, Yahya made a third attempt which finally overran much of the Idrisid territory before the British could intervene and he forced them into agreements that accepted his suzerainty over the territory. By 1927, the imam's forces had reached the British protectorate of Aden, but there, again, he was decisively crushed by air attacks over five days. Sensing an opportunity, the Idrisids appealed to the Saudis for support against the imam, and a new crisis developed in 1933 when anti-Saudi dissidents took refuge in the area under the imam's control. Britain supplied the Saudis with aircraft and munitions as they mounted their own offensive that year. Eventually, after many months of negotiations, Imam Yahya agreed to relinquish control of several provinces in the interior and agreed to respect British control of territories adjacent to Aden, but the tension with the Saudis continued.

Ibn Saud had waged his own war against Al-Rashid in Nejd, the desert region of the interior of southern Arabia which he secured in 1921, followed by the Hejaz, which was incorporated in 1925. The successful Saudi Arabian tribal army, the Ikhwan, inspired by Wahhabi ideology, wanted to press on and assert itself across the region including Yemen, leading to several raids into Transjordan, Kuwait, and Iraq, but Ibn Saud, knowing the military power of the British, aimed to avoid direct confrontation. In 1928, angered by Ibn Saud's domestic agenda, the Ikhwan turned on their sponsor but Ibn Saud defeated the revolt in 1930 at the Battle of Sabilla, whereupon the ringleaders were executed. Thereafter the Saudis became cautious partners of the British in that they shared a desire to maintain the status quo.

The occupation of Mesopotamia continued after the Great War and was administered by military authority as an occupied enemy territory until the establishment of British civil government under Sir Arnold Wilson. This arrangement disappointed the Arabs, but the San Remo Conference (1920), which made the new Iraq a Mandate territory, sparked mass demonstrations. Iraqis feared that, despite wartime assurances of liberation, the British intended to turn Iraq into a colony and they accused Sir Arnold of extending wartime powers rather than relinquishing them. Wilson had told the British government that no aspirations for independence existed.[32] Gertrude Bell, the indomitable traveller and Oriental Secretary to Wilson's administration, concurred that the Arabs only wanted the British, rather than the Ottomans or the French. The Secretary of State for India asked Wilson to obtain popular support for a single Arab state of Iraq with British tutelage, in order to conform to the new spirit of self-determination being sought by the peacemakers in Europe.[33] Wilson and his political officers made attempts to win over prominent sheikhs in the search for a consensus, and extended the patronage system which had been the mainstay of British influence in the Gulf for the previous hundred years.

Fearful of the sort of takeover then underway in Syria, Iraqi protests were led by prominent religious figures and orchestrated by former Ottoman Army officers and tribal elders. They felt that evidence was mounting of British permanent control. The establishment of a British Revenue Secretariat and assessments of land and local rents seemed to herald further control, not autonomy. The Indian rupee, which had been the currency in Basra during the occupation, was extended to the whole country and Indian officials were prominent in the administration. Yet, Wilson's desire to portray universal backing for the British authorities meant there was little consideration of the growing opposition, despite the criticism of Gertrude Bell.[34] A delegation entitled the Haras al-Istiqlal al-'Iraqiyin (Iraq Guards for Independence) had, like the Egyptians and Palestinians, been prevented from attending the Paris peace conferences.[35] But, unlike previous anti-Ottoman nationalists, these young men wanted nothing to do with the British. Most dangerous of all, amongst the ranks of the discontented were Iraqis who had served in

Emir Feisal's army against the Ottomans. Seasoned by war and fully expecting a reward for their service, their participation was a crucial factor in the violence that occurred.

In May 1920, at a series of mass meetings and demonstrations, other grievances were added to the Iraqi nationalist agenda, including the demand to repeal taxation and land-ownership legislation. Sunni and Shi'a leaders shared the same objectives, even though close cooperation between them was always difficult. There was some inspiration from protests in Egypt, and from the Kurdish north, both of which had begun the previous year, and enthusiastic demonstrations in Baghdad soon spread to other cities. The rejection of Iraqi demands for representative governance by Sir Arnold Wilson was the spark that led to an outbreak of violence in June that year. Ayotallah Muhammad Taqi Al-Shirazi, a Shi'a leader, subsequently issued two fatwa: one declared that Iraqi service in the British administration was *haram* (forbidden) and the second authorized resistance if Iraqi demands were not met. As rioting worsened, the British authorities moved to arrest ringleaders, but the springing from prison of an elder from the Zawalim clan, who had been arrested for refusing to pay taxes, by armed followers ignited a general revolt. By July, most settlements along the Euphrates were in rebel hands, and so were the districts around Baghdad.[36]

The suppression of the revolt was successful, and given the capability of the British forces, inevitable. Two squadrons of RAF aircraft, later augmented to ninety aircraft, conducted extensive operations against rebel bands, and the fighters were dispersed with explosives and machine-gun fire. A number of Indian Army battalions were brought in as reinforcements. The army's armoured cars and infantry, some mounted in lorries for additional mobility, were also active in every region, assisted in many cases by Iraqi levies in British service. Despite subsequent attempts by Iraqi nationalists to portray the uprising as a 'great, national struggle', the unrest actually revealed the deep fissures within Iraqi society. When Kurds in the north revolted, their objectives and actions were not aligned with the Arab Sunni and Shi'a populations in the south. Various clans tended to join the revolt in an uncoordinated and piecemeal manner, allowing the British to defeat them in detail. Sunni elites also failed to participate, seeing greater advantage in remaining with the British. Their decision deterred the participation of many thousands of Sunnis. The rising caused considerable consternation in London because the numbers of troops required and the cost of the suppression put great strain on budgets that were already depressed after the war.

Sir Arnold Wilson told London: 'What we are up against is anarchy plus fanaticism. There is little or no nationalism.' He asserted, rather implausibly, that the trouble was caused by foreign agencies including Kemal Atatürk, the Germans, pan-Islamists, Standard Oil, the Jews, and the Bolsheviks.[37]

In October 1920, the rebels were defeated. Short of funding and support, the leaders surrendered Karbala and Najaf. Some 6,000 rebels had been killed, and 312 British and Indian personnel had also perished in the fighting. The cost of the counter-insurgency had been considerable: the £40 million bill represented twice the annual budget for Iraq's administration. Churchill, now the Secretary of State for the Colonies, was particularly incensed at the cost of suppressing a tribal uprising.[38] The imperative at the end of the fighting was to find a cheaper dispensation that was more acceptable to the Iraqi people. As a result of a conference in Cairo, the British garrison was reduced and security was placed into the hands of the RAF. Government was put into the hands of Feisal. He was rendered dependent on British advisors which ensured London's influence in the country was maintained, but the relationship was often strained. His dependence was not only to keep him in line in Iraq; it was also to prevent him making another attempt to contest French control of Syria. Elevating him to become king of Iraq, they reasoned, ensured he possessed an alternative source of power and prestige amongst the Arabs.

The Cairo Conference was an attempt to reorder not only Iraq but other parts of the Middle East. The Iraq Revolt, the unrest in Egypt, the Syrian conflict, and the fighting still unfolding in southern Arabia, against a background of falling budgets and reduced military means, demanded a strategic review. Churchill was assisted by Lawrence, his special advisor, and the conference itself was attended by the British civil and military leadership of Mesopotamia, the Gulf, Egypt, and Palestine, including Arnold Wilson, Sir Percy Cox, General Edmund Allenby, and Sir Herbert Samuel. Also in attendance were Feisal and Abdullah of the Hashemite dynasty. Gertrude Bell was one of the specialist representatives of Iraq but so was Jafar al-Askari, the veteran of the Sharifian operations and pro-British Iraqi officer. The conference met to approve the decision that the kingdoms of Iraq and Transjordan would be awarded to Feisal and Abdullah respectively.[39] The monarchy of Iraq was compensation for Feisal, but it was still a curious decision given the absence of any family, clan, or patronage links to Mesopotamia. The conference approved of the French control of Syria and Lebanon, but there was little comment on any other aspect of Arab nationalism in Syria for another four years, until a revolt broke out. The final settlement between Britain and France came two years later, when agreements were concluded over the future of Mosul.

Meanwhile, Afghanistan, the one regional state that had apparently remained unaffected by the war, was on the cusp of collapse. Amir Habibullah expected a generous reward from the government of India after the war, not least because he had remained aligned to Britain despite the arrival of Ottoman and German delegations in 1915. What the Afghans wanted was full independence, since, by the treaty agreed in 1879, the British controlled Afghan foreign policy in return for protection of Afghanistan's territorial integrity. Concerned that this issue might be raised in Paris, the British discouraged Habibullah from sending a delegation to Europe. Soon after, they were preoccupied by unrest in the Punjab, and, at the time, the government of India did not consider Afghanistan to be a priority. However, the viceroy, Lord Chelmsford, was sympathetic to the amir's request that British control should be relinquished.[40] After all, it had been impossible, in spite of the 1879 treaty, to prevent foreign emissaries reaching Kabul or a treaty being signed with two countries with which Britain was actually at war. For the sake of better future relations, Chelmsford thought that removing an irksome clause might be safer. The calculation came too late. Amir Habibullah was murdered on 20 February 1919.

Habibullah's brother, Nasrullah Khan, claimed the throne as amir and ensured that Habibullah's eldest son and heir apparent, Inyatullah, submitted to him. The announcement was greeted with enthusiasm by the *ulema* and by the Ghilzai clans of eastern Afghanistan.[41] However, Amanullah, the third son of the late amir, refused to accept Nasrullah's accession. His command of the military garrison at Kabul proved to be decisive. Offering to immediately increase soldiers' pay enticed the army to declare themselves for Amanullah. Nasrullah and his allies were arrested. The government of India accepted the accession of Amanullah as amir, but the mullahs of Afghanistan protested. Expressions of concern spread rapidly to the rest of the population and the army began to look unreliable. Amanullah needed to establish his legitimacy with the people. His long and outspoken criticism of his father's close relations with the British offered the chance to harness public support. Within days, Amanullah declared war on Britain.

The Afghan assumption was that the British Empire was weakened by the First World War. In March and April 1919, British authorities in India were facing serious unrest in the Punjab. One Afghan verdict was that:

> The English are distracted in mind on account of the European war, and have not the strength to attack the Afghans. The people of India too are much dissatisfied with the English on account of their tyranny and oppression. They will never hesitate to raise a revolt, if they can find the opportunity, as their hearts are bleeding at their hands.[42]

There was a great deal of anger with the wartime restrictions of the Criminal Law Amendment Act, popularly known as the Rowlatt Acts, and there were riots in Delhi and Lahore. In Amritsar, Brigadier General Reginald Dyer imposed martial law, and subsequently opened fire on an unauthorized and unarmed meeting of several hundred Punjabis, killing over 300 civilians.[43]

To seize advantage of the unrest, the Afghan 'post master' in Peshawar, Ghulam Hayder, reported that he was prepared to 'begin a Holy War in Peshawar City'.[44] He wrote that 8,000 men, both Hindus and Muslims, were at his call with a further 2,000 from the neighbouring villages. He even claimed that 'Sikh regiments have assured Hindus that they look on Moslems as brethren and will not fire on them.' More importantly he reported, quite erroneously, that there were 'not sufficient troops in India and [the government] often moves about one regiment, consisting of 2 or 3 companies, [*sic*] to make a display'. He claimed that, despite efforts to get more men, none had arrived in the Peshawar area and that even 'British subjects will not supply recruits', which was perhaps a reference to the unwillingness of Territorial battalions that had served on the North West Frontier during the war to stay on much longer in India. The post master reported enthusiastically that there were 'disturbances throughout India' and added that, if Afghanistan did not act in favour of the people of India, the 'public will be displeased with the Amir'. He concluded, 'it is not expedient to delay and to give the English time to collect troops'.[45]

In fact the Peshawar insurrection failed almost immediately because the city was quickly subdued by the threat that if the ringleaders of the unrest were not handed over the population would have its water supply cut off.[46] The unrest of April was also crushed by armed police while Dyer's action at Amritsar had a salutary effect on rioters elsewhere. The British, for all the talk of their war weariness, were showing that they were as determined as ever to maintain security and control of the region and they were prepared to use considerable force to do it. If the Afghan strategy had been to exploit unrest in India hoping it would tie down hundreds of British and Indian troops, then it failed even before their war got fully underway.

At the outbreak of hostilities on 6 May 1919, the amir made a declaration of jihad against British injustices and claimed he had the right to intervene in India in accordance with international law. He stated that the British had inflicted injustices of all kinds, but especially against religion, honour, and modesty. The same day, Afghan troops seized a peak above the strategically important Khyber Pass and killed a party of labourers.[47] Mustering a total of 50,000 men, the Afghan Army outnumbered the British forces along the frontier, but with no experience of formation-level manoeuvres, Afghan units tended to remain on the defensive and make only tactical assaults when opportunities arose.

The Afghan Army had concentrated in four locations: at the head of the Khyber Pass in the north; in Khost and in Kunar, both in eastern Afghanistan; and at Kandahar in the south, while a reserve was kept at Kabul. The amir's strategy was based on exploiting a narrow window of opportunity and achieving a rapid if limited success against British forces in the border area, in order to bolster his domestic position. Not all of his forces were in position by the time the war broke out, and there is no doubt that prompt counter-offensives by the British disrupted the Afghan strategy. The main Afghan offensive on the 'central front' near Thal did not get underway until 26 May, by which time Afghan forces at the Khyber Pass and Kandahar had already been defeated.

To oppose the Afghans, the British had a number of Territorial Army battalions whose personnel were eager for demobilization, and there were some inexperienced Indian Army regiments, stiffened with mountain artillery, armoured cars, and, most importantly, aircraft of the Royal Air Force. From the outset, the RAF were envisaged as the decisive arm against the Afghans. Despite being checked in their first attempt to clear the Khyber Pass on 9 May, the British were in a position to make a second assault just two days later.[48] The second attack was made at night and the leading units were within yards of the Afghan positions when firing broke out. The British made their attacks by hurling grenades into unsuspecting Afghan sangars, and then followed up with bayonet charges and close-range fire support. The Afghan positions were overrun and five Afghan guns captured, and as they withdrew they were strafed by British aircraft or shot down by carefully placed cut-off groups. It was estimated that in this, the Second Battle of Bagh, on 11 May 1919 the Afghans lost 100 killed and 300 wounded.

To follow up their attack, the British maintained their air bombardment of Dakka, en route to Kabul, dropped propaganda leaflets urging local clans to stay out of the fighting, and pushed on westwards, across the border, with ground forces. The amir protested, claiming he had not sought to interfere in the unrest in India, but soon initiated a serious counter-attack. Even against inexperienced troops, it was with some difficulty that the British held on to the surrounding hills. In the end, it was the sustained air campaign and the inability of the Afghans to dislodge the British and Indian troops that caused the amir's men to withdraw towards the capital.

The British decided to make a surprise counter-offensive against Kandahar to prevent the Afghans from stirring the Baluchis of British India to resistance, but also to put pressure on the Afghan government and draw reserves away from the northern theatre of operations. The result was the defeat of the Afghan garrison at Spin Boldak, the southern border town, by a combined ground and air attack.[49] With both their northern and southern wings defeated, the Afghans made one last attempt to drive into British India through Waziristan. Their hope was that the Waziris, who had shown support for the amir's jihadist declarations, would accompany the Afghan Army as it advanced through British territory. They believed that an offensive towards Peshawar might force the British to abandon any hope of reaching Kabul. The offensive was to use overwhelming force, with two axes of advance via the Kurram and Matun valleys converging at the town of Thal at the heart of the North West Frontier Province, consisting of fourteen battalions of infantry and forty-eight guns, augmented by irregulars. The British had almost no forces in this sector to oppose the onslaught. Indeed, the full strength of the Afghan Army that descended on Thal numbered 19,000. The British garrison mustered ninety.

Occupying the high ground around the settlement, General Nadir ringed three sides of the hastily dug British defences. The small British garrison were able to resist a number of probing attacks, but it was clear that, without supplies, they could not hold out for long. As a result, Brigadier General Dyer assembled a relief force at Kohat and implemented a deception plan, whereby he assembled dummy artillery from logs and used brushwood on the mud flaps of his motor vehicles, which raised great clouds of dust, to give the impression that a large force was approaching. Dyer made a forced march with his composite force and arrived on 31 May. He used artillery fire to distract the Afghans from his true intentions, and attacked with all his forces against irregulars stationed in the southern hills.[50] After several hours of fighting, they were dispersed. Nadir Khan sent a message to Dyer arguing that an armistice had been concluded and he asked that hostilities be suspended while negotiations were underway. Dyer was right to suspect that Nadir Khan intended to withdraw the bulk of his force without engaging the British and responded abruptly: 'My guns will give an immediate reply.' Nadir Khan's men fled, and stores and equipment were abandoned in the retreat. The RAF assisted in the harassment of Nadir Khan's forces, but perhaps their most important contribution was the bombing of Kabul and Jalalabad. Just over a ton of explosives were dropped on the two cities, creating panic. Amanullah requested an immediate ceasefire.

With his nationalist credentials established against Britain and his domestic reputation sealed, Amanullah also tried to champion the Basmachi cause against the Soviets in Central Asia. During the war, rumours that the tsar was about to impose conscription were sufficient to ignite a revolt in 1916, and, while this wartime resistance was crushed, sufficient numbers remained defiant throughout 1917 to organize a subsequent and more sustained guerrilla war. During the revolution, the focus of fighting was the independent Islamic and leftist authority in Kokand. To suppress this bid for self-government, the Bolsheviks used Caucasian, especially Armenian, irregulars, but the massacres they inflicted mobilized even larger numbers of Central Asians to form resistance groups, collectively known as the Basmachi, with Irgash Bey as one of its more prominent leaders.

Despite the loss of the fertile Ferghana Valley early on, and some defections, the Basmachi movement continued to radiate across the region, and Khiva and Bokhara were soon engaged in the conflict. Enver, who had volunteered initially to assist the Soviets to put down the revolt in 1921, took the opportunity to defect to the resistance and he came to command the Basmachi with a corps of 16,000. His pan-Turanian appeal was blended with an Islamist call to arms with such success that, for a time, he appeared to dominate Turkestan. Soviet policies of reconciliation, concessions to Islamic law and custom, and overwhelming military force led by General Frunze, the Soviet commander, eventually defeated Enver's movement at Kafrun in June 1922, although Afghanistan remained a base of operations for Basmachi fighters until 1926. The government in Moscow pressured Amanullah to abandon his war by proxy, and so the Afghans shifted their strategy to embrace the communists. Yet, in the case of Amanullah and many Afghan officers, there was initially more enthusiasm for the achievements of Kemal Atatürk in Turkey than for either the communists or Enver.[51] The modernization and nationalism of the Turkish army, their series of victories against the Greeks in Smyrna, and a successful confrontation with Britain over the Chanak Straits all seemed to indicate the direction for Afghanistan.

Not everyone in the region was in awe of Atatürk. In June 1920, some 18,000 Muslims in British India attempted to emigrate to Afghanistan in the hope of being the vanguard of a new *Khalifat* (caliphate), but Atatürk's destruction of the old Ottoman system and Amanullah's unwillingness to lead a *ghaza* (offensive holy war) to restore the caliphate, or even accommodate the *Khalifat* emigrants, caused the movement to collapse.[52]

Domestic unrest forced Amanullah out of office on 14 January 1929. His zeal for reform and modernization had generated great resistance. His successor Inyatullah held on for only three days and had to be evacuated on a British aircraft. Amanullah tried to regain the throne but was defeated and forced into exile. Afghanistan remained plagued with unrest for years.

One by one, the jihadist revolts, initiated or encouraged by the Ottomans and the Germans, were petering out. The risings in Libya, Sudan, Sinai, Afghanistan, and Turkestan had all been crushed. The nationalists too had foundered in the face of opposition by the European powers. The uprisings in Egypt, Syria, Iraq, and the Caucasus had been put down. The pathetic nature of the resistance was exemplified by one of the last struggles that had been linked to Ottoman inspiration during the war. In Somaliland, Mullah Abdullah Hassan was regarded by the British as a peripheral figure, a fanatic of little lasting consequence. In 1900, this little-known alam had made himself notorious for anti-British rhetoric. That same year, the mullah moved his followers to the strategic watering hole at Burao and declared jihad, initially against Somalis who failed to heed him, but his continuing defiance led to the despatch of British columns to intercept him. There was a brief interlude when the Italians agreed to settle his followers at Ilig, but this 'recognition' only increased his prestige and his movement came to be seen as a form of resistance to all non-Somalis. Mindful of the power he was acquiring, Abdullah Hassan made extensive use of 'emissaries' to spread his message. Yet, the strongest support was limited to his own Darod clan and his mother's tribe, the Dolbohanta. He found it difficult to get much backing outside these groups (which were admittedly large ones in the Somali context).

Just as he seemed to be at the peak of his popular appeal, one of his former acolytes, Abdullah Shahari, had him condemned by the religious authorities in Mecca, but this only seemed to increase levels of violence and the interior of Somaliland was practically abandoned to his jihadists. Hoping for protection, some groups, even the Dolbohanta, looked to the British for support. Resistance continued sporadically into the war, but sensing that the British might soon turn against him in a more sustained way, Abdullah Hassan voluntarily placed himself under Ottoman protection. He claimed to have answered the caliph's call to jihad, hoping for external backing. But the Ottoman Empire's defeat in 1918 and a popular Somali desire for peace and reform after years of war in the interior meant support drained away. The mullah was soon in retreat and confined to the south-eastern corner of British Somaliland.

In 1920, at Jid Ali, the British brought in the RAF and drove the remnants of the mullah's forces into retreat. The mullah himself escaped to the Ogaden, but was pursued by 3,000 Somali auxiliaries commissioned by the British. On the run, many of the mullah's remaining followers died of a smallpox epidemic, and he too was struck down in January 1921. The movement he had led collapsed immediately. As in so many examples in the Great War, aspirations and ideals withered under the machinery of war or wasted away through infection, deprivation, and disease. The last flame of the wartime jihad had been finally extinguished.

In this way, by the mid-1920s, the Middle East was brought under the control of the British and French Empires. The military operations that had restored peace after 1918 nevertheless elicited a strongly worded reproach from the Afghans, which spoke for many across the region: 'it is a matter for great regret', they wrote, 'that the throwing of bombs . . . and bombardment of places of worship and sacred spots was considered a most abominable operation [in the World War] while we now see with our own eyes that such operations were a habit which is prevalent amongst all civilized people of the West'.[53]

12

Making Strategy in War and Peace

The British had not intended to dismember the Ottoman Empire before the war, as their national interests were better served by its preservation. The Ottoman territories acted as buffer zones for the British commercial arteries that ran between the United Kingdom and its maritime empire. The Straits had contained Russia, the Suez Canal was in its possession, and the supremacy of the Royal Navy had ensured that the eastern Mediterranean, Arabian Sea, Gulf, and Indian Ocean were under Britain's control. Even regimes that resented British influence and power, such as Persia and Afghanistan, were unwitting components in Britain's defence schemes for India and the empire in Asia. British garrisons or partners in Aden, Kuwait, the Trucial States, and Cyprus also acted as bridgeheads for greater influence in the interior of the Middle East.

Yet, even before the war, there had been a challenge to Britain's grand strategy. The constellation of France and Russia, its chief colonial rivals, had forced the government to confront the country's isolation. Prime Minister Lord Salisbury had hinted in 1900 that Britain's diplomatic independence could no longer be considered 'splendid'. Within a decade, not only had there been a comprehensive review of Britain's relations with France and Russia, but secret military talks with France implied some 'Continental commitment' against the new aggressive foreign policy of Germany. And it was Germany's combined battleship building programme and posturing in the Middle East against Britain's interests that confirmed the government's determination to respond to a new threat. In 1912, Lord Haldane, the Secretary of State for War, had attempted to halt the arms race, but Lloyd George, the Chancellor of the Exchequer, was less conciliatory. In his Mansion House speech that year, he roundly condemned the Germans' apparent intention to build a naval base in Morocco which would threaten Gibraltar. The language of the Agadir Crisis was belligerent on both sides, and there is some indication that, as a result, Germany felt it needed to prepare for war within two years.

The alignment of the Ottoman Empire with the Central Powers and the outbreak of war in 1914 transformed the 'ways' in which Britain fulfilled its national interests in the Middle East. Initially there was optimism. The Ottomans failed to prevent a British landing in the Gulf in the course of protecting oil installations in southern Persia. The Ottoman naval attack against Russia in Odessa was short-lived, and when an Ottoman offensive was launched against Egypt in late 1914, it was checked and defeated. Indeed, the Ottoman menace to the Suez Canal failed to interrupt the great movement of men, materials, and shipping from the British Empire to Europe. Egypt proved to be an important staging post and training ground for troops bound for other theatres, and furthermore the Ottoman Empire had seemingly failed to defend itself when the Royal Navy had bombarded the port of Aqaba and the forts at the tip of Gallipoli. Indeed, the spectacular detonation of the magazine at the Sedd el-Bahr fortress gave the impression that naval gunfire would be very effective against land defences.

The reputation of the Ottoman Empire for defeats, including the Balkan Wars (1912–13) and the disaster at Sarıkamış (1914), further encouraged the idea that it could be knocked out of the war relatively easily. Plans were considered for an assault on Alexandretta, which would cut off the Arabian possessions from the Anatolian heartland and cause serious dislocation to any attempt to reinforce the garrison in Mesopotamia. But objections by France prevented the Alexandretta plan from being initiated. Instead, with pressure mounting to counterbalance another Ottoman thrust against Suez via Sinai, and urgent calls from Russia for support, it was decided to launch a naval attack through the Dardanelles. If successful, Istanbul would be at the mercy of the Royal Navy's guns and it would be forced to capitulate. This would persuade other Balkan and neutral nations to reject the Central Powers and complete the encirclement of Germany and Austria-Hungary. Instead of more costly engagements on the Western Front, the Entente could remove the kaisers' 'props'.

The naval operations were hampered by bad weather, the density of sea mines, insufficient 'means' for mine sweeping, and determined, skilful use of artillery by the Ottomans. The loss of three significant vessels to mines on 18 March 1915 brought to an end all idea of success with naval power alone.

Amphibious operations were thus executed at Gallipoli but the 'means' were inadequate and the steady build-up of manpower came too late to achieve local superiority. Since the British and imperial forces were unable to get across the Gallipoli peninsula, so the Ottoman guns covering the Dardanelles remained inviolate. The stalemate that developed suggests a form of stasis, but that would be misleading. Both sides made Herculean efforts to drive the other back. The cost in lives, both from combat and disease, was inordinately high for such limited results.

The Gallipoli battles also exposed a brutal but stark truth about the character of war in this period. It was a question of ruthless mathematics in juxtaposition to the moral force of human will. The higher volumes, rates of fire, longer ranges, flatter trajectories, and accuracy of modern artillery, machine guns, and magazine-fed rifles could cut down men attempting to cross open ground far more efficiently than in the past. This tactical reality impinged upon operational plans repeatedly. In turn, strategic ambitions were curtailed. Urgent solutions were sought and deployed, producing enhanced artillery coordination, new technologies, and, eventually, all-arms synchronization. In spite of saturating bombardments with overwhelming volumes of fire, determined bands of survivors could often provide sufficient resistance to stall even large-scale attacks, while vigorous counter-attacks against depleted assaulting formations could recover ground that was lost.

The idea of the 'culminating point of strength', articulated by Carl von Clausewitz in the early nineteenth century, was played out not only at the tactical level, but also at the operational and strategic level. The British offensive up the Tigris in 1914–15 swept aside the Ottoman defenders. The rapidity of the advance encouraged the belief that Baghdad might be taken. The loss of this city would, it was hoped, not only discredit the Ottoman Empire but, in the estimation of the British colonial authorities, produce a beneficial effect on the minds of their Muslim subjects. It was widely held that 'the Oriental' was impressed with strength and would offer his allegiance to the side that seemed the strongest. The capture of Baghdad was thus a reassuring prospect to British imperial governors from Cairo to Calcutta, as it held out the possibility of neutralizing one uncomfortable fact: the British were confronted with a specifically anti-colonial call to arms by the caliph of Istanbul, with German encouragement.

In fact, the subsequent failure of the overextended dash to Baghdad, and the fall of Kut, was accompanied by even more alarming intelligence about

German and Ottoman attempts to foment unrest in Egypt, Sudan, British Somaliland, Persia, Afghanistan, and India. German agents, replete with gold, tried to buy the loyalty of British colonial subjects or those they were convinced had grievances against London or New Delhi. In places, the advocates of jihad had some success. There were serious insurgencies in western Egypt, Sudan, and southern Persia. But these were only marginally concerned with esoteric ideas of holy war. Far more pragmatic considerations shaped the allegiances of the people of the Middle East, and some were existential. Armenian and Hashemite resistance to the Ottomans, for example, was driven by the desire to survive. Others made their decisions on the basis of power. Nationalists saw opportunities in the war, but were often confronted by the overwhelming force of occupying armies. The Persians, for example, were frequently forced into retreat by Russian, Ottoman, or British troops. Syrian nationalists lacked the means to subvert the Ottomans' imposition of martial law. Egyptian nationalists were similarly weak but they were also bitterly divided and barely organized.

Contrary to all expectations, the British struggled to overcome the Ottomans in 1915–16. They were forced to evacuate from Gallipoli, and failed to make headway in Palestine in 1917 despite a promising campaign in Sinai. Limits on resources meant there were strict instructions to remain on the defensive in Mesopotamia. Shifts in the relationship between the Prime Minister Lloyd George and the Chief of the Imperial General Staff, Sir William Robertson, reflecting a difference in preferred emphasis on the eastern theatres and the Western Front respectively, broke the deadlock in the Middle East. With Lloyd George's backing, Maude was allowed to press on past Kut to Baghdad and Allenby was permitted to take Jerusalem. By the end of 1917, both of these ancient cities were in British hands. In 1918, the British achieved even more significant military victories in northern Mesopotamia, at Hit and Khan Baghdadi, and in Palestine, at Meggido. The Ottoman forces were routed, enveloped, or destroyed.

Allenby later noted that, in late 1917, it had not been at all apparent that the Allies would win the war. Russia had withdrawn from the war, and the Americans had not yet arrived in force in Europe. There was every chance that France and Italy, both of whom had suffered significant military set-backs, might seek a compromise peace, not least because there was the prospect of a major German offensive in the west, and possibly also in the Middle East, in 1918. The British offensive into Palestine and Syria was seen as a way to ensure a better bargaining position at the peace talks—and would give Britain a buffer for India against a German-dominated Middle East.

After the war, Palestine and Sinai became more important in Britain's imperial defence. In 1924, the Colonial Office concluded:

> Previous to 1914 and during the critical phases of the Great War, Egypt was the essential link between Europe and our Eastern possessions. The Suez Canal assumed an importance which rendered its defence of vital consequence. Nevertheless, the Turk reached the Canal, and at one point succeeded in crossing it. Such success was in part due to our inability to find troops in that period of the war for detachments outside the vital theatre and the undeveloped state of our resources. But the factor which rendered invasion of Egypt and an attack on the canal possible for the Turks was the close proximity of the Turkish base and railhead to Egypt. The geographical defence of Egypt, namely, the Sinai desert, had proved itself inadequate in modern warfare, and still more apparent will this become in any future war.
>
> As the Great War developed and military operations in the Middle East expanded, it soon became apparent that not only Egypt but Palestine rose in importance in the political and strategic world. Palestine, hitherto only a country of interest to us, assumed the proportion of the strong enemy base, both naval, military and air, whose occupation became necessary for our security in the East and Mediterranean.
>
> The security of Egypt depends on isolation from both physical and moral attack. Any occupation of Palestine had proved too close to render such isolation complete. Many as were the advantages of defending Egypt along the line of the Suez Canal, a line some 80 miles long, and with a desert glacis stretching to the East, there were disadvantages. The line was too attenuated except for a large body of troops. Any strategic counter-attack was impossible owing to lack of water in Sinai Desert except by a slow methodical advance. The Canal was too close to Egypt, and Turkish successes would be at once felt in a country which reacts with mercurial effect [to] local circumstances. The bombing of Cairo was undertaken by the Turk in days when aeronautics were in their infancy.[1]

The Hashemite Arabs participated in the enterprise to secure Palestine and Syria, something which had given them, as they saw it, a right to rule Arabia in the post-war settlement. This view was not shared by London or Paris, which qualified their response. Britain had envisaged that the Ottoman Empire would survive, with autonomous regions, not unlike Egypt, under Allied supervision. This would ensure that Russia or Turkey did not try to make a bid for control of the region. London also felt obliged to accommodate its French ally, and that meant relinquishing control of Syria. The British strove for compromise, hoping to satisfy the Arab factions, especially Ibn Saud and Sharif Hussein, and those Britain sought to support, namely the Kuwaitis, Idrisids, and Trucial Sheikhs. It also tried to accommodate the Jews in a homeland in Palestine, not least because of their wartime support. The answer to the overlapping claims in the post-war Middle East appeared to lie in two solutions: one, Mandate authorities, which ensured British influence but permitted time for the preparation of self-government; and two, the appointment of Emir Feisal as king of Syria and Abdullah as king of Transjordan, which rewarded two allies and created a bloc alongside the domains of the king of the Hejaz, their father Hussein. The former was achieved, but the latter seemed to unravel within a decade of the war's conclusion. Hussein lost the Hejaz, Feisal was ejected from Syria, and compensated with the ill-fated monarchy of Iraq, and only Abdullah's regime survived.

Figure 12.1 Sharif Hussein, the Guardian of the Holy Places, king of Hejaz, whose aspiration to become caliph was ultimately unsuccessful

The wartime destabilization of traditional power relationships was crucial in developing the opportunities for new political factions, but at the same time, caused a revision of wartime strategies. The collapse of the tsarist regime in Russia released the nationalities of the Caucasus to make new polities, and removed the constraints on northern Persians. The conclusion of the European war and the chance to remake the region through the peace conference at Paris also created expectations. For certain minorities, these hopes would be dashed. Some groups ultimately went down to defeat: the Georgians, the Iraqis, the Kurds, the Azeris, the Syrians, the Senussi, and the Idrisids. For others, including Kemal Atatürk and Ibn Saud, there would be new wars to fulfil their aspirations.

The British emerged as the most successful from the Great War in the Middle East. Their interests were secure and they possessed strategically important territory to further those interests, including the oil fields in Mosul, the landward approaches to India, the Suez Canal, and even the Straits and Dardanelles. France had established its presence in Syria, which ensured that, in all future consideration of the region, the French would have to be consulted. Strategically, they also now possessed a base in the eastern Mediterranean, and therefore a balance to British domination in those waters.

By contrast, Russia had fulfilled none of her pre-war strategic ambitions for the Middle East. The Caucasus would eventually fall under Soviet domination, and Central Asia too, but this was merely the recovery of territories the Russians had possessed before 1914. Checked in Poland in 1920, the Bolshevik regime had to concentrate on consolidating its domestic power. Its influence in the Middle East was limited in the inter-war years. Even Afghanistan, a Soviet partner from 1921, was convulsed by internal disorder and when it emerged in 1933 as a more secure state once more, it was a monarchy aligned to Britain.

The Ottomans had also achieved none of their war aims. The Ottoman thrusts against Britain in Egypt and against the Russians in the Caucasus had both ended in ignominy and merely encouraged these two empires, which had been content to remain on the strategic defensive in the region, to consider greater offensive action against the regime. While the Ottomans defended Gallipoli, Palestine, Mesopotamia, and eastern Anatolia successfully in 1915, these operations could not create indefinitely the strategic security they sought. Indeed, it could be argued that it was only a matter of time before the resources of the Entente powers could be brought to bear against the Ottomans, and that their relative success in defence was only achieved when the British and Russians were forced to deploy their strength elsewhere.

If one is to accept that pan-Turanianism was no more than the establishment of Turkish control of the Caucasus, rather than the foundation of a new Turkic empire across Persia and Central Asia, then we would still conclude that Enver's ambitions were unfulfilled. Djemal's aspirations too were never realized. The relegation of the idea of the caliphate was, however, already very well advanced even before the war broke out. The secularists had won power over the sultan before 1914, and it was likely that the war only accelerated the termination of the institution of monarchy. Triumvirate member Mehmet Talaat's desire to suppress all internal disorder with terror during his time as Ottoman Minister of the Interior was the greatest failure of all: it generated more resistance and utterly discredited both the Committee of Union and Progress and the Ottoman Empire. The other war objectives were certainly failures. The Ottomans did not recover the Balkans, the islands of the Aegean, Egypt, or Libya. Indeed, it was Atatürk as leader of Turkey who recovered part of the lost provinces of the Caucasus, not the Ottoman Empire.

The surprise of the Great War in the Middle East was nevertheless the resilience of the Ottoman Empire. It had fought a war on four fronts simultaneously, it had endured a steady erosion of its capacity to fight, and yet it had clung on, exhibiting a characteristically defiant and stubborn resistance. In every theatre, this will to fight on, especially by the *Mehmetçik* (Ottoman soldiers), earned the praise even of their enemies. It was a feature of the

Figure 12.2 Istanbul: stacks of arms in the Arsenal 1919

Turkish soldier in subsequent wars and came to epitomize the strong relationship of the Turkish people with their armed forces, although periods of military control in domestic politics later produced anguish and suspicion. The reaction in recent years, of a more pronounced Islamist political agenda, has been more detrimental and divisive. Turkey has found itself on the front line against Kurdish irredentists, jihadist terrorism and the collapse of its neighbours, including the Soviet Union in the 1990s, Iraq in the 2000s, and Syria in the 2010s. Its relationship with Europe has been equally troubled. Yet from a security perspective, Turkey has remained a staunch NATO ally. Here lies the paradox: the embittered enemies of 1914–18, Britain and its Western military partners, have since become the guarantors of Turkey's future security, thereby fulfilling a line of reasoning that Britain had articulated before the Great War.

Immediately after the war, Sir Henry Wilson had written to Allenby to sum up the war and he concluded that the German strategic plan had been 'command of the sea [and] the Near and Middle East'. Wilson believed Britain had prevented German command of the sea and 'I was always casting about in my mind how this second objective [German domination of the Middle East] could be frustrated.'[2] He concluded: 'You [Allenby] and [General] Franchet [D'Esperay, the commander in the Balkans] did that. The collapse of the main theatres followed almost automatically.' This generous verdict he reached by attributing the ruination of the enemy's strategic plans to a loss of will: 'With the loss of both Prizes the Governing Class of the Boch[e] lost heart—as well he might—and was no longer able to buoy up his Army and Navy. Hence this indescribable crash. It is a wonderful story.' Naturally some of Wilson's thoughts can be attributed to the feelings of relief and euphoria that the war had been concluded successfully, but it is a view which indicates something of contemporaries' sense of the priorities in this war, and the strategies by which it had been fought.

Epilogue

Some of the strategic decision-makers did not survive the war. Kitchener had died at sea in 1916. Colmar von der Goltz, the German commander with the Ottoman Sixth Army in Mesopotamia, also died that year of disease. General Stanley Maude had succumbed in that same unhealthy theatre of operations to cholera in 1917. The Ottoman sultan, Mehmet V, who had presided over his empire's entry into the Great War, did not live to see the end of the conflict. He died in June 1918 and was succeeded by his brother, Sultan Mehmet VI, but the Ottoman dynasty was abolished in 1922. Baron Hans von Wangenheim, the German ambassador to the Ottoman Empire, who endorsed the brutal reprisals against the Armenians, died in 1915.

Despite winning the British General Election of 1918 on the promise of social reform and punishment of Germany, David Lloyd George had taken a conciliatory line with Germany at the Paris peace conference. Over British policy in Ireland too, he had merged a fiery rhetoric with the willingness to compromise with the Republican movement. The contradictions continued. He had seemed to support the British Empire yet arranged for the implementation of the Montagu Commission's recommendation to devolve power in India. In May 1920, despite advocating that Poland and Germany should be supported as a 'bulwark to Bolshevism', he received a Soviet trade delegation and concluded a commercial agreement the following year. The decision prompted Sir Henry Wilson to condemn Lloyd George as a 'traitor and Bolshevist'.[1] The Prime Minister's unwillingness to attend Cabinet meetings, his high-handed treatment of departments, and accusations that he had been selling peerages in 1922 to create loyalists all contributed to a general distrust amongst his colleagues in government. The economic downturn in Britain, worsened by the demobilization of the armed forces and the end of wartime contracts in 1921, deepened the gloom and mocked his post-war promise to make Britain a 'land fit for heroes to live in'. The Chanak Crisis was the final straw: Austen Chamberlain, Andrew Bonar Law, and Stanley Baldwin convinced the Conservatives to drop Lloyd George as Prime Minister. In the subsequent election of 1924, Lloyd George's Liberal party was bitterly divided, but Asquith, his rival, lost his seat and by default Lloyd George became the leader. Despite expectations of a return to power, the Liberals were eclipsed by Labour, and Lloyd George lost influence in British politics. His final years were marked by misjudgement. He became enamoured with Hitler in the 1930s, and in 1940 he advocated a negotiated peace with Nazi Germany. He died, aged 82, just months before the war came to an end.

Winston Churchill fared better than Lloyd George. After the war he served as Secretary of State for the Colonies (1921–2), then Chancellor of the Exchequer (1924–9). It was his decision to return Britain to the Gold Standard in 1925 that would prove of even greater significance than his advocacy of the Dardanelles operations, for the consequences for the British economy were severe and the cuts to defence deeper than perhaps might otherwise have been the case. As a result of the Great Depression, Churchill found himself in the political wilderness, and his dire warnings of future German aggression earned him further condemnation. When the next European war seemed imminent, the Prime Minister, Neville Chamberlain, could no longer keep him out of Cabinet. Despite further criticism in his career for championing hopelessly idealistic strategic schemes, he was ably served, and restrained, in the Second World War by his Chief of the Imperial General Staff, Alan Brooke. Churchill committed a great proportion of the British armed forces to the defence of India and the Middle East, which, by extension, necessitated operations in East Africa and Libya against the Italians. Perhaps his greatest achievement was not in designing any particular strategy, but in mobilizing the English language and personifying the resolve of the British people when defeat seemed likely. This was, in essence, an aspect of the Clausewitzian 'trinity', which others had underestimated: the alignment of effort by the government, armed forces, and the people in defence and in the pursuit of victory.

Herbert Asquith was snubbed by Lloyd George after the war, by the latter's refusal to let him participate in the Paris peace conference. He re-entered parliament after a by-election but lost his seat for a second time in 1924. He made a bid to become the Chancellor of Oxford University in 1925, having been granted a peerage, but was not selected. Soon after, he suffered a stroke which left him confined to a wheelchair and he died at home in Berkshire in 1928.

Sir William Robertson, who had been forced out as CIGS in February 1918, was reassigned to Eastern Command. Lloyd George and his closest associates thought that Robertson was planning a military *coup d'état*, such was the depth of antagonism that had developed between the CIGS and the Prime Minister, but, aside from a great deal of bad temper on both sides, there is no evidence that Robertson would have contemplated such a desperate act. Indeed, within weeks, Robertson was appointed to command the Home Forces, including London, in June 1918 which was hardly the safest course of action if there had been genuine doubts about his loyalty. When the war came to an end, Robertson was made Commander-in-Chief of the British Army of Occupation on the Rhine, and when, in June 1919, it looked as if Germany would refuse to sign the Treaty of Versailles, Robertson readied his inexperienced formations (the veterans having been demobilized) to advance deeper into the country. There was some expectation that irregular warfare would develop, but the crisis passed. Finding a suitable reward for Robertson's war service caused further controversy. He was thought unsuitable for the delicate task of pacifying Ireland and was instead promoted to field marshal in 1920, which was interpreted widely as a 'consolation prize'. Nevertheless Parliament recognized him and he was made baronet of Beaconsfield. He took up various appointments in civilian life, including president of the British Legion, and died in 1933, aged 73.

Sir Henry Wilson had a far shorter career. He was made a field marshal and baronet, retiring from the army in 1922. His pre-war interest in Irish politics never abated and he was shot dead by two paramilitary gunmen on his own doorstep on 22 June 1922.

General Edmund Allenby was made a field marshal on 31 July 1919, and entitled Viscount Allenby of Megiddo and Felixstowe. He continued to serve as high commissioner for Egypt and the Sudan until his retirement in 1925. After many accolades to his achievements in Palestine, he took up residence in South Kensington in London, and a blue plaque commemorates him there. He died in 1936, aged 75, while on a fishing trip in South America. General Archibald Murray had been reassigned from his Egyptian Expeditionary Force (EEF) in 1917 and was sent to Aldershot. In 1919 he was granted the rank of general and retired from the army soon after. He died in January 1945. Colonel T. E. Lawrence took up a fellowship at All Souls College Oxford, and then, unable to come to terms with his celebrity, tried to adopt a new persona first as Shaw and then Ross. He retired after service in the RAF in 1935 and died soon after in a road traffic accident near his home in Dorset.

General William Marshall took the Ottoman surrender at Mosul in 1919 and after the war he accepted the post of General Officer Southern Command in India until 1923, after which he retired. General Philip Chetwode also returned to India as a great advocate of modernization and reform. In 1930 he became Commander-in-Chief in India and ended his career as Field Marshal Baron Chetwode with an honorary degree from Oxford University. Major General Charles Townshend, who had been taken prisoner at Kut and released to present the Ottoman armistice in 1918, tried to establish himself as an expert on Turkey and offered to be the liaison with Kemal Atatürk. Resentment at the relative luxury of his imprisonment nevertheless embittered many commentators, and he found himself without work. General Sir Ian Hamilton had also suffered humiliation in the Gallipoli campaign and he was given no further command appointments after 1916. He died in 1947. General Sir John Nixon, who had first commanded in Mesopotamia, was blamed for the failures of the campaign in the commission of 1917 which effectively ended his career and he died four years later. Percy Lake, who succeeded him, retired from the army in 1919. Sir Arthur Barrett, the divisional commander who had been replaced by Townshend, returned to India in 1916 as General Officer Commanding Northern Command and he played a prominent part in the Third Anglo-Afghan War of 1919. He was promoted to field marshal for his services in 1921, a year after his retirement, and he died in 1926.

Immediately after the armistice, Ismail Enver and the rest of the Ottoman leadership had gone into exile in Germany. The new Turkish government had him tried *in absentia* for driving the Ottoman Empire into the war and he was condemned to death. Enver established good working relations between the Germans and the Soviets, and even had a hand in ensuring that the new Turkey was left unmolested by the Bolsheviks despite attending the communist-inspired 'Congress of Eastern Peoples' in Baku in September 1920 which advocated a worldwide jihad. In 1921 Enver tried to return to Anatolia via Moscow, but his presence was rejected by Mustapha Kemal (Atatürk), and there was, of course, the deterrence of the outstanding death penalty. On his return to Moscow he volunteered his services to suppress the Basmachi revolt but, after negotiations with the resistance, he became their leader. Despite a successful campaign, he was killed by the Soviets. Various accounts exist of the manner of his death but the Soviets claimed he had been surprised and shot dead by one of their agents who had infiltrated his refuge. In 1996, his body was recovered and buried in Şişli cemetery in Istanbul.

Mehmet Talaat abandoned the capital of the Ottoman Empire on 8 November 1918, carried secretly away by U-boat to Germany. Like Enver, in his absence he was tried by court martial and condemned to death. The charges were notable in two respects: first, for the charge that he had carried the Ottoman Empire into a ruinous war, and secondly, that he had issued the instructions that led directly to the massacres of Armenians and other minorities. He was tracked by both Soviet and British intelligence services, the latter being conscious of his intentions to generate an anti-British front. It proved too difficult to apprehend him while he resided in Germany but in 1921 he was murdered on his doorstep by Soghomon Tehlirian, an Armenian revolutionary from Erzurum.

Ahmed Djemal, one of Talaat's fellow pashas in the triumvirate that ruled the Ottoman Empire during the war, had also fled Istanbul in November 1918 and escaped to Germany, and then Switzerland. In 1920 he travelled to Afghanistan to assist in the development of the Afghan Army. In his capacity as liaison officer for the Afghans with the Soviets, following their Treaty of Friendship in 1921, he made a visit to Tiflis (Tblisi), where on 21 July 1922 he was assassinated by three Armenian gunmen. His body was returned to Turkey and he was buried at Erzurum.

Mustapha Kemal Atatürk was far more successful, becoming the undisputed master of his country in the 1920s. His reforming zeal swept away the old bureaucracies, traditional practices, and even the *ancien régime's* alphabet and language. He purged his internal adversaries and established new practices in education, economics, social relations, and culture. He can be attributed with having laid the foundations of an entirely new, secular nation. As such he became an inspiration for thousands of intellectuals, ideologues, and reformers across the Middle East and beyond. The hagiography only seemed to be magnified as the decades passed, culminating in the UN year of Atatürk in 1981. His achievements were undoubtedly great, but his methods were uncompromising, and much of the celebration can be attributed to the desire to find an icon who resisted Western influences and power.

Liman von Sanders had been captured in the pell-mell rout of Ottoman forces in Palestine in 1918 and in 1919 he was in Malta, still in captivity, charged with association with the Armenian massacres. Nevertheless, he was released and returned to Germany where he published his memoirs. He died in 1927, aged 73. General Erich von Falkenhayn had been reassigned after failing to defend Jerusalem from Allenby in November 1917 and was deployed to Belarus in February 1918. After the war he turned to writing his memoirs, recording the decisions that he and others had taken at the highest levels between 1914 and 1916. He died in 1922. General Kress von Kressenstein had also been reassigned from Palestine. In the summer of 1918 he was tasked to defend Georgia against the Bolsheviks and he deterred the annexation of Abkhazia. In 1929 he retired from the German Army and died in Munich in 1948.

Kaiser Wilhelm II was compelled to abdicate in November 1918, largely because the German Army and Navy would no longer support him, and he went into exile in the Netherlands. He never returned to the Middle East although he did visit Corfu. Following the rise of Hitler, he entertained ideas of a restoration, but the Nazis had little use for him, even when they occupied the Netherlands in 1940. The old kaiser died, cursing the 'British and Jewish conspirators', just before the invasion of Soviet Russia in 1941.

Russia's Grand Duke Nicholas went into exile because of the Bolshevik revolution in March 1919, first in Italy and then in France. He refused to join the Russian civil war and died in 1929. Tsar Nicholas II was murdered by the Bolsheviks while in captivity in 1918, in order to prevent a restoration. The new communist regime lurched from crisis to crisis until the late 1920s, but its propaganda message of worldwide revolution, in unity with pan-Islamic jihadism, was contained and gradually withered. General Nikolai Nicholayavich Yudenich had been reassigned from the Caucasus in 1917 by Alexander Kerensky's government to Petrograd and he was a supporter of the anti-Bolshevik Kornilov Revolt. Forced to flee in 1919, he took refuge in Finland. There he organized a small force known as the North-western Army, and, coordinating his operations with other White forces, he was nominated as the regional political leader. However, his offensive against Petrograd was checked by the city's Bolsheviks and their reinforcements. His army was compelled to retreat to Estonia where it was disarmed. Yudenich was arrested but the British secured his release, and he went into exile in France, where he died in 1933.

Arabia and Persia had been significantly influenced by a handful of British officers and diplomats. Sir Mark Sykes, who had done so much to shape Arab and Jewish interests in the Middle East, fell victim to the Spanish influenza epidemic while in Paris during the peace talks. He died in his hotel room in February 1919. By contrast Georges Picot survived the war and the peace, but saw the French capital fall to the Nazis in 1940, and died in 1951. Lieutenant Colonel Sir Henry McMahon, who had initiated the correspondence with Sharif Hussein during the war, retired from the Indian

Army in 1916 and played no further part in the diplomacy of the region, although his name came to be associated with the border dispute between India and China in 1962, the so-called McMahon Line drawn up in 1914. Sir Percy Sykes was recalled from his role leading the South Persia Rifles in 1918 amid much acrimony but he did not retire from the army until 1924. His interest in the Middle East remained keen and he became the honorary secretary of the Royal Society for Asian Affairs, having published thirteen books between 1919 and 1940, including histories of Persia and Afghanistan. His literary achievements led to the Society's decision to establish a medal bearing his name.[2] Sir Percy Cox, after his efforts to have King Feisal installed as the monarch of Iraq, continued to influence the direction of politics in the country, but, when he retired in 1923 he too retained his interest in the region, and served as president of the Royal Geographical Society between 1933 and 1936. He died while hunting the following year.

Max von Oppenheim, the 'Abu Jihad' ('father of holy war'), returned to Germany in 1917 and experienced regular periods of bankruptcy. He tried to return to his pre-war archaeological excavations in Syria but met resistance from the French authorities, and when, eventually, he was granted access, he found his old excavation site of Tell Halaf badly damaged by the French–Syrian conflict. He struggled to establish a museum in Germany dedicated to his work, but both this establishment and his home, containing many artefacts and papers, were destroyed by RAF bombing in 1943. He lost almost everything, narrowly survived the bombing of Dresden, and died in Bavaria in 1946. Wilhelm Wassmuss was captured at the end of the war in Persia and released in 1920. Having failed to secure funds from the new German government to pay the southern Persian fighters whom he had promised recompense, he attempted to establish a profitable farm near Bushehr with which to generate funds himself. When the farm failed and disputes arose with locals, he returned to Germany penniless and died a broken man in 1931. Oskar von Niedermayer had made a perilous escape from Afghanistan in 1916 and was initially re-tasked to raise a revolt against the British amongst the Arabs of Mesopotamia. In 1918 he was recalled to Berlin and at the end of the war found himself on the Western Front. In the inter-war years he oscillated between academic study and military service, showing a particular interest in Russia and Eastern Europe. In the Second World War he raised a division of Eastern European troops against the Soviets and then Slovene partisans but he was arrested by the Nazi authorities for criticisms of the regime. He was imprisoned for the rest of the war, and, when he tried to make his way home in 1945, he was arrested by the Soviets. He died in a labour camp in 1948.

When Emir Feisal was ejected from Syria, his former British allies appointed him as king of Iraq. His reputation for leadership in the 1916–18 revolt accorded him respect but he had no link to the Iraqi people. His desire to rule independently of British influence caused friction with Sir Percy Cox, the high commissioner. Worse still, his insistence on bringing Syrian and Lebanese exiles into his administration stirred resentment with locals, despite his efforts to mollify opinion. Nevertheless he developed schemes for roads and an oil pipeline through Syria to the Mediterranean, hoping this would be the basis of an infrastructure that would unify the Middle East. Relations with Britain worsened prior to the settlement of an Anglo-Iraqi Treaty in 1932, not least because Feisal regarded this bilateralism as an obstacle to establishing a single Arab state. His increasing frustration with governing Iraq resulted in bouts of authoritarianism and ill-temper, prompting Sir Henry Dobbs, Cox's successor, to describe him as 'puerile and petulant'. He died in 1933, an exhausted man.

Emir Abdullah was also granted his position as king of Transjordan by the British in 1921. He accepted the Mandate authority placed over him until 1946, but ruled an independent Jordan for several years. Tragically, he was assassinated by a Palestinian gunman in 1951 while at prayers on a visit to Jerusalem. The motive was ostensibly the fear that the king was about to negotiate a peace settlement with Israel, but there was also a conspiratorial group, led by Colonel el-Tell and associated with the former grand mufti of Jerusalem, Amin al-Husayni, which detested Abdullah's regime for being orientated towards Britain. The monarchy survived the murder and the Hashemite dynasty continued through his grandson, His Royal Highness, King Hussein.

The king of Hejaz, Hussein bin Ali, declared himself caliph the moment the institution was abolished by the Turkish National Assembly in 1924. The announcement received a mixed reaction. It incensed Abdulaziz Ibn Saud who regarded it as a claim to rule all Arabia. The conflict that followed drove Hussein out of Mecca and Medina, forcing him to take refuge in Jordan. Britain could not choose between two allies and refused to drive the Saudis from the Hejaz, and Hussein abdicated in favour of his son, Ali, although he retained the title of caliph. He died, still in exile, in 1931 and was buried in Jerusalem. Ibn Saud obtained Britain's recognition of the independence of Saudi territories in 1927, and the kingdom of Saudi Arabia was formally established in 1932. The fate of the country seemed to be no different from the other peripheries of the former Ottoman Empire until the discovery of oil in 1938 transformed the economy. Ultimately, of course, the growth of the oil industry changed the world's relationship not only with Saudi Arabia, but the entire Middle East. It was a development that would ensure the entire region remained of paramount strategic importance to the world.

Endnotes

CHAPTER 1

1. *Hansard*, 5th series, vol. C, col. 2211 [1917].
2. Carl von Clausewitz, *On War* (Princeton, NJ: Princeton University Press, 1976), Book VIII, Part iii, p. 588.
3. Robert Johnson, *Spying for Empire: The Great Game in Central and South Asia, 1757–1947* (London: Greenhill, 2006), p. 51.
4. Quoted in K. Schilling, *Beitrage zu einer Geschichte des radikalen Nationalismus in der Wilhelimischen Ära* (Cologne, 1968) p. 60, cited in *The American Historical Review* 75(3) (February 1970).
5. *Nauticus* (1900), p. 73, cited in Volker R. Berghahn, 'On the Social Function of Wilhelmine Armaments Policy' in Georg Iggers (ed.), *The Social History of Politics* (Leamington Spa: Berg, 1985), p. 166.
6. Mueller to Tirpitz, 8 February 1905, in V. R. Berghahn, *Germany and the Approach of War in 1914* (London: Macmillan, 1973), p. 53.
7. *The War: German Attempts to Fan Islamic Feeling*, L/PS/11/99 P 4180/1915, India Office Records, British Library.
8. Spenser Wilkinson, 'Britain at Bay', based on the *Morning Post* articles (New York, 1909), Part XI.
9. David Gilmour, *Curzon* (London: John Murray, 1994), p. 203.
10. Britain concluded a separate agreement with China, recognizing its sovereignty over Lhasa, but there was widespread disgust when the Chinese invaded Tibet and pursued a policy of brutal repression in 1910–11 until the revolution of Xinhai drove the Qing forces out in 1912. Melvyn Goldstein, *A History of Modern Tibet* (Berkeley: University of California Press, 1989).
11. E. F. Chapman and Cyprian A. G. Bridge, 18 March 1892, Joint Report of the DMI and DNI. CAB 37/31/10, The National Archives, Kew [TNA].
12. Firuz Kazemzadeh, *Russia and Britain in Persia, 1864–1914* (New Haven, CT: Yale University Press, 1968), p. 334.
13. R. A. Johnson and C. R. Moran, 'In the Service of Empire: Imperialism and the British Spy Thriller', *Studies in Intelligence*, 54(2) (June 2010).
14. F. Ahmad, *The Young Turks: The Committee of Union and Progress in Turkish Politics, 1908–1914* (Oxford: Oxford University Press, 1969).
15. A. L. Macfie, *The End of the Ottoman Empire, 1908–1923* (London: Longmans, 1998), p. 27.

16. F. McCullagh, *The Fall of Abdul Hamid* (London: Methuen, 1910), p. 48.
17. One of the Young Turks who accompanied Enver was Mustapha Kemal, the future Atatürk. Andrew Mango, *Atatürk* (London: John Murray, 2004).
18. Misha Glenny, *The Balkans, 1804–1999: Nationalism, War and the Great Powers* (London: Granta, 1999), pp. 228–43.
19. Hew Strachan, *The First World War*, I: *To Arms* (Oxford: Oxford University Press, 2001), pp. 50–1.
20. Macfie, *The End of the Ottoman Empire*, p. 78; David Fieldhouse, *Western Imperialism in the Middle East 1914–1958* (Oxford: Oxford University Press, 2006), p. 16.
21. Glenny, *The Balkans*, pp. 243–8.
22. Eugene Rogan, *The Fall of the Ottomans* (New York: Basic Books, 2015), p. 32.
23. 'Dnevnik A. N. Kuropatkina', *Krasnyi Arkhiv*, 2 (1922), p. 31, cited in Firuz Kazemzadeh, *Russia and Britain in Persia, 1864–1914* (New Haven, CT: Yale University Press, 1968), p. 339.
24. Ibid.
25. L. Albertini, *The Origins of the War of 1914* (Oxford: Oxford University Press, 1967), I, pp. 547–9.
26. L.C.F. Turner, 'The Russian Mobilisation in 1914' in Paul Kennedy (ed.), *War Plans of the Great Powers* (London: Allen and Unwin, 1979), p. 257.
27. Strachan, *First World War*, I: *To Arms*, p. 84.
28. Berghahn, *Germany and the Approach of War*, p. 143.
29. Strachan, *First World War*, I: *To Arms*, p. 61.
30. Berghahn, *Germany and the Approach of War*, p. 144.
31. Carl von Clausewitz, *On War*, trans. M. Howard and P. Paret (Princeton, NJ: Princeton University Press, 1976), I, ii, p. 75; Donald Stoker, *Clausewitz: His Life and Work* (Oxford: Oxford University Press, 2014).
32. Clausewitz, *On War*, I, xxviii, p. 89.
33. Ibid., I, iii, p. 77.
34. Ibid., I, vii, p. 78, and xvii, p. 88.
35. Ibid., XIII, iii, p. 592.
36. Bernard Lewis, *The Middle East* (London: Weidenfeld and Nicolson, 1995), p. 289.
37. Ibid., pp. 298–9.
38. Sir Lawrence Freedman, *Strategy: A History* (Oxford: Oxford University Press, 2013), p. xi; Raymond Aron, 'The Evolution of Modern Strategic Thought' in Alastair Buchan (ed.), *Problems of Modern Strategy* (London: Chatto and Windus, 1970); Edward Luttwak, *Strategy: The Logic of War and Peace* (Cambridge, MA: Belknap, 2001); Williamson Murray, MacGregor Knox, and Alvin Bernstein (eds.), *The Making of Strategy: Rulers, States and War* (Cambridge: Cambridge University Press, 1994); Wilkinson Dent Bird, *The Direction of War* (Cambridge: Cambridge University Press, 1920), p. 43.
39. Freedman, *Strategy: A History*, p. 119.
40. David Lloyd George, *War Memoirs* (London: Odhams, 1936), II, pp. 1755, 1773.

41. Salisbury, cited by Count Hatzfeldt to Otto von Bismarck, 13 August 1887, in E. T. S. Dugdale, *German Diplomatic Documents, 1871–1914* (London: Methuen, 1928), I, p. 249.
42. Michael Howard, *The Continental Commitment* (London: Harmondsworth, 1974), p. 149; Hew Strachan, 'The British Way of Warfare Revisited', *Historical Journal*, 26(2) (1983), pp. 447–61.
43. Naval Intelligence Division, 1892 cited in Arthur J. Marder, *The Anatomy of British Sea Power: A History of British Naval Policy in the Pre-Dreadnought Era, 1880–1905* (Hamden, CT: Archon Books, 1964), pp. 159–60.
44. David French, *The British Way of War, 1688–2000* (London: Unwin Hyman, 1990), p. 148.
45. Avner Offer, 'The British Empire, 1870-1914: A Waste of Money?', *Economic History Review*, 46(2) (1993), pp. 215–38.
46. Iain R. Smith, *The Origins of the South African War* (London: Longmans, 1995); Keith Surridge, *Managing the South African War* (London: Royal Historical Society, 1999).
47. Berghahn, *Germany and the Approach of War in 1914*.
48. Geoffrey Till, 'Sir Julian Corbett and the Twenty-First Century: Ten Maritime Commandments' in Andrew Dorman, Mike Smith and Matthew Uttley (eds.), *The Changing Face of Maritime Power* (Basingstoke: Macmillan, 1999).
49. Julian Corbett, 'Note on naval strategy', 1906, revised 1909, Corbett Papers, box 6, National Maritime Museum.
50. Eric Grove, 'Introduction' to Julian Corbett, *Some Principles of Naval Maritime Strategy* (London: Brassey's, 1988 [1911]), p. xxiv.
51. Halford Mackinder, 'The Geographical Pivot of History', 23(4), *The Geographical Journal* (1904), pp. 421–37.
52. *Morning Post*, 24 April 1912, cited in Gove, 'Introduction', p. xxxix.
53. Julian Corbett, 'The Teaching of Naval and Military History', address to the Historical Association, 7 January 1916, *History*, pp. 17–18. Corbett Papers, box 6, National Maritime Museum.
54. Major G. W. Redway, *The Great War* (London: Amalgamated Press, 1916), VI, p. 513.
55. Redway's assessment associated strategy with a military objective, but there was an acknowledgement that strategy had also to incorporate industrial and economic considerations, not least for the purpose of meeting exponential demands for munitions. He wrote: 'It is the business of strategy to ensure superiority of force and to count the cost of a campaign before undertaking it.' He continued: 'The British expedition to Gallipoli will remain a monument of error in this respect.' Ibid., VI, p. 521.
56. Critical of press optimism, Redway added: 'The Great War would have been over in a twelvemonth if even a tithe of the reported 'decisive' battles had had any foundation in fact.' Ibid., VI, p. 526.
57. Ibid., VI, pp. 529–30.
58. Ibid., VI, p. 530.

59. Fieldhouse, *Western Imperialism*, pp. 47–8.
60. Committee of Imperial Defence: Asiatic Turkey, Report of a Committee, 30 June 1915, CAB 42/3/12, TNA.
61. Fieldhouse, *Western Imperialism*, p. 47.
62. Ibid., p. 49.
63. Ziya Golkap, *The Principles of Turkism*, trans. Robert Devereux (Leiden, 1968 [Ankara, 1920]), pp. 12–15.
64. Fieldhouse, *Western Imperialism*, p. 19.

CHAPTER 2

1. Robert Gerwarth and Erez Manela (ed.), *Empires at War, 1911–1923* (Oxford: Oxford University Press, 2014).
2. 'Far from Jihad' Colloquium, Cité nationale de l'histoire de l'immigration, Paris, May 2014.
3. See, for example, CIGS to GOC Mesopotamia, 7 December 1917, L/Mil/7/18848, India Office Records, British Library.
4. Hew Strachan, *The First World War* (London: Simon and Shuster, 2003), p. 101.
5. Ibid., p. 104.
6. Yusuf Hikmet Bayur, *Türk İnkılâbı Tarihi* (Ankara: TTK Basımevi, 1952), II, Part IV, p. 626. For detailed information on the negotiations see Alpay Kabacalı, İletişim Yayınları (eds.), *Talat Paşa'nın Anıları*, 3rd edn (Istanbul: Türkiye İş Bankası Yayınları, 1993), p. 29.
7. H. J. Mackinder, 'The Geographical Pivot of History', *The Geographical Journal*, 23(1) (1904), pp. 421–37.
8. See intercepted letter from Bethmann-Hollweg to the Maharaja of Jodhpur, Chelmsford Papers, Mss Eur E264/52, India Office Records, British Library; see also Peter Hopkirk, *On Secret Service East of Constantinople* (Oxford: Oxford University Press, 1994), pp. 55–6.
9. Robert Johnson, *Spying for Empire: The Great Game in South and Central Asia, 1757–1947* (London: Greenhill, 2006), pp. 217–21, 225–7.
10. Hew Strachan, *The First World War*, I: *To Arms* (Oxford: Oxford University Press, 2001), pp. 644–51, 670–3.
11. David French, 'The Dardanelles, Mecca and Kut: Prestige as a Factor in British Eastern Strategy, 1914–1916', *War and Society*, 5(1) (1987), p. 50.
12. Feroz Ahmad, *The Young Turks: The Committee of Union and Progress in Turkish Politics, 1908–1914* (Oxford: Clarendon Press, 1969), pp. 1–50.
13. Edward J. Erickson, *Ordered to Die: A History of the Ottoman Army in the First World War* (Westport, CT: Greenwood Press, 2001), p. 4.
14. Ulrich Trumpener, 'Turkey's Entry into World War I: An Assessment of Responsibilities', *The Journal of Modern History*, 34(4) (1962), pp. 378–9.
15. J. Jenkins, 'Fritz Fischer's "Programme for Revolution": Implications for a Global History of Germany in the First World War', *Journal of Contemporary History*, 48(2) (2013), pp. 397–418.

16. Mustapha Aksakal, 'Holy War Made in Germany? Ottoman Origins of the 1914 Jihad', *War in History* 18(2) (2011), pp. 184–99; Hew Strachan, 'The First World War as a Global War', *First World War Studies*, 1(1) (2010), p. 9.
17. Strachan, *The First World War*, I: *To Arms*, p. 729.
18. Djemal Pasha, *Memories of a Turkish Statesman: 1913–1919* (London: Hutchinson and Co., 1922), p. 154; P. J. Vatikiotis, *The History of Modern Egypt: From Muhammad Ali to Mubarak* (Baltimore, MD: Johns Hopkins University Press, 1991), pp. 169–74.
19. Jacob M. Landau, *Pan-Turkism: From Irredentism to Cooperation* (Indiana: Indiana University Press, 1995), pp. 28–35; Michael Reynolds, 'Buffers, Nor Brethren: Young Turk Military Policy in the First Word War and the Myth of Pan-Turanism', *Past and Present*, 203 (May 2009), 137–79.
20. Strachan, *The First World War*, I: *To Arms*, p. 735.
21. Ibid., p. 734.
22. Djemal Pasha, *Memories of a Turkish Statesman*, pp. 156–60.
23. Israel Gershoni and James P. Jankowski, *Egypt, Islam, and the Arabs: The Search for Egyptian Nationhood, 1900–1930* (New York: Oxford and New York: Oxford University Press, 1986), pp. 4–24.
24. Vatikiotis, *The History of Modern Egypt*, p. 256.
25. *Osmanlı Ordu Teşkilatı*, pp. 147–61, cited in Mehmet Beşikçi, 'Mobilising Military Labor in the Age of Total War: Ottoman Conscription Before and During the Great War' in Erich-Jan Zürcher (ed.), *Fighting for a Living: A Comparative History of Military Labour 1500–2000* (Amsterdam: Amsterdam University Press, 2013), p. 555.
26. Erickson, *Ordered to Die*, p. 7.
27. Beşikçi, 'Mobilising Military Labor', p. 557.
28. Erickson, *Ordered to Die*, p. 243.
29. Beşikçi, 'Mobilising Military Labor', p. 562, n. 62.
30. Ibid., p. 576.
31. Mesut Uyar, *The Ottoman Defence against the Anzac Landing, 25 April 1915* (Canberra: Army History Unit, 2015), p. 137.
32. Captain Thomas Walter White, *Guests of the Unspeakable: The Odyssey of an Australian Airman* (London: John Hamilton, 1928).
33. In the Mediterranean, there were four heavy cruisers and four light cruisers, as well as numerous supporting vessels, destroyers, torpedo boats, and submarines.
34. Admiral Sir Roger Keyes, *Memoirs of Admiral of the Fleet, Sir Roger Keyes* (London: Thornton Butterworth, 1934–5).
35. Paul Guinn, *British Strategy and Politics, 1914–1918* (Oxford: Clarendon Press, 1965), p. 11.
36. Ibid., pp. 31–2.
37. Revd O. Creighton, *With the 29th Division in Gallipoli* (Uckfield: Naval and Military Press, 2009 [London, 1916]), p. 46.
38. H. S. Gullet, *The Australian Imperial Force in Sinai and Palestine* (Sydney: Angus and Robertson, 1939); D. A. Kent, 'The Anzac Book and the Anzac Legend: C. E. W. Bean as Editor and Image-maker', *Historical Studies*, 21(84) (1985), pp. 376–90; S. Brugger, *Australians in Egypt, 1914–1919* (Carleton: Melbourne

University Press, 1980); C. E. W. Bean, *The Story of Anzac*, II: *The Official History of Australia in the War of 1914–18* (Queensland: Angus and Robertson, 1924; republished St Lucia: University of Queensland Press, 1981).

39. C. Pugsley, *Gallipoli: The New Zealand Story* (Auckland: Hodder and Stoughton, 1984); C. G. Powles, *The New Zealanders in Sinai and Palestine* (Uckfield: Naval and Military Press, 1956).
40. Redistribution of the Army in India, 1904, Committee of Imperial Defence 58-D, CAB 6/2, The National Archives [TNA].
41. Caste Returns, 1 January 1904, L/Mil/7/17084, India Office Records, British Library.
42. George Morton-Jack, *The Indian Army on the Western Front: India's Expeditionary Force to France and Belgium in the First World War* (Cambridge: Cambridge University Press, 2014), p. 3.
43. Auchinleck served with the 62nd Punjabis and was decorated for his dedication and courage in actions at Suez, the Hanna, Kut, and in northern Mesopotamia between 1915 and 1919. Charles Allen, *Plain Tales From the Raj* (London: Andre Deutsch-Penguin, 1975), pp. 239–40.
44. There were two examinations, with further training in specialist languages as required.
45. Incidentally, Auchinleck succeeded; Montgomery failed. Charles Chenevix Trench, *The Indian Army and the King's Enemies, 1900–1947* (London: Thames and Hudson, 1988), p. 25.
46. There is an extensive literature on the martial races, but a clear explanation is given in David Omissi, *The Sepoy and the Raj: The Politics of the Indian Army, 1860–1940* (London: Macmillan, 1994). For a more contemporaneous view, see George MacMunn, *The Martial Races of India* (London: Sampson Low, 1933).
47. Francis Ingall, *The Last of the Bengal Lancers* (London: Leo Cooper, 1988), p. 5.
48. The 129th Baluchis, for example, despite the title, contained no Baluchis but was made up of Pashtuns, Mahsuds, and Punjabis. In Wilde's Rifles, there were companies consisting of Dogras, Pathans, Punjabis, and Sikhs.
49. The most significant losses of the frontier wars occurred in the 1897–8 Pathan Rising. On the Tirah expedition, some 287 were killed and a further 853 were wounded, but this was exceptional. Captain H. L. Nevill, *Campaigns on the North West Frontier* (London: John Murray, 1912), p. 301.
50. A further five cavalry brigades could be deployed with sufficient notice. Indian Expeditionary Force A, War Diary, Simla, October 1914, p. 136, L/Mil/17/5/3088, British Library.
51. Charles Townshend, *When God Made Hell: The British Invasion of Mesopotamia and the Creation of Iraq, 1914–1921* (London: Faber and Faber, 2010), pp. 3–4.
52. Kristian Coates Ulrichsen, *The Logistics and Politics of the British Campaigns in the Middle East, 1914–22* (Basingstoke: Palgrave Macmillan, 2010), p. 33.
53. Ghassan Atiyyah, *Iraq: 1908–1921. A Socio-Political Study* (Beirut: The Arab Institute for Research and Publishing, 1973), p. 41.

54. CAB 19/2-27: War Cabinet Commission on the Mesopotamia Campaign (1917), TNA; Stuart Cohen, 'The Genesis of the British Campaign in Mesopotamia, 1914', *Middle Eastern Studies*, 12 (1976), pp. 119–32; V. H. Rothwell, 'Mesopotamia in British War Aims, 1914–1918', *The Historical Journal*, 13(2) (1970), pp. 273–94.
55. John Pollock, *Kitchener* (London: Constable, 1998), pp. 417–18.
56. John Grigg, *Lloyd George: War Leader* (London: Allen Lane, 2002), p. 239.
57. David Lloyd George, *War Memoirs* (London: Odhams, 1936), II, p. 2032.
58. Ibid.
59. Ibid., II, p. 2033.
60. Ibid., II, p. 2034.
61. Paul Guinn, *British Strategy and Politics, 1914–1918* (Oxford: Clarendon Press, 1965), p. 183.
62. Ibid., p. 192.
63. Ibid., p. 194.
64. Ibid., p. 197.
65. Lloyd George, *War Memoirs*, II, p. 2036.
66. Ibid., II, p. 2037.
67. Guinn, *British Strategy*, p. 117.
68. Ibid., p. 116.
69. The author wishes to thank the Royal College of Defence Studies, London, for sharing their ideas on *Thinking Strategically* (London: RCDS, 2012), pp. 24–5.
70. Alfred Lord Milner, 'England in Egypt', p. 30 cited in George McMunn and Cyril Falls, *Military Operations, Egypt and Palestine* (London: HMSO, 1927), I, p. 7.
71. Ronald Robinson and John Gallagher, 'The Partition of Africa' in F. H. Hinsley (ed.), *The New Cambridge Modern History*, II: *Material Progress and World-wide Problems, 1870–1898* (Cambridge: Cambridge University Press, 1962), p. 599.
72. Martin Thomas, *Empires of Intelligence: Security Services and Colonial Disorder after 1914* (Berkeley, CA: University of California Press, 2008), p. 26; Priya Satia, *Spies in Arabia: The Great War and the Cultural Foundations of Britain's Covert Empire in the Middle East* (Oxford: Oxford University Press, 2008), p. 7.
73. David M. Anderson and David Killingray (eds.), *Policing the Empire: Government, Authority and Control, 1830–1940* (Manchester: Manchester University Press, 1991), p. 6.
74. Scott Anderson, *Lawrence in Arabia: War, Deceit, Imperial Folly and the Making of the Modern Middle East* (London: Atlantic, 2013), pp. 139–43.
75. Thomas, *Empires of Intelligence*, p. 49.
76. Antony Wynn, *Persia in the Great Game: Sir Percy Sykes: Explorer, Consul, Soldier, Spy* (London: John Murray, 2003).
77. C. A. Bayly, *Empire and Information: Intelligence-Gathering and Social Communication in India, 1780–1870* (Cambridge: Cambridge University Press, 1996), pp. 3–6, 365.
78. Thomas, *Empires of Intelligence*, p. 27.
79. *Private Letters between General Sir William Robertson and General Sir Archibald Murray*, CAB 44/15, TNA.

80. *The Papers of General Sir Archibald Murray*, 79/48/3, Imperial War Museum.
81. Strachan, *The First World War*, I: *To Arms*, p. 694.
82. Peter Hart, *Gallipoli* (London: Profile Books, 2011), pp. 7–12; French, 'The Dardanelles, Mecca and Kut', p. 50.

CHAPTER 3

1. Robert Holland, 'The British Empire and the Great War, 1914–1918' in Judith Brown and William Roger Louis, *The Oxford History of the British Empire*, IV: *The Twentieth Century* (Oxford: Oxford University Press, 1999), p. 133.
2. David French, 'The Dardanelles, Mecca and Kut: Prestige as a Factor in British Eastern Strategy, 1914–1916', *War and Society*, 5 (1987), p. 46.
3. Martin Gilbert, *Winston S. Churchill*, III, *1914–1916* (London: Heinemann, 1971), p. 220.
4. Ibid.
5. Ibid., III, p. 222.
6. Francis Robinson, 'The British Empire and the Muslim World' in Judith M. Brown and William Roger Louis (eds.), *The Oxford History of the British Empire*, IV: *The Twentieth Century* (Oxford: Oxford University Press, 1999), p. 405.
7. Committee of Imperial Defence, 1907, CAB 5/2, The National Archives [TNA].
8. Bethmann Hollweg to Auswärtiges Amt, 4 September 1914, GFM 397/00326, cited in Richard J. Popplewell, *Intelligence and Imperial Defence: British Intelligence and the Defence of the Indian Empire, 1904–1924* (London: Frank Cass, 1995), p. 176.
9. General Sir Archibald Murray, 'Memorandum on Martial Law in Egypt', 26 November 1916, FO 371/2930, TNA.
10. Popplewell, *Intelligence and Imperial Defence*, pp. 182, 226. The subversion mission had been led by German, Ottoman, and Indian personnel, and included Tarak Nath Das and Tirumal Acharya. The British counter-intelligence effort in the Canal Zone was led by Lieutenant Colonel C. E. Wilson under the Arab Bureau. See FO 37/2790, part 242004, TNA.
11. Ahmed Djemal Pasha, commander of Fourth Army, was known as 'Biyuk' ('The Great'). He should not be confused with Mohammed Djemal Pasha, referred to by British accounts as Djemal III, who commanded the garrison at Medina, or Mohammed Djemal Pasha, 'Kuchuk' ('little')/'Merslinli', commander of VIII Corps.
12. Djemal Pasha, *Memories of a Turkish Statesman, 1913–1919* (London: Hutchinson and Co., 1922), p. 154; General Kress von Kressenstein gave the figure for the Ottoman force at 19,000 but did not include the irregulars or volunteers that accompanied the column.
13. Moltke to Wangenheim, 4 September 1914, R 22402; Wangenheim to Auswärtiges Amt, 6 September 1914, no. 725, R 1914, Politisches Archiv des Auswärtiges Amts, Berlin.
14. Kress von Kressenstein to Karl Sussenheim, 20 August 1920, Karl Sussenheim Papers, Library of Congress, cited in Mustafa Aksakal, *The Ottoman Road to War*

in 1914: The Ottoman Empire and the First World War (Cambridge: Cambridge University Press, 2008), p. 147.

15. Eugene Rogan, *The Fall of the Ottomans* (New York: Basic Books, 2015), p. 100.
16. Djemal, *Memories*, p. 154.
17. Philip Knightly and Colin Simpson, *The Secret Lives of Lawrence of Arabia* (London: Thomas Nelson, 1969), p. 41. Although Lawrence did not officially join the Cairo intelligence service until December 1914, authorities agree that the Sinai survey was a military intelligence task.
18. Hew Strachan, *The First World War*, I: *To Arms* (Oxford: Oxford University Press, 2001), p. 738.
19. W.T. Massey, *The Great War in the Middle East* (London: Leonaur, 2009 [London, 1918]), I, p. 22.
20. Roger Ford, *Eden to Armageddon: World War I in the Middle East* (London: Weidenfeld and Nicholson), p. 300.
21. George McMunn and Cyril Falls, *Military Operations: Egypt and Palestine from the Outbreak of War with Germany to June 1917* (London: HMSO, 1928), p. 29.
22. Massey, *The Great War in the Middle East*, I, p. 22.
23. Rogan, *The Fall of the Ottomans*, p. 121.
24. Massey, *The Great War in the Middle East*, I, p. 21.
25. Strachan, *The First World War*, I: *To Arms*, p. 744.
26. Rogan, *The Fall of the Ottomans*, p. 238.
27. George McMunn and Cyril Falls, *Military Operations, Egypt and Palestine* (London: HMSO, 1927), I, pp. 66, 105.
28. Ibid., I, p. 108.
29. Rogan, *The Fall of the Ottomans*, p. 240.
30. Ibid., p. 252.
31. McMunn and Falls, *Military Operations, Egypt and Palestine*, I, p. 145.
32. R. J. M. Pugh, *Wingate Pasha* (Barnsley: Pen and Sword, 2011), p. 130.
33. McMunn and Falls, *Military Operations, Egypt and Palestine*, I, p. 150.
34. Ibid., I, p. 152.
35. Strachan, *The First World War*, I: *To Arms*, p. 753.
36. Donald M. McKale, *War by Revolution: Germany and Great Britain in the Middle East in the Era of World War I* (Kent, OH: Kent State University Press, 1998), p. 104.
37. Ali Abdullatif Ahmida, *The Making of Modern Libya: State Formation, Colonization, and Resistance, 1830–1932* (Albany: State University of New York Press, 1994), pp. 121–2.
38. Strachan, *The First World War*, I: *To Arms*, p. 730.
39. Kress von Kressenstein, *Mit den Türken zum Suezcanal* (Berlin, 1938), pp. 75–6, cited in Strachan, *The First World War*, I: *To Arms*, p. 732; McKale, *War by Revolution*, p. 98.
40. McMunn and Falls, *Military Operations, Egypt and Palestine*, I, p. 208.
41. Ibid., I, p. 222.
42. Ibid., I, p. 224.

43. Shakespeare to Sir Percy Cox, 17 January 1915, cited in James Barr, *Setting the Desert on Fire* (London: Bloomsbury, 2006), p. 58.
44. McKale, *War by Revolution*, pp. 99–100.
45. Barr, *Setting the Desert on Fire*, p. 13.
46. Fritz Fischer, *Germany's Aims in the First World War* (New York: Norton, 1967), p. 121.
47. Gottfried Hagen, 'German Heralds of Holy War: Orientalists and Applied Oriental Studies', *Comparative Studies of South Asia, Africa and the Middle East*, 24(2) (2004), p. 146.
48. The German War, Persia and Afghanistan, L/PS/10/592–4, India Office Collection, British Library.
49. The War: German Attempts to Fan Islamic Feeling, L/PS/11/99, P4180/1915, India Office Records, British Library.
50. See Christopher Sykes, *Wassmuss: 'The German Lawrence'* (London: Longmans Green and Co., 1936).
51. C. J. Edmonds, 'The Persian Gulf Prelude to the Zimmerman Telegram', *Royal Central Asian Journal*, I (1960).
52. Weekly Report, 21 December 1915 Home Department, Political Proceedings, B series (December 1915), pp. 709–11, POS 9841, India Office Records, British Library.
53. Touraj Atabaki (ed.), *Iran and the First World War* (London: I. B. Tauris 2006), p. 2.
54. William Edward David Allen and Paul Muratoff, *Caucasian Battlefields: A History of the Wars of the Turko-Caucasian Border, 1828–1921* (Cambridge: Cambridge University Press, 2010 [1953]), p. 298.
55. Allen and Muratoff, *Caucasian Battlefields*, p. 298.
56. Ibid., p. 373.
57. It proved difficult to get intelligence from Europe directly. Richard Popplewell, *Intelligence and Imperial Defence: British Intelligence and the Defence of the Indian Empire, 1904–1924* (London, 1995) p. 185.
58. Revolt in Persia: Expenditure of Secret Service Funds, L/PS/8/71–3 and 75, British Library.
59. Brigadier General F. J. Moberly, *History of the Great War, Operations in Persia, 1914–1918* (London: Historical Section of the Committee of Imperial Defence, 1929), L/Mil/17/15/28, British Library.
60. Hopkirk, *On Secret Service*, p. 146.
61. Report on the Working of the Military Mission in East Persia, L/Mil/17/15/34 and 35, British Library.
62. Bushire, Operations in Persia, L/PS/10/650, file 464 and O'Conner and the Shiraz Prisoners, L/PS/10/582 file 334 (1916), British Library.
63. McKale, *War by Revolution*, p. 132.
64. Ibid., p. 133.
65. Antony Wynn, *Persia in the Great Game: Sir Percy Sykes* (London: John Murray, 2003), pp. 258–62; The South Persia Rifles, L/PS/10/690, British Library.

66. Wynn, *Persia in the Great Game*, p. 265; Sykes Mission, L/PS/10/579; see also Despatch by Brigadier General Sykes on Minor Operations in South Persia, Nov. 1917–Mar. 1918 and May–Jul. 1918, L/Mil/17/15/29 and 30, British Library.
67. Wynn, *Persia in the Great Game*, p. 261.
68. Ibid., p. 263.
69. Ibid., p. 267.
70. McKale, *War by Revolution*, p. 142.
71. F.J. Moberly, *The Campaign in Mesopotamia, 1914–1918* (London: HMSO, 1923–7) and L/Mil/17/15/66–72, British Library.
72. Roos-Keppel to Hardinge, 13 February 1915, Hardinge Papers, Printed Letters and Telegrams, vol. 89, p. 69, Cambridge University Library.
73. Undated and unsigned letter, Hardinge Papers, Printed Letters and Telegrams, vol. 91, p. 21, Cambridge University Library.
74. Mehendra Pratap, *My Life Story of Fifty-Five Years*, ed. Vir Singh (Delhi: Originals, 2004 [1947]), p. 51.
75. James Campbell Ker, *Political Trouble in India, 1907–1917* (Calcutta: Oriental Publishers, 1973 [1917]), p. 307.
76. Sir Michael O'Dwyer, *India as I Knew It, 1885–1925* (London: Constable, 1925), p. 179.
77. Popplewell, *Intelligence and Imperial Defence*, p. 186; *Afghanistan: The Silk Letter Case*, L/PS/10/633, British Library.
78. Wynn, *Persia in the Great Game*, p. 270.

CHAPTER 4

1. Peter Hart, *Gallipoli* (London: Profile Books, 2013), p. vii.
2. John Laffin, *Damn the Dardanelles: The Agony of Gallipoli* (Gloucester: Alan Sutton, 1980), p. 214.
3. Another compelling reason to doubt the standard Anglophone orthodoxy of Gallipoli is the limited number of available Ottoman sources against which a balanced assessment of the Allies' performance can be made. There has been considerable reliance on the Turkish General Staff History and some translated works in the Rayfield Papers of the Imperial War Museum in London. Robin Prior, who has written an outstanding operational history, noted recently: 'it is still the case that there is no depth to sources in Turkish, or more accurately, Ottoman. We just do not have the war diaries, after action reports and operations orders on the Turkish side to place against those on the Allied side.' Robin Prior, *Gallipoli: The End of the Myth* (New Haven, CT and London: Yale University Press, 2010), p. xv.
4. Sean McMeekin, *The Russian Origins of the First World War* (Cambridge, MA: Harvard University Press, 2011), p. 115.
5. M.T. Florinsky, *The End of the Russian Empire* (New York: Collier Books, 1961), pp. 209–10. See also Joshua A. Sanborn, *Imperial Apocalypse: The Great War and the Destruction of the Russian Empire* (Oxford: Oxford University Press, 2015).
6. Brian Bond, *War and Society in Europe* (London: Fontana, 1984), p. 110.

7. C.F. Aspinall-Oglander, *Military Operations: Gallipoli* (London: William Heinemann, 1929), I, pp. 51–3.
8. Lloyd George, *War Memoirs* (London: Odhams, n.d. [1933–4]), I, pp. 219–26; Lord M. Hankey, *The Supreme Command, 1914–1918* (London: George Allen and Unwin, 1961), I, pp. 260–2.
9. Robert Johnson, *Spying for Empire: The Great Game in Central and South Asia, 1757–1947* (London: Greenhill, 2006), pp. 55–6.
10. David French, *The British Way of War, 1688–2000* (London: Unwin Hyman, 1990), pp. 169–70.
11. The Constantinople Agreement, concluded on 10 April 1915, see 'The Constantinople Agreement' in J. C. Hurewitz (ed.), *The Middle East and North Africa in World Politics*, II: *1914–1945* (New Haven, CT: Yale University Press, 1979), pp. 16–21; Martin Gilbert, *Winston S. Churchill*, III, *1914–1916* (London: Heinemann, 1971), p. 222.
12. Gerhard Ritter, *The Sword and the Sceptre* (Coral Gables, FL: University of Miami Press, 1970), II, pp. 68–71.
13. Gilbert, *Winston S. Churchill*, p. 218.
14. Selahattin Adil, *Çanakkale Cephesinden Mektuplar-Hatıralar* (Istanbul: Yeditepe Yayınevi, 2007), p. 21.
15. Edward J. Erickson, 'Strength against Weakness: Ottoman Military Effectiveness at Gallipoli, 1915', *Journal of Military History*, 65(4) (2001), p. 991.
16. Tim Travers, *Gallipoli, 1915* (Stroud: Tempus, 2001), p. 21; Paul Guinn, *British Strategy and Politics, 1914 to 1918* (Oxford: Clarendon Press, 1965), p. 55.
17. Naval Intelligence Department, *Turkey Coast Defences, 1908: Part II, Coast Defences*, Admiralty 231/49, The National Archives [TNA].
18. G. J. Wolseley, 'Secret Memorandum', 2 March 1878, Sir Henry Stafford Northcote, First Earl of Iddesleigh Papers, Add MSS 50022, The British Library; Robert Johnson, '"Russians at the Gates of India?" Planning the Defence of India, 1885–1900', *Journal of Military History*, 67 (2003), p. 731.
19. Guinn, *British Strategy*, p. 56.
20. David French, 'Dardanelles, Mecca and Kut: Prestige as a Factor in British Eastern Strategy, 1914–1916', *War and Society* 5(1) (1987), pp. 45–62, 51.
21. Gilbert, *Winston S. Churchill*, III, p. 221.
22. Guinn, *British Strategy*, p. 50.
23. W. S. Churchill to H. Asquith, 29 December 1914, in Gilbert, *Winston S. Churchill*, III, p. 226.
24. Hankey, *Supreme Command*, I, pp. 248–9, 267.
25. M. Hankey, *Memorandum*, 28 December 1914, cited in Gilbert, *Winston S. Churchill*, III, p. 230.
26. Aspinall-Oglander, *Military Operations: Gallipoli*, I, p. 59; Basil Liddell Hart, *A History of the World War, 1914–1918* (London: Faber and Faber, 1938), p. 218.
27. Martin Gilbert, *A History of the Twentieth Century*, I: *1900–1933* (London: Harper Collins, 1997), pp. 362–3.

28. Huw Strachan, *The First World War* (London: Simon and Schuster, 2003), p. 113.
29. Guinn, *British Strategy*, p. 57.
30. Richard Haldane served as Lord Chancellor, but was forced out of public life after a press campaign alleged a close association with Germany.
31. Sir John French, Memorandum, 5 January 1915, Kitchener Papers, TNA.
32. Guinn, *British Strategy*, p. 52.
33. Ibid., p. 58.
34. Dardanelles Commission, First Report, Cd 8490 (1917), pp. 17–18, 21–2, 29–30; Hankey, *Supreme Command*, I, pp. 277–9; Lloyd George, *War Memoirs* (London: Odhams, 1934), I, p. 104; Guinn, *British Strategy*, p. 60.
35. Dardanelles Commission, First Report, pp. 29, 32–3; Lloyd George, *War Memoirs*, I, pp. 104, 259.
36. The Possibility of a Joint Naval and Military Attack Upon the Dardanelles, I; Memorandum, General Staff, II; with Note by the DNI, 20 December 1906, in The Final report of the Dardanelles Commission, Part II: Conduct of Operations, Cmd 371 (1919), pp. 7–8; Hankey, *Supreme Command*, I, pp. 279–80.
37. Strachan, *The First World War*, p. 114, citing General Groener.
38. Erickson, 'Strength against Weakness', pp. 998–9.
39. Hilmi Kendircioğlu, 'Ottoman Artillery' in Robert Johnson and Metin Turcan (eds.), *Gallipoli: The Turkish Perspective* (London: Ashgate, 2016).
40. Lt Robert Blackie, cited in Travers, *Gallipoli*, p. 23.
41. Aspinall-Oglander, *Military Operations: Gallipoli*, I, p. 57.
42. Gibson, Diary, 13 March 1915, Gibson Papers, Imperial War Museum.
43. Trumbull Higgins, *Winston Churchill and the Dardanelles* (London: Heinemann, 1963), p. 118.
44. Travers, *Gallipoli*, p. 33.
45. Dardanelles Commission, First Report, p. 38; Final Report, pp. 13–14.
46. Guinn, *British Strategy*, p. 69.
47. Eugene Rogan, *The Fall of the Ottomans* (New York: Basic Books, 2015), p. 135.
48. Ibid., p. 141.
49. Hart, *Gallipoli*, p. 46.
50. Aspinall-Oglander, *Military Operations: Gallipoli*, I, pp. 101–10; Guinn, *British Strategy*, p. 67.
51. Ibid., I, pp. 101–2.
52. Ibid., I, p. 24; Ian Hamilton, *Gallipoli Diary* (London: Edward Arnold, 1920), I, p. 15; Guinn, *British Strategy*, p. 72.
53. *Mezhdunarodnie Otnosheniya v epokhou imperialisma* [International Relations in the Era of Imperialism], 3rd ser., 1914–1917 (Moscow: Mezhdunarodnie Otnosheniya, 1930), VII, (2), nos. 569 and 736.
54. Aspinall-Oglander, *Military Operations: Gallipoli*, I, p. 98.
55. Ferhat Çalişkan, 'Critique of the Defense Plans' in Robert Johnson and Metin Turcan (eds.), *Gallipoli: The Turkish Perspective* (London: Ashgate, 2016).
56. Aspinall-Oglander, *Military Operations: Gallipoli*, I, p. 132.

57. Royal Dublin Fusiliers Association, 'Irish Battalions Major Battles: Helles Landings, Gallipoli, April 1915'; Aspinall-Oglander, *Military Operations: Gallipoli*, I, p. 232.
58. The recipients were Captain Richard Raymond Willis; Sergeant Alfred Richards; Lance Corporal William Keneally: Aspinall-Oglander, *Military Operations: Gallipoli*, I, p. 227.
59. Hasan Tahsin Vanli, 'Seizing the Initiative at the Tactical Level' in Robert Johnson and Metin Turcan (eds.), *Gallipoli: The Turkish Perspective* (London: Ashgate, 2016).
60. Rogan, *The Fall of the Ottomans*, p. 151.
61. Edward J. Erickson, *Ordered to Die: A History of the Ottoman Army in the First World War* (Westport, CT: Greenwood Press, 2001), p. 83.
62. Rogan, *The Fall of the Ottomans*, p. 155.
63. Aspinall-Oglander, *Military Operations: Gallipoli*, I, pp. 196–8.
64. Cited in John Laffin, *Damn the Dardanelles* (Gloucester: Allen Sutton, 1989), p. 55.
65. Edward Erickson, *Gallipoli: The Ottoman Campaign* (Barnsley: Pen and Sword, 2010), p. 83.
66. Erickson, *Ordered to Die*, p. 84.
67. Bernard Montgomery, *A History of Warfare* (London: George Rainbird, 1968), p. 487.
68. Guinn, *British Strategy*, p. 75.
69. Letter from General Sir Ian Hamilton to Lord Kitchener, 15 July 1915, Papers of General Sir Ian Hamilton, 7/1/6, King's College London, Liddell Hart Centre for Military Archives.
70. Rogan, *The Fall of the Ottomans*, p. 188.
71. Robert Rhodes James, *Gallipoli* (London: B. T. Batsford Ltd, 1965), p. 221.
72. Hamilton, *Gallipoli Diary*, I, pp. 264, 266, 267.
73. Hankey, *Supreme Command*, I, p. 340.
74. Guinn, *British Strategy*, p. 95.
75. Rhodes James, *Gallipoli*, pp. 236–7.
76. Ibid., pp. 246–7.
77. John Lee, 'Sir Ian Hamilton and the Dardanelles, 1915,' in Brian Bond (ed.), *Fallen Stars: Eleven Studies of Twentieth Century Military Disasters* (London: Brassey's, 1991), pp. 45–6.
78. Aspinall-Oglander, *Military Operations: Gallipoli*, II, pp. 168–77.
79. Rogan, *The Fall of the Ottomans*, p. 202.
80. Aspinall-Oglander, *Military Operations: Gallipoli*, II, p. 282.
81. Ronald Robinson, 'Imperial Theory and the Question of Imperialism after Empire', *Journal of Imperial and Commonwealth History*, 12(2) (1984), p. 44.
82. Cited in French, 'Dardanelles, Mecca and Kut: Prestige as a Factor in British Eastern Strategy, 1914–1916', p. 54.
83. Donad M. McKale, *War by Revolution: Germany and Great Britain in the Middle East in the Era of World War I* (Kent, OH: Kent State University Press, 1998), pp. 79, 122–3.
84. Cited in French, 'Dardanelles, Mecca and Kut', p. 54.

85. Telegram from Sir Austen Chamberlain to the viceroy of India, 21 October 1915, Hardinge Papers, vol. 94, Cambridge University Library.
86. Ibid.
87. Aspinall-Oglander, *Military Operations: Gallipoli*, II, p. 402; Hankey, *Supreme Command*, I, pp. 303–6.
88. Aspinall-Oglander, *Military Operations: Gallipoli*, II, p. 417.
89. Strachan, *The First World War*, p. 120.
90. Winston Churchill, *The World Crisis*, II: *1915* (New York: Charles Scribner and Sons, 1923), p. 541.
91. Strachan, *The First World War*, I: *To Arms* (Oxford: Oxford University Press, 2001), p. 994.
92. Guinn, *British Strategy*, p. 83.
93. Mehmet Akif Okur, 'The Impact of War' in Robert Johnson and Metin Turcan (eds.), *Gallipoli: The Turkish Perspective* (London: Ashgate, 2016).
94. Erickson, *Gallipoli: The Ottoman Campaign*, pp. xiv–xv.
95. Ulrich Trumpener, 'The Turkish War, 1914–18' in John Horne (ed.), *A Companion Volume to World War I* (Oxford: Wiley-Blackwell, 2010), pp. 102–3.

CHAPTER 5

1. George McMunn and Cyril Falls, *Military Operations, Egypt and Palestine* (London: HMSO, 1927), I, p. 77.
2. Ibid., I, pp. 80–1.
3. Ibid., I, p. 81.
4. Kristian Coates Ulrichsen, *The Logistics and Politics of the British Campaigns in the Middle East, 1914–22* (Basingstoke: Palgrave Macmillan, 2010), pp. 144–5.
5. McMunn and Falls, *Military Operations, Egypt and Palestine*, I, p. 74.
6. Reginald Wingate to G. N. Curzon, 20 January 1919, FO 371/3713, The National Archives [TNA].
7. McMunn and Falls, *Military Operations, Egypt and Palestine*, I, p. 64.
8. Ibid., I, p. 84.
9. The 42nd, 52nd, 53rd, and 54th.
10. Letter from Sir John Maxwell to Sir William Robertson (Chief of the Imperial General Staff, London), 4 March 1916, Papers of Sir William Robertson, File 4/5/1, Liddell Hart Centre for Military Archives, King's College London.
11. CIGS to Lieutenant General Sir A. Murray, 29 December 1915, cited in McMunn and Falls, *Military Operations, Egypt and Palestine*, I, pp. 99–100.
12. Sir A. Murray to CIGS, 15 February 1916, cited in McMunn and Falls, *Military Operations, Egypt and Palestine*, I, p. 171.
13. Letters between CIGS and Sir A. Murray, 16 October 1916, CAB 44/15 TNA.
14. McMunn and Falls, *Military Operations, Egypt and Palestine*, I, p. 173.
15. W. T. Massey, *The Great War in the Middle East*, pub. as *The Desert Campaigns* (New York: Putnam's, 1918; repub. London: Leonaur, 2009), p. 23.

16. McMunn and Falls, *Military Operations, Egypt and Palestine*, I, p. 49.
17. Kress von Kressenstein, cited in McMunn and Falls, *Military Operations, Egypt and Palestine*, I, 'Sinai', p. 21; Otto Liman von Sanders, *Five Years in Turkey* (Annapolis, MD: US Naval Institute Press, 1927), p. 181; both cited in McMunn and Falls, *Military Operations, Egypt and Palestine*, I, p. 157.
18. EEF Intelligence Diary, 13 April 1916; RFC Resumé of Operations, 8–14 April 1916, attached to EEF Intelligence Summary, 16 April 1916, WO 157/703, TNA.
19. Eugene Rogan, *The Fall of the Ottomans* (New York: Basic Books, 2015), p. 313.
20. McMunn and Falls, *Military Operations, Egypt and Palestine*, I, p. 182.
21. Ibid., I, p. 202.
22. Ibid., I, p. 199.
23. Massey, *The Great War in the Middle East*, p. 67.
24. Ibid., pp. 60, 68.
25. McMunn and Falls, *Military Operations, Egypt and Palestine*, I, p. 199.
26. James Kitchen, *The British Imperial Army in the Middle East: Morale and Military Identity in the Sinai and Palestine Campaigns, 1916–1918* (London: Bloomsbury, 2014).
27. John Grigg, *Lloyd George: War Leader* (London: Allen Lane, 2002), pp. 12–13.
28. Elizabeth Greenhalgh, *Victory Through Coalition: Britain and France During the First World War* (Cambridge: Cambridge University Press, 2009), p. 89.
29. Grigg, *Lloyd George*, p. 37.
30. William Robertson, *Soldiers and Statesmen, 1914–1918* (London, 1926), II, pp. 213–14.
31. Hew Strachan, *The First World War* (London: Simon and Schuster, 2003), p. 177.
32. Grigg, *Lloyd George*, p. 34.
33. Intelligence, General Headquarters, Egyptian Expeditionary Force, March 1917, pp. 8–14, AWM4 1/8/11, Australian War Memorial, Canberra [AWM].
34. The estimates of the main defences were correct but the garrison of Gaza was assessed as half the actual numbers. Formation Headquarters, Intelligence Summary, GHQ, EEF, p. 56, AWM4 1/9/3.
35. Matthew Hughes, 'General Allenby and the Palestine Campaign, 1917–1918', *Journal of Strategic Studies*, 9 (1996), p. 62.
36. Matthew Hughes, *Allenby and British Strategy in the Middle East, 1917–1919* (London; Portland, OR: F. Cass, 1999), p. 18.
37. Private Letters between CIGS and Sir A. Murray, pp. 177–8, CAB 44/15, TNA.
38. Ibid., pp. 182–3.
39. McMunn and Falls, *Military Operations, Egypt and Palestine*, I, pp. 281, 284; Formation Headquarters, Intelligence Summary, GHQ, EEF, p. 68, AWM4 1/9/3, AWM.
40. War Diary, 158th Brigade, 53rd Welsh Division, 26 March 1917, WO 95/4626, TNA.
41. McMunn and Falls, *Military Operations, Egypt and Palestine*, I, p. 293.
42. Ibid., I, p. 294.
43. AWM4 1/60/14 Part 1, pp. 15–17, AWM.
44. McMunn and Falls, *Military Operations, Egypt and Palestine*, I, pp. 305–11.

45. Lord Carver, *The Turkish Front* (London: Sidgwick and Jackson, 2003), p. 198.
46. John D. Grainger, *The Battle for Palestine 1917* (Woodbridge and New York: Boydell Press, 2006), p. 37; James E. Kitchen, *The British Imperial Army in the Middle East: Morale and Military Identity in the Sinai and Palestine Campaigns, 1916–18* (London: Bloomsbury, 2014), pp. 118–19; Matthew Hughes, *Allenby and British Strategy in the Middle East, 1917–1919* (London: F. Cass, 1999), p. 20.
47. War Diary 158th Brigade, 53rd Welsh Division, 27 March 1917, WO 95/4626, TNA.
48. Ibid.
49. McMunn and Falls, *Military Operations, Egypt and Palestine*, I, p. 318.
50. CAB 24/11, 146, TNA.
51. Ibid.
52. CAB 23/13/23, 8, TNA.
53. McMunn and Falls, *Military Operations, Egypt and Palestine*, I, p. 321.
54. Djemal Pasha, *Memories of a Turkish Statesman: 1913–1919* (London, Hutchinson and Co., 1922), p. 179.
55. McMunn and Falls, *Military Operations, Egypt and Palestine*, I, p. 329.
56. Ibid., I, p. 331.
57. Ibid., I, p. 338.
58. Carver, *Turkish Front*, p. 204.
59. McMunn and Falls, *Military Operations, Egypt and Palestine*, I, p. 348.
60. Ibid., I, p. 355.
61. Ibid., I, p. 357.
62. Zachary Foster, 'The 1915 Locust Attack in Syria and Palestine and Its Role in the Famine During the First World War', *Middle Eastern Studies*, 51(3) (2015).
63. Tilman Lüdke, 'Loyalty, Indifference, Treason: The Ottoman-German Experience in Palestine During World War 1' in Haim Goren, Eran Dolev, and Yigal Sheffy (eds.), *Palestine and World War I: Grand Strategy, Military Tactics and Culture in War* (London: I. B. Tauris, 2014), pp. 83–4.

CHAPTER 6

1. Proceedings of the Sub-Committee of Imperial Defence, 5 August 1914, Asquith Papers, Bodleian Library, Oxford; Sir Julian Corbett and Sir Henry Newbolt, *Naval Operations* (London, 1920), I, pp. 128ff; Paul Guinn, *British Strategy and Politics, 1914–1918* (Oxford: Clarendon Press, 1965), p. 40.
2. Brigadier General F. J. Moberly, *The Campaign in Mesopotamia* (London: Historical Section of the Committee of Imperial Defence, 1923), I, p. 87; IOR/L/Mil/17/15/66, India Office Records, British Library.
3. Charles Townshend, *When God Made Hell: The British Invasion of Mesopotamia and the Creation of Iraq, 1914–1921* (London: Faber and Faber, 2010), pp. 3–4.
4. Kristian Coates Ulrichsen, *The Logistics and Politics of the British Campaigns in the Middle East, 1914–22* (Basingstoke: Palgrave Macmillan, 2010), p. 33.

5. Moberly, *The Campaign in Mesopotamia*, I, pp. 75–153; *Mesopotamia Commission Report*, Cd 8610 (1917), pp. 12–15; Colonel Richard Meinertzhagen, *Army Diary 1899–1926* (London: Oliver and Boyd, 1960), p. 82.
6. Eugene Rogan, *The Fall of the Ottomans* (New York: Basic Books, 2015), p. 81.
7. Ibid., p. 82.
8. Ghassan Atiyyah, *Iraq: 1908–1921. A Socio-Political Study* (Beirut: The Arab Institute for Research and Publishing, 1973), p. 41.
9. Fourth Army consisted of two corps, XII (with its two divisions, the 35th and 36th at Mosul) and XIII (with its two divisions, 37th and 38th, at Baghdad). The 37th Division was sent to the Caucasus; XII Corps was deployed to Sinai and Palestine. Fourth Army Headquarters went to Syria. Only the 38th Division remained and that was at brigade strength.
10. Rogan, *The Fall of the Ottomans*, p. 217.
11. Townshend, *When God Made Hell*, p. 133; Coates Ulrichsen, *The Logistics and Politics of the British Campaigns*, p. 33.
12. David French, 'The Dardanelles, Mecca and Kut: Prestige as a Factor in British Eastern Strategy, 1914–1916', *War and Society*, 5(1) (1987), pp. 54–5.
13. Guinn, *British Strategy and Politics*, p. 105.
14. Rogan, *The Fall of the Ottomans*, p. 222.
15. Townshend, *When God Made Hell*, p. 120.
16. F. J. Moberly, *Campaign in Mesopotamia* (London: Historical Section of the Committee of Imperial Defence, 1925), II, p. 525.
17. Ibid., II, pp. 49–58; Edward J. Erickson, *Ordered to Die: A History of the Ottoman Army in the First World War* (Westport, CT: Greenwood Press, 2001), pp. 112–13.
18. Rogan, *The Fall of the Ottomans*, p. 232; Moberly, *The Campaign in Mesopotamia*, II, p. 59.
19. Charles Townshend, *My Campaign in Mesopotamia* (London: Thornton Butterworth, 1920); Moberly, *The Campaign in Mesopotamia*, II, pp. 167 and 278; Mesopotamia Dispatches, Parliamentary Command Papers, Cd. 8074 East India (Military); WO 32/5204: Report on Siege of Kut-al-Amara by Lieutenant H. McNeal, Royal Field Artillery, Dec. 1915–Apr. 1916, The National Archives [TNA].
20. Byron Farwell, *Armies of the Raj: From the Great Indian Mutiny to Independence, 1858–1947* (New York: W. W. Norton and Company, 1989), p. 250.
21. Regimental records of the Oxford and Buckinghamshire Light Infantry, Woodstock, Oxfordshire.
22. Colonel E. A. E. Lethbridge, Narrative of the Siege of Kut El Amara, 1915–1916, Regimental Archives of The Oxfordshire and Buckinghamshire Light Infantry, Woodstock, Oxfordshire.
23. The supply question remains disputed, and there has been much criticism of Townshend's refusal to enforce strict measures of rationing from the outset. Major General T. L. Davison, Mesopotamia Commission, 28 November 1916, statement.

24. Rogan, *The Fall of the Ottomans*, p. 259.
25. *Birinci Dunya Harbi'nde Türk Harbi* [The First World War, Turkey's War] (Ankara: Genekuurmay, 1993), III, pt 1, p. 800.
26. K.3698, D. 1/235-4, F. 1-1, and F. 1-162, ATASE Archives, Ankara.
27. Hikmet Özdemir, *The Ottoman Army, 1914–1918: Disease and Death on the Battlefield* (Salt Lake City: University of Utah Press, 2008 [orig. pub. in Turkish, 2005]), p. 90.
28. Report on state of nutrition of garrison at Kut-al-Amara, 1916, WO 32/5113; Report on siege of Kut-al-Amara by Lieutenant H. McNeal, Royal Field Artillery, Dec. 1915–Apr. 1916, WO 32/5204, TNA.
29. Townshend, *When God Made Hell*, pp. 250–3.
30. Paul Davis, *Ends and Means: The British Mesopotamia Campaign and Commission* (Cranbery, NJ: Associated University Presses, 1994), p. 141.
31. Ibid., p. 148.
32. Hardinge to Cox, 20 December 1915, Hardinge Papers, vol. 94/2/155, University Library, Cambridge.
33. Robert Johnson, *Spying for Empire* (London: Greenhill, 2006), p. 219; Revolt in Persia: Expenditure of Secret Service Funds, L/PS/8/71.72,73,75, India Office Records, British Library.
34. Rogan, *The Fall of the Ottomans*, pp. 236–7.
35. Touraj Atabaki, *Iran and the First World War: Battleground of the Great Powers* (London: I. B. Tauris, 2006).
36. Antony Wynn, *Persia in the Great Game: Sir Percy Sykes: Explorer, Consul, Soldier, Spy* (London: John Murray, 2003).
37. Townshend, *When God Made Hell*, p. 335.
38. Moberly, *The Campaign in Mesopotamia* (London: Historical Section of the Committee of Imperial Defence, 1926), III, pp. 3–4.
39. Robertson to Duff, telegram, no. 15955, Military Operations 30 April 1916, WO 106/906, TNA.

CHAPTER 7

1. S.D. Sazonov, in his *The Fateful Years, 1909–16* (New York: F.A. Stokes, 1928), p. 49.
2. Hugh Seton Watson, *The Decline of Imperial Russia* (London: Methuen, 1952).
3. Hew Strachan, *The First World War*, I: *To Arms* (Oxford: Oxford University Press, 2001), pp. 717–18.
4. William Edward David Allen and Paul Muratoff, *Caucasian Battlefields: A History of the Wars of the Turko-Caucasian Border, 1828–1921* (Cambridge: Cambridge University Press, 2010 [1953]), p. 240.
5. Ibid., p. 243.
6. Edward J. Erickson, *Ordered to Die: A History of the Ottoman Army in the First World War* (Westport, CT: Greenwood Press, 2001), p. 72.
7. Allen and Muratoff, *Caucasian Battlefields*, p. 248.

8. Otto Liman von Sanders, *Five Years in Turkey* (Annapolis, MD: US Naval Institute Press, 1927), p. 37.
9. Erickson, *Ordered to Die*, p. 53.
10. Donald M. McKale, *War by Revolution: Germany and Great Britain in the Middle East in the Era of World War I* (Kent, OH: Kent State University Press, 1998), p. 79.
11. Liman von Sanders, *Five Years in Turkey*, pp. 37–9; Eugene Rogan, *The Fall of the Ottomans* (New York: Basic Books, 2015), p. 101.
12. Rogan, *The Fall of the Ottomans*, p. 102.
13. Allen and Muratoff, *Caucasian Battlefields*, p. 253.
14. Ibid., p. 258; Rogan, *The Fall of the Ottomans*, p. 109.
15. The Russians were outnumbered locally by 50 per cent. Allen and Muratoff, *Caucasian Battlefields*, p. 252.
16. Ibid., p. 261.
17. Ibid., p. 267.
18. Ibid., pp. 261, 265.
19. Ibid., p. 269.
20. Ibid., p. 284.
21. Russian losses were 16,000 with 12,000 sick.
22. Tevfik Sağlam, *Cihan Harbinde*, III: *Ordu'da Sıhhî Hizmete Ait Küçük Bir Hulâsa* [The World War, III: The Medical Services: A Selection] (Istanbul: Askerî Tibbiye Publishers, 1940), p. 6.
23. Strachan, *The First World War*, I: *To Arms*, p. 729.
24. Hikmet Özdemir, *The Ottoman Army, 1914–1918: Disease and Death on the Battlefield* (Salt Lake City: University of Utah Press, 2008), pp. 51, 60.
25. Sağlam, *Cihan Harbinde*, III: *Ordu'da*, p. 6.
26. Özdemir, *The Ottoman Army*, p. 54.
27. Rogan, *The Fall of the Ottomans*, p. 163.
28. Taner Akçam, *The Young Turks' Crime Against Humanity: The Armenian Genocide and Ethnic Cleansing in the Ottoman Empire* (Princeton, NJ: Princeton University Press, 2012), pp. 183–4.
29. Rogan, *The Fall of the Ottomans*, pp. 172–3.
30. Donald Bloxham, *The Great Game of Genocide: Imperialism, Nationalism and the Destruction of the Ottoman Armenians* (Oxford: Oxford University Press, 2005), pp. 97–8.
31. Justin McCarthy, *Muslims and Minorities: The Population of Ottoman Anatolia and the End of Empire* (New York: New York University Press, 1983), pp. 121–30; Richard Hovannisian (ed.), *The Armenian Genocide: History, Politics, Ethics* (Basingstoke: Palgrave, 1992).
32. Strachan, *The First World War*, I: *To Arms*, p. 714. The Musavat Party was founded in 1911 as a secret organization pledged to unite all Muslims, and was established in emulation of the Young Turks.
33. Ibid., I, p. 715.
34. Ibid., I, p. 728.

35. Allen and Muratoff, *Caucasian Battlefields*, p. 298.
36. Ibid., p. 302.
37. Ibid., p. 303.
38. Ibid., p. 307.
39. Ibid., p. 311.
40. Ibid., p. 312.
41. Ibid., p. 320.
42. Ibid., p. 332.
43. Ibid., p. 326.
44. Ibid., p. 334.
45. Yudenich was furious that the envelopment had not been complete: ibid., p. 340.
46. Estimates are that the Ottomans lost 15,000 casualties and 5,000 taken prisoner, with some twenty guns in Russian hands: ibid., p. 342.
47. There were eleven individual forts and two co-located groups of forts. These were interspersed with trenches and gun batteries, and protected by wire, cliffs, and bluffs. Each fort consisted of up to fifty guns although only half of these were considered 'modern' types.
48. Enver also ordered two divisions to Mesopotamia, two to Syria, and two to Alexandretta to anticipate a possible British landing. The divisions allocated to the Caucasus would have to be moved by rail and then cover 500 miles on foot.
49. Allen and Muratoff, *Caucasian Battlefields*, p. 345.
50. Rogan, *The Fall of the Ottomans*, p. 256.
51. Allen and Muratoff, *Caucasian Battlefields*, p. 361.
52. Russian casualties at Erzurum were 5,000 killed and wounded, with the same number suffering frostbite and cold injuries.
53. Allen and Muratoff, *Caucasian Battlefields*, p. 372.

CHAPTER 8

1. *Memoirs of King Abdullah of Jordan* (London: Jonathan Cape, 1950), p. 112; Ronald Storrs, *Orientations* (London: Readers' Union, 1939), p. 129; Eugene Rogan, *The Fall of the Ottomans* (New York: Basic Books, 2015), p. 276.
2. C. E. Dawn, *From Ottomanism to Arabism: Essays on the Origins of Arab Nationalism* (Urbana: University of Illinois Press, 1973), p. 26; Donald McKale, *War by Revolution* (Kent, OH: Kent State University Press, 1998), p. 75.
3. McKale, *War by Revolution*, p. 75.
4. Efraim Karsh and Inari Karsh, 'Myth in the Desert, or Not the Great Arab Revolt', *Middle Eastern Studies*, 33(2) (1997), pp. 267–312.
5. J. C. Hurewitz (ed.), *The Middle East and North Africa in World Politics: A Documentary Record* (New Haven, CT: Yale University Press, 1979), II, pp. 46–56.
6. Ibid., II, pp. 60–4.
7. Correspondence between Sir Henry McMahon and the sharif of Mecca July 1915–March 1916, Cmd 5957 (London, 1939), p. 3; Elie Kedourie, *In the Anglo-Arab*

Labyrinth: The McMahon–Hussein Correspondence and its Interpretations, 1914–1939 (Cambridge: Cambridge University Press, 1976), Wingate to Balfour, 25 December 1917, FO 371/3395/12077, The National Archive [TNA]; see also Karsh and Karsh, 'Myth in the Desert, or Not the Great Arab Revolt', pp. 289–90; Ali Allawi, *Faisal I of Iraq* (New Haven, CT: Yale University Press, 2014), pp. 138–41.

8. Linda Schilcher, 'The Famine in 1915–1918 in Greater Syria' in John Spagnolo (ed.), *Problems of the Middle East in Historical Perspective* (Reading, NY: Ithaca Press, 1992), pp. 229–52.
9. Rogan, *The Fall of the Ottomans*, p. 291.
10. *Memoirs of King Abdullah of Jordan*, p. 136; Djemal Pasha, *Memories of a Turkish Statesman, 1913–1919* (London: Hutchinson and Co., 1922), p. 215.
11. This was certainly the view of the Arab Bureau in Cairo. 'Note on the Conference at Ismailia', 12 September 1916, FO 882/4, TNA.
12. Eliezer Tauber, *The Arab Movements in World War* (London: Frank Cass, 1993), I, pp. 102–17; Rogan, *The Fall of the Ottomans*, p. 302.
13. Edouard Brémond, *Le Hedjaz dans la Guerre Mondiale* (Paris: Payot, 1931), p. 35; James Barr, *Setting the Desert on Fire: T. E. Lawrence and Britain's Secret War in Arabia, 1916–118* (London: Bloomsbury, 2006), p. 47.
14. Robin Bidwell, 'The Brémond Mission in the Hijaz, 1916–17: A Study in Inter-Allied Co-operation' in Robin Bidwell and Rex Smith (eds.), *Arabian and Islamic Studies* (London: Longman, 1983), pp. 182–95.
15. Robertson to Murray, 16 October 1916, Add 52463, British Library.
16. George McMunn and Cyril Falls, *Military Operations, Egypt and Palestine* (London: HMSO, 1927), I, pp. 230, 233–4.
17. Ibid., I, pp. 240–1.
18. The near collapse of the Arab force appears in T. E. Lawrence, *Seven Pillars of Wisdom* (London: Jonathan Cape, 1935), pp. 116–32. Inactivity also affected Feisal: 'With the Northern Army', Secret Despatches from Arabia, 15 February 1917, cited in Malcom Brown, *T. E. Lawrence in War and Peace* (London: Greenhill, 2005), p. 99.
19. Details of the actions are in Lawrence, *Seven Pillars*, pp. 294–302.
20. The Ottoman garrison was only 600 strong. McMunn and Falls, *Military Operations, Egypt and Palestine*, I, p. 240.
21. Barr, *Setting the Desert on Fire*, p. 166.
22. Rogan, *The Fall of the Ottomans*, p. 339.
23. McMunn and Falls, *Military Operations, Egypt and Palestine*, I, p. 354.
24. Hikmet Özdemir, *The Ottoman Army, 1914–1918: Disease and Death on the Battlefield* (Salt Lake City: University of Utah Press, 2008), p. 84.
25. 4/10832, box 3709, F I, 34; and 4/11007, box 3772, box H-7, F I, *Birinci Dunya Harbi'nde Turk Harbi* [The First World War: The Turkish War], vol. 4, part 2, p. 752, ATASE Archives, Ankara.
26. Cited in Özdemir, *The Ottoman Army*, p. 160.

27. McMunn and Falls, *Military Operations, Egypt and Palestine*, I, pp. 355, 356.
28. The A and NZ, Australian, and Yeomanry Mounted Divisions. Ibid., I, pp. 357.
29. Hew Strachan, *The First World War*, I, *To Arms* (Oxford: Oxford University Press, 2001), p. 702.
30. Cyril Falls and A. F. Becke, *Military Operations, Egypt and Palestine* (London: HMSO, 1930), II, pp. 4–6.
31. Rogan, *The Fall of the Ottomans*, p. 342.
32. Matthew Hughes (ed.), *Allenby in Palestine* (Stroud: Sutton, 2004), p. 8.
33. Falls and Becke, *Military Operations, Egypt and Palestine*, II, p. 9.
34. Allenby to Robertson, 11 July 1917, 8/1/63, Robertson Papers, Liddell Hart Centre for Military Archives, London.
35. R. J. M. Pugh, *Wingate Pasha: The Life of General Sir Francis Reginald Wingate, 1861–1953* (Barnsley: Pen and Sword, 2011), p. 172.
36. David Lloyd George, *War Memoirs* (London: Odhams, 1936), II, p. 1090.
37. Robertson to Allenby, Secret, 10 August 1917, WO 158/611, TNA.
38. Falls and Becke, *Military Operations, Egypt and Palestine*, II, p. 15; Lloyd George, *War Memoirs*, II, pp. 1091–2.
39. Archibald Wavell, *Allenby: A Study in Greatness* (London: 1940), p. 186; John Grigg, *Lloyd George: War Leader* (London: Allen Lane, 2002), p. 150.
40. Allenby to Robertson, 9 October 1917, WO 158/611; WO 106/718/102–4, TNA.
41. Lloyd George, *War Memoirs*, II, p. 1092.
42. Falls and Becke, *Military Operations, Egypt and Palestine*, II, p. 27.
43. Robertson to Allenby, 1 August 1917, 8/1/67, Robertson Papers, Liddell Hart Centre for Military Archives, London.
44. Allenby to Robertson, 8 August 1917, WO 106/718/182–7, TNA.
45. *Hansard*, 5th series, vol. C., col. 2211 [1917]; Grigg, *Lloyd George*, p. 344.
46. Edward J. Erickson, *Ottoman Army Effectiveness in World War I: A Comparative Study* (London: Routledge, 2007), p. 118.
47. Falls and Becke, *Military Operations, Egypt and Palestine*, II, p. 30.
48. Michael Occleshaw, *Armour Against Fate: British Military Intelligence in the First World War* (London: Columbus, 1989), pp. 130–1.
49. The orders were found after the fall of Gaza. R. M. Meinertzhagen, *Army Diary, 1899–1926*, XXVII, 1 June 1926 (Edinburgh: Oliver and Boyd, 1960), p. 285.
50. Falls and Becke, *Military Operations, Egypt and Palestine*, II, p. 50.
51. Ibid., II, p. 56.
52. Ibid., II, p. 59.
53. Ibid., II, p. 60.
54. Yigal Sheffy, *British Military Intelligence in the Palestine Campaign, 1914–1918* (London; Portland, OR: Frank Cass, 1998), pp. 237–8.
55. Falls and Becke, *Military Operations, Egypt and Palestine*, II, pp. 66–9.
56. Ibid., II, p. 74.
57. Ibid., II, pp. 95–101.
58. Ibid., II, pp. 75, 104, 110.

59. See Matthew Hughes, *Allenby and British Strategy in the Middle East, 1917–1919* (London; Portland, OR: Frank Cass, 1999), pp. 35–40; Clive Garsia, *A Key to Victory: A Study in War Planning* (London, 1940).
60. Falls and Becke, *Military Operations, Egypt and Palestine*, II, pp. 127–9, 158–74.
61. Ibid., II, p. 201.
62. Hughes, *Allenby in Palestine*, p. 4.
63. On Allenby's willingness to engage see War Diary of 161st Infantry Brigade, 54th (East Anglian) Division, 6th July, WO 95/4649, TNA.
64. Robertson to Allenby, 13 June 1917, WO 106/718/313–14, TNA. See, for example, *SS135 Instructions for the Training of Divisions for Offensive Action*, which insisted that brigade formations should not advance too far, allowing one to 'leap frog' another in attack to counter the effects of fatigue and attrition.
65. First Annual Report of the British Mandate, Department of Health, 1921. Naomi Shepherd, *Ploughing Sand: British Rule in Palestine, 1917–1948* (New Brunswick, NJ: Rutgers University Press, 2000).
66. Edward J. Erickson, *Ordered to Die: A History of the Ottoman Army in the First World War* (Westport, CT: Greenwood Press, 2001), p. 169.
67. Erickson, *Ottoman Army Effectiveness in World War I*, p. 107.
68. Ibid., p. 103.
69. Sir William Robertson, Future Operations in Palestine, 26 December 1917, CAB/24/37/12, TNA.
70. Robertson to Allenby, 13 November 1917, WO158/611, TNA; Robertson to Allenby, 23 November 1917, Robertson Papers 8/1/81, Liddell Hart Centre for Military Archives, London.
71. James E. Kitchen, *The British Imperial Army in the Middle East: Morale and Military Identity in the Sinai and Palestine Campaigns, 1916–18* (London: Bloomsbury, 2014), p. 191.
72. Cited in Grigg, *Lloyd George*, p. 344.
73. Hughes, *Allenby in Palestine*, p. 11; Grigg, *Lloyd George*, p. 343; Rogan, *The Fall of the Ottomans*, p. 352.
74. Joint Note no. 12, J. E. Edmonds, Cyril Falls, and Wilfred Miles, *Military Operations France and Belgium 1918* (1922), I, Appendices, no. 9, pp. 37–42.
75. See, for example, Minutes of Imperial War Cabinet Meeting, 21 June 1918, CAB/23/44A/1, TNA.

CHAPTER 9

1. Hew Strachan, *The First World War*, I: *To Arms* (Oxford: Oxford University Press, 2001), pp. 655–70, 694–712.
2. David French, 'British Strategy and Winning the Great War' in B. A. Lee and K. F. Walling (eds.), *Strategic and Political Rationality: Essays in Honour of Michael I. Handel* (London: Routledge, 2003), p. 207; Strachan, *First World War*, I: *To Arms*, pp. 674–5.

3. John Darwin, *Britain, Egypt and the Middle East: Imperial Policy in the Aftermath of War, 1918–22* (London: Palgrave Macmillan, 1981), p. 144.
4. David French, 'The Dardanelles, Mecca and Kut: Prestige as a Factor in British Eastern Strategy', *War and Society*, 5(1) (1987), p. 45.
5. S. A. Cohen, *British Policy in Mesopotamia, 1903–1914* (London: Ithaca, 2008), p. 308.
6. Robert Johnson, *Spying for Empire: The Great Game in Central and South Asia, 1757–1947* (London: Greenhill, 2006), pp. 218–22; Keith Neilson, '"For Diplomatic, Economic, Strategic and Telegraphic Reasons": British Imperial Defence, the Middle East and India, 1914–1918' in G. Kennedy and K. Nielson (eds.), *Far Flung Lines: Essays on Imperial Defence in Honour of Donald Mackenzie Schurman* (London: Routledge, 1996), pp. 103–23.
7. P. W. Long, *Other Ranks of Kut* (London, 1938), p. 103, cited in Eugene Rogan, *The Fall of the Ottomans* (New York: Basic Books, 2015), p. 271.
8. Captain Reynolds Lecky, cited in Rogan, *The Fall of the Ottomans*, p. 268.
9. F. J. Moberly, *The Campaign in Mesopotamia, 1914–1918* (London: Historical Section of the Committee of Imperial Defence, 1923), I, p. 48, India Office Records, British Library and CAB 19/26, The National Archives [TNA].
10. Andrew Syk, 'The Mesopotamia Commission: Britain's First Iraq Inquiry', *RUSI Journal*, 154(4) (2009), pp. 94–101. See also Paul K. Davis, *Ends and Means: The British Mesopotamian Campaign and Commission* (Cranbery, NJ: Associated University Presses, 1994).
11. Hardinge to Sir Percy Cox, 14 March 1916, cited in Andrew Syk, 'Command and the Mesopotamia Expeditionary Force, 1915–1918' (Oxford, DPhil thesis, 2009), p. 5.
12. Marian Kent, *Oil and Empire: British Policy and Mesopotamian Oil, 1900–1920* (London: Macmillan, 1976).
13. Mesopotamia Commission, Statements of Evidence, CAB 19/8, p. 127, TNA.
14. Cyril Falls, *The Great War* (New York: G. P. Putnam and Sons, 1959), p. 179.
15. Edward J. Erickson, *Ordered to Die: A History of the Ottoman Army in the First World War* (Westport, CT: Greenwood Press, 2001), pp. 164–6; Rogan, *The Fall of the Ottomans*, pp. 318–19.
16. Memorandum on India's Contribution to the War in Men, Material, and Money: August 1914 to November 1918, L/Mil/17/5/2381, British Library; Kristian Coates Ulrichsen, *The Logistics and Politics of the British Campaigns in the Middle East, 1914–22* (Basingstoke: Palgrave Macmillan, 2010), p. 65.
17. George Barrow, *The Life of General Sir Charles Carmichael Monro* (London: Hutchinson, 1931), p. 132.
18. Moberly, *The Campaign in Mesopotamia* (London: Historical Section of the Committee of Imperial Defence, 1926), III, pp. 79, 86–90; William Robertson, *Soldiers and Statesmen, 1914–1918* (London, 1926), II, pp. 79, 227; Paul Guinn, *British Strategy and Politics, 1914–1918* (Oxford: Clarendon Press, 1965), p. 219.
19. Rogan, *The Fall of the Ottomans*, p. 322.

20. Guinn, *British Strategy*, pp. 113–14.
21. Moberly, *The Campaign in Mesopotamia*, III, pp. 204–11.
22. Guinn, *British Strategy and Politics*, p. 157; Robertson, *Soldiers and Statesmen*, II, p. 74.
23. Moberly, *The Campaign in Mesopotamia*, III, pp. 125–6, 159, 199; Robertson, *Soldiers and Statesmen*, II, p. 77; Guinn, *British Strategy*, p. 200.
24. Rogan, *The Fall of the Ottomans*, p. 323.
25. Consul Heizer's miscellaneous record, NARA, cited in Rogan, *The Fall of the Ottomans*, p. 325.
26. David Fromkin, *A Peace to End All Peace: The Fall of the Ottoman Empire and the Creation of the Modern Middle East* (New York: Henry Holt and Company, 2001).
27. Ghassan R. Atiyyah, *Iraq: 1908–1921, A Socio-Political Study* (Beirut: The Arab Institute for Research and Publishing, 1973), p. 227.
28. Memorandum from Arnold Wilson to the Chief of the General Staff, G.H.Q., 17 September 1918, L/PS/10/619, British Library.
29. Major General Dunsterville, the inspiration for Kipling's 'Stalky and Co', was tasked to secure northern Persia and Baku on the Caspian with a brigade known as 'Dunsterforce': see Chapter 10 and L. C. Dunsterville, *The Adventures of Dunsterforce* (London: E. Arnold, 1920).
30. Moberly, *The Campaign in Mesopotamia*, I, preface.
31. Davis, *Ends and Means*; John S. Galbraith, 'No Man's Child: The Campaign in Mesopotamia, 1914–1916', *International History Review*, 6(3) (1984), pp. 358–85; David Gould, 'Lord Hardinge and the Mesopotamia Expedition and Inquiry, 1914-1917', *The Historical Journal*, 19(4) (1976), pp. 919–45.
32. Kaushik Roy, 'The Army in India in Mesopotamia from 1916 to 1918: Tactics, Technology and Logistics Reconsidered' in I. W. F. Beckett (ed.), *1917: Beyond the Western Front* (Leiden and Boston, MA: Brill, 2009), pp. 131–58.
33. This is also the verdict of E. A. Cohen and J. Gooch, *Military Misfortunes: The Anatomy of Failure in War* (London: Macmillan, 1990), pp. 156–63.
34. Philip Graves, *The Life of Sir Percy Cox* (London: Hutchinson and Co., 1941).
35. See Peter Slugett, *Britain in Iraq, 1914–32* (London: Ithaca, 1976). A. L. Macfie, 'British Intelligence and the Causes of Unrest in Mesopotamia, 1919–21', *Middle Eastern Studies*, 35 (1999), pp. 165–77.
36. Aylmer Haldane, *The Insurrection in Mesopotamia, 1920* (London and Edinburgh: Blackwood and Sons, 1922).
37. *Critical Study of the Campaign in Mesopotamia up to April 1917: Compiled by Officers of the Staff College, Quetta, October–November 1923* (Quetta: Government of India Publishing, 1925). An analysis of the Study can be found in Edwin Latter, 'The Indian Army in Mesopotamia, 1914–18', *Journal of the Society for Army Historical Research*, 72 (1994).
38. T. R. Moreman, *The Army in India and the Development of Frontier Warfare* (London: Macmillan, 1998); Kaushik Roy, 'Modernisation or Demodernisation of the Army in India: Cavalry from the First World War to the Third Afghan War,

1914–1919', paper presented to the First World War Studies Conference, Imperial War Museum, 11 September 2009.

39. This is challenged by Kaushik Roy, 'The Historiography of the Colonial Indian Army', *Studies in History*, 12(2) (1996). See also the longer studies: T. A. Heathcote, *The Military in British India: The Development of Land Forces in South Asia, 1600–1947* (Manchester: Manchester University Press, 1995); and Daniel Marston and C. S. Sundaram (eds.), *A Military History of South Asia: from the East India Company to the Nuclear Era* (Westport, CT: Praeger, 2007).
40. Mark Harrison, 'The Fight Against Disease in the Mesopotamian Campaign' in Peter Liddle and Hugh Cecil (eds.), *Facing Armageddon: The First World War Experienced* (Barnsley: Leo Cooper, 1996), pp. 475–89.

CHAPTER 10

1. Nasir Yuceer, *Birinci Dünya Savaşi'nda Osmanlı Ordusu'nun Azerbaycan ve Dağistan Harekatı* [The Ottoman Army's Azerbaijani and Daghestani Operations in the First World War] (Ankara: Genelkurmay Basımevi, 1996), p. 189.
2. William Edward David Allen and Paul Muratoff, *Caucasian Battlefields: A History of the Wars of the Turko-Caucasian Border, 1828–1921* (Cambridge: Cambridge University Press, 2010), p. 447.
3. Allen and Muratoff, *Caucasian Battlefields*, p. 449.
4. Eugene Rogan, *The Fall of the Ottomans* (New York: Basic Books, 2015), p. 356.
5. Allen and Muratoff, *Caucasian Battlefields*, p. 457.
6. Ibid., p. 459.
7. Ibid., p. 467.
8. Yuceer, *Birinci Dünya Savaşi'nda Osmanlı Ordusu'nun Azerbaycan ve Dağistan Harekatı*, p. 72.
9. Robert Service, *Lenin* (Cambridge, MA: Harvard University Press, 2000), p. 256.
10. Ibid., pp. 284–5, 294.
11. V. I. Lenin, *Imperialism: The Highest Stage of Capitalism*, 18th edn (Moscow: Progress, 1982 [1916]), p. 118.
12. R. H. Ullman, *Anglo-Soviet Relations, 1917–21* (Princeton, NJ: Princeton University Press, 1961–72), I, ch. 8.
13. Ullman, *Anglo-Soviet Relations*, II, p. 23.
14. Rogan, *The Fall of the Ottomans*, p. 358; James Barr, *Setting the Desert on Fire* (London: Bloomsbury, 2006), p. 209.
15. Leonard Stein, *The Balfour Declaration* (London, 1961), p. i; Barr, *Setting the Desert on Fire*, p. 201.
16. The key lobbyist in Britain, Chaim Weizmann, was a research chemist at Manchester University and when he invented a new formula to make explosives more effective he asked for no reward except the British government's consideration for a Jewish homeland: Chaim Weizmann, *Trial and Error* (New York: Harper, 1949).

17. D. K. Fieldhouse, *Western Imperialism in the Middle East, 1914–1958* (Oxford: Oxford University Press, 2006), p. 49.
18. Barr, *Setting the Desert on Fire*, p. 210.
19. Djemal to Feisal, November 1917, FO 686/38 The National Archives, TNA.
20. Scott Anderson, *Lawrence in Arabia: War, Deceit, Imperial Folly and the Making of the Modern Middle East* (London: Atlantic, 2013), pp. 270–2.
21. Barr, *Setting the Desert on Fire*, p. 217.
22. E. H. T. Robinson, *Lawrence the Rebel* (London: Lincolns-Prager, 1946), p. 119.
23. T. E. Lawrence, *Seven Pillars of Wisdom* (London: Jonathan Cape, 1935), p. 326; 'Arabia-Hejaz', Intelligence Report, 24 July 1917, cited in Malcolm Brown, *T. E. Lawrence in War and Peace* (London: Greenhill, 2005), p. 200.
24. Barr, *Setting the Desert on Fire*, pp. 216–17.
25. Lawrence claimed to have been betrayed by an Ottoman agent of Moroccan descent, Abd el Kadir: Philip Knightly and Colin Simpson, *The Secret Lives of Lawrence of Arabia* (London: Nelson, 1969), p. 83.
26. Barr, *Setting the Desert on Fire*, pp. 225–7.
27. Rogan, *The Fall of the Ottomans*, p. 362.
28. Otto Liman von Sanders, *Five Years in Turkey* (Annapolis, MD: US Naval Institute Press, 1927), p. 211.
29. Cyril Falls and A. F. Becke, *Military Operations, Egypt and Palestine* (London: HMSO, 1930), II, p. 337.
30. Liman von Sanders, *Five Years in Turkey*, p. 213.
31. Falls and Becke, *Military Operations, Egypt and Palestine*, II, p. 346.
32. Ibid., II, p. 347.
33. David Lloyd George, *War Memoirs* (London: Odhams, 1936), II, p. 1726.
34. Ibid., II, p. 1728.
35. Falls and Becke, *Military Operations, Egypt and Palestine*, II, pp. 411–21.
36. Yuceer, *Birinci Dünya Savaşi'nda Osmanlı Ordusu'nun Azerbaycan ve Dağistan arekatı*, p. 41.
37. Antony Wynn, *Persia in the Great Game* (London: John Murray, 2003), p. 299.
38. The massacres were known as the 'March Events', Allen and Muratoff, *Caucasian Battlefields*, p. 481.
39. Yuceer, *Birinci Dünya Savaşi'nda Osmanlı Ordusu'nun Azerbaycan ve Dağistan Harekatı*, p. 124.
40. Allen and Muratoff, *Caucasian Battlefields*, p. 469.
41. Ibid., p. 471.
42. Ibid., p. 477.
43. Allegedly, Enver approved of collision with Germans over Georgia: see Yuceer, *Birinci Dünya Savaşi'nda Osmanlı Ordusu'nun Azerbaycan ve Dağistan Harekatı*, pp. 93–6; Allen and Muratoff, *Caucasian Battlefields*, p. 479.
44. Yuceer, *Birinci Dünya Savaşi'nda Osmanlı Ordusu'nun Azerbaycan ve Dağistan Harekatı*, p. 76.
45. Firuz Kazemzadeh, *The Struggle for Transcaucasia* (New York and Oxford: George Ronald, 1951), pp. 135, 142, 150.

46. Allen and Muratoff, *Caucasian Battlefields*, p. 484.
47. Report by General Malleson on Operations in Transcaspia, including the Battle of Dushakh (Delhi: Government of India Publishing, 1919), L/Mil/17/14/88; The Turko-German Advance into the Caucasus, Secret, War Office, 1918, L/Mil/17/14/88, British Library.
48. Allen and Muratoff, *Caucasian Battlefields*, p. 485.
49. Reginald Teague Jones, *The Spy who Disappeared*, Introduction and Epilogue by Peter Hopkirk (London: Gollancz, 1990), pp. 62–8. Teague Jones went on to work in Persia in the 1920s and in the American Consulate in the Second World War.
50. Ibid., pp. 71–6.
51. Aidyn Balaev, *Azerbaidzhanskoe natsional'noe dvizhenie v 1917–1918 gg* [The Azerbaijani National Movement in 1917–1918] (Baku: Elm, 1998), p. 207.
52. The militias were mainly untrained groupings of civilians, a few survivors of the Ottoman reprisals, and some more experienced volunteers. There were rifles but no machine guns and only a handful of obsolete artillery pieces. Allen and Muratoff, *Caucasian Battlefields*, p. 486.
53. Yuceer, *Birinci Dünya Savaşi'nda Osmanlı Ordusu'nun Azerbaycan ve Dağistan Harekatı*, p. 114.
54. Allen and Muratoff, *Caucasian Battlefields*, p. 492.
55. Rogan, *The Fall of the Ottomans*, p. 371.
56. For examples of Bolshevik propaganda in this period see L/PS/10/836–7 and L/PS/12/2273–7, Collection 10, British Library.
57. Liman von Sanders, *Five Years in Turkey*, pp. 268–9.
58. Erik-Jan Zürcher, 'Little Mehmet in the Desert: The Ottoman Soldier's Experience' in Peter Liddle and Hugh Cecil (eds.), *Facing Armageddon: The First World War Experienced* (London: Leo Cooper, 1996), pp. 233–4.
59. See, for example, Rafael de Nogales Méndez, *Four Years beneath the Crescent* (New York; London: C. Scribner's Sons, 1926).
60. Edward J. Erickson, *Ottoman Army Effectiveness in World War I: A Comparative Study* (London: Routledge, 2007), p. 130. Intelligence Report, General Headquarters, Egyptian Expeditionary Force, 4 July 1918, AWM4 1/8/25, AWM, Canberra.
61. Erickson, *Ottoman Army Effectiveness in World War I*, p. 145.
62. Edward J. Erickson, *Ordered to Die: A History of the Ottoman Army in the First World War* (Westport, CT: Greenwood Press, 2001), p. 196.
63. Lloyd George to M. Pichon, Quai d'Orsay, 30 October 1918, F120–1; I.C./84, Lloyd George Papers.

CHAPTER 11

1. John Grigg, *Lloyd George: War Leader* (London: Faber, 2011), p. 632.
2. Sevket Pamuk, 'The Ottoman Economy in World War I' in Stephen Broadberry and Mark Harrison (eds.), *The Economics of World War I* (Cambridge: Cambridge University Press, 2009), p. 120.

3. Serezli Ismail, *Diary*, January 1918, Imperial War Museum, trans. Leo Gough.
4. Eugene Rogan, *The Fall of the Ottomans* (New York: Basic Books, 2015), p. 382.
5. Margaret MacMillan, *Peacemakers: The Paris Conference of 1919 and Its Attempt to End War* (London: John Murray, 2001).
6. David Fieldhouse, *Western Imperialism in the Middle East, 1914–1958* (Oxford: Oxford University Press, 2006), p. 65.
7. Ibid., pp. 64–5; MacMillan, *Peacemakers*, pp. 460–2.
8. Erik-Jan Zürcher, *Turkey: A Modern History* (London: I. B. Tauris, 2004).
9. Kristian Coates Ulrichsen, *The Logistics and Politics of the British Campaigns in the Middle East, 1914–22* (London: Palgrave Macmillan, 2010), p. 178.
10. Laurence Grafftey-Smith, *Bright Levant* (London: John Murray, 1970), p. 59.
11. Kristian Coates Ulrichsen, *The First World War in the Middle East* (London: Hurst, 2014), p. 180.
12. Allenby to Wilson, 21 April 1919, HHW2/33B/13, Wilson Papers, Imperial War Museum.
13. Allenby to Wingate, 21 April 1919, 173/3/15, Wingate Papers, Sudan Archives, University of Durham.
14. Ibid.
15. Allenby to Wilson, 21 April 1919, HHW2/33B/13, Wilson Papers, Imperial War Museum.
16. Allenby to Wilson, 17 May 1919, HHW2/33B/16, Wilson Papers, Imperial War Museum; Allenby to Curzon, 4 May 1919, VI/D/444/3, Milner Papers, Bodleian Library, Oxford.
17. Allenby to War Office, 6 October 1918, WO 33/960, 133, The National Archive [TNA].
18. James Barr, *A Line in the Sand: Britain, France and the Struggle that Shaped the Middle East* (London: Simon and Schuster, 2011), p. 62.
19. Allenby to War Office, 7 October 1918, WO 33/960, 136, TNA.
20. Eugene Rogan, *The Arabs* (London: Penguin, 2009), p. 214.
21. Allenby to Wilson, 19 October 1918, HHW2/33A/28, Wilson Papers, Imperial War Museum.
22. Allenby to Wilson, 9 November 1918, HHW2/33A/29, Wilson Papers, Imperial War Museum.
23. Wilson to Allenby, 7 December 1918, HHW2/33B/1, Wilson Papers, Imperial War Museum.
24. Allenby to Wilson, 4 February 1919, WO 33/960, 290, TNA.
25. Allenby to Wilson, 17 May 1919, HHW2/33B/16, Wilson Papers, Imperial War Museum.
26. Barr, *Line in the Sand*, pp. 71–2.
27. Fieldhouse, *Western Imperialism*, p. 253.
28. Ibid., p. 63.
29. 'Photos, Plans and Cuttings to the League of Nations relating to incidents around the Wailing Wall and Jerusalem, June–August 1929', CO 733/160/19/4,

TNA; Bernard Wasserstein, *The British in Palestine: The Mandatory Government and Arab–Jewish Conflict, 1917–1929* (London: Basil Blackwell, 1991).

30. Memo on Report by Jewish Agency for L(eague of) N(ations), CO 733/192/1, TNA.
31. Steven Wagner, 'British Intelligence and Policy in the Palestine Mandate 1920-39' (Oxford, DPhil thesis, 2014).
32. Arnold Wilson, *Mesopotamia, 1917–20: A Clash of Loyalties* (Oxford: Oxford University Press, 1931), p. 103.
33. Edwin Montagu to Arnold Wilson, 28 November 1918, L/Mil/5/761, British Library.
34. Gertrude Bell to Sir Hugh Bell, 10 January 1919, Bell Papers, Newcastle University.
35. Haras was led by Muhammad al-Sadr, son of one of the most prominent Shi'a *Mujtahids*.
36. Thair Karim, 'Tribes and Nationalism: Tribal Political Culture and Behaviour in Iraq, 1914–20' in Faleh Abdul-Jabar and Hosham Dawod (eds.), *Tribes and Power: Nationalism and Ethnicity in the Middle East* (London: Saqi Books, 2003), p. 292.
37. David Fromkin, *A Peace to End All Peace* (New York: Henry Holt, 1989), p. 452.
38. Charles Townshend, *When God Made Hell: The British Invasion of Mesopotamia and the Creation of Iraq, 1914–21* (London: Faber and Faber, 2010), p. 453; Martin Gilbert (ed.), *Winston S. Churchill* (London: Heinemann, 1975), IV, p. 490.
39. Fromkin, *A Peace to End All Peace*, p. 503.
40. Copies of Parliamentary Papers, House of Commons, 1919, XXXVIII, Cd 324, L/Mil/17/14/61 IOR.
41. Percy Sykes, *A History of Afghanistan* (London: Macmillan, 1940), II, p. 266.
42. Ibid., II, p. 269.
43. Report of the Hunter Committee: Disturbances in the Punjab, Cmd 681, 1920; D. George Boyce, 'From Assaye to *The Assaye*: Reflections on British Government, Force and Moral Authority in India', *Journal of Military History*, 63(3) (1999), p. 660.
44. Afghan Post Master to the Amir, 7 May 1919, cited in *The Third Afghan War: Official Account* (Calcutta: Government of India Publication, 1926), p. 29.
45. *The Third Afghan War: Official Account*, p. 30.
46. Sykes, *A History of Afghanistan*, p. 275; T. A. Heathcote, *The Afghan Wars, 1839–1919* (Staplehurst: Spellmount, 2003), p. 180.
47. *Third Afghan War: Official Account*, p. 25.
48. Ibid., pp. 33–4; Third Afghan War, Report on the Action at Bagh, L/Mil/17/14/63 IOR, British Library.
49. *Third Afghan War, Official Account*, p. 104.
50. Relief of Thal, L/Mil/17/14/65 IOR, British Library.
51. Turkey and the Khalifat, 26 May 1919, L/PS/11/153, file P3464 IOR, British Library.

52. Sykes, *A History of Afghanistan*, p. 286.
53. Cited in Heathcote, *The Afghan Wars*, p. 198.

CHAPTER 12

1. *The Strategical Importance of Palestine*, secret, 199—C, Committee of Imperial Defence, The National Archives [TNA].
2. Wilson to Allenby, 7 December 1918, Wilson Papers, HHW2/33B/1.

EPILOGUE

1. Travis Crosby, *The Unknown Lloyd George: A Statesman in Conflict* (London: I. B. Tauris, 2014), p. 278.
2. Hugh Leach and Susan Farrington, *Strolling About on the Roof of the World: The First Hundred Years of the Royal Society for Asian Affairs* (London: Routledge, 2003).

Picture Acknowledgements

1.1 © The Keasbury-Gordon Photograph Archive/Alamy Stock Photo
1.2 Photo by General Photographic Agency/Hulton Archive/Getty Images
2.1 © Robert Hunt Library/Mary Evans
2.2 © IWM
2.3 Heritage Images/Glowimages.com
3.1 © IWM
3.2 Underwood Archives/Age Fotostock
4.1 © GL Archive/Alamy Stock Photo
5.1 Photo by APIC/Getty Images
5.2 © Illustrated London News Ltd/Mary Evans
5.3 © IWM
6.1 © IWM
7.1 © ITAR-TASS Photo Agency/Alamy Stock Photo
8.1 © 2003 Credit: Topham Picturepoint
8.2 © TopFoto.co.uk
8.3 © IWM
8.4 © Robert Hunt Library/Mary Evans
9.1 The Print Collector/Heritage Images/Age Fotostock
9.2 © IWM
10.1 © IWM
10.2 © IWM
10.3 Mary Evans Picture Library
11.1 Heritage Images/Glowimages.com
11.2 © Art Directors & TRIP/Alamy Stock Photo
12.1 © Bettmann/Corbis
12.2 © IWM

Select Bibliography

NATIONAL ARCHIVES AND RECORDS ASSOCIATION, COLLEGE PARK, WASHINGTON DC (NARA)

T-137 Auswärtigen Amt (The Middle East).
T-149 Auswärtigen Amt, NfdO (Information Service for the East).

POLITISCHES ARCHIV DES AUSWÄRTIGEN AMTS, BONN

Ägypten.
Turkei 165 (Arabien).
Weltkrieg, Nr.IIg (Unternehmungen und Aufwiegelungen gegen unsere Feinde in Ägypten, Syrien und Arabien).
Weltkrieg, Nr.IIg Geheim (Ägypten, Syrien und Arabien).

ASKERÎ TARIH VE STRATEJIK ETÜT BAŞJANLIĞI ARŞIVI (ATASE) [ARCHIVE OF THE DIRECTORATE OF MILITARY HISTORY AND STRATEGIC STUDIES], ANKARA

Harp cerideleri [Military Records of the Ottoman Army].
K 526; K 1859; K 2918–3121; K 3920.

THE NATIONAL ARCHIVES, KEW, LONDON (TNA)

CAB 19/2–27: War Cabinet Commission on the Mesopotamia Campaign.
CAB 24 War Cabinet.
CAB 25 Supreme War Council.
CAB 27 War Cabinet Committees.
FO 371 Foreign Office (Egypt, Persia, Ottoman Empire).
FO 882 The Arab Bureau.
FO 395 Consular Papers.
WO 33 Reports and Miscellaneous.
WO 106 Directorate of Military Operations.
WO 106/52: Various materials on operations in Mesopotamia, 1914–16.
WO 106/914: Gen. F. S. Maude's dispatches on operations of Mesopotamia Expeditionary Force, Apr.–Oct. 1917.
WO 157 Intelligence Summaries, 1914–21.
WO 302: Various maps from Mesopotamia campaign, 1914–18.

INDIA OFFICE RECORDS (IOR), POLITICAL AND SECRET, AND MILITARY DEPARTMENT RECORDS, BRITISH LIBRARY, LONDON

L/PS/8 Political and Secret Files.
L/Mil/7/16624–19656 Military Department Records.
L/Mil/7/5/2421–4321 Military Department Records.
L/Mil/17 Military Department Records.

IMPERIAL WAR MUSEUM, LONDON

Collections: http://www.iwm.org.uk/collections.
Atatürk's Memoirs of the Anafartalar Battles, K 03/1686.
Bishop of Nagpur, *Mesopotamia Revisited* (Nagpur: Government Press, 1917), Acc. No: K. 84/2304.
'Black Tab', *On the Road to Kut* (London: Hutchinson, 1917), Acc. No: 6668
Captured Turkish Documents, Doc. 12809.
Dane, Edmund, *British Campaigns in the Near East*, 2 vols. (London: Hodder and Stoughton, 1917–19).
Hewett, Sir John, *Report for the Army Council on Mesopotamia* (London: HMSO, 1919), Acc. No: 7317.
Indian Army Expeditionary Force, *Operations of Indian Expeditionary Force D*, IEF, 1917 Acc. No: K67 496.
Indian Army General Staff, *Field Notes: Mesopotamia* (Calcutta, 1917) Acc. No: 82/3010.
Moberly, F. J., *The Campaign in Mesopotamia*, 4 vols. (London: HMSO, 1924–7).
Mesopotamia Despatches, Parliamentary Command Papers CD. 8074 East India (Military).
IWM 79/48 *The Papers of General Sir Archibald Murray*.
Staff College Quetta, *Critical Study of the Campaign in Mesopotamia up to April 1917*, Parts I and II, 2 vols. (Calcutta: General Staff Army Headquarters, 1925), Acc. No: 13506.
Townshend, Charles, *My Campaign in Mesopotamia* (London: Thornton Butterworth, 1920).

MIDDLE EAST CENTRE ARCHIVE, ST ANTONY'S COLLEGE, OXFORD

Sir R. Wingate Papers.

KING'S COLLEGE LONDON, LIDDELL HART CENTRE FOR MILITARY ARCHIVES

Papers of Gen. Sir Ian Hamilton.
Papers of Sir William Robertson.
Papers of Capt. Sir Basil Liddell Hart.

CAMBRIDGE UNIVERSITY LIBRARY

Lord Hardinge Papers.

REGIMENTAL ARCHIVES OF THE OXFORDSHIRE AND BUCKINGHAMSHIRE LIGHT INFANTRY, WOODSTOCK, OXFORDSHIRE

Col. E. A. E. Lethbridge, *Narrative of the Siege of Kut El Amara, 1915–1916.*

OFFICIAL HISTORIES

Aspinall-Oglander, Brig.-Gen. C. F., *History of the Great War, based on Official Documents: Military Operations: Gallipoli:* 2 vols. (London: William Heinemann, 1929 and 1932).

Bean, C. E. W., *Official History of Australia in the War of 1914–1918*, 2 vols. (Angus and Robertson, 1921 and 1924).

Falls, Cyril and A. F. Becke, *Official History of the Great War Military Operations: Egypt and Palestine*, II: *From June 1917 to the End of the War* (London: HMSO, 1930).

General Staff Headquarters India, *Critical Study of the Campaign in Mesopotamia up to April 1917: Compiled by Officers of the Staff College, Quetta, Oct-Nov 1923* (Calcutta: Government of India Press, 1925).

Genelkurmay Baskanligi, T. C., Harp Tarihi Başkanığı, *Birinci Dünya Harbinde Türk Harbi* [The Turkish War in the First World War], *V inci Cilt* [5 vols.], *Çanakkale Cephesi* [Gallipoli] and *Kafkas Cephesi üçüncü Ordu Harekati* [Caucasus] (republished in Ankara: Gnkur. Basımevi, 1978–80).

Lepsius, J., A. Bartholdy, and F. Thimme (eds.), *Die Grosse Politik der Europäischen Kabinette, 1871–1914, Sammlung der Diplomatischen Akten des Auswärtigen Amtes* [The Grand Strategy of the European Cabinets, 1871–1914, Collection of Diplomatic Documents of the Foreign Office], 40 vols. (Berlin: Deutsche Verlagsgesellschaft für Poltik und Geschichte, 1925–6).

MacMunn, Lt. Gen. Sir George and Capt. Cyril Falls, *Official History of the Great War Military Operations: Egypt and Palestine* (London: HMSO, 1927–9), I.

Moberly, F. J., *The Campaign in Mesopotamia*, 4 vols. (London: HMSO, 1924–7).

SELECTED PUBLISHED BOOKS AND ARTICLES

Abdullah, *Memoirs of King Abdullah of Jordan* (London: Jonathan Cape, 1950).

Aboul-Enein, L. C. D. R. Youssef, 'The First World War Mesopotamian Campaigns: Military Lessons on Iraqi Ground Warfare', *Strategic Insights*, 4(6) (2005).

Adil, Selahattin, *Çanakkale Cephesinden Mektuplar-Hatıralar* [Letters and Memorabilia from the Chanakkale Front] (Istanbul: Yeditepe Yayınevi, 2007).

Ahmad, Feroz, *The Young Turks: The Committee of Union and Progress in Turkish Politics, 1908–1914* (Oxford: Oxford University Press, 1969).

Ahmad, Kamalmadhar, *Kurdistan during the First World War*, trans. Robert Burton and Ali Maher Ibrahim (London: Saqi Books, 2001).

Ahmida, Ali Abdullatif, *The Making of Modern Libya: State Formation, Colonization, and Resistance, 1830–1932* (Albany: University of New York Press, 1994).

Akçam, Taner, *The Young Turks' Crime Against Humanity: The Armenian Genocide and Ethnic Cleansing in the Ottoman Empire* (Princeton, NJ: Princeton University Press, 2012).

Aksakal, Mustapha, 'Holy War Made in Germany? Ottoman Origins of the 1914 Jihad', *War in History*, 18(2) (2011), pp. 184–99.

Aksakal, Mustapha, *The Ottoman Road to War in 1914: The Ottoman Empire and the First World War* (Cambridge: Cambridge University Press, 2008)

Allen, Charles, *Plain Tales From the Raj* (London: Andre Deutsch-Penguin, 1975).

Allen, William Edward David and Paul Muratoff, *Caucasian Battlefields: A History of the Wars of the Turko-Caucasian Border, 1828–1921* (Cambridge: Cambridge University Press, 2010 [1953]).

Allworth, Edward A. (ed.), *Central Asia* (New York: Columbia University Press, 1967).

Anderson, D. M. and D. Killingray (eds.), *Policing the Empire, 1830–1940* (Manchester: Manchester University Press 1991).

Andrew, C. M., *Secret Service: The Making of the British Intelligence Community* (London: Heinemann, 1985).

Askari, Jafar al, *A Soldier's Story: From Ottoman Rule to Independent Iraq* (London: Arabian Publishing, 2003).

Atabaki, Touraj, *Iran and the First World War: Battleground of the Great Powers* (London: I. B. Tauris, 2006).

Atiyyah, Ghassan, *Iraq: 1908–1921. A Socio-Political Study* (Beirut: The Arab Institute for Research and Publishing, 1973).

Balaev, Aidyn, *Azerbaidzhanskoe natsional'noe dvizhenie v 1917–1918 gg* [The Azerbaijani National Movement in 1917–1918] (Baku: Elm, 1998).

Bargut, Şemsettin, *Birinci Dünya Harbi'nde ve Kurtuluş Savaşı'nda Türk Deniz Harekâtı* [The First World War and War of Independence: Naval Operations] (Ankara: Deniz Kuvvetleri K.lığı Basımevi, 2000).

Barış, Yusuf İzzettin, *Çanakkale Savaşları* [The Chanakkale Battles] (Ankara: Matsa Basımevi, 2000).

Barker, A. J., *The First Iraq War, 1914–1918: Britain's Mesopotamian Campaign* (London, 2009 [1967]).

Barr, James, *Setting the Desert on Fire: T. E. Lawrence and Britain's Secret War in Arabia, 1916–1918* (New York: W. W. Norton 2008).

Başbakınlık, T. C., *Devlet Arşivleri Genel Müdürlüğü, Osmanlı Belgelerinde Çanakkale Muharebeleri-i* [The General Directorate of State Archives, Chanakkale Battles in Ottoman Documents] (Ankara, Başbakanlık Basımevi, 2005).

Bayly, C. A., *Empire and Information: Intelligence-Gathering and Social Communication in India, 1780–1870* (Cambridge: Cambridge University Press, 1996).

Bayur, Yusuf Hikmet, *Türk İnkılâbı Tarihi* [History of the Turkish Revolution] (Ankara, TTK Basımevi, 1952), II(4).
Bean, C. E. W., *Gallipoli Mission* (Canberra: ABC Books, 1990 [1948]).
Beesly, Patrick, *Room 40: British Naval Intelligence, 1914–18* (London: Hamish Hamilton, 1982).
Belen, Fahri, *Birinci Cihan Harbinde Türk Harbi* [The Turkish War in the First World War] (Ankara: General Staff Printing, 1965), III.
Beloff, Max, *Imperial Sunset 1897–1921* (London: Methuen and Co., 1969).
Berghahn, Volker R., *Germany and the Approach of War in 1914* (London: Macmillan, 1973).
Berghahn, Volker R., *Imperial Germany, 1871–1914: Economy, Society, Culture and Politics* (Oxford: Berghahn Books, 1994).
Berghahn, Volker R., 'On the Social Function of Wilhelmine Armaments Policy' in Georg Iggers (ed.), *The Social History of Politics* (Leamington Spa: Berg, 1985).
Bidwell, Robin, 'The Turkish Attack on Aden, 1915-1918', *Arabian Studies*, 6 (1982), pp. 171–94.
Bloxham, Donald, *The Great Game of Genocide: Imperialism, Nationalism and the Destruction of the Ottoman Armenians* (Oxford: Oxford University Press, 2005).
Bourne, K. and D. C. Watt (eds.), *British Documents on Foreign Affairs: Reports and Papers from the Foreign Office Confidential Print: Near and Middle East. Part I: From the Mid-Nineteenth Century to the First World War*, Series B: The Near and Middle East, 1856–1914, series B (University Publications of America, 1984–5); and *Part II, From the First World War to the Second World War*, Series B: Turkey, Iran and the Middle East, 1918–1939 (University Publications of America, 1985–97).
Bovykin, V. I., *Ocherki istoriivneshnei politiki Rossii* [Essays in the History of Russia's Foreign Policy] (Moscow: Uchpedgiz, 1960).
Bowman-Manifold, M. G. E., *An Outline of the Egyptian and Palestine Campaigns, 1914 to 1918*, 2nd edn (Chatham: W. and J. Mackay, 1923).
Brémond, Edouard, *Le Hedjaz dans la Guerre Mondiale* (Paris: Payot, 1931).
Briton Cooper Busch, *Britain, India, and the Arabs 1914–1921* (Berkeley, Los Angeles and London: University of California Press, 1971).
Bruce, Anthony, *The Last Crusade: The Palestine Campaign in the First World War* (London: John Murray, 2002).
Buchan, John, *Greenmantle* (London: Hodder and Stoughton, 1916).
Busch, B. C., *Britain, India and the Arabs, 1914–21* (Berkeley, Los Angeles and London: University of California Press, 1971).
Callwell, C. E., *The Dardanelles: Campaigns and Their Lessons* (London: Constable and Co., 1919.)
Callwell, C. E., *Field-Marshal Sir Henry Wilson: His Life and Diaries* (London: Cassell, 1927).
Carr, E. H., *The Bolshevik Revolution, 1917–1923* (London: Macmillan, 1953), III.
Carver, Michael, Field Marshal Lord, *The National Army Museum Book of The Turkish Front 1914–1918: The Campaigns at Gallipoli, in Mesopotamia and in Palestine* (London: Sidgwick and Jackson, 2003).

Churchill, Winston S., *The Great War* (London, 1934).

Churchill, Winston S., *The World Crisis*, 5 vols. (New York: Charles Scribner and Sons, 1923–31).

Cohen, E. A. and J. Gooch, *Military Misfortunes: The Anatomy of Failure in War* (London: Macmillan, 2006).

Cohen, Stephen P., *The Indian Army* (Berkeley: University of California Press, 1971).

Cohen, Stuart, *British Policy in Mesopotamia, 1903–1914* (London: Ithaca, 2008 [1976]).

Cohen, Stuart, 'The Genesis of the British Campaign in Mesopotamia, 1914', *Middle Eastern Studies*, 11 (1976), pp. 119–32.

Cohen, Stuart, 'Mesopotamia in British Strategy, 1903–1914', *International Journal of Middle East Studies*, 9(2) (Apr 1978), pp. 171–81.

Cooper, Bryan, *The Tenth Irish Division in Gallipoli* (London: H. Jenkins, 1918).

Corrigan, Gordon, 'The Gurkhas at Gallipoli' in Rob Johnson (ed.), *The British Indian Army: Virtue and Necessity* (Cambridge: Cambridge Scholars Publishing, 2014).

Dawn, C. E., *From Ottomanism to Arabism: Essays on the Origins of Arab Nationalism* (Urbana: University of Illinois Press, 1973).

Darwin, John, *Britain, Egypt and the Middle East: Imperial Policy in the Aftermath of War, 1918–22* (London: Palgrave Macmillan, 1981).

Davis, Paul, *Ends and Means: The British Mesopotamia Campaign and Commission* (Cranbery, NJ: Associated University Presses, 1994).

Dickson, Brig. Gen. W. E., *East Persia: A Backwater of the Great War* (London: E. Arnold and Co., 1924).

Djemal Pasha, *Memories of a Turkish Statesman: 1913–1919* (London: Hutchinson and Co., 1922).

Donaldson, Robert H., *Soviet Policy toward India: Ideology and Strategy* (Cambridge, MA: Harvard University Press, 1974).

Dunsterville, Maj. Gen. M. H., *The Adventures of Dunsterforce* (London: E. Arnold, 1920).

Dyer, Brig. Gen. R., *The Raiders of the Sarhad* (London: H. F. and G. Witherby, 1921).

Earle, Meade, *Turkey, the Great Powers and the Baghdad Railway* (New York: Macmillan, 1923).

Edmonds, C. J., 'The Persian Gulf Prelude to the Zimmerman Telegram', *Royal Central Asian Journal*, I (1960).

Ellis, C. H., *The Transcaspian Episode, 1918–19* (London: Hutchinson, 1963).

Enver Pasha, *Kendi Mektuplarinda Enver Paşa* [Enver Pasha in His Own Letters], ed. M. Sükrü Hanioğlu (Istanbul: Der Yaylinlari, 1989).

Erickson, Edward, *Gallipoli and the Middle East, 1914–1918: From the Dardanelles to Mesopotamia* (London: Amber, 2008).

Erickson, Edward, *Ordered to Die: A History of the Ottoman Army in the First World War* (Westport, CT: Greenwood, 2000).

Erickson, Edward, 'Strength against Weakness: Ottoman Military Effectiveness at Gallipoli, 1915', *Journal of Military History*, 65(4) (2001).

Ethem, Hasan, 'Last Letter', *The Gallipolian*, 76 (Winter 1994).

Fair, John D., 'Politicians, Historians and the War: A Reassessment of the Political Crisis of December 1916', *The Journal of Modern History*, 49(3) (1977), pp. 1329–43.

Farwell, B., *Armies of the Raj: From the Great Indian Mutiny to Independence, 1858–1947* (New York: W. W. Norton and Company, 1989).

Ferguson, A. C., 'Gallipoli, 1915', *The Gallipolian*, 85 (Winter 1997).

Fieldhouse, D. K., *Western Imperialism in the Middle East, 1914–1958* (Oxford: Oxford University Press, 2006).

Ford, Roger, *Eden to Armageddon: World War I in the Middle East* (New York: Pegasus, 2010).

Foster, Zachary, 'The 1915 Locust Attack in Syria and Palestine and its Role in the Famine During the First World War,' *Middle Eastern Studies* 51(3) (2015).

French, David, *British Strategy and War Aims, 1914–1916* (London: Allen and Unwin, 1986).

French, David, 'British Strategy and Winning the Great War' in B. A. Lee and K. F. Walling (eds.), *Strategic and Political Rationality: Essays in Honour of Michael I. Handel* (London: Routledge, 2003).

French, David, *The British Way in Warfare* (London: Allen and Unwin, 1990).

French, David, 'The Dardanelles, Mecca and Kut: Prestige as a Factor in British Eastern Strategy, 1914–1916', *War and Society*, 5 (1987).

French, David, *The Strategy of the Lloyd George Coalition, 1916–1918*, 2 vols. (Oxford: Clarendon Press, 1995).

Fromkin, David, *A Peace to End All Peace* (London: Andre Deutsch, 1989).

Fuller, W., *Strategy and Power in Russia, 1600–1914* (New York, 1992).

Galbraith, John S., 'No Man's Child: The Campaign in Mesopotamia, 1914–1916', *International History Review*, 6(3) (1984), pp. 358–85.

Gehrke, Ulrich, *Persien in der Deutschen Orientpolitik während des ersten Weltkrieges* [Persia in the German Eastern Policy during the First World War], 2 vols. (Stuttgart: Kohlhammer, 1960).

Geiss, Imanuel, *German Foreign Policy, 1871–1914* (London: Routledge and Kegan Paul, 1976).

Gershoni, Israel and James P. Jankowski, *Egypt, Islam, and the Arabs: The Search for Egyptian Nationhood, 1900–1930* (Oxford and New York: Oxford University Press, 1986).

Geyer, D., *Russian Imperialism* (Leamington Spa: Berg, 1987).

Gilbert, Martin, *A History of the Twentieth Century*, I: *1900–1933* (London: Harper Collins, 1997).

Gilbert, Martin, *Winston Churchill: The Challenge of War, 1914–1916* (London, 1971), III.

Gillam, Maj. John, *Gallipoli Diary* (London: George Allen and Unwin, 1918).

Gilmour, David, *Curzon* (London: John Murray, 1994).

Goate, John, 'Diary', *The Gallipolian*, 91 (Winter 1999).

Goltz, Colmar von der, *Denkwürdigkeiten* [Memoirs] (Berlin: E. S. Mittlar und Sohn, 1929).

Göncü, Gürsel and Şahin Aldoğan, *Çanakkale Muharebe Alanları Gezi Rehberi, MB Yayınevi* (Istanbul: MB Yayinevi, 2006).

Gooch, G. and H. Temperley, *British Documents on the Origins of the War* (London, 1926–38), I–IV.

Gould, David, 'Lord Hardinge and the Mesopotamia Expedition and Inquiry, 1914–1917', *The Historical Journal*, 19(4) (1976), pp. 919–45.

Grainger, John D., *The Battle for Palestine 1917* (Woodbridge and New York: Boydell Press, 2006).

Graves, Philip, *The Life of Sir Percy Cox* (London: Hutchinson, 1941).

Greenhalgh, Elizabeth, *Victory through Coalition* (Cambridge: Cambridge University Press, 2005).

Grigg, John, *Lloyd George: War Leader* (London: Allen Lane, 2002).

Günesen, Fikret, *Çanakkale Savaşları* [Chanakkale Battles] (Istanbul: Kastaş Yayınları, 1986).

Hamilton, Sir Ian, *The Commander*, ed. A. Farrar-Hockley (London: Hollis and Carter, 1957).

Hamilton, Sir Ian, *Gallipoli Diary*, 2 vols. (New York: George H. Doran, 1920).

Hankey, Lord M., *The Supreme Command, 1914–1918*, 2 vols. (London: George Allen and Unwin Limited, 1961).

Harris, J. P., *Men, Ideas and Tanks: British Military Thought and Armoured Forces, 1903–1939* (Manchester: Manchester University Press, 1995).

Harrison, Mark, 'The Fight Against Disease in the Mesopotamian Campaign' in Peter Liddle and Hugh Cecil (eds.), *Facing Armageddon: The First World War Experienced* (Barnsley: Leo Cooper, 1996).

Hart, Peter, *Gallipoli* (London: Profile Books, 2013).

Heathcote, T. A., *The Military in British India: The Development of Land Forces in South Asia, 1600–1947* (Manchester: Manchester University Press, 1995).

Higgins, Trumbull, *Winston Churchill and the Dardanelles* (London: Heinemann, 1963).

Holland, Robert, 'The British Empire and the Great War, 1914–1918' in Judith M. Brown and William Roger Louis (eds.), *The Oxford History of the British Empire*, IV: *The Twentieth Century* (Oxford: Oxford University Press, 1999).

Hopkirk, Peter, *On Secret Service East of Constantinople* (Oxford: Oxford University Press, 1994).

Hopkirk, Peter, *Setting the East Ablaze: On Secret Service in Bolshevik Asia* (Oxford: Oxford University Press, 1984).

Hovannisian, Richard (ed.), *The Armenian Genocide: History, Politics, Ethics* (Basingstoke: Palgrave, 1992).

Hughes, Matthew, *Allenby and British Strategy in the Middle-East 1917–1919* (London: Frank Cass, 1999).

Hughes, Matthew, 'General Allenby and the Palestine Campaign, 1917–1918,' *Journal of Strategic Studies*, 9 (1996).

Hurewitz, J. C. (ed.), *The Middle East and North Africa in World Politics: A Documentary Record* (New Haven, CT: Yale University Press, 1979).

Ingall, Francis, *The Last of the Bengal Lancers* (London: Leo Cooper, 1988).

James, Robert Rhodes, *Gallipoli* (London: B. T. Batsford Ltd, 1965).

Jeffrey, K., 'The Eastern Arc of Empire: A Strategic View, 1850–1950', *Journal of Strategic Studies*, 5 (1982).

Jeffrey, K., *Field Marshal Sir Henry Wilson: A Political Soldier* (Oxford: Oxford University Press, 2006).

Jelavich, B., *The Ottoman Empire* (Bloomington, IN: Indiana University Press, 1973).

Jenkins, J., 'Fritz Fischer's "Programme for Revolution": Implications for a Global History of Germany in the First World War,' *Journal of Contemporary History*, 56(3) (2013).

Johnson, Robert, *The Afghan Way of War* (London: Hurst; New York: Oxford University Press, 2011).

Johnson, Robert, 'Contested Historiography: The Causes and the Consequences of the Gallipoli Campaign' in Robert Johnson and Metin Gurcan (eds.), *Gallipoli: The Turkish Perspective* (London: Ashgate, 2016).

Johnson, Robert, *Spying for Empire: The Great Game in Central and South Asia, 1757–1947* (London: Greenhill, 2006).

Joint Doctrine Note 3/11, 'Decision Making and Problem Solving; Human Factors and Organisational Factors', https://www.gov.uk/government/publications/joint-doctrine-note-3-11-decision-making-and-problem-solving-human-and-organisational-factors.

Joll, James, *The Origins of the First World War* (London, 1984).

Jordan, G., *British Military History: A Supplement to Robin Higham's Guide to the Sources* (London: Garland, 1988).

Judd, Alan, *The Quest for C: Mansfield Cumming and the Foundation of the Secret Service* (London: Harper Collins, 1999).

Kabacalı, Alpay (eds.), *Talat Paşa'nın Anıları* [Memoirs of Talat Pasha], 3rd edn (Istanbul: Türkiye İş Bankası Yayınları, 1993).

Kannengeiser, Col. Hans, *The Campaign in Gallipoli* (London: Hutchinson, 1927).

Karsh, Efraim and Inari Karsh, *Empires of the Sand: The Struggle for Mastery in the Middle East, 1789–1923* (Cambridge, MA: Harvard University Press, 1999).

Karsh, Efraim and Inari Karsh, 'The Myth of the Desert, or Not the Great Arab Revolt', *Middle Eastern Studies*, 33(2) (1997), pp. 267–312.

Kazemzadeh, Firuz, *Russia and Britain in Persia, 1864–1914* (New Haven, CT: Yale University Press, 1968).

Kazemzadeh, Firuz, *The Struggle for Transcaucasia, 1917–21* (New York and Oxford: George Ronald, 1951).

Kedourie, Elie, *England and the Middle East: The Destruction of the Ottoman Empire 1914–1921* (London: Harvester Press, 1956).

Kemal 'Atatürk', Mustafa, *Zabit ve Kumandan ile Hasbihal* [Conversation with Officers and Commanders] (Istanbul: Türkiye İş Bankası Yayınları, 2011).

Kendirciglu, Hilmi, 'Ottoman Artillery in the Gallipoli Straits' in Robert Johnson and Metin Gurcan (eds.), *Gallipoli: The Turkish Perspective* (London: Ashgate, 2016).

Kenez, Peter, *Civil War in South Russia, 1919–20* (Berkeley, Los Angeles, and London: University of California Press, 1977).

Kennedy, Paul, *The Realities Behind Diplomacy* (London: Fontana, 1985).

Kennedy, Paul, *The Rise and Fall of British Naval Mastery* (London: Fontana, 1991).

Kennedy, Paul, *The Rise and Fall of the Great Powers* (New York: Random House, 1987).

Kennedy, Paul (ed.), *The War Plans of the Great Powers* (London: Allen and Unwin, 1979).

Kent, Marion (ed.), *The Great Powers and the End of the Ottoman Empire* (London: Allen and Unwin, 1984).

Kent, Marion, *Oil and Empire: British Policy and Mesopotamian Oil, 1900–1920* (London: Macmillan, 1976).

Ker, James Campbell, *Political Trouble in India, 1907–1917* (Calcutta: Oriental Publishers, 1973 [1917]).

Kerr, Greg (ed.), *Private Wars: Personal Records of the ANZACs in the Great War* (Melbourne and Oxford: Oxford University Press, 2000).

Kitchen, James, *The British Imperial Army in the Middle East: Morale and Military Identity in the Sinai and Palestine Campaigns, 1916–1918* (London: Bloomsbury, 2014).

Knightly, Philip and Colin Simpson, *The Secret Lives of Lawrence of Arabia* (London: Thomas Nelson, 1969).

Kress von Kressenstein, Friedrich Freiherr, *Mit den Türken zum Suezkanal* (Berlin: Vorhut-Verlag, 1938).

Laffin, John, *Damn the Dardanelles* (Gloucester: Allen Sutton, 1989).

Landau, Jacob M., *Pan-Turkism: From Irredentism to Cooperation* (Bloomington and Indianapolis: Indiana University Press, 1995).

Landau, Jacob M., *The Politics of Pan-Islam: Ideology and Organisation* (Oxford: Clarendon Press, 1990).

Larcher, Maurice, Mehmed Emin Bey, and Murat Çulcu, *Çanakkale 1915-Boğaz Harekâtı* [Chanakkale: Operations at the Narrows] (Istanbul: E.Yayınları, 2008).

Latter, Edwin, 'The Indian Army in Mesopotamia, 1914–18', *Journal of the Society for Army Historical Research*, 72 (1994).

Lawrence, T. E., *Seven Pillars of Wisdom: A Triumph* (London: Jonathan Cape, 1935)

Lee, John, 'Sir Ian Hamilton and the Dardanelles, 1915' in Brian Bond (ed.), *Fallen Stars: Eleven Studies of Twentieth Century Military Disasters* (London: Brassey's, 1991).

Lee, John, *A Soldier's Life, General Sir Ian Hamilton 1853–1947* (London: Macmillan, 2000).

Lenin, V. I., *Imperialism: The Highest Stage of Capitalism*, 18th edn (Moscow: Progress, 1982 [1916]).

Liddell Hart, Basil, *A History of the World War, 1914–1918* (London: Faber and Faber, 1938).

Liman von Sanders, Otto, *Five Years in Turkey* (Annapolis, MD: US Naval Institute Press, 1927).

Lobonov-Rostovsky, A., *Russia and Asia* (New York: G. Wahr, 1951).

Longer, V., *Red Coats to Olive Green: A History of the Indian Army 1600–1974* (New Delhi: Allied, 1975).

Lüdke, Tilman, 'Loyalty, Indifference, Treason: The Ottoman-German Experience in Palestine During World War I' in Haim Goren, Eran Dolev, and Yigal Sheffy (eds.), *Palestine and World War I: Grand Strategy, Military Tactics and Culture in War* (London: I. B. Tauris, 2014).

Lushington, R. F., *A Prisoner with the Turks, 1915–1918* (London: Marshall, 1923).

McCarthy, Justin, *Muslims and Minorities: The Population of Ottoman Anatolia and the End of Empire* (New York: New York University Press, 1983).

MacDonell, Aeneas Ranald, *And Nothing Long* (London: Constable, 1938).

McDowell, David, *A Modern History of the Kurds* (London: I. B. Tauris, 1996).

McKale, Donald M., *War By Revolution: Germany and Great Britain in the Middle East in the Era of World War I* (Kent, OH: Kent State University Press, 1998).

McLean, D., *Britain and Her Buffer State: The Collapse of the Persian Empire 1890–1914* (London: Royal Historical Society, 1979).

McMeekin, Sean, *The Berlin–Baghdad Express: The Ottoman Empire and Germany's Bid for World Power, 1898–1918* (London: Allen Lane, 2010).

McMeekin, Sean, *The Russian Origins of the First World War* (Cambridge, MA: Harvard University Press, 2011).

Macmillan, Margaret, *Peacemakers: The Paris Conference of 1919 and Its Attempts to End War* (London: John Murray, 2001).

MacMunn, George, *The Martial Races of India* (London: Sampson Low, 1933).

Majd, Mohammad Gholi, *Iraq in World War I: From Ottoman Rule to British Conquest* (Lanham, MD: University Press of America, 2001).

Malleson, Maj. Gen. Sir Wilfred, 'The British Military Mission to Turkestan, 1918–1920', *JCAS*, IX (1922).

Marder, A., *The War at Sea*, 5 vols. (Oxford: Oxford University Press, 1961–70).

Marshall, Lt. Gen. Sir William, *Memories of Four Fronts* (London: Ernest Benn Ltd, 1929).

Maslovsky, E.V., *Mirovaya voina na Kavkazskom fronte, 1914–1917 g* [The World War on the Caucasian Front, 1914–1917] (Paris: Renaissance, 1933).

Massey, William T., *The Great War in the Middle East*, I: *The Desert Campaigns and How Jerusalem Was Won* (orig. pub. as *The Desert Campaigns*) (London: Leonaur, 2009 [1917]).

Massey, William T., *The Great War in the Middle East*, II: *Allenby's Final Triumph* (London: Leonaur, 2009).

Massie, R. K., *Dreadnought: Britain, Germany and the Coming of the Great War* (London: Pimlico, 1993).

Menan, K., *The Russian Bogey and British Aggression* (Calcutta: Eastern Trading Co., 1957).

Menning, B.W., *Bayonets before Bullets: The Russian Imperial Army, 1861–1914* (London, 1992).

Mericli, Iskender, 'Memories of a Turkish soldier', *The Gallipolian*, 75 (Autumn 1994).

Mitrokhin, Leonid, *Failure of Three Missions: British Efforts to Overthrow Soviet Government in Central Asia* (Moscow: Progress, 1987).

Mollo, B., *The Indian Army* (Poole: Blandford Press, 1981).

Morgan, Kenneth, 'Lloyd George and Germany', *Historical Journal*, 39(3) (1996), pp. 755–66.

Morton-Jack, George, *The Indian Army on the Western Front: India's Expeditionary Force to France and Belgium in the First World War* (Cambridge: Cambridge University Press, 2014).

Mousley, E. O., *The Secrets of a Kuttite: An Authentic Story of Kut, Adventures in Captivity and Stamboul Intrigue* (London and New York: John Lane Co., 1922).

Mühlmann, Carl, *Der Kampf um die Dardanellen* [The Struggle for the Dardanelles] (Oldenburg: Stalling, 1927), XVI.

Murphy, Lt. Col. C. C. R., *A Mixed Bag* (London: John Hogg, 1921).

Murphy, Lt. Col. C. C. R., *Soldiers of the Prophet* (London: William Clowes, 1921).

Nadeem, Gen. Shukry Mahmood, *Harb Al-Iraq 1914–1918: Dirasa Ilmiyah* [The War in Iraq, 1914–1918: An Analytical Study] (Baghdad: Al Nibras, 1954).

Nath, Ashok, *Izzat: Historical Records and Iconography of Indian Cavalry Regiments 1750–2007* (New Delhi: USII, 2009).

Neidermayer, Oskar von, *Unter der Glutsonne Irans* [Under the Blazing Sun of Iran] (Hamburg: Curt Brenner, 1925).

Neilson, Keith, '"For Diplomatic, Economic, Strategic and Telegraphic Reasons": British Imperial Defence, the Middle East and India, 1914–1918' in G. Kennedy and K. Nielson (eds.), *Far Flung Lines: Essays on Imperial Defence in Honour of Donald Mackenzie Schurman* (London: Routledge, 1996).

Nyman, Lars-Erik, *Great Britain and Chinese, Russian and Japanese Interests in Sinkiang, 1918–34* (Malmo: Esselte Studium, 1977).

O'Dwyer, M., *India As I Knew It, 1885–1925* (London: Constable, 1926).

Okse, Necati, 'Atatürk in the Dardenelles Campaign', *Revue Internationale d'Histoire Militaire*, 50 (1981).

Olsen, William J., *Anglo-Iranian Relations During World War I* (London: Frank Cass, 1984).

Omissi, David, *Indian Voices of the Great War: Soldiers' Letters, 1914–1918* (London: Macmillan, 1999).

Oppenheim, Max von, *Die Nachrichstelle der Kaiserliche Deutschen Botschaft und die Deutsche wirtsschaftliche Propaganda in Türkei* [The Reports of the German Imperial Embassy and German Economic Propaganda in Turkey] (Berlin: Reichsdruckerei, 1916).

Özdemir, Bulent, *Assyrian Identity and the Great War: Nestorian, Chaldean and Syrian Christians in the Twentieth Century* (Dunbeath: Whittles, 2012).

Özdemir, Hikmet, *The Ottoman Army, 1914–1918: Disease and Death on the Battlefield* (orig. pub. in Turkish, 2005; Salt Lake City: University of Utah Press, 2008).

Pamuk, Sevket, 'The Ottoman Economy in World War I' in Stephen Broadberry and Mark Harrison (eds.), *The Economics of World War I* (Cambridge: Cambridge University Press, 2005).

Peters, Rudolph, *Islam and Colonialism* (The Hague: Mouton, 1979).

Pollock, John, *Kitchener* (London: Constable, 1998).

Popplewell, Richard, 'British Intelligence in Mesopotamia, 1914–1916', *Intelligence and National Security*, V (1990), pp. 139–72.

Popplewell, Richard, *Intelligence and Imperial Defence: British Intelligence and the Defence of the Indian Empire, 1904–1924* (London: Frank Cass, 1995).

Pratap, Mehendra, *My Life Story of Fifty-Five Years* (Delhi: Originals, 2004).

Pratt, E. A., *The Rise of Rail Power in War and Conquest* (London: P. S. King and Son, 1915).

Preston, R. M. P., *The Desert Mounted Corps: An Account of the Cavalry Operations in Palestine and Syria 1917–1918* (London: Constable, 1921).

Prior, Robin, *Gallipoli: The End of the Myth* (New Haven, CT and London: Yale University Press, 2010).

Ralston, David B., *Importing the European Army: The Introduction of European Military Techniques and Institutions into the Extra European World* (Chicago, IL: University of Chicago Press, 1990).

Redway, Maj. G. W., *The Great War* (London: Amalgamated Press, 1916), VI.

Reynolds, Michael A., 'Buffers, Not Brethren: Young Turk Military Policy in the First World War and the Myth of Pan-Turanism', *Past and Present*, 203 (May 2009), pp. 137–79.

Robertson, William, *Soldiers and Statesmen, 1914–1918*, 2 vols. (London: Cassell and Co., 1926).

Robinson, Francis, 'The British Empire and the Muslim World', in Judith M. Brown and William Louis, *The Oxford History of the British Empire*, IV: *The Twentieth Century* (Oxford: Oxford University Press, 1999).

Robinson, Ronald, 'Imperial Theory and the Question of Imperialism After Empire', *Journal of Imperial and Commonwealth History*, 12(2) (1984).

Rogan, Eugene, *The Fall of the Ottomans: The Great War in the Middle East, 1914–1920* (London: Allen Lane, 2015).

Roger Louis (ed.), *The Oxford History of the British Empire*, IV: *The Twentieth Century* (Oxford: Oxford University Press, 1999).

Roshwald, Aviel, *Ethnic Nationalism and the Fall of Empires: Central Europe, Russia and the Middle East, 1914–1923* (London and New York: Routledge, 2001).

Rothwell, V. H., 'Mesopotamia in British War Aims, 1914–1918', *The Historical Journal*, 13(2) (1970), pp. 273–94.

Roy, Kaushik, 'The Army in India in Mesopotamia from 1916 to 1918: Tactics, Technology and Logistics Reconsidered' in I. W. F. Beckett (ed.), *1917: Beyond the Western Front* (Leiden and Boston, MA: Brill, 2009), pp. 131–58.

Roy, Kaushik, 'The Historiography of the Colonial Indian Army', *Studies in History*, 12(2) (1996).

Sağlam, Tevfik, *Cihan Harbinde*, III: *Ordu'da Sıhhî Hizmete Ait Küçük Bir Hulâsa* [In the World War, vol. III: The Army Medical Service: An Extract] (Istanbul: Askerî Tibbiye Publishers, 1940).

Samra, Chattar Singh, *India and Anglo-Soviet Relations, 1917–1947* (London: Asia Publishing House, 1959).

Sanders, Liman von, *Five Years in Turkey* (Annapolis, MD: US Naval Institute Press, 1927).

Sanyal, Usha, *Devotional Islam and Politics in British India* (New Delhi and Oxford: Oxford University Press, 1996).

Satia, Priya, *Spies in Arabia* (Oxford: Oxford University Press, 2008).

Savory, Sir Reginald, 'Some Gallipoli Memories', *The Gallipolian*, 15 (1974).

Schilcher, Linda, 'The Famine in 1915–1918 in Greater Syria' in John Spagnolo (ed.), *Problems of the Middle East in Historical Perspective* (Reading: Ithaca Press, 1992).

Schilling, K., *Beitrage zu einer Geschichte des radikalen Nationalismus in der Wilhelimischen Ara* (Cologne: Gouder and Hansen, 1968).

Schneer, Jonathan, *The Balfour Declaration* (New York: Random House, 2010).

Seton Watson, Hugh, *The Decline of Imperial Russia* (London: Methuen, 1952).

Sheffy, Yigal, *British Military Intelligence in the Palestine Campaign, 1914–1918* (London; Portland, OR: Frank Cass, 1998).

Singha, P. B., *Indian National Liberation Movement and Russia, 1905–17* (New Delhi: Sterling, 1975).

Skrine, Sir Clarmont, *World War in Iran* (London: Constable, 1962).

Sluglett, Peter, *Britain in Iraq, 1914–1932* (London and Oxford: Ithaca, 1976).

Steel, Nigel and Peter Hart, *Defeat at Gallipoli* (London: Macmillan, 1994).

Steinberg, E. L., *Ocherki istorii Turkmenii* [Essays in the History of Turkmenistan] (Moscow: Ministry of Education, 1934).

Still, John, *A Prisoner in Turkey* (London: John Lane, 1920).

Storrs, Ronald, *Orientations* (London: Nicholson and Watson, 1943).

Strachan, Hew, *The First World War*, I: *To Arms* (Oxford: Oxford University Press, 2001).

Strachan, Hew, *The First World War* (London: Simon and Schuster, 2003).

Strachan, Hew, 'The First World War as a Global War', *First World War Studies*, 1(1) (2010).

Syk, Andrew, 'Command and the Mesopotamia Expeditionary Force, 1915–1918' (Oxford, DPhil thesis, 2009).

Syk, Andrew, 'The Mesopotamia Commission: Britain's First Iraq Inquiry', *RUSI Journal*, 154(4) (2009), pp. 94–101.

Sykes, Christopher, *Wassmuss: 'The German Lawrence'* (London: Longmans Green and Co., 1936).

Sykes, Brig. Gen. Sir Percy, *A History of Afghanistan*, 2 vols. (London: Macmillan, 1940).

Sykes, Brig. Gen. Sir Percy, *A History of Persia*. 2 vols, 3rd edn (London: Macmillan, 1930).

Tauber, Eliezer, *The Emergence of Arab Movements* (London: Frank Cass, 1993).

Teague Jones, Reginald (alias Ronald Sinclair), Introduction and Epilogue by Peter Hopkirk, *The Spy Who Disappeared* (London: Gollancz, 1990).

Thomas, Martin, *Empires of Intelligence: Security Services and Colonial Disorder after 1914* (Berkeley, CA: University of California Press, 2008).

Thornton, A. P., 'Rivalries in the Mediterranean, The Middle East and Egypt' in F. H. Hinsley (ed.), *Material Progress and World-wide Problems, 1870–1898* (Cambridge: Cambridge University Press, 1962).

Tod, Col. J., 'The Malleson Mission to Transcaspia in 1918', *JRCAS*, 27 (1940).

Toker, Hülya, 'Naval Operations' in Robert Johnson and Metin Gurcan (eds.), *Gallipoli: The Turkish Perspective* (London: Ashgate, 2016).

Townshend, Charles, *When God Made Hell: The British Invasion of Mesopotamia and the Creation of Iraq, 1914–1921* (London: Faber and Faber, 2010).

Trask, David, *The United States in the Supreme War Council: American War Aims and Inter-Allied Strategy* (Middletown, CT: Wesleyan University Press, 1961).

Travers, Tim, 'Command and Leadership Styles in the British Army: The 1915 Gallipoli Model', *JCH*, 29(3) (1994).

Travers, Tim, *Gallipoli, 1915* (Stroud: Tempus, 2001).

Travers, Tim, 'The Other Side of the Hill', *Military History Quarterly*, 12(3) (2000).

Travers, Tim, 'The Ottoman Crisis of May 1915 at Gallipoli', *War in History*, 8(1) (2001).

Trench, Charles Chenevix, *The Indian Army and the King's Enemies, 1900–1947* (London: Thames and Hudson, 1988).

Trumpener, Ulrich, *Germany and the Ottoman Empire, 1914–1918* (Princeton, NJ: Princeton University Press, 1968).

Trumpener, Ulrich, 'Liman von Sanders and the German-Ottoman Alliance', *JCH*, 1(4) (1996).

Trumpener, Ulrich, 'Turkey's Entry into World War I: An Assessment of Responsibilities', *The Journal of Modern History* (1962).

Tuncoku, Mete, *Anzaklarin Kaleminden Mehmetçik, Canakkale, 1915* [Turkish Soldiers in the Words of the ANZACs at Chanakkale] (Ankara: Atatürk Araştırma Merkezi, 1997).

Turner, John, *British Politics and the Great War: Coalition and Conflict, 1915–1918* (London; New Haven, CT: Yale University Press, 1992).

Ullman, R. H., *Anglo-Soviet Relations, 1917–21*, 3 vols. (Princeton, NJ: Princeton University Press, 1961–72).

Ulrichsen, Kristian Coates, *The Logistics and Politics of the British Campaigns in the Middle East, 1914–22* (Basingstoke: Palgrave Macmillan, 2010).

Uyur, Mesut, 'Ottoman Arab Officers between Nationalism and Loyalty during the First Word War', *War in History*, 20(4) (2013), pp. 526–44.

Vanli, Hasan Tahsin, 'Taking the Initiative in the Gallipoli Campaign' in Robert Johnson and Metin Gurcan (eds.), *Gallipoli: The Turkish Perspective* (London: Ashgate, 2016).

Vatikiotis, P. J., *The History of Modern Egypt: From Muhammad Ali to Mubarak* (Baltimore, MD: Johns Hopkins University Press, 1991).

Wavell, Field Marshal Earl, *The Palestine Campaigns* (London: Constable, 1968).

Wilcox, Ron, *Battles on the Tigris* (Barnsley: Pen and Sword, 2006).

Wilson, Arnold T., *Loyalties: Mesopotamia, 1914–1917: From the Outbreak of War to the Death of General Maude* (New York: Greenwood, 1969 [1930]).

Winter, Denis, *Making the Legend: The War Writings of C. E. W. Bean* (St Lucia: University of Queensland Press, 1992).

Winter, Denis, *25 April 1915: The Inevitable Tragedy* (St Lucia: University of Queensland Press, 1994).

Winter, Jay and Antoine Prost, *The Great War in History* (Cambridge: Cambridge University Press, 2005).

Woodward, David R., *Hell in the Holy Land: World War I in the Middle East* (Lexington: University of Kentucky, 2006).

Wynn, Antony, *Persia in the Great Game: Sir Percy Sykes: Explorer, Consul, Soldier, Spy* (London: John Murray, 2003).

Yuceer, Nasir, *Birinci Dünya Savaşi'nda Osmanlı Ordusu'nun Azerbaycan ve Dağistan Harekatı* [The Ottoman Army's Azerbaijani and Daghestani Operations in the First World War] (Ankara: Genelkurmay Basımevi, 1996).

Zurcher, Erik-Jan, *Turkey: A Modern History* (New York: I.B. Tauris, 1993).

Index

Page references followed by an '*f*' are to illustrations; military formations are listed at the end of their respective country or army entries.